The Harrier Story

In its former life as an FRS.1, Sea
Harrier ZD615 was operated by 801 NAS.
It has served with the OEU and 899 NAS
since its delivery as an F/A.2 conversion
in August 1993, though its deck number
changed to 723 in April 1994. Deck
numbers are usually painted on easily
removable panels so that they can be
switched between aircraft. (BAe)

THE
Harrier
STORY

PETER E. DAVIES &
ANTHONY M. THORNBOROUGH

Foreword by John Farley

ARMS AND
ARMOUR

For John Farley, an unfailing guide and
mentor throughout this project, and for our
patient wives, Lucy and Maggie

ARMS & ARMOUR PRESS
An imprint of the Cassell Group
Wellington House, 125 Strand, London WC2R 0BB

British Library Cataloguing-in-Publication data:
A catalogue record for this book is available from the British Library.

ISBN 1 85409 248 0

Edited and designed by Roger Chesneau/DAG Publications Ltd

Printed and bound in Great Britain
by Hillman Printers (Frome) Ltd, Somerset

Contents

Left to right: Fred Sutton (Chief Flight Development Engineer, HSA Dunsfold), John Farley (Chief Test Pilot, HSA), Sir Stanley Hooker (Director of Engineering, Rolls-Royce), John Dale (Chief Pegasus Development Engineer) and Bill Bedford (Former Chief Test Pilot, HSA).

John Dale has just been given his first Harrier flight (in G-VTOL, 31 August 1976), an experience which he described as 'being borne on my own hot air at last!' Ten years earlier, to the day, the RAF's first pre-production Harrier had made its maiden flight. (BAe)

Foreword

John Farley OBE AFC CEng,
former Chief Harrier Test Pilot, BAe

Quite a bit has been written about the Harrier since its origins back in the late 1950s and the authors necessarily fall into two categories—programme insiders, who are long on personal knowledge but short on objectivity, and outsiders, who tend to be the opposite.

So, when Peter Davies first contacted me and asked if I would mind answering a few questions, I was totally unprepared for what arrived. His questions showed a depth of knowledge of the subject that any insider would have been proud of! Finding all the answers was going to mean Peter contacting many of the senior people who had been involved, not just one or two.

That was eighteen months ago. Not surprisingly, the result of the authors' efforts is a book than even insiders will learn much from. For those not lucky enough to have first-hand knowledge of the Harrier, there is everything they could ask for in one balanced story. As a final point, if anybody still feels that the Harrier is only about improving the quality of air shows, I ask them to read the accounts of the Falklands and Gulf War operations word by word. They are an eye opener and a fitting tribute to the servicemen and women who daily use their Harriers to protect you and me.

John Farley

Preface

Forty-three years after VTOL in Britain began with the 'Flying Bedstead', and twenty-seven years after entering service with the Royal Air Force, the unique Harrier remains in production and development. About 390 examples serve with the armed forces of Great Britain, the United States, Italy, India, Spain and Thailand, with several more export prospects. Initially a private venture by Hawker Aircraft, the Harrier is now manufactured on an international basis. It is still powered by its 'dedicated' engine, the Rolls-Royce Pegasus—one of the few instances where a major engine design has been used in only one aircraft type (the Dornier Do 31 prototype research aircraft has been the only other user to date).

Progressive updates to the powerplant, airframe and avionics (sometimes requiring the complete 're-lifing' of the aircraft) have taken the Harrier several generations beyond the basic Kestrels and Harrier Is which set the parameters for forward rough-field and seafaring V/STOL operations.

From its original role as a self-contained, self-starting close-support attacker (it was one of the first fighters to feature an APU), the Harrier has become a truly multi-role aircraft. Radar-equipped versions can match the best of the world's existing fighters, while sophisticated attack systems and advanced internal electronic warfare protection enable Harriers to deliver substantial warloads over long distances by day and night. All this has been accomplished without sacrificing the aircraft's unique vertical take-off and landing characteristics. Once viewed as little more than a technology demonstrator, the Harrier has steadily evolved into an extremely flexible and potent warplane.

This book describes the development of an outstanding product of Anglo-American engineering and attempts to identify the select group of individuals whose ingenuity made it happen. Some of them have contributed to this volume. The authors are extremely grateful to David Andrews, Alan Baxter, Maj. Michael C Berryman USMC, Col John 'Hunter' Bioty (CO MAG-13 FWD), Lt-Gen. Harry Blot USMC, Phil Boyden, John Crampton, John Dale, Dale Donovon (RAF CPRO), Mike Downing, Capt. Steve M. Dunkin USMC, Andy Evans, John Farley, John Fawcett, Rod Frederiksen, Lt-Cdr Simon Hargreaves, Ralph Hooper, G. W. Johnson, David Kamiya, Tim Laming, Gordon Lewis, Lt-Gen. Tom Miller USMC Ret., Frank Mormillo, Tim Perry, Lt Hugh Rathbone RN, Richard Read, Martin Rogers, Jim Rotramel, Andy Sephton, Cdr V. G Sirrett. RN Ret. and Richard L. Ward.

Peter E. Davies &
Anthony M. Thornborough

1. 'Like a Humming Bird'

*The Aeroplane won't amount to a damn until they get a machine that will act like a hummingbird—
go straight up, go forward, go backward, come straight down and alight. It isn't easy but someone is going
to do it.*—Thomas Edison (1847–1931)

Although early forms of the helicopter had begun to achieve parts of Edison's vision within his lifetime it was not until nearly thirty years after his death that the first fixed-wing aircraft with real military potential began to behave in the ways he advocated. The evolution of VTOL aviation was a lengthy process which yielded many part-solutions and painful failures over half a century. Vectored thrust, the key to the Harrier's success, probably dated back to 1909 when Mr Edgar Simpson suggested fitting aircraft with propellers in 'side funnels' which could be directed downwards for take-off and backwards for horizontal flight. Ralph Hooper, who was largely responsible for the Harrier's forerunner, the P.1127, recalled that as early as 1911 someone had suggested directing the air flow from the Wright Brothers' biplane's propellers downwards through ducts to allow vertical take-off. Then, and for many years afterwards, the central problem was to generate enough power to produce a favourable thrust-to-weight ratio.

Between these early, speculative days and the first practicable V/STOL designs there were many attempts at solving the problems of power and stability which made vertical flight a hard trick to perform. During the Second World War the Germans created many far-reaching design initiatives, including the Bachem Ba 349 Natter, a stub-wing, rocket-powered bomber-interceptor which blasted off vertically. Its pilot baled out when the fuel ran out. Focke-Achgelis did preliminary studies for their Fa 269, a conventional monoplane but with two large, swivelling propellers which swung aft of the wing for conventional flight and downwards for VTOL. Prophetically, it was intended to

operate from shipboard platforms in the air defence role half a century before the Harrier actually performed that mission. The concept eventually found realization in the 1980s with Bell-Boeing's V-22 Osprey, designed to support the US Marine Corps' Harrier force as a light transport.

The 1950s brought a fresh burst of innovation, initially based on small, 'tail-sitting' turboprop-powered designs such as the 1951 Lockheed XFV-1 and Convair XFY-1 'Pogo'. Although their lack of development potential caused their termination in 1956, these two aircraft did fly and they generated lasting interest in VTOL for their sponsors, particularly the US Navy.

Jet engines began to generate enough power to offer favourable thrust/weight figures and the final phase of 'tail-sitter' interest centred on the Rolls-Royce Avon-powered Ryan X-13. Funded by the USAF, this little delta flew with a conventional undercarriage in 1955 and thereafter with none. Instead, it hooked itself on to a nylon 'washing line' rig from a hover, making its vertical take-offs and 'landings' from that posture. Transitions from vertical to horizontal flight were accomplished by both the X-13 and the Convair 'Pogo'. All were exclusively technology demonstrators with no real growth potential: the X-13, for example, had fuel for only 15 minutes' flight. Controlling the aircraft in a vertical hover placed the pilot virtually on his back and placed unusual demands on his skill and judgement.

The focus then shifted to 'flat-rising' aircraft powered by smaller, downward-venting lift jets and adding conventional wing lift for short take-off (STO). Various designs emerged, some using ingenious 'buried fans' to augment thrust for take-

off. Others employed 'jet augmentor' ducts to decrease pressure on the upper surfaces of the aircraft, thereby generating extra lift. Ryan's XV-5A and the Lockheed XV-4B for the US Army pioneered augmentation techniques which re-emerged in the 1970s with the Rockwell XFV-12A naval V/STOL fighter project and more recently in some of the 1990s designs for the Advanced STOVL aircraft to succeed the Harrier.

Although many millions of dollars were expended by all three US Armed Forces on these experiments, nothing with real military potential emerged. More fruitful research was begun in Great Britain, initially with Rolls-Royce's Thrust Measuring Rig (TMR) XJ314, in 1953. Powered

With a configuration which earned it the inevitable nickname 'Flying Bedstead', the Rolls-Royce Thrust Measuring Rig (TMR) XJ314 hovers noisily, its pilot protected only by his goggles and a rudimentary roll-bar pyramid. Boom-mounted puffer jets were the forerunners of the Harrier Reaction Control System. (Via HMS *Heron*)

by a pair of 5,000lb thrust Nene turbojets with their exhausts venting downwards near the centre of this open-plan 'flying bedstead' apparatus, the TMR was controlled by 'puffer jets' directing high-pressure air downwards from booms located at four points around the device. A second TMR (XK426) was allocated to the Royal Aircraft Establishment (RAE) at Bedford in 1957 where it performed 157 tethered flights and four 'free' flights before crashing at Hucknall and killing RAE Bedford's Commanding Officer. Similar test rigs appeared in France and in Russia later in the 1950s. Rolls-Royce's TMR was built for research into the commercial potential of VTO. The company's Chief Scientist, Dr A. A. Griffith, conjectured Concorde-like supersonic airliners which would be blasted off the runway not conventionally by reheated turbojets but vertically by batteries of small lift engines. His lightweight RB.108 jet engine, with an 8:1 thrust/weight ratio, was used in the Short Bros SC.1 'flat-riser', ordered in 1954 by the British Ministry of Supply (Spec. ER.143). Two prototypes were built (XG900 and XG905) using four downward-pointing RB.108s and a fifth, rearward-directed unit. The aircraft had a conventional delta wing, a blunt fin and a complex three-axis autostabilisation sys-

tem. Its integrated reaction control ('puffer jet') system, electronic control system, HUD and blind-landing data-link (installed later in the 1960s) made it a very advanced and valuable research tool for its time. 'Tethered' hovering, with the SC.1 attached to safety lines, began in May 1958, a year after its first conventional flight. A steel grid over an exhaust-gas dispersal pit was used as a 'launch pad' to avoid the recirculation of hot gases. Full transitions from horizontal to vertical flight, and vice versa, were achieved in April 1960 (six months before the P.1127 flew). The two prototypes, flown by a selection of company and RAE test pilots, conducted a series of VTOL and STOL trials to explore ground erosion problems.

Short's SC.1 was the first design to inspire widespread belief in the long-term value of research into the V/STOL concept. Like all its American forbears it was purely a research vehicle. Its success led Rolls-Royce to adhere to the lift-jet concept for their future military V/STOL proposals. In 1954 they had experimented briefly with deflected thrust, using the Vickers Beryl-Meteor test-bed (RA940) with two RN.4 Nene engines featuring thrust deflectors beneath their nacelles. Engine thrust could be redirected downwards by 60 degrees. This installation enabled the Gloster fighter to achieve forward airspeeds as low as 65kt, though with intense buffeting, and actually pointed the way to the eventual P.1127/Harrier line

of development. However, Rolls-Royce's RB.108 and its successors had attracted the British Government's attention, and also that of the NATO Mutual Weapons Development Team (MWDT) under the fiery Colonel Johnnie Driscoll USAF. Established by the United States, the team's mission was to encourage and finance promising European defence projects. Rolls-Royce decided to follow that route, entering into a collaborative project with Dassault in France which led in 1963 to the Mirage-based Balzac powered by eight RB.108s and a single BS Orpheus.

At the Bristol Aero Engine Company, Stanley Hooker took a very different view. He rejected the notion of lugging around the dead weight of up to eight lift engines which were used only for take-off and landing. Failure of an engine in either of these situations would, he felt, require at least two 'spares' to maintain equilibrium, or at least a large burden of automatic interconnecting gear to preserve engine power balance. Although the idea of equipping each aircraft with eight or nine engines rather than one might appeal to Rolls-Royce shareholders, there were obvious limitations when military payloads and range were considered. But NATO was interested in V/STOL. General Lauris Norstad, NATO Supreme Commander, wanted light fighters which would operate from short runways; Colonel Driscoll wanted aircraft which would fly from 'cow pastures'. The preference for

Gordon Lewis's memo, dated 2 August 1956, and his accompanying sketch of the BE.48 proposal.

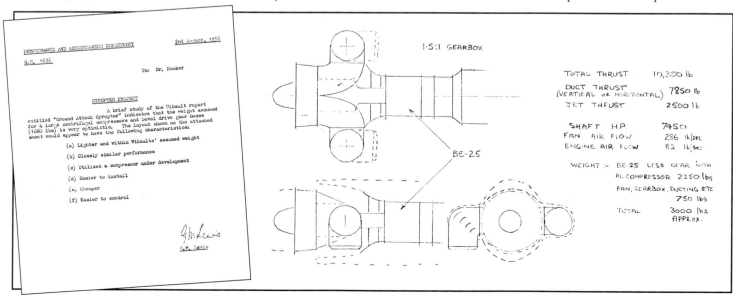

Michel Wibault's Gyropter design, with four 'centrifugal blowers' and thrust deflector at the end of the jet-pipe. The proof that the Gyropter was envisaged as a combat aircraft is seen in the internal gun and missile armament which Wibault included. (Gordon Lewis)

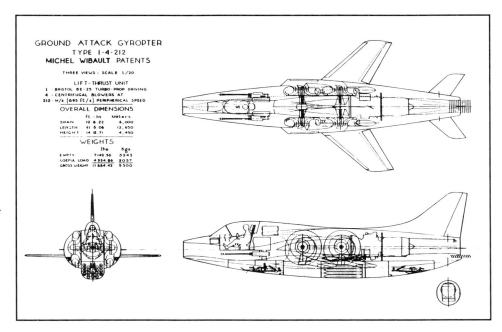

lightweight fighters led MWDT to pay 75 per cent of the Bristol Orpheus jet engine's development costs. This powerplant was destined for the Folland Gnat 'feather-weight fighter' which would also have attracted funding had it been capable of rough-field operation. Instead, the Orpheus powered the Fiat G.91 'Gina' for the *Luftwaffe*, Italy and Portugal benefited. Winner of the NATO lightweight fighter contest, the 'Gina' was kept in production for 557 copies.

These NATO dealings brought Dr Hooker into contact with a French designer, Michel Wibault. He had run his own aircraft company which had produced the first biplane fighter, the WIB 1, in 1918, followed by a series of parasol-wing fighters which pioneered lightweight duralumin structures. He became a consultant engineer to Vickers (who adapted several of his fighter designs) and then sold out to Breguet in 1934 and moved to the United States. There he met millionaire Winthrop Rockefeller who helped to establish him as a freelance designer back in Paris. In the mid-1950s he completed a design called Le Gyropter (not Gyroptère as is often thought). Based on Bristol Aero Engines' proposed BE.25 Orion turbo-prop, Wibault's concept had a fat, tubular fuselage and a small, swept wing. The Orion's propshaft drove two centrifugal 'blowers' on each side. Built into circular, rotating volute casings, they could direct jet efflux downwards for VTOL or aft for forward flight.

Wibault produced an inch-thick brochure (dated March 1956) which gave a full description of his Gyropter. It contained extensive performance calculations and exquisitely detailed engineering drawings, executed by Wibault with great difficulty because of an illness which had left him with badly deformed hands. He had offered his idea to elements of the French aircraft industry but he was still *persona non grata*, having left France just before it fell to the Germans. He therefore presented it to MWDP, who expressed a strong interest.[1] Dr Hooker became involved because his 8,000hp Orion was central to the design. His first reaction was that Wibault's arrangement of gearboxes, shafts and compressors was unnecessarily heavy and potentially unreliable. Nevertheless, he took the idea, christened 'vectored thrust' by NATO research adviser Theodore von Kármán, back to Bristol and discussed it with his design team. Project engineer Gordon Lewis (later to become Technical Director of Rolls-Royce) suggested some crucial changes. He proposed that Wibault's four 'centrifuges' should be replaced by a single axial compressor with one pair of rotating nozzles and a single rear deflecting jet-pipe. He saw this as a 'simple and elegant way of doing what Wibault was trying to do'. He also recognized the potential of Wibault's project which, in retrospect 'described all the principal operating characteristics of the Harrier'. Gordon Lewis drew out his revised powerplant (BE.48) proposal in August 1956. It was rather more than an academic exercise. As he explained to the authors, NATO's lightweight fighter programme, beginning with the Fiat G.91, was to have included two further stages. Breguet's 1001 *Taon* (translated as 'Horse-fly' but also an anagram of NATO) was a swept-wing fighter based on the same Orpheus BOr.3 as the G.91. It flew successfully in prototype form, even capturing a couple of closed-circuit speed records, but never entered production. Stage Three was for a V/STOL light attack aircraft with an unspecified powerplant.

Gordon Lewis drew his BE.48 around the Orion engine, 'driving the first two stages of the Olympus low pressure compressor through an epicyclic reduction gear, the fan and engine having a separate air intake to reflect the thermodynamic cycle defined in Wibault's calculations. The fan air was exhausted through two rotating nozzles, one each side, while the residual thrust from the turboprop exhaust could be diverted by deflecting cascades at the rear of the aircraft'. Lewis calculated that this axial-fan proposal would yield much the same engine (and aircraft)

[1] MWDP's Col Johnny Driscoll sent Dr Hooker the Wibault brochure in early April 1956 because he wanted MWDP to initiate a V/STOL project. Thereafter he continued to encourage Bristol Engines to work on the Wibault proposals, at a time when the company was already fully engaged on other major projects such as the Olympus, Orpheus and Proteus. Gordon Lewis remarked that, with only about half a dozen senior design engineers on strength at that stage, 'they needed a new project like a hole in the head!'. Driscoll and his successor Colonel Chapman were not convinced by Rolls-Royce's lift engine designs.

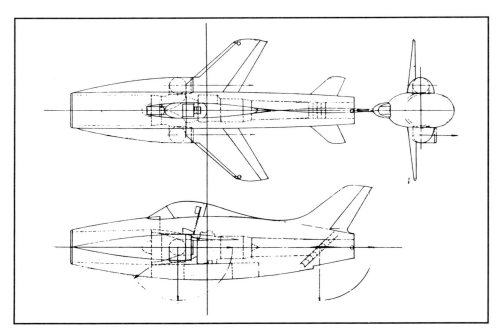

Wibault's revised Gyropter design, using Gordon Lewis's BE.25/BE.48 proposals. Note the 'cascade' thrust deflector in the jet-pipe. (Gordon Lewis)

performance as Wibault's original concept, and it was therefore put to MWDP and to Wibault. 'Surprisingly, he accepted our major change to his original project with enthusiasm. The meeting with Wibault resulted in a scheme for a Gyropter Ground Attack Fighter using the BE.48.'

This new engine proposal inspired much more interest among the engineers at Bristol. 'It is relevant to the eventual success of the Pegasus and Harrier to recall that in the 'fifties many new projects were being generated and there was an extremely productive exchange of ideas among the technical specialists and designers which carried worthwhile projects forward with little structured programming or task definition.' As they explored the potential of the system it was soon realised that the reduction gear was an undesirable feature which would be heavy, expensive and hard to develop. The Orion 'core' already had two spools and could not have accepted a third low-speed shaft (to power a low-speed turbine in place of the gearing) without major redesign.

A solution was found in the MWDP-funded Orpheus, a single-spool turbojet using the same compressor as the LP spool of the Orion. It offered lighter weight for the same power, albeit with higher fuel consumption. The redesign was labelled BE.52 and it was based as far as possible on existing components in order to produce a demonstration engine as quickly as possible without substantial cost.

The Orpheus alone provided insufficient thrust, so a two-stage fan (adapted from Bristol's Olympus engine) was fitted in front of it, driven by an extra two-stage turbine. Its connecting shaft passed through the large-diameter Orpheus centre shaft. Bypass air from the front fan was directed to the two vectoring 'cold' nozzles while the hot 'core' gases discharged rearwards through a single deflecting nozzle. The design matured rapidly and received approval from Colonel Willis Chapman, Driscoll's successor at MWDP. He arranged for Gordon Lewis to meet Wibault in Paris. Shortly before Wibault's death he and Lewis took out a joint patent on the engine with its vectored thrust concept, in January 1957. In this form the rear nozzle configuration was left open to adaptation, allowing either for a single nozzle or for another pair of vectoring nozzles at the end of a jetpipe.

MWDP's interest in the project enabled it to go ahead and in June 1958 they agreed to fund 75 per cent of the development costs. Sir Reginald Verdon Smith,

Bristol Aero Engines' far-sighted Chairman, agreed to put up the rest from company resources. In the absence of a specific airframe to use the engine, Bristol explored possibilities which, a few years later, led to the BE.58 (a proposed civil version) and BE.61, a scaled-down version aimed at the Hawker Siddeley Trident airliner. It would have had a higher bypass ratio (non-vectored) than the RB.163/1 Spey originally selected for that design, and it would also have met noise abatement regulations right up to the 1990s. The BE.52 was initially offered to Short Brothers (in which Bristol Aero Engines had a financial stake) in the hope that it might be favourably evaluated as an alternative to the Rolls-Royce lift-jet arrangement in their SC.1 test-bed. However, Shorts produced a scheme based on the BE.53 (Bristol's 'datum configuration' engine, with three fan stages driven by an uprated Orpheus) and then took it to MWDP. There they took the chance to promote the SC.1 with its existing lift-jets for MWDP money and showed no enthusiasm for the single vectored thrust engine. This was rather a slap in the face for the Bristol team, but another, far more feasible solution was shortly to emerge.

Sir Sidney Camm, Chief Designer for the Hawker Aircraft Company for 41 years, had for some time been studying the various British and US attempts at V/STOL flight. In May 1957 he wrote to Dr Stanley Hooker at Bristol expressing his scepticism about Rolls-Royce's lift-jet ideas and asking whether Hooker had any alternative proposals. Gordon Lewis assured the authors that it was this letter which began the crucial 'VTOL' link between Hooker and Camm and led directly to the Harrier. Hooker responded by sending Sir Sidney details of the Wibault-Lewis engine. Camm passed the brochure to his design office, where doubts were expressed about the 11,000lb thrust claimed for the engine and, therefore, its practicability as a VTOL 'thruster'. However, one of the designers, Ralph Hooper, found the engine's simplicity and novelty sufficiently interesting to sketch out a basic airframe around it. A small, high-wing aircraft with a tailwheel undercarriage was drawn, us-

John Dale, credited by Sir Stanley Hooker for 'converting the early Pegasus into a reliable service engine'. He also played a major role in the worldwide acceptance of the Pegasus concept as Pegasus Project Manager. (Via John Farley)

ing the three-nozzle layout. If there was to be any operational application, Hooper foresaw that the straight-wing, high-tail two/three seater might be a reconnaissance platform, operating from short, forward airstrips. It seemed possible that the three-nozzle/tail-sitting format might just allow a nose-high vertical landing, but inadequate thrust seemed to rule out the VTO-with-load option, given only two vectoring nozzles. Initially referred to as the P.1127 High Speed Helicopter, the outline design was shown to Dr Hooker and his team at Hawker's Kingston offices in June 1957. They met Camm, Ralph Hooper, John Fozard and Roy Chaplin (who was on the verge of retirement but supervised the early stages of P.1127 study). Camm indicated that he intended to build a prototype based on a later version of Hooper's design, using company funding.

As Ralph Hooper refined his initial design he was aware that the three-nozzle layout precluded effective hovering. Recalling the bifurcated jetpipe of the company's Sea Hawk fighter, he divided the rear jet-pipes with a second pair of noz-

zles (as Wibault and Lewis's patent had already included as a possibility). Placing these rear vectoring nozzles at the end of a jetpipe as they had assumed obviously limited the amount of 'hot' jet thrust that they could handle without causing thrust-centre problems and instability. Hooper therefore moved the rear nozzles much closer to the front, cold pair, thereby eliminating these problems, saving weight and internal fuselage space and greatly increasing the engine's potential thrust. Hooker's team was then able to tackle the definitive four-nozzle BE.53 development. Chief Designer Charles Marchant took over the management of the project, and working hardware appeared in July 1959. The engine was then handed over to Chief Development Engineer John Dale to develop to flight standard. He stayed with it for seventeen years until his retirement, and Dr Hooker (later Sir Stanley Hooker) gave him the credit for converting the embryonic BE.53 into a dependable service powerplant.

There was an unwritten rule at Bristol that a new engine was not named until it became a committed programme. The name 'Pegasus' would have been conferred upon the BE.53 shortly after its first bench-run in October 1959. Neither Gordon Lewis nor John Dale could specifically recall for the authors the exact timing or origin of the name, but they as-

sumed that Stanley Hooker would have coined it.[2] Although it had previously been used for the nine-cylinder radial engine which powered countless Second World War bombers, the name Pegasus, conjuring up a winged horse on four columns of air, could not have been more appropriate.

Hawker and Bristol Engines together began to work on other challenging features of the evolving P.1127 concept. A 'puffer jet' reaction control system (RCS), similar in principle to that of the 'Flying Bedstead', used air bled from the low pressure (LP) compressor, piped to outlets under the nose, tail and wingtips. In the hover, stability was maintained by these blasts of air, released in response to movements of the pilot's control column and rudder pedals. At first a constant-bleed system was designed, but this was subsequently replaced by an RCS which was triggered only when the controls were moved from the 'neutral' position. It soon became obvious that the relatively small fuselage and thin wing could not accommodate pipes large enough for the required volume of air. Instead, high-pressure 'hot' air was ducted through smaller-diameter pipes made from rolled, welded Nimonic 75 alloy.[3] The system was activated when the nozzles' angle reached 18 degrees downwards.

Hooper's original drawings were soon replaced by a very different configuration, still labelled P.1127, which featured a small, undrooped delta wing, a swept tail, a single-seat cockpit and the four-nozzle BE.53/2 engine. Twin undercarriage units retracted into the fuselage—rather close

---

[2] One of the names in circulation was Janus, the Roman deity with two faces—one in front and one behind—who guarded the gate of heaven.
[3] The use of high-pressure air bled from the outlet from the engine compressor solved the installation problem but had severe performance penalties. The solution emerged from the technical teams who took advantage of thermal lag to allow a significant increase in turbine inlet temperature during the brief periods of maximum bleed demand without exceeding the limiting temperature acceptable to the turbine blades. This concept led to the unique engine rating system peculiar to the Pegasus which allows high peaks of bleed demand to be met without overall thrust loss.

to the hot nozzles—and a nosewheel unit was introduced. When the first P.1127 brochure was published for the September 1957 SBAC display it portrayed an aircraft grossing 8,500lb and carrying a 2,000lb external load from a 600ft take-off roll. Colonel Willis Chapman approved the specification but felt that it offered only half the required range. It was suggested to Bristol Aero Engines that water injection would give the required extra thrust to carry more fuel for this purpose. Estimates of potential thrust advanced from 11,000lb to over 13,000lb as a result, though it would be several years before a production Pegasus with water-injected turbine cooling appeared.

Another worry at Kingston was the presumed control stability problem resulting from the gyroscopic effect of the large Olympus fan fronting the engine and rotating in the same direction as the Orpheus 'core' turbine. An autostabilisation system like those used on the lift-jet test-beds would have coped with the problem, but with increased weight and complexity. Like that of his American counterpart Kelly Johnson, Camm's design philosophy was to 'keep it simple'. He once said that 'sophistication means complication, then in turn escalation, cancellation and ruination'—an all-too-familiar pattern in the post-war aviation industry. Ralph Hooper suggested counter-rotation of the fan and core to provide that simple solution.

In fact, counter-rotation had already been envisaged in the original Wibault-Lewis patent, where the stability problem had been anticipated. However, while the engine was made up from 'off the shelf' components in order to make it acceptable internally on cost grounds, Lewis had to use fans and turbines which were constructed to Bristol's usual 'left hand tractor' (clockwise rotation) pattern. Reblading the Olympus fan to rotate the other way would have been prohibitively expensive, but when interest in the project became strong enough it was possible to justify designing a completely new counter-rotating fan.

Chapman's MWDP delegation visited Kingston again in March 1958 to view the revisions to the P.1127. By that time

Hooper had rethought the undercarriage and decided on a neater 'zero track' single-leg for the main gear, with two small 'outrigger' legs on the wingtips. It was an arrangement reminiscent of Boeing's jet bombers and it would require similar no-flare, four-square landing techniques in the conventional landing mode. Although this configuration was probably lighter than any wide-track gear option, it presented difficulties. In test pilot John Farley's opinion, it took from 1960 to 1967 to make it work properly for take-off and landing. The P.1127's frontal area was reduced by moving the engine's gearbox, pump and generators from the bottom of the engine to a position above its top casing. The small delta wing was cropped for strength and weight reduction, and triangular sections were removed from the inboard ends of the flaps to avoid interference with the hot nozzles. These 'cutaways' were later filled in. At the rear end, the tailfin took on the distinctive Hawker 'family' look which has survived throughout Harrier's evolution. Another distinctive feature, the anhedral wing, was introduced originally to keep the outriggers as short as possible, but wind-tunnel tests showed that the droop was also necessary for stability.

Sir Sydney Camm's involvement in the P.1127 was quite minor in its early stages and the aircraft's birth was delegated to a small team of designers headed by Ralph Hooper and John Fozard. Camm's principal concern in 1957–58 was to develop a successful design to fill the gap caused by the premature end of Hunter production and development following Duncan Sandys' notorious 1957 White Paper on Defence. This had stated, with support from experts in Government and the armed forces, that the RAF would be unlikely to require manned bomber or fighter aircraft in future. The Ministry of Defence's Operational Requirement (OR) 339 for a Canberra replacement was the only substantial contract still in circulation by the year's end. Hawker's bid (with Avro) was the P.1129, a large, twin-engine supersonic striker. Camm focused the company's design effort on this major prize, but lost to BAC's TSR.2. Work on the P.1127 was then revived in January 1959,

partly in response to the encouraging progress at Bristol with the fully funded Pegasus. In the shadow of the Sandys White Paper it was important to refer to P.1127 as a 'research' aircraft in order to dodge the cancellation axe, and this 'experimental' label tended to stick to the design long after it became a true combat aircraft. As Ralph Hooper explained to the authors, P.1127 had actually been at a very low key, but in 1959, with TSR.2 settled, there was at last a hint of Government interest and possible funding for the P.1127. Hawker's P.1129 venture had eaten up £1m of company money and there was an understandable reluctance to commit much more to a new-risk venture without hope of official support.

Meanwhile detail design work on the P.1127 had begun in mid-1958 and progress had been made with wooden models, initially at Kingston Technical College's wind tunnel and then at the RAE. Robin Balmer, another of the nucleus of P.1127 designers, produced a computer-operated simulator of the aircraft's control systems. Although official support still remained vague, Camm decided to push ahead, as he had done with another private venture, the Hurricane, twenty-five years before. With no order or Operational Requirement in prospect, he decided to construct a prototype. He was aware that there was still limited Government approval for the Rolls-Royce/short lift engine concept too, and he probably saw the construction of some working hardware as the best means of attracting attention Hawker's way. In March 1959 the Hawker management took the plunge and supported the cutting of metal for two P.1127s.

A month later the RAF issued GOR.345, a requirement for a Hunter replacement to enter service in 1965. It was substantially written around the P.1127 brochure and signified genuine service interest. There also seemed to be a hope of NATO support, but later discussions in Paris revealed that NATO thinking had already moved towards a larger, all-weather V/STOL type. MWDP interest still remained strong and drew increasing attention from the US defence industry as

Sporting a trendy white-walled nose-wheel, the stripped-down P.1127 proto-type XP831 hovers over its exhaust-gas dispersal grid. Tethers and telemetry cables dangle from the aircraft. Wool tufts measured airflow over the rear fuselage and jury-rigged metal strips on the outrigger wheels improved stability with wheels in contact with the ground. (BAe)

well. Links with America came at an important time. Not only were Ralph Hooper and Robert Marsh (Head of Projects at Hawker) able to study the jet-deflection powered Bell X-14, which had some similarities to P.1127, they were also to visit NASA's Langley Field installation, where it was agreed that a vital programme of 'free flight' P.1127 model testing could be carried out in the 16ft transonic tunnel there. John Stack, Director of Aeronautics at Langley, was a P.1127 enthusiast from the outset and he arranged for the tests, using a 1/6th scale balsa model, complete with simulated Pegasus, provided by V/STOL researcher Marion McKinney. Towards the end of 1959 this model was 'flown' by a team of 'pilots', each one remotely controlling one of its control axes. Model tests settled one of the designers' main worries—that the aircraft would become totally unstable during the transition phase of flight. Earlier tunnel testing at RAE Farnborough had suggested that serious instability would occur in transition to horizontal flight because of downwash beneath the tailplane as the

nozzles deflected aft. Further tunnel tests ensued, with British Government funding at last available for continuation design and research.

At NASA the P.1127 made an important, lasting impression. Among those who were attracted to the aircraft were Jack Reeder and Fred Drinkwater, two men in influential research positions at NASA Langley and NASA Ames. They became the first two non-British pilots to fly the real P.1127 at Dunsfold in July 1962. Reeder became instrumental in ensuring that NASA obtained examples of the second-generation P.1127, the Kestrel, for testing and he helped to introduce the US Marines to the aircraft. Having flown many of the US V/STOL prototypes, he quickly appreciated that P.1127 was far in advance of them.

At Kingston contracts were issued for cockpit, electrical and navigation equipment by the end of 1959 and Bristol Siddeley (as they had then become) ran the BS.53/2 engine on a test-bed in September. Although the engine's initial thrust was only 9,000lb, Bristol engineers were confident that power increases would be available quite quickly. By February the following year power had been boosted to 11,000lb, just enough for Hawker Siddeley (as they, in turn, became) to foresee that the P.1127 could conceivably make a vertical take-off.

Preparations were made for the first flight. Hawker test pilots Bill Bedford and

Hugh Merewether visited the United States, where they had valuable flying experience in the variable-stability Sikorsky HO35-1 helicopter, the Bell X-14 and the NASA Ames V/STOL simulator. Despite a landing accident in which Merewether damaged the X-14's undercarriage after a pilot-induced oscillation near to the ground, the Hawker pilots resisted the idea of using extensive autostabilisation in the P.1127. In fact, a simple system giving 20 per cent authority in the roll axis was installed, but not always used. As part of his preparation, Bedford also 'did time' on the heavily auto-stabilized Short SC.1 in Ireland.

June 1960 brought very welcome Government funding for the two prototype P.1127s (serial numbers XP831 and XP836). The first of these was delivered to Hawker's Dunsfold airfield on 15 July 1960. Bristol Siddeley delivered the first of six Pegasus engines in September, knowing that it still suffered many development problems which would make the flight test programme a prolonged business. Engine thrust exceeded the aircraft's tare weight by a mere 1,000lb, achieved by stripping XP831 of anything that could be removed to save a few pounds. Radios, the ram air turbine (RAT), the air brake and undercarriage fairings, the nose boom, cabin ventilation, even the windshield (replaced by perspex) were all unscrewed. Paint was restricted to a few small camera alignment markers. Large bell-

mouth intakes were fitted to encourage the airflow into the engine. At the final weigh-in the prototype registered 9,243lb, which included enough fuel for only three minutes' engine running. Half of that was used to start up and check the controls. The first Pegasus engines had a one-hour life span with nozzles deflected (25 hours with nozzles aft) at full power before they had to return to Bristol for strip-overhaul said to cost £60,000. That worked out at £1,000 per minute in engine depreciation.

After XP831 had completed its first ground-runs, in a special pen with a gridded floor and huge metal exhaust shrouds, Chief Test Pilot Bill Bedford prepared to make its first vertical 'lift' on 21 October 1960. A few days previously he was in Germany demonstrating the company's two-seat Hunter. On his way back to the hotel his driver misjudged a bend and the car ran into some trees. Bedford's right ankle was broken and the resultant plaster cast seemed to imply that the first flight would be seriously delayed. Undaunted, Bedford was ferried home in the Hunter, demonstrated his comparatively unhindered dexterity to the RAF Central Medical Board by flying a glider, a helicopter and several other aircraft, and was certified to fly the P.1127—but only in 'tethered mode'.

He was not overly impressed by the aircraft's looks on first acquaintance, but he found the cockpit pleasingly straightforward (a sentiment which would not have been shared by pilots of later 'Harrier I' variants!). VTOL required only one extra control, a nozzle angle-setting lever situated in the same cockpit 'box' as the throttle control. XP831 was placed on a specially built 40ft by 45ft steel grid over a pit to reduce jet efflux recirculation, similar to the Short Brothers structure. The first flight took place on time: the aircraft reached an altitude of one foot, restrained by tethering lines of that length, but it had achieved VTO. The lines were increased to 4ft for the next hop, but broke. Shorter, stronger tethers were attached and the aircraft's outrigger wheels were propped on platforms to keep it 'wings-level', and later extended for the same reason. Like the Boeing bombers, the P.1127 originally tilted on to one outrigger when at rest. For hovering trials even a slight tilt caused problems, particularly when the main undercarriage began to 'unload' while still on the ground, thereby increasing the tilt angle. The P.1127 then tended to skid sideways as it left the ground. Even a 6-degree tilt was enough to induce 0.1g of horizontal acceleration. Brief two- or three-minute hops gave Bedford little time to explore handling techniques, though he began to experience the inlet momentum drag phenomenon. This became a primary concern for all Harrier pilots and it occurred when the aircraft was not kept pointing into 'relative' wind. With tethers in place it began to pirouette about. Inadequate thrust in the RCS did not help, though some easing of the problem came with the re-gearing of the control column to give greater roll control. After a month of gyrations in these confined conditions ('like a balloon on a string', as Stanley Hooker saw it), Camm agreed to the first untethered flight on 19 November.[4] Bill Bedford was still operating XP831 with hardly any instruments and sometimes with autostabilisation disconnected. The

system was in any case 'saturated' with commands most of the time and made little difference to the handling. He also had to avoid running the engine continuously in certain rpm bands because of blade vibration.

XP831 was then grounded after five weeks while conventional intakes were refitted, optimised for conventional flight. Its reaction control system was modified to give more response and the outrigger wheels were locked with shear pins to counter shimmying while taxying. The main undercarriage, with Sea Hawk wheels, was strengthened after a fracture occurred during a high-speed taxy. The wheels also juddered alarmingly until their brake pads were swapped around, though rather weak mainwheel brakes were destined to be a handicap in all first-generation Harriers. Nosewheel steering was reported to be 'unreliable and deficient in handling'.

Hugh Merewether had become the second test pilot on the P.1127 by the time the first conventional take-off was made on 13 March 1961. Camm had seen little point in making this proof test earlier on the assumption that the P.1127, like previous Hawker designs, would naturally behave well in the air. Its two test pilots did, nevertheless, comment on a few deficiencies—excessive noise and vibration in the cockpit, buffeting, lack of longitudinal stability and a tendency to pitch nose-down when the flaps were lowered for landing.

The year 1960 had ended with more good news at Kingston. Government funding was provided for four more prototypes, and Bristol Siddeley's quarter share of Pegasus development costs were paid off. Although the four new P.1127s

were described as a development batch (DB), it was also made clear that the Government still saw the aircraft as a research device, despite GOR.345 which demonstrated direct RAF interest. To the pilots who had flown the P.1127 it was an embryonic fighter from the outset, but, post-Sandys, such suggestions were still risky!

Hovering trials continued into 1961, with a more powerful 12,000lb Pegasus 2 for the May–June trials. Some of the 51 flights could then be made from solid surfaces rather than the grid with this extra power, and it was possible to gain a better impression of the effects of jet downwash on stability. In hovering flights up to 100ft altitude the aircraft's lack of directional stability at forward speeds up to 50kt became apparent, and it remained a quirk of the 'breed' for years to come. It resulted from the high intake momentum drag, situated ahead of the aircraft's centre of gravity, and the tailfin's lack of stabilizing effect at such low speeds. A second aircraft, XP836, flew on 7 July 1961 and began test-flying to explore the aircraft's 'conventional flight' performance at speeds up to Mach 1.02 and 40,000ft altitude at one end of the envelope and down to the threshold of transition to the hover at around 90kt at the other.

Serious port wing drop was noted at transonic speeds and was partially alleviated by fixing thirteen vortex generators above the wings. Fixes for the other stability problems were more difficult. The original small, clipped delta was seen to need a swept trailing edge and the tailplane clearly needed modification so that it would not be exposed to wing wake but at the same time did not extend into the engine 'wash' either. XP836's 'high speed' intake produced an unacceptable loss of thrust at low speeds and led to an ingenious solution—variable geometry rubber intakes. Simple rubber bags were fixed to the intake edges and inflated to 10psi at low speeds, preventing airflow separation inside the intake lip. At higher speeds they

---

[4]Pegasus Project engineer John Dale also remembered these tethered flights as 'very alarming to watch' and, like Bill Bedford, he was relieved when the much safer untethered 'hops' were sanctioned.

were deflated. Obviously rather fragile structures, the 'rubber lips' tended to flap about at speeds above 250kt when deflated and tore off at higher speeds, though they were flown to 335kt on one occasion. It was an ingenious way of compromising the 'elephant-ear' profiles used originally on XP831 and the sleeker 'forward flight' inlet shape, but something more radical was needed.

XP831 meanwhile continued to explore the lower end of the performance envelope up to 90kt, and Bill Bedford made the first complete transition from vertical to horizontal flight on 12 September 1961. A real flavour of Hawker tradition was given by one of the chase planes on these flights—an earlier Camm design, the company's Hurricane PZ865. Short take-offs followed in October, and by the end of that year, as John Farley reported, 'the P.1127 worked. It was full of ifs and buts, and there was a great deal to be sorted out, but it required only engineering and not black magic to progress to the point where the thing would be seen to have some style.'

Technical success took place against a background of shifting political support for the project. Interest in a joint P.1127-based development programme had been shown by both West Germany and Italy at the start of 1961, and the RAF's

Bill Bedford makes the first P.1127 deck landing, on HMS *Ark Royal* in February 1963. (Via HMS *Heron*)

GOR.345 was still current. However, by November that Operational Requirement had been cancelled and it was obvious that the RAF and its NATO partners were becoming more interested in a larger, faster, more capable aircraft. NATO's NBMR-3 (NATO Basic Military Requirement) competition was launched in April 1961. From the outset it seemed that no specific funding would be available for the winning design, but manufacturers throughout Europe responded energetically, with visions of extensive worldwide sales before them. The result was a prolonged, largely unproductive detour from the P.1127/ Harrier development story. NBMR-3 called for a supersonic strike-fighter capable of delivering a 2,000lb warload over a 250-mile radius from a take-off run not exceeding 500ft. Despite reservations among the Air Staff, the RAF was immediately attracted to the idea of bypassing the P.1127 subsonic phase of V/STOL development and going for a Mach 2 derivative which could allow nuclear strike operations from dispersed sites in the event of a full frontal attack on Europe. Although Stanley Hooker had indicated in 1960 that the Pegasus 5, with an extra stage to its LP fan, could be expected to generate 18,000lb of thrust, this was only sufficient to meet GOR.345's target—carrying a 2,000lb warload over a 150-mile radius from a 50ft take-off, and strictly subsonically.

Kingston was not unprepared for this eventuality and was well aware that the

RAF had long preferred faster, longer-ranging strikers. Early in 1961 Ralph Hooper had drawn out the P.1150, a 52ft long P.1127 derivative using a Pegasus 6 with plenum chamber burning (PCB). Gordon Lewis's original 1956 patent (with M. Wibault) included the possibility of fuel burning in the front nozzles as a means of increasing thrust. This technique introduced 1,200°K fuel combustion to the 'cold' air flow which normally bypassed the core compressor and was ejected unheated by fuel from the cold nozzles. Thrust ratings of up to 33,000lb were forecast for a developed PCB Pegasus 6, which eventually became the BS.100 engine. A prototype BS.100 was built and test-run in October 1964, yielding over 30,000lb, while the PCB Pegasus 6 had generated 25,000lb. In all, five out of the twelve engines ordered had been constructed by the time it was cancelled. Gordon Lewis, who was in charge of the BS.100 project with John Dale as Chief Development Engineer, received notice of its termination in a Government letter which totalled one and a half lines of writing. BS.100 was to have been a huge engine programme and it cost £18 million up to cancellation.

Hooper used the BS.100 idea for a redesign of the P.1150, the larger, heavier P.1154. In order to manage both projects successfully John Fozard then took over the P.1154 while Ralph Hooper retained control of P.1127. RAF interest was strong, and in keeping with the current fashion of 'commonality' the Royal Navy was persuaded (reluctantly) by H M Government to specify the P.1154 as a replacement for its Sea Vixen strike fighter. Ralph Hooper remembered that the Royal Navy had its own V/STOL requirement in 1961, to which Hawker responded with a multi-lift-engine design, the P.1152. De Havilland, Blackburn and the HSA Advanced Projects Group also submitted designs. The Royal Navy was told to compromise with the RAF by H M Government, but a delegation led by 'Winkle' Brown arrived at Kingston on 2 April 1962 with a set of 'minimum demands' without having discussed the issue with the RAF at all. At the time, Hooper advised against compromising the RAF P.1154 design.

Ark Royal **provided a large audience for Bill Bedford's arrival on board. The ship's namesake successor became one of the most active Sea Harrier 'bases' in the 1980s.** (BAe)

Prolonged wrangling ensued as the RAF and RN attempted to define a single aircraft for their very different requirements. For the Navy, catapult launching (and therefore a new tricycle undercarriage), a two-man cockpit and—towards the end of the process—twin Spey engines were proposed, but this was contested strongly by Ralph Hooper and the BS.100 was retained as the intended powerplant. None of these features fitted the RAF's specification and eventually, in 1964, the Navy pulled out and the RAF P.1154 was cancelled a year later.

There is little doubt that P.1154 could have achieved some of its original design objectives, but the insoluble problem of ground erosion caused by the huge increase in jet thrust, concentrated on a small 'footprint' area, could not have been resolved. The P.1154 could only have operated in V/STOL mode from specially prepared sites, and without the flexibility of VTOL and forward site operation there was no reason to buy the aircraft in preference to the type which actually filled the bill—the F-4 Phantom. Certainly, the NBMR-3 selectors had felt that the design's technical merit, backed by Hawker's V/STOL experience, qualified it as the winner of the 1962 competition. Its rival, the Mirage IIIV, was an international

project involving Dassault, Rolls-Royce (it had eight RB.162 lift engines), BAC and Boeing. Pressure was brought to bear on all selectors to declare the Mirage to be 'of equal merit' to the all-British design. After fruitless attempts by Hawker to delegate P.1154 work on a European basis it was realised that the French would stick by the jumping Mirage whatever the other participants decided. In a situation worthy of a Feydeau farce, NBMR-3 was then withdrawn altogether. Development of the Mirage IIIV was suspended in 1966 after the loss of both prototypes and the whole idea faded away. The P.1154, denied its original *raison d'être*, staggered on through a couple of years of inter-service indecision until it became a ripe target for Labour defence cuts—just as metal was being cut for the first aircraft.

Despite the delays and disappointments, valuable lessons were taken on board in the study period for the 'supersonic P.1127', many of which were carried over into the next stage of Harrier development. Although P.1127 work had slowed down, testing continued and the Kingston/Dunsfold team steadily established the rule book of V/STOL flying using the six prototypes. Of these, the second was lost in unusual circumstances on 14 December 1961. Two days earlier the jet had gone supersonic in a shallow dive. On the 14th Bill Bedford was making a flight to check for flutter problems, with Hugh Merewether observing from a Hunter T.7. Climbing to 8,500ft, he no-

ticed an increase in cockpit noise level and a tendency to roll. He descended towards RNAS Yeovilton's runway but increasingly had to struggle with XP836 to keep it in the air. At 300ft and 170kt he lost it and ejected through the canopy with the aircraft at a 30-degree roll angle. Bedford was lucky to escape this inauspicious introduction of the aircraft to the base from which so many of its successors were destined to operate.

The accident lacked explanation until a local farmer appeared at Yeovilton's main gate with an unusual object which turned out to be XP836's port 'cold' nozzle. It had dropped off the aircraft four miles from its fiery end in another farmer's former barn. Merewether had been able to carry out a visual check of the jet when trouble was first reported, but had not been able to inspect the port side. Some cross words passed between the senior designers' offices at Kingston and Patchway (Bristol). It seemed that the fibreglass laminations did not extend satisfactorily into the flange by which the nozzle was bolted to the aircraft. Replacement nozzles in aluminium sheet were tried but they cracked with air vibration, as did titanium specimens. John Dale suggested using steel, as in the perfectly reliable 'hot' nozzles, and this was done, despite a 50lb weight penalty.

Other unfortunate incidents followed. Hugh Merewether himself survived a brilliantly executed forced landing in XP972 after his engine caught fire during a 5g turn at high speed and low level. During these violent manoeuvres the titanium blades at the back end of the HP compressor had rubbed against the engine casing, causing the world's first titanium friction fire.[5] The metal has very low thermal conductivity and heat from friction built up in the rotating blades until they ignited, causing a fire and an engine surge. Molten titanium burned a hole through the bottom of the engine. Unable to lock his undercarriage down in the 90 seconds between the 'bang'

[5]Titanium fires caused by heavy rubbing of blade tips on a compressor casing distorted by high-g turns became a problem once again in 1991 when USMC AV-8Bs suffered several similar incidents. See Part 3, 'Super Harrier Plus'.

through the engine smoothly at the correct speed. This caused flame-outs, or at worst fire damage to turbines, possibly preventing a relight. The first production Valiant bomber (WP199) was made available having just completed successful trials of the rearward-facing ejector seats which the Ministry of Aviation unwisely chose not to install in its V-bomber fleet. A Pegasus 3 was installed in a structure which protruded slightly from the Valiant's bomb bay, limited by minimal ground clearance, and Tom Frost took it aloft on 11 March 1963. On its third flight the belly installation began to disintegrate in flight, as witnessed by Flight Lieutenant Prithee Singh (Indian Air Force), flying the Jet Provost chase plane. Pegasus engineer Alan Baxter recalled the incident: 'As the bottom skin of the Pegasus intake began to peel back the Valiant crew were unaware of the damage until the Jet Provost crew informed them. Singh's excitement caused him to lapse into his native tongue, and it fell to his co-pilot to apprise the Valiant of the problem.' The damage caused a three-month delay. Testing was further inhibited by the engine's location immediately aft of the Valiant's nosewheel bay, which connected directly to an avionics bay deep in the upper fuselage known as the 'organ loft'. This really contained a wealth of undetectable small objects in nooks and crannies, all of which tended to drop out and get sucked into the Pegasus intake while ground-running, causing compressor damage. The Valiant was retired after only fifty of the planned seventy flights because of problems associated with the installation. Clearly, a P.1127 was the best place to test a Pegasus.

and touchdown, he put the powerless P.1127 down on to the hallowed Battle of Britain turf of Tangmere aerodrome and walked away. A more public and embarrassing forced landing ended Bill Bedford's 1963 Paris Air Show demonstration in XP831. In the hover, his nozzles began an uncommanded rotation aft and the aircraft flopped down (on the French V/TOL platform) causing extensive airframe damage—but none to its pilot. The aircraft's international image (and sales prospects) had been damaged by a tiny piece of grit jamming a valve in the system which regulated nozzle angles.

Reliable coordination and operation of the nozzles had been one of Sir Stanley Hooker's main priorities in the Pegasus design. Plessey's control system was normally extremely reliable, setting angles quickly and exactly. Hooker chose motorcycle drive chains to rotate the nozzles. The bearing rings for the rear 'hot' nozzle mountings had to be cooled, using air piped from the front nozzles.

Bristol Siddeley decided to acquire a flying test bed (FTB) to sort out some of the persistent difficulties with the engine, particularly surging, when the airflow was disturbed, stalled and unable to pass

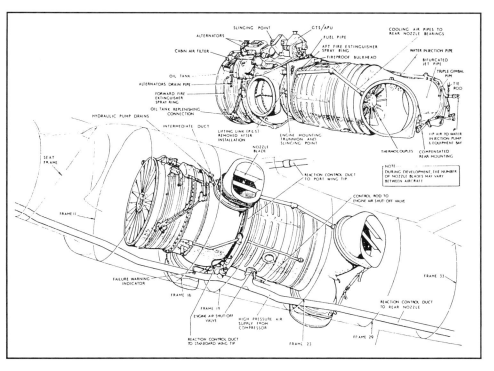

Bristol's next Pegasus variant was a big advance. The 'Peggy Five' (BS.53/5) had variable inlet guides in front of the HP compressor, an annular combustion chamber and 15,500lb of thrust. It led to the Pegasus 6, with a three-stage fan and water-cooled first-stage HP turbine which cranked up the power to 19,000lb thrust, over twice the original output. It was intended for the production version of the P.1127 which the manufacturers hoped would follow its immediate successor—the Kestrel.

KESTRELS

Each of the DB P.1127s introduced different improvements to the design. Several, including XP831, received the drooped tailplane which became another visual trademark for the 'family'. It improved longitudinal control, though it 'left the aircraft short of forward stick in V/STOL flight and so the tailplane range had to be increased in the nose-down sense'. John Farley, who commented on this change, joined the programme in 1964 and began his Harrier career on XV831 in comparative tests with the Short SC.1. At that time there were six P.1127s flying, no two of them the same. Engine life had increased to the point where de-

velopment flying could be advanced more rapidly. XP980 introduced Küchemann 'streamwise' wingtip fairings, to combat transonic wing-drop, and hydro-mechanical nosewheel steering. XP976 had the 'spade-blade' rear nozzle heat shields in place of the Sea Hawk-type 'pen-nib' fairings. Both aircraft had the 13,500lb Pegasus 3.

XP984, the last of the 'pure' P.1127s, was different in that it received the swept wing trailing edge, a thicker wing root and leading edge extensions, plus the uprated Pegasus 5 with no restrictions on rpm 'bands' for continuous running. It also had improved wheel brakes, drop-tank pylons and a spin-test parachute fairing. Both XP980 and XP984 were eventually passed to RAE Bedford, where one of the pilots was John Fawcett. XP980 was used to test the effectiveness of a new runway arrester net. It had radio-controlled brakes, throttle and nosewheel steering because it was feared that the arresting net wires might cut into the aircraft's canopy and hurt the pilot. XP984 tested 'nozzle-inching', a limited HOTAS ('hands-on-throttle-and-stock') concept allowing the nozzles to be moved forward and aft by a few degrees using a spring-loaded switch on the throttle. The idea was to allow fore and aft con-

trol of position in the hover without changing pitch attitude.

John Fawcett had the unfortunate experience of seeing the aircraft meet its end at Bedford in October 1975. 'My successor at Bedford was John Bolton, a test pilot with a lot of Harrier experience. I authorized him for a familiarization flight in XP984. He carried out a partially jet-borne approach for a slow landing in a crosswind which was close to the P.1127's 10kt limit. The aircraft didn't have the self-shortening modification on the main undercarriage, and limited nosewheel steering. It bounced into a position where only the nosewheel was in contact with the ground (commonly called "wheel-barrowing"). John Bolton was then unable to control the aircraft, which swerved off the runway, dug its nose into the grass, reared up in the air and eventually fell the right way up on its wheels. To those of us watching it seemed to balance for an eternity on its nose, with us convinced that it was going to land on its back-end and the pilot's head.' He escaped unhurt apart from facial 'splatter' injuries caused by triggering the canopy-shattering MDC (miniature detonating cord).

XP984 had already been badly damaged when it suffered total engine failure during a dive from 30,000ft at Mach 1.15. Hugh Merewether made his second 'dead stick' P.1127 recovery: in heavy cloud conditions he managed to belly-land on grass at Thorney Island with a fire in the engine bay. The P.1127 had also done early trials with the HUD and yaw autostabilisation. Its only other appearance after the Bedford crash was at Sotheby's saleroom in 1994. It was an important 'bridge' between the original P.1127 and Hawker's next venture, the Kestrel. Two more modifications were made ahead of Kestrel production. One was the introduction of up-and-down blowing valves for the RCS, in XP984. Previously they had only vented downwards, and the new increased sensitivity made pitch and roll autostabilisation unnecessary. Finally, the intake problem was resolved with a new design which worked well across the speed range.

The Kestrel was originally known as the 'P.1127 Development Aircraft'. In Ralph

Kestrel FGA.1 XS694, with TES markings. The aircraft was subsequently shipped to the USA as 64-18267, later NASA 520. It suffered a hard landing during early deck-suitability trials, then ground-looped at Wallops Island, Virginia, in 1967 and was eventually scrapped. Its wings were used to restore XS689 for the Smithsonian Institution exhibition. (BAe)

Hooper's opinion, 'the pressure to give it a new name came from the marketing people'. Nine were built, specifically for an evaluation squadron in response to an Instruction to Proceed from the Government dated 22 May 1962. Negotiations for a full service evaluation model began in 1960, when an RAF P.1127 was very much on the agenda of several RAF 'top brass', leading to GOR.345. As early as January 1960 the Central Fighter Establishment (CFE) at RAF West Raynham had been asked to study V/STOL in an operational context, with a view to full service evaluation. American-inspired support for the project also came from Germany (particularly from *Herr* Strauss, the Defence Secretary) and crucially from the United States itself via MWDP. Another key figure was Larry Levy, who had made a fortune in the US aviation accessories business and joined MWDP in 1961. He had an important role in persuading the three

governments to support a P.1127 evaluation on a three-nation basis.

Interest had lapsed during the NBMR-3 interlude but was revived thereafter. January 16, 1963 was the date of a Tripartite Agreement between Britain, Federal Germany and the United States in which each country agreed to pay for three aircraft and a third of the development costs. Based on XP984 with its enlarged wing and Pegasus 5, the Kestrel had an extra 2 sq ft of fin area to improve stability in forward flight with the undercarriage down. Rear fuselage length was increased by 9in (as in XP984 also) to restore CG, given the Pegasus 5's different thrust centre, and a small gunsight was added to allow evaluation of gun-tracking. Wheel brakes were operated by foot rather than hand, nosewheel steering was modified to prevent 'backlash' and a nose-mounted camera with 'eyelid' fairings was included to give a token, but misleadingly small, mission capability.

As Ralph Hooper pointed out to the authors, 'the Kestrel was the OR.345 aircraft with most of the operational equipment removed. It was designed and stressed for an 18,000lb thrust Pegasus, but to save money and time HMG agreed to de-rate it to only 15,500lb as adequate for trials purposes (just).[6] It was also designed

and stressed for five 1,000lb weapons stations, but only two (inboard) wing stations were fitted. Harrier GR.1 was the Kestrel in a refined form.'

The first Kestrel F(GA).1, XS688, still with 'rubber lips' intakes, flew on 7 March 1964. Flight trials showed that an increase in tailplane span to 14ft was needed to improve stability even more. The aircraft was named on 30 September and received CA release in December for use by the Tripartite Evaluation Squadron (TES). Ten pilots for the unit were selected in January 1964 and began conversion courses using the DB P.1127s and XP831 which was returned to service in October. The Americans nominated a test pilot from each of their three services, the USMC being represented by Commander J.J. Tyson USN. Two US Army pilots were included as there was a possibility of the P.1127 replacing their OV-1 Mohawk battlefield surveillance aircraft. Both *Luftwaffe* pilots were line (rather than test) pilots, though that description did scant justice

---

[6]The extra thrust potential of Pegasus 5 came out of day-long discussions between Gordon Lewis and Bristol Engines' Chairman in which Lewis argued that such a move would save time and cost if the 'production P.1127' (Harrier) went ahead, requiring the increased power. He was proved correct.

Another Kestrel, XS688, still with 'rubber lips' intakes, raises a cloud of grass and leaves as it rises out of a woodland site. This Kestrel was used for USAF tests as 64-18262 and is currently displayed at the USAF Museum, Wright-Patterson, Ohio. (Via R. L. Ward)

to *Oberst* Gerhard Barkhorn, Deputy Commander of the TES. He had destroyed 301 enemy aircraft on the Eastern Front during the Second World War as a fighter pilot—the second highest score ever! The RAF contingent comprised three squadron pilots and the TES commander, Wing Commander David Scrimgeour, a 38-year-old with considerable jet fighter experience. All pilots went through Hunter conversion training to experience handling characteristics similar to the Kestrel's conventional aspects and a five-hour helicopter course at Ternhill.

The TES evaluation began at West Raynham on 1 April and the only serious mishap occurred the same day. One of the US Army pilots, whose only fast jet experience had been his Hunter course of ten hours, forgot to release the aircraft's parking brake on a STO. The huge acceleration from the Pegasus 5 virtually ripped

off the mainwheel tyres and an outrigger collapsed. There was a fire after the aircraft cartwheeled at 60kt and fractured its back. Major Lon Salt, who had flown the US Army's XV-4A 'Hummingbird' and Ryan XV-5A flat-risers, was dragged clear by David Scrimgeour and two other RAF officers. The brand-new Kestrel, XS696, was written off. A modification was introduced to release the parking brake automatically when the throttle was pushed to

the gate. The TES pilots, particularly those from the RAF, also had to get used to nosewheel steering and much taxying around the field was done to this end. Kestrel was given a selector button on the control stick to give +/−5-degree nosewheel directional variation with full rudder pedal and another button on the throttle to give +/−35-degree for steering at low speeds. Even *Oberst* Barkhorn had difficulty with the new flying techniques. On one flight he inadvertently closed the throttle too soon as the aircraft was about to touch down, causing a more-than-heavy landing but no permanent damage.

The West Raynham trials were a long-awaited chance to prove the P.1127 concept. Although thrust was still marginal for VTOL due to the de-rated Pegasus (by then lasting up to 30hr between overhauls), the pilots practised vertically from a whole range of sites. Other small airfields and an Army battle training area were in the vicinity of West Raynham. Square VTOL platforms made of steel or aluminium planks were used, as was an American in-

A pair of Tripartite Kestrels, showing the type's sleek, fighter-like silhouette. As NASA 521 (64-18263), XS689 was used to develop VIFF tactics in 1970 and was eventually put on display at the Smithsonian Institution. XS695 was retained at the A&AEE, was displayed (static) at the 1966 Hanover Air Show and then passed to the Culdrose School of Aircraft Handling. It is currently stored at Cardington for the RAF Museum. (BAe).

Left: Kestrels in a tidy quartet. Aircraft No 1 (XS691) went to Edwards AFB for trials and was accidentally dropped into the James River from a helicopter while being transferred to the Hampton Virginia Aerospace Park. (BAe)

Right: Bristol Siddeley's trials Kestrel XS693, with company test pilot Harry Pollitt. The interior configuration of the blow-in doors can be clearly seen. (Via Alan Baxter)

vention—the polyester resin self-hardening VTOL pad. This was spread on grass, often from a helicopter, and hardened in a few hours.

In all, 340 sorties were flown from grass sites, with attendant FOD ingestion and consequent thrust reduction. Pilots learned to approach grass landing sites at a steady 30kt to keep the cloud of grass, leaves and other woodland debris behind the aircraft's intakes as they landed. Many of the techniques practised were the result of three years of planning by the CFE and Hawker Aircraft. The effects of nozzle scorching marks on grass sites as a means of detecting a Kestrel operating site from the air were studied, as were the problems of logistical support of forward sites, of operating in winter conditions, establishing minimum turnaround times and disguising personnel and support gear from detection. Many of these exercises formed the basis of RAF V/STOL doctrine for the next three decades.

Although the Kestrel was stressed for a warload it was not equipped to deliver weapons and the TES trials did not, in any case, call for this. Possibly the expenditure of a little live ordnance in front of some journalists would have made the trials bit impressive for prospective customers, but the aircraft were able to demonstrate at least a nominal recce capability with their onboard cameras. Many flights were simulated strike and close-support sorties with only the avionics and ordnance missing. Drop tanks (100gal) were carried on the two available pylons towards the end of the trials, though they were seen to cause some deterioration in longitudinal stability. Pilots even began to explore the technique later known as VIFF, deflecting their nozzles slightly to tighten a turn.[7] Bill Bedford flew the first P.1127 night sortie on 1 February 1965, giving TES pilots effective clearance for limited night operations which at one stage involved help from the RAE Blind Landing Experimental Unit.

Left: Kestrels XS695 and XS694 hovering in close proximity during the TES trials. (NASA)

Right: The cockpit of Kestrel XS693. Comparison with the 'office' of a Harrier GR.7 or AV-8B+ (see later) shows that things have changed radically, apart from the basic throttle and nozzle control arrangement. Armament master switch and recce camera controls (top left) testify to the Kestrel's combat capability. (Via Alan Baxter)

Far right: The Kestrel's throttle and nozzle controls are in the centre of this photograph of XS693's left cockpit consoles. The large black disc on the left is the LP fuel cock. XS693 crashed en route to Boscombe Down during Pegasus 6 Test Flight 53 on 21 September 1967. (Via Alan Baxter)

In all, 930 sorties totalling 600 hours were flown in the eight months of the TES's existence. Personnel from all three nations involved reported back in glowing terms. However, the German participation ended there. Their three Kestrels went to the USA with the three American-funded examples and continued to provide useful research data.[8] For the Germans, the trials were seen as useful background experience for the pilots who were to fly Germany's own V/STOL aircraft, the VFW 1262 (VAK-191), powered by a combination of Rolls-Royce lift-jets and a vectored thrust engine.[9] After three prototypes were constructed, VAK-191 was abandoned. So was the Dornier Do 31 V/STOL transport which used two underwing Pegasus 5s and eight Rolls-Royce lift engines.

HARRIER

For the RAF, West Raynham was a timely vindication of its rather tentative V/STOL plans and aspirations. The P.1154 had finally been cancelled during the tri-

---

[7]The development of VIFF techniques is discussed more fully in 'It Changes Everything'.
[8]See 'It Changes Everything'.
[9]The engine was originally the Bristol BS.94, a military version of the BS.75 with vectored nozzles. In the end, the Government decided to support the Rolls-Royce bid, designated RB.193, for which Rolls-Royce would have required a licence from Bristol to use vectored nozzles for patent reasons.

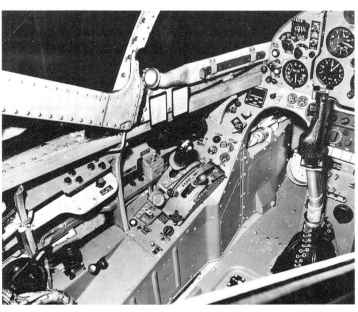

als, and interest focused once again on a developed P.1127, though some tended to view it as consolation prize. The design had actually matured considerably during the five years of development. For the next step in the progress towards an operational version a good deal of P.1154 experience was used for the redesign which was at first called P.1127(RAF). Once again the engine-led P.1127 programme was permit-ted to advance further because of new increases in Pegasus power. Bristol's BS.53/6 (Pegasus 6) was test-flown in one of the UK-owned Kestrels (XS693). The aircraft was modified at Brough to receive the new engine (Serial 922, Build 15) which arrived there in December 1966. Test flights by pilots Harry Pollitt and Duncan Simpson included experiments with water injection for VTOL. After fur-ther complimentary assessments by Hugh Merewether the test-bed was flown by an A&AEE pilot, Squadron Leader Hugh Rigg (brother of actress Diana Rigg). During Flight 53 of the programme he experienced an engine surge severe enough to need the fuel HP cock momen-tarily turned off to enable the engine to recover. Rigg did not realise this in time and the resulting high JPTs burned the HP

Left, upper: In clean condition, the fourth DB Harrier GR.1 (XV279) folds up its landing gear after a VTO. After a lengthy career as a test airframe this aircraft ended its days with RAF Wittering's Fire Section. (Via Alan Baxter)

Left, lower: Still mainly in lurid yellow primer paint, the first production Harrier GR.1 (XV738) performs engine trials at Filton in 1968. Later it was delivered to No 3 Squadron and subsequently served with all the RAF's front-line Harrier units. It was stored at Bruntingthorpe in 1995. (Via Alan Baxter)

blades too badly to allow a relight. He ejected safely at very low level and XS693 crashed near Boscombe Down.

The new Pegasus (known as Mk 101 in its production form) had demonstrated enough power for a combat-capable P.1127 variant, although it was almost a year before Patchway received a replacement test-bed to prove the engine finally. Fitting a pressure ratio limiter helped to prevent such severe surges in future.

Design work pressed ahead at Kingston to satisfy a new RAF requirement, ASR.384. Issued in February 1965, the same month as the P.1154 cancellation, it defined the revised P.1127(RAF) and was accompanied by an order for six DB aircraft. Detail redesign of 90 per cent of the Kestrel airframe was needed, under the leadership of John Fozard. Ralph Hooper relinquished direct supervision of the project, having taken it from rough sketch to near-operational status, and became overall Chief Engineer at Kingston. As part of the effort to improve Pegasus 6 airflow problems, new intakes were designed with rows of auxiliary 'blow-in' doors, six per side at first, then eight. They increased airflow to the more powerful engine and its successors in hovering and partially jet-borne flight. The airframe was built for a minimum 3,000hr fatigue life. Kestrel's wing, optimised for high-speed cruise, was given a 15in tip extension to move the aerodynamic pressure centre aft to improve handling with underwing stores. It also had a new leading edge with fences and vortex generators. It was stressed for two 1,200lb inboard and two 650lb outboard pylons and was tested to an equivalent 15,000hr fatigue life.

A redesigned undercarriage, based on the P.1154 model, gave greater stability for fast taxying and was further modified by Dowty-Rotol in 1967 to include a 'self-shortening' main leg. This was meant to overcome the 'bounce' factor which had caused many P.1127 landing mishaps (including John Bolton's). While absorbing normal energy on touchdown, it provided no rebound force for the first seven inches of travel, by which time the strengthened outriggers were in contact. A four-square touchdown was assured, effective up to a sink rate of 12ft per second, and cross-wind taxying was far better. Nosewheel steering was tweaked once again and a stronger nose oleo was used. The tailplane, with its distinctive kinked extensions and 15-degree droop, was similar to the Kestrel's but stronger and heavier. The Kestrel's combined main undercarriage door and air brake was replaced by a separate air brake under the rear fuselage and undercarriage doors which closed after gear extension or retraction to minimise the ingress of FOD at forward sites.

In the cockpit, the Kestrel's Martin-Baker Mk 6 HA seat was replaced by a much more advanced zero-zero Mk 9. Its ejection sequence was speeded up by the inclusion of MDC in the canopy to shatter it immediately before ejection. Such refinements would have been appreciated by the first P.1127 pilots: hovering in XP831, they were aware that at least 90kt of forward speed was needed for its seat to function successfully in ejection. Autostabilisation was reintroduced for service with a new low-authority pitch and roll control system.

Although the P.1127(RAF) still resembled the Kestrel externally, there were major internal changes to equip it for service. Whereas the Kestrel had been largely devoid of avionics, the RAF required its aircraft to carry much of the 'kit' developed for the P.1154, albeit rather more slowly and not quite so far. Suddenly the new aircraft required a 'crash programme' at Kingston to adapt a huge range of equipment from one evolutionary pattern to another. Pressure was also applied at the various establishments which had to clear all its systems and weapons for use.

A new communications suite was ordered from Plessey and Marconi, providing VHF/UHF facilities. Great difficulty was experienced in locating the aerials in the aircraft's structure for such wide frequency bands without mutual interference, or interference from external stores. Four were fitted in the tail, with a detachable tactical VHF antenna on the spine, though this was seldom used by the RAF. Cossor's 1520 IFF transponder, a cockpit voice recorder (using standard C60 cassettes) and a Hoffman Mk 5 tacan completed the comprehensive set-up.

The radar which was under development for P.1154 was briefly considered, but rejected as unnecessarily expensive and weighty for the aircraft's anticipated roles. The heart of P.1154's nav-attack system in 1961 was to have been Ferranti's FE.541 inertial system, based on a four-gimbal platform and still under development in Edinburgh as the P.1127(RAF) was being defined. In all, the nav-attack fit comprised FE.541, a head-up-display (HUD) designed by a new company called Specto (and one of the first to be installed in a combat aircraft), a Smiths Industries air data computer, a Sperry magnetic compass and a Telford camera recorder. A present-position computer (PPC) worked from data supplied by the FE.541's inertial accelerometers. Ferranti's navigation display and computer (NDC) received data from the PPC and presented it as a direct numerical display of latitude/longitude.

A major innovation was the moving map display. Map images were stored on 35mm strip film and driven across a circular screen on the cockpit front panel by lat/long servos in the NDC. Each strip represented a 28 or 56nm wide band of territory (depending on scale). Up to 20 strips could be joined end-to-end to give a 1,200nm latitude coverage, with the aircraft usually 'placed' centre of screen. The NDC could accept offsets from fix points in addition to set-and-computed steering routes to them. It showed heading, drift, range and bearing to target, all of which were transmitted to the HUD or viewed in a single instrument display at '10 o'clock' to the moving map screen.

Before each mission the FE.541 was aligned so that its three accelerometers were orientated along north, east and vertical axes (azimuth orientation and vertical erection, to be exact) after the platform had been heated to its correct operating temperature. Avionics were installed in bays in the nose and rear fuselage to preserve CG. The rear bay, accessed via a chemically etched, load-bearing door requiring 22 screws to be removed, enclosed equipment on two cooled, shock-proofed shelves.

Central to the offensive capability was the weapons aiming computer (WAC), also deriving its data from the PPC, INAS and air data computer. It calculated weapons aiming mark deflections for the HUD and gave an automatic weapons release signal if required. Its 'knowledge' of the weapons actually carried came from a unique 'ballistics box'. Into this were inserted 'plugs' carrying the ballistics information for each pylon-load of ordnance and a fixed plug for guns, if they were fitted. Since the aircraft had no room for internal weapons, two standard 30mm Aden cannon, mainstay of the Hunter's armament, together with 130 rounds each were installed in detachable pods below the fuselage. The total weight of 900lb was distributed around the CG, avoiding handling problems. The Aden possessed considerable destructive force and great reliability.[10] Ammunition was pre-loaded into boxes which were then installed in the pods, obviating the need to load rounds directly into the aircraft in austere, mucky forward site conditions. Each box had an inbuilt wheel at its rear end so that it could be dragged over hard ground rather like a shopping trolley. No special handling gear was needed for the guns apart from a belt-loading strop and a screwdriver.

To enhance the aircraft's reconnaissance capability, Vinten supplement their sideways-looking F95 Mk 7 camera in the nose with a detachable pod containing four more F95s and an Aeronautical and

Ferranti's FE.541 INAS and associated black boxes beside an early Harrier GR.1 with a modified nose cone. (Via Alan Baxter)

General Instruments F135 with a 1.5in lens. An EMI signal data converter enabled encoded positional information from the INAS to be printed on each negative.[11]

In order to increase the aircraft's self-sufficiency at forward-site locations a gas turbine starter/auxiliary power unit (APU) delivering around 100hp was designed in. It incorporated a 2kVA, 400Hz three-phase AC generator which would be used instead of the Pegasus to power the aircraft's systems on the ground. Rather than needing powered external equipment, the aircraft's APU could actually supply power to ground servicing machinery. Essentially, it provided autonomous start-up of the engine and could keep the battery nicely charged to work the radios and other gear, freeing the forward sites of cumbersome trolleys and similar small-wheeled accessories, in keeping with the aircraft's 'footloose and fancy-free' philosophy.

As a means of increasing range, principally for ferry purposes, a detachable refuelling probe was designed to be fitted using four bolts in a position above the left intake. With its proboscis placed in the pilot's view, 'plugs' could be made by day, or by night using a light built into the left wing root and focused on the tanker's trailing 'basket'. Ferry range could be increased further with bolt-on extended wingtips, though it is unlikely that these were ever used operationally.

A final touch to make the aircraft more user-friendly for RAF pilots was much less technical than the avionics, but potentially just as useful. A small wind-vane was located just ahead of the windshield so that the pilot could readily see the direction of wind relative to the direction of his aircraft's nose in jet-borne flight. He could therefore avoid 'weathercock' instability problems which could lead to unequal lift over the two wings and an uncontrollable roll.

This wide-ranging redesign in the light of Kestrel experience, and some well-defined RAF needs, took time to execute. ASR.384 specified a four-year period up to service entry and six DB aircraft (XV276–281), the first of which flew on 31 August 1966. Shortly afterwards it borrowed one more thing from the defunct P.1154—the name 'Harrier' which was to have been applied to its supersonic sister. There was a political process behind the christening too, according to Ralph Hooper: 'Harrier was first described as the "Kestrel Development Aircraft", but pressure for change came from HM Government who had taken money from the USA and Germany to develop the Kestrel and feared that, if the UK was seen to have benefited towards further development of the type, these Governments might want some repayment!'

With 3–4,000lb of fuel and stores, the Harrier (DB) was already close to the thrust limits for the Pegasus Mk 101, although a 4,000lb warload was possible using STO. Bristol Siddeley came under further pressure to deliver still more power. Meanwhile the DB jets went about proving the redesign and clearing the aircraft's

Harrier GR.1 XV741, the fourth built, fitted with refuelling probe and extended wingtips for the Transatlantic Air Race. (Authors' collection)

systems for service use. Duncan Simpson took XV281 south for tropical trials, calling at Sigonella and arousing interest in the Italian Navy. XV278 was used extensively for stores clearance trials, while XV277 became the workhorse test-bed for a whole series of engine and airframe updates over a 22-year period.

The first true production Harrier GR Mk 1 (XV738) flew with Duncan Simpson aboard on 28 December 1967 following receipt of the RAF's initial contract for squadron Harriers placed at the start of that year. Five more DB aircraft followed, taking on their share of service evaluation at Boscombe Down and Dunsfold. XV738 went straight to Bristol, where it was urgently required for Pegasus 6 development flying, the urgency underlined by the fact that it remained in yellow primer paint for some time. In 1971 it flew the first Pegasus 10 (Mk 102) rated at 20,500lb thrust and then the Pegasus 11 (Mk 103) at 21,500lb, ensuring operational growth potential for future Harriers. Spreading the pre-service testing across a fleet of aircraft in this way ensured that Harrier entered service with the RAF exactly on target.

---

[10]The Aden and other armament loads are described in the Appendix dealing with Harrier weapons.

[11]See Appendix on Harrier weapons.

2. Harriers with Roundels

The RAF's original order for the Harrier GR.1 was for sixty aircraft (as indeed was the order for its replacement, the Harrier II, fourteen years later), amended to 61 after the loss of XV743 on a pre-delivery flight accident which killed Major Charles Rosburg USAF. When they were ordered, early in 1967, the Harriers were supposed to equip one RAFG unit and one in the UK. Subsequent orders and attrition replacements almost doubled that quantity:

118 first-generation, single-seat Harriers were to be produced for the Royal Air Force in all. Their first delivery, XV746, flew into RAF Wittering on 18 April 1969. The Harrier Conversion Team (HCT) began its training at Dunsfold in January 1969, moving to Wittering as the nucleus of No 233 OCU on 1 April.

No 1(F) Squadron, chosen in August 1968 as the first unit to receive the revolutionary aeroplane, made its last APC on

the Hunter FGA.9 and prepared to leave its West Raynham base for Wittering in June 1969. One pilot, Squadron Leader 'Porky' Munro, already had Kestrel TES experience, but only four pilots at Wittering had any Harrier qualifications—the team of QFIs (led by Squadron Leader Richard Le Brocq) of the Harrier Conversion Team. They had received their V/STOL indoctrination from HSA pilots at Dunsfold, using Harrier XV745 extensively (later to be lost in a mid-air accident). Munro was put in charge of 'A' Flight which went through its ground school and taxying sorties in July. He and Flight Lieutenant Sowler made the squadron's first Harrier flights at the end of the month and both were amazed by the aircraft's projectile-like acceleration off the runway. They were also impressed by the handling qualities and by the nosewheel steering (absent from their previous Hunters), but missed the rear view from the former Hawker product.[1]

Conventional take-offs and landings were made at first and pilots learned to tame the Harrier's 165kt landing speed (the same as the BAC Lightning's) by using a 10-degree nozzle deflection. To many of them the aircraft was otherwise a 'Hunter that goes straight up and down'.

Wittering's VTOL pads and dispersed sites had not been completed in July 1969 so 'A' Flight returned to the old concrete Kestrels' nest at West Raynham for their first 'jumps'. They were joined by Wittering's Station Commander, Group Captain P. Williamson, who had overseen the

Blasting a cloud of coal dust aloft, XV741 (with ferry wingtips and 100gal tanks), settles on to St Pancras Station's coalyard in London at the end of a 5hr 31min record transatlantic flight. (BAe)

squadron's very impressive entry for the *Daily Mail* Transatlantic Air Race between 4 and 11 May 1969. Two Boscombe Down test pilots, Squadron Leader T. Lecky-Thompson and Squadron Leader Graham Williams, flew XV741 and XV744 from St Pancras station yard in London to a disused wharf on Manhattan Island in record time, using motorcycles to complete the final 'legs' each end between the two objectives, the Post Office Tower and the Empire State Building. They took 5hr 57min westbound, reduced to 5hr 31min eastbound, but a Royal Navy combination of FG.1 Phantoms and Wessex helicopters won the west-to-east race, mainly by over-using the Phantoms' afterburners. The RAF Harrier team won the westbound race despite numerous 'air stops' for flight refuelling. Their two jets were fitted with 'jousting lance' bolt-on refuelling probes, 100gal tanks and detachable 'ferry' wingtip extensions—one of the very few examples of their use—which were supposed to add 11 per cent to the range.[2] Tremendous popular interest was generated in Britain, and locally in the United States. Harrier's service entry could not have had a more dramatic flourish, or a better indication that the 'Jump Jet' was not just an expensive gimmick. Subtly, the point was made that air wars could be fought from station coalyards and derelict dockland. Demonstrating commendable toughness, both contenders had long, active service lives: XV741 remained in use in June 1995, still bearing its '20th Anniversary Transatlantic Air Race' logo, although by then it was relegated to ground-handling duties at SAH Culdrose, where trainee Sea Harrier deck-handlers pulled it around. XV744 also gave a lifetime of service: it was still flying at Wittering as '3K' when Harrier GR.3 operations wound down in 1992, moving on to the Royal Military College of Science at Shrivenham as '9167M'.

At West Raynham the Harrier students' syllabus included a 'press-up' on their second sortie with an instructor in radio contact, and they gradually learned to manoeuvre the aircraft in the hover during the following three sorties, preparing them for transition to level flight. Flight Lieu-

tenant Sowler misjudged an early transition to vertical landing on 5 August 1969 and XV751 rolled over on landing in a cabbage field. After some Cat-4 damage repair work at HSA it reappeared at No 233 OCU (successor to the HCU) but its pilot prudently transferred to Chivenor, returning to his preferred mount, the Hunter. No 1 Squadron's new CO, Wing Commander Duncan Allison (an old hand on the squadron), also found that he could not easily adapt his piloting skills to the Harrier's strange ways and he handed back command to his predecessor, Squadron Leader Bryan Baker. At the end of October 1969 a new CO was found among the Phantom FGR.2 instructors at No 228 OCU, RAF Coningsby. Wing Commander Ken Hayr AFC accepted the challenge of the RAF's premier Harrier squadron on 1 January 1970. He went through the conversion process, initially gaining 'hover' experience in a Whirlwind helicopter with the side windows blanked off, before transitioning to the Harrier GR.1. He was to prove a tireless and inspiring leader and his role in establishing the new type in service was considerable.

When Wing Commander Hayr arrived in the job the Harrier was experiencing a number of 'shake-down' problems. It had just emerged from a two-month grounding after a Pegasus had thrown some com-

XV753, from the first production block in 1969, with four Matra 155 pods underwing. The aircraft has the original paint scheme of Gloss Dark Green (BS381C: 641) and Gloss Dark Sea Grey (BS381C:638), with undersides in Light Aircraft Grey (BS381C:627) and Type D roundels. This aircraft spent most of its career with No 1 Squadron and No 233 OCU. (Via R. L. Ward)

pressor blades and caught fire on take-off. An anomaly in the hydraulic system was signalling the tailplane hydraulic boosters to run up to maximum power uncommanded, causing sudden pitch-up. That problem was not rooted out until April 1970. In the same month the aircraft began to receive the HUD, INAS and moving map which they had lacked on delivery due to development delays.[3] This naturally increased the training workload considerably. An early enthusiasm for

[1] Nosewheel steering is effected through the rudder pedals after squeezing a little flap on the stick. In most other contemporary RAF fighters, including the Lightning, the rudder pedals were used for differential braking of the main gear to the same end, a cruder method which described bigger turning circles. The Harrier's undercarriage arrangement made nosewheel steering essential.

[2] Another aircraft which could use such devices was the American F-111 series, though they were seldom employed.

[3] These avionics are described later in this chapter.

33

Wing Commander Ken Hayr (with hat), CO of No 1 Squadron, and his pilots look pleased to receive replica Harriers from one of Britain's major toymakers. Each one was carefully marked with squadron colours supplied by decal artist Richard Ward. He also advised Ken Hayr on the best ways of applying squadron badges to the real Harriers so that they were not sucked into their engines. The solution involved strong glue and varnish! (Via R. L. Ward)

showing how the aircraft could operate from grass surfaces was resulting in bogged-down undercarriages and 'FOD-ded' engines.

No 1 Squadron took nine aircraft (less HUDs and INAS) to RAF Akrotiri, Cyprus, for their first detachment from 3 to 25 March 1970, at a time when most of the pilots had little more than 25 hours on the type. On their return they had doubled that time. Their visit was remembered for the nine-aircraft 'bow', arranged in a line-abreast hover along the length of Akrotiri's runway. When the squadron returned for a full Armament Practice Camp (APC) in June–July the absent avionics had been installed, but pilots found some difficulty in using HUD/INAS techniques to equal the bombing and rocketry scores which they had achieved with the old-fash-

ioned 'eyeball' methods! Their CO kept noses to HUDs (revolutionary devices at the time) and also took his men on their first dispersed-site operation abroad—a series of flights from the local, dusty, Army airstrip at Dhekalia.

The first of these 'off-base' exercises had actually taken place from a makeshift site at the edge of the Wittering base in May. Several other locations were used, including local farmers' fields, woods and the disused Bruntingthorpe airfield. Suitably camouflaged ground equipment was prepared for the larger site practices and, progressing from the groundwork done by the TES Kestrels, the squadron developed tactics for operating four aircraft at a rate of six sorties daily from each site. As confidence grew the squadron reached its total complement of eighteen Harrier GR.1s in July 1970, declared itself fully operational in September and ventured abroad to Bardufoss, Norway, in support of NATO's ACE Mobile Force. This was to be the first of very many similar deployments to Scandinavia for the defence of NATO's northern flank. Harrier personnel began to accept that tents in the snow and aircraft servicing in chilly mountain caves were part of the admission price to No 1 Squadron.

A less auspicious 'first' occurred on 6 October 1970 while the squadron was on one of its first major dispersed-site exercises at Ouston, Norfolk. Flight Lieutenant Neil Wharton ejected from XV496 on approach with a fuel system problem that caused a flame-out and the RAF lost its first Harrier. Under Ken Hayr the Squadron pioneered most of the land-based techniques for the world's first operational VTOL aircraft. His pilots were the first to grapple with what were to become familiar hazards for Harrier flyers, including low-level bird-strikes. Flight Lieutenant John Feesey became the first of many to be 'shot down' by a feathered adversary when his aircraft ate a seagull on take-off and flopped into a field from an altitude of 20ft. Both Feesey and his Harrier flew again. There were also cases of flying MEXE (alloy landing pad sections disturbed by the Pegasus' downwash and irritating the aircraft), flying FOD and superficial dents and scrapes as the techniques of VTOL in enclosed rural spaces were thrashed out.

Having amazed the crowds at the 1970 SBAC Display with a varied four-ship demonstration, the No 1 Squadron flying circus appeared at the 1971 Paris *Salon* to similarly ecstatic public response. In the same summer the first of many appearances by No 1 Squadron aboard a Royal Navy ship was arranged. Ken Hayr led four Harrier GR.1s aboard HMS *Ark Royal* in April–May 1971 for a convincing demonstration of the aircraft's all-weather capability.[4] An isolated fault caused the second Harrier loss for the Squadron on 3 August. Captain Louis Distelzweig (on exchange from the USAF after a Vietnam combat tour on F-100D Super Sabres) took off in XV803/Y to lead a four-ship, but his nozzles jammed in the lift-off position. As he struggled to maintain control for a landing the nozzles suddenly swung forward to the braking stop angle and stuck there. The American attempted an ejection as his Harrier stalled and sank, but it is likely that his ejection seat pins had not been removed and tragically he died in the crash.

[4]See Sea Jet, two chapters on.

Still bearing the original Harrier OCU grasshopper logo, GR.1 XW919 hovers at Chivenor on 5 August 1972. This aircraft was rebuilt after a crash at RAF Lyneham in June 1973 in which the pilot ejected following loss of power. It served time in Belize, ending its days at SAH Culdrose in 1995. (R. L. Ward)

Wing Commander Hayr's last major exercise before he stepped down on 6 January 1972 was a second visit to Norway. The entire squadron, with snow-camouflaged Harriers, took part in Exercise 'White Tent' at Gardermoen the previous December. 'White tents' there were aplenty as the visit dug itself and its equipment into the snowy woods in temperatures well below the comfort line. Flight Lieutenant Steve Jennings' unique inverted landing on arrival raised anxiety levels somewhat. His nosewheel steering remained frozen as he passed through lower-altitude air (in which it would have

In March 1972 Exercise 'Snowy Owl' at Milltown, near RAF Kinloss, was the first major dispersed site exercise in which No 1 Squadron Harriers flew quick-reaction CAS sorties. A Taskmaster tractor manoeuvres its charge on MEXE and PSP runway surfaces in its woodland hide. (R. L. Ward)

thawed out in warmer climates). His aircraft skidded off the iced runway and came to rest upside-down in a snowdrift. XV292 went home in a Belfast transport for Cat-4 damage repair and reissue to No 3 Squadron while Steve Jennings returned to flying duties unscathed.

March 1972 brought Exercise 'Snowy Owl' for No 1's further education, with their new CO Wing Commander Eric Smith. For the first time they operated quick-reaction CAS (close air support) and recce sorties from two dispersed sites under simulated wartime conditions. One site adjoined RAF Kinloss, the other was at the nearby disused Milltown airfield. Eight Harrier GR.1s flew up to 25 sorties daily, firing live SNEB and 30mm on the local Tain ranges. The sites were set up by Army sappers, hammering down the MEXE 'tin' taxiways, or Second World War-vintage PSP (pierced steel planking) in some cases, in the hides and access paths, then spraying it green to match the terrain. MEXE VTOL 'pads', camouflage-net hides and 12ft square RAF frame tents ('The Hessian Hilton') were then provided. The rest arrived in about thirty C-130 Hercules loads, although for later exercises this total was gradually reduced as more airportable lightweight equipment became available. Standard fire trucks (three per site) and two-ton mobile generators were among the first pieces of kit to be replaced by less bulky items. Live weapons and other stores were kept at a central logistics park ('logs park') at a safe distance and trucked in as required, usually at night.

A No 1(F) Squadron pilot awaits instructions for his next sortie at Milltown. Green 'lo-viz' helmets were becoming fashionable at this time, as were red/blue Type B roundels (on camouflaged surfaces) and matt paintwork (introduced November 1970). The glossy paint was initially oversprayed with matt varnish, the aircraft being resprayed with matt polyurethane later. (R. L. Ward)

Maintenance tended to be confined to daylight hours to avoid compromising the site by using artificial lighting. Few problems were experienced with the Harrier's mechanical parts, although the more delicate INAS and electrical systems caused a good deal of work during the first few years.

Although two-week exercise detachments were standard practice, in wartime the location of each forward operating base (FOB) would have been changed more frequently, both to keep up with the FEBA (forward edge of battle area) position and to minimise site detection by hostile infra-red or sideways-looking radar-equipped reconnaissance aircraft. If a site had been approached by enemy ground forces, all personnel, including aircrew, were supposed to double as light infantrymen and pick up a rifle to aid the RAF Regiment Field squadron at the outer screen of defence. Pilots often flew up to four sorties daily on field exercises. A taceval (tactical evaluation) in 1974 produced sortie rates of one per aircraft per

hour for three days, giving a total of 364 sorties by fourteen Harriers.

While No 1(F) Squadron blazed many trails during their first two years—as befitted the world's longest-established military flying unit—the training effort continued at Wittering. The Harrier Conversion Unit became No 233 OCU on 1 October 1974, with the Welsh motto *Ymlaen* (meaning 'Forward'), which described only one of the Harrier's many tricks but aptly pointed the way for the next stage of the V/STOL re-equipment programme. No 233 OCU with its Welsh wildcat unit badge dated back to 1952 (four decades after No 1 Squadron was formed) and the need to expand the 2 TAF Vampire Det pilot supply in the atmosphere of the Korean War. The unit then trained Hunter pilots at Pembrey until 1957, re-forming at Wittering where it ran six courses to convert the first generation of RAF Harrier aircrew by February 1971. Having worked its way through the backlog of RAF Hunter aircrew to provide most of that requirement, it began its first *ab initio* course for pilots straight from basic training at the Tactical Weapons Unit (TWU) on 1 March, introducing three-month courses. No 1 Squadron had passed through in six batches from July 1969 to October 1970. The next two courses (Nos 3 and 4) produced pilots for the two RAF Germany (2 ATAF) squadrons which were to place the Harrier squarely on NATO's front line.

TWO SEATS FOR TRAINING

With only single-seat aircraft available, No 233 OCU made use of HSA Hunters at first so that an instructor could fly 'wing' on a trainee Harrier pilot's early sorties. A far better solution was the introduction of the two-seat Harrier. A year after the initial order for Harrier GR.1s the RAF ordered a pair of development batch two-seaters to meet Air Staff Requirement 386. Although it was clear that the task of converting pilots to the Harrier would be more demanding than for conventional jets, there was no two-seater version available at Wittering until eighteen months after training began. By that time most of the first round of pilots for all three operational squadrons had passed through the OCU. The delay was not of Hawker Siddeley's making. Their design for a two-seater, designated T.2, progressed alongside the single-seater, evolving from Ralph Hooper's two-seat studies which had accompanied the P.1154 project. It was intended to carry exactly the same operational weapons system as the GR.1, providing the same stores carriage and combat envelope. Despite the inclusion of a second cockpit, and the tail ballast necessary to maintain the CG around the fixed engine datum, the aircraft weighed only 1,400lb more than the GR.1. For combat use the removal of the rear seat reduced this differential to 800lb. The earliest design studies had shown that a tandem-seat arrangement, rather than the side-by-side Hunter T.7 configuration, was inevitable because the air intake could not be widened. A 47in plug was added to the front fuselage to take the rear 'stepped up' cockpit. A rear seat was positioned seven inches further aft than the GR.1 equivalent, over the nosewheel bay, so that the cabin air-conditioning had to be relocated to a large 'hood' fairing behind the canopy. This arrangement did little for the aircraft's aesthetic attributes but it provided the rear-seat instructor with an extremely clear view ahead. Unusually for a trainer, there was a view 10 degrees down from the horizontal, straight ahead from the back seat. Relocated under the rear Martin-Baker Type 9 Mk 1 seat, which was set 18in higher than the single-seat position, were the

0.75in steel tubes filled with chilled iron grit. This meant that wings could be swapped between single and two-seaters, but not tailplanes.

Weathercock stability, crucial in the Harrier, was clearly going to be affected by the major changes 'up front'. An enlarged ventral fin was added, aligned with the trailing edge of the rudder. A row of detachable ballast weights was fitted to an extended tail boom which increased the aircraft's overall length to 56 ft (17.04m) over the pitot. The tailfin was moved aft 33in and raised to increase its area by fitting an 11in plinth beneath it. Trials of various tailfin configurations were carried out with the two development T.2s after the first flight of XW174 on 24 April 1969 and XW175 on 14 July. The first aircraft was able to contribute little to the programme. Six weeks after its maiden flight it crashed near Boscombe Down with a fuel system problem. Duncan Simpson, on his first T.2 flight, sustained neck injuries in the ejection process after failing to persuade his 'Peggy' to relight. MDC was installed in canopies subsequently, along with a manual back-up relight system. Continued tests with XW175 showed that the aircraft was difficult to hold 'wings level' at high angles of attack. At first it was thought that airflow breakaway from the new rear canopy was to blame and the large air scoops behind it were removed—without improvement. A series of fin enlargements was then trialled. First was a rectangular extension stretching back over the tailboom. Kingston's sheet metal workers then produced a series of height extensions to place the fin more effectively in the airflow at high AOA (angles of attack). A 6in growth made no difference. Small improvements resulted from an 18in

INAS, q-feel unit, F95 camera and windscreen washer reservoir, all to maintain balance with the engine thrust centre. To help it cope with the heavier fuselage, the front RCV was moved forward, close to the tip of the nose. However, the rear cockpit did not have the moving map and INAS nav/attack HUD displays. In the front cockpit, equipment and instrumentation was identical to that in the GR.1. Even the windshield was the same, with minor reinforcement to cope with increased canopy side-loads from the two

massive clamshell canopy hoods. An internal windshield was situated ahead of the rear cockpit in case of damage to the front canopy.

Early in the design process it was realised that there was a resonant frequency problem with the standard Harrier tailplane. On the GR.1 the fuselage's natural frequency was not a sub-harmonic of the tailplane, so the phenomenon was not apparent. In the T.2 installation there was interaction, which was cured by installing four dampers in each tailplane tip—three extension stuck on to the fintip aerial mounting. Then an extreme 23in version appeared, but it would have required other reinforcement for production use and expensive alterations to the 'plans'. Kingston's philosophy, inherited from Sir Sidney Camm, was 'FIBDATD'—'Fix It But Don't Alter (many of) The Drawings'.

The eventual solution was a compromise. An 18in, broad-chord extension was made possible by removing the fin-cap aerial 18in up the fin trailing edge and refairing its leading edge into the dorsal fin fillet, using slightly revised internal structure. Additionally, 'Fozard's Flipping Air Brake' came to the rescue. From the earliest days of Harrier flying it had been found that partially extending the air brake improved dutch roll stability. It was automatically part-extended for this purpose when the undercarriage was lowered in any case. For the T.2, it was established that a 26-degree air brake extension would prevent

Gas flow diagram for the Pegasus Mk 101.

FRONT NOZZLES

REAR NOZZLES

H.P. COMPRESSOR

ANNULAR COMBUSTION CHAMBER

L.P. COMPRESSOR

H.P. TURBINES

L.P. TURBINES

Jet Characteristics

	Front	Rear
Velocity	1200 fps (365 m/sec)	1700 fps (520 m/sec)
Temperature	110°C (220°F)	680°C (1200°F)

at Sea Level VTO rating.

lateral and directional oscillation at high AOA, in conjunction with the revised fin. A final, welcome modification in the trainer version was the addition of an extending foot step to help entry and exit. In the GR.1 this was only possible with ladders or gymnastics.

The first of twelve production T.2s flew on 3 October 1969 and was used by HSA to test a variety of stores configurations and the RWR (radar warning receiver) installation, as well as for continued 'weathercock' trials. It was force-landed in July 1970 while still with the manufacturer, in the month when No 233 OCU began to receive their two-seaters. Several of the early production aircraft, like the early TAV-8As for the USMC, had the tall, scimitar-like 18in fin extension, causing a variety of side-views on the flightlines at Cherry Point and Wittering when later deliveries appeared with the lower-profile model. Several T.2s were retrofitted with the later design. In due course No 1 Squadron received its T.2 allocation, as did RAF Wildenrath for the RAFG squad-

rons. Each squadron had one or two 'family models' on charge for instrument ratings, weapons delivery and other training functions. The RAFG aircraft were eventually pooled.

The Harrier T.2's extra weight inhibited its VTO performance with the original Pegasus 6 Mk 101. Of the first twelve aircraft built, the final pair had the more powerful Mk 102 engine and were designated T.2A. Earlier aircraft were retrofitted to a similar standard. A further engine upgrade to the 21,500lb Mk 103 resulted in the T.4, of which fourteen were new-build aircraft and rest upgraded T.2As. At the same time most had RWR and LRMTS installed.[5] As in the GR.3 upgrade, the RWR tail installation meant an increase of five inches in fin height so that all GR.3/T.4 aircraft eventually had the same basic fin assembly. Four aircraft were used without the LRMTS installation and they were known as T.4As and utilised for handling training, where their 300lb lighter weight and better VTOL performance was useful. In 1987 the tentative designation T.6 was given to a night-attack version of the T.4, but this was to be superseded by a later Harrier II derivative, the T.10, described later in the book.

An early demonstration of the two-seater's undiminished performance was put on by No 1 Squadron during a NATO exchange with the *Luftwaffe's* JBG-31. In order to find the winner of a time-to-10,000ft contest a Harrier T.4 was pitted against one of German squadron's hot-rod TF-104Gs. Both had back-seat 'referees'. The Harrier won by 7 seconds and, to rub in a little salt, it went on to complete a one-hour sortie while the Starfighter crew headed home, gasping for fuel.

HARRIERS IN GERMANY
NATO's 2 ATAF was responsible for the defence of some 60,000 square miles of territory in Central Europe, drawing upon West German, Dutch, Belgian and RAF units. Its striking power had rested partly in the Canberra B(I).8, including those of No 3 (formerly No 59) Squadron at

[5]Laser Rangefinder and Marked-Target Seeker, described later in this chapter.

Geilenkirchen, and the Hawker Hunter which was operated by several squadrons. Among them was No IV (formerly 79) Squadron which flew the fighter/recce Hunter FR.10 with its nose-mounted cameras, at RAF Gütersloh. No IV Squadron therefore had a reconnaissance background which was to be carried over into their Harrier era. The third unit earmarked for conversion to Harriers had been flying the Pioneer communications aircraft for a year before disbandment in 1979, and fifteen years on Hunters prior to that.

No IV (AC) Squadron received its first Harrier, XV779, at RAF Wildenrath in August 1970 and fourteen more over the following year. Four of No 1 Squadron's experienced Harrier pilots were posted to the German base to form the nucleus of the first 2 ATAF VTOL squadron. No 20 Squadron was re-formed at Wildenrath, a move made possible by the second Harrier order, for seventeen GR.1s (XW763–770 and XW916–924), built to the same standard as the first batch and delivered

from September 1971, though not all to No 20 Squadron. This second Wildenrath unit received XV801 in November 1970, the first Harrier to be delivered direct to RAFG, and officially re-formed the following month. Wildenrath's Harrier Wing was completed by No 3 Squadron, which initially drew aircraft from the other two squadrons so that it could convert in time for the Wing's official operational date, 1 January 1972. At the time the station commander was a VTOL veteran, Group Captain David Scrimgeour, former commander of the Kestrel TES at West Raynham.

During its six years at Wildenrath the Harrier Wing expanded upon all the FOB operating techniques pioneered at Wittering and West Raynham. In early 1971 the RAF decided to establish thirty forward-base training sites within 50km of Wildenrath, including several in Holland and Belgium, with another twenty carefully researched locations for potential use in wartime. Extensive aerial surveillance (up to 700 sorties were made) narrowed

the choice down to sites where aircraft could be concealed in such a way as to elude an enemy strike pilot, with his two-second average target-sighting time during a fast, low pass. They enabled the Harrier men involved to become thoroughly familiar with local terrain, reducing the stresses of navigation over what otherwise would comprise mostly unfamiliar ground.

Harriers stood up well to their intensive use at Wildenrath. No IV Squadron had only one engine change in its first six months and no recurrence of the compressor blade failure which had hampered training the previous year. Ferranti's INAS also performed as advertised. The Wing's major problem was the location of Wild-

Pegasus nozzles and RCS ducts are clearly displayed on XV281, the last of six GR.1 (DB) aircraft. Like all the development aircraft, '281 performed a variety of test programmes at A&AEE, Filton and Dunsfold. It flew all-weather trials, ski-jump launches and deck-trials on HMS _Eagle_. (Via Alan Baxter)

enrath itself. With a nominal 200-mile maximum operational radius assumed for most Harrier training purposes, the airfield's location some 150 miles from the most likely area of combat engagement in time of war meant potentially small warloads and brief loiter times. When the Harrier Wing relocated to Gütersloh in 1977, placing them on NATO's most easterly airfield (only 75 miles from the East German border), its commanders were able to construct a more realistic war-plan for their 'survivable tactical air power' scenario. The rearrangement was a simple base-swap with Gütersloh's two fighter squadrons, which had recently changed from the BAC Lightning to the longer-ranged Phantom FGR.2. No IV Squadron made the move on 4 January 1977, followed by No 3 Squadron on 4 April. This transfer also brought about a change in the Wing's composition. RAFG's requirement for five Jaguar GR.1 squadrons, and the more limited crew and administrative accommodation at Gütersloh, were

compelling reasons for the switch of No 20 Squadron to the Jaguar and the dispersal of their Harriers among the other two 2 ATAF units, giving totals of 18 per squadron. Another factor was attrition (26 losses by 1977), which caused some difficulty in supporting four squadrons and an OCU with appropriate numbers of aircraft.[6]

During its Wildenrath days the three-squadron Wing took part in many forward-based exercises which refined the techniques of concealed-site tactics. One such outing, 'Autumn Leaves', held on the Sennelager training area in 1973, involved such effective camouflage that not one of the forest hides was discovered by the frequent recce overflights from 'hostile' forces. Wing Commander Philip Champniss's No 20 Squadron detachment took over disused farm buildings as their HQ, with briefing 'rooms', communications, stores and accommodation in camouflaged tents. Their HQ vehicles were parked in barns while the Harriers settled

Above: Rising out of its forest FOB, 'Y' of No 20 Squadron was one of the GR.1As from the three RAFG squadrons which participated in Exercise 'Heath Fir', June 1976. (Via R. L. Ward)

Right, upper: A close examination of this print reveals large numbers of fingers in ears as NATO officials observe a hovering Harrier. Also in the frame are a second No 3 Squadron example, refuelling, and a third, just visible behind its hide-netting in the centre. The occasion was the RAF Exercise 'Oak Stroll'. (Via R. L. Ward)

Right, lower: From the outside it looks like a haystack, but there's a Harrier inside. Dispersed-site trials at Watton in May 1974 included XV756/34 of No 1 Squadron in Exercise 'Big Tee'. (R. L. Ward)

[6]No 20 Squadron's insignia were to reappear on Harriers in 1992 when the nameplate became available again and it was applied to No 233 OCU as an RAF Reserve designation (each OCU having a Reserve or 'shadow' designation for combat duties).

down under trees or netting attached to farm buildings and operated from a very uneven grass airstrip. The Harrier's undercarriage, designed for a sink rate of 12fs, coped with the bumps and mud admirably. Fuel came from 10,000-gal plastic pillow tanks with disguised fuel lines running to each of the individual aircraft hides. Vertical take-offs from a small forest clearing were technically possible but prohibitive in terms of reduced payloads. Instead, a small area of road or a field served as the common runway, with vertical (or rolling vertical) landings on a 75ft square, green-painted MEXE pad or longer strip.

On one of the secondary 'Autumn Leaves' sites Harriers had to taxy up a sloping scrub area to reach their take-off strip, throwing up mud and stones, but usually without self-inflicted FOD damage. A much bigger problem was the risk of bird-strikes in the vicinity of woods. Harriers had an 8mm thick canopy and the windshield was stressed to take a one-pound bird hitting its centre at 600kt. A bird in the engine via the aircraft's necessarily vast air inlets was usually more serious. While the actual damage to the front fan or compressor would probably be slight, the ingestion of a bird disturbed the airflow through the compressor, causing a surge. On early marks of Pegasus the surge margins were very tight and a comparatively small disturbance in the compressor could easily trigger a surge and flame-out. At low altitude a pilot would have little time to react and a bale-out might be his only recourse. Given time and altitude, he could pick up the indication of a surge on his central warning panel (CWP) to the right of the cockpit (red for 'serious', accompanied by an aural warning in the headphones). There would also be plenty of 'noises off' from an engine in surge to confirm the warnings too. Test pilot John Fawcett pointed out that in extreme cases the hinged blow-in doors around the intake could actually blow out! A relight could then be attempted by shutting the engine down to stop the surge and reduce JPT (jet-pipe temperature) to safer levels. The throttle was then advanced, with the manual fuel control system engaged, to open the HP fuel cock and achieve a relight, slowly building up thrust. If the igniters worked and powered flight could be resumed, the pilot would then seek a diversionary airfield as soon as possible after making a PAN call (next in level of urgency down from a 'Mayday') on his radio.

Most FOD ingested by the aircraft's intakes, including birds, was spat out via the cold nozzles at the front end of the engine with little damage to the deeper regions of the turbine. However, FOD can cause blade separation and ingestion, which in turn could lead to penetration of the engine casing and a fire. Blades in the low-pressure compressor had to be

Hard-working test-bed GR.1 (DB) XV277, with a GR.3 nose-shape and instrument boom. In its long career this aircraft flew stores clearance trials at Boscombe Down, Martel missile tests, the LERX installation and a whole succession of Pegasus updates between November 1978 and November 1988. It then spent over six years at Yeovilton's AMG before being sold to the collector Dick Everett in Ipswich. (Via Alan Baxter)

The spine of Harrier GR.1 XV804/45 of No 233 OCU provides a useful vantage point for Yeovilton's Air Display in September 1975. This Harrier served with every front-line Harrier Force unit. (Authors)

checked frequently for nicks in their leading edges, with a hand-held mirror for dentist-style inspections deeper in the engine. This type of inspection was carried out mainly by the Harrier Servicing Flight (HSF) at each main base, or in the field.

On a forward site, mission tasking was handled from the Forward Wing Operations Centre (FWOC), the Wing's HQ in the field which was usually crammed into a vehicle. Targets and approach routes were issued and data on the state of readiness of each squadron was passed back to it by an Army Ground Liaison Officer (GLO). He in turn relayed instructions to each pilot about his mission. Once over the target the pilot's CAS control passed to a FAC. Pilots on strike sorties usually flew in pairs, armed with two 1,000lb bombs or SNEB rockets.

Reconnaissance sorties were usually solo affairs for a No IV Squadron Harrier with a Vinten five-camera pod slung between its guns. All Harriers could provide useful recce data from their 70mm F95 fixed camera, triggered on a panel fixed to the cockpit wall and operated from a button on the left of the control stick grip. The pilot used an IP (Initial Point) to start his photo run and a stopwatch to time it. In the field No IV Squadron took along its mobile processing and intelligence unit, contained in several camouflaged trailer vehicles. As soon as the aircraft returned, its Vinten pod was swung open and film from the five cameras was removed and rushed to be developed in a matter of a few minutes before being run across a light-box, usually with the pilot on hand to help with interpretation. Imprinted data from the aircraft's INAS gave relevant location and heading information. Usually the process was completed in around twenty minutes from landing so that the information could be supplied to the FWOC and used for targeting.

The Harrier's attack role in NATO's Central European area was essentially similar to that of the Jaguar, Alpha Jet or, later, the A-10A. NATO tank forces in the mid-1970s were outnumbered 2.5 to 1 and the Warsaw Pact forces were estimated to have 40 per cent more fighting units, not including reserves within Soviet Russia. NATO's chosen response was in the form of aircraft which could repel, or at least slow down, a hostile tank advance until reinforcements could be brought in from the United States. The Harrier's anti-armour tactics involved flying low and delivering CBU or bombs on to the advancing tanks, reaching their targets via time-sequenced 'gates' in the friendly missile belts. Unlike the other RAFG offensive squadrons, the Harrier units did not have a strike (i.e. nuclear) capability.

Mission planning for a typical GR.3 CAS sortie was done in great detail, even in FOB conditions, which might include full chemical warfare protection gear for all personnel and an open-air 'briefing room'. Attack headings, target details and

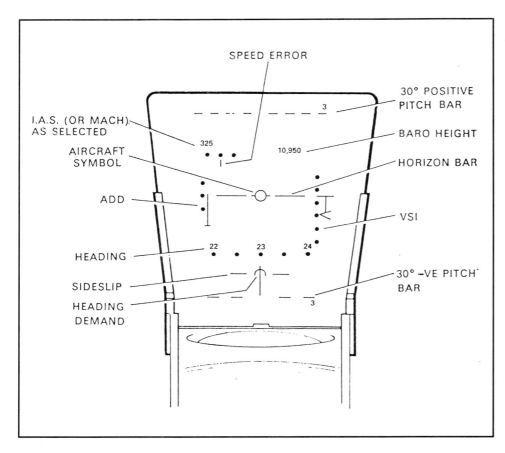

Data format on the HUD in the Navigation mode

start-up and take-off times were calculated, so were nozzle angles and fuel weights for a typical vertical landing with the possibility of stores still aboard. A typical training load was a pair of 100gal combat tanks on the inboard pylons, two ML practice bomb carriers outboard and 100 rounds of 30mm in each gun pod. Attacks were normally made by pairs flying at around 480kt and 250ft AGL, with 1,500–2,000yds' separation between the pair.

Having signed the aircraft's Form 700 record sheet, a Harrier pilot would climb aboard and check his Mk 9 ejection seat for correct installation of 'safety pins'. (One of the authors recalls witnessing a tragic incident where this was not done and a GR.3 pilot was fired 300ft into the air when he started to get out of the aircraft without putting in the pins first, with fatal consequences.) INAS alignment was the next job. The FE.541 inertial system took 8–12 minutes to settle on true north. In peacetime it could be updated in flight

using tacan bearings and overflight of a prominent feature built into the flight plan (such as a bridge) with known coordinates. Weapons panel switch checks were also completed for safety, as was the freedom of the fuselage-mounted ADD probe and the yaw vane ahead of the windshield. While a Houchin APU powered up the systems, external walk-round checks were completed, with special attention to control surfaces, undercarriage components and 'puffer jet' RCS outlets. Back in the cockpit the FE.541 was turned to 'nav' mode and the APU disconnected. With cockpit checks completed, the pilot signalled removal and stowage of his five cockpit and ejection seat safety pins and initiated engine start-up. Fuel cocks were turned on, the starter button pressed and the igniters lit up the engine. Electric power then came on line, enabling the pilot to set his radio frequency, check in and turn on his oxygen supply.

The pre-take-off check covered trim, air brakes, fuel, flaps, instrument readings, oxygen flow, hood secured, harnesses fastened and hydraulics showing correct pres-

sures. Engine run-ups were done against a stopwatch to check acceleration of the engine fan-speeds. Inadequate acceleration time could mean a scrubbed mission. With power held at 55 per cent rpm the nozzles were lowered, thereby pressurizing the hot air ducts to the RCS, and duct pressures could be checked. With nozzles swung aft, the nozzle-stop setting was inserted in the nozzle control box to preset their take-off angle, usually 55 degrees for STO. Power was pushed to 99 per cent and the Harrier lifted off at between 110 and 125kt from a 700–800ft run, with the nozzles slammed to the take-off position at the optimum speed. With his eye on the AOA indicator, the pilot balanced nozzle position against speed to avoid stalling, raising flaps and undercarriage before 250kt was reached. Normal cruise speed was about 420kt and power could be reduced to 80–85 per cent to maintain this.

From then on the Harrier pilot took his airspeed, altitude and heading instructions from his HUD, checking his position via the fixed cursor overlying the circular moving map display, which was driven by the INAS. At low altitude the radar altimeter could be set to give audio pull-up instructions at a selected minimum height AGL. Paper maps, stowed in a clip by the pilot's left knee, were kept handy in case the INAS went down. If all systems were running properly, the INAS gave a precise position reference. Waypoints or IPs could be 'repeated' on the HUD, with appropriate 'distance to run' indications. At the IP the stopwatch came into use again. Weapons switches were set, pylons switched on and weapons delivery mode selected on the weapons control panel to the left of the moving map display.

Inertial systems like the FE.541 were designed to enable strike aircraft to make first-pass attacks on their targets. Combined with an effective HUD, an inertial system enabled the pilot to line up his aircraft for the attack run before his target was visible. With the system switched to 'Navigate', a pilot was free to fly wherever he wished: the INAS would continue to show his direction to his next waypoint or target from any position, including a deviation from the planned route (within limits). Closer to the target he switched the system to 'Close Navigation' and a range circle marking in the HUD unwound anti-clockwise from a distance of twelve miles out from the target. The altitude of the target was already entered into the navigation display computer (NDC), and armament options could then be selected on the WCP knowing that release altitudes and trajectories would be correctly computed. With the NDC switched to 'Plan' at six miles from the target, the HUD indication entered its transition phase, showing the distance-to-target 'clock' at the top of the combining glass and a stabilised target bar at the bottom. As soon as the target appeared in the area indicated by the target bar, a central vertical aiming line was 'placed' over the target bar visually by aligning the aircraft accurately. Both target bar and aiming line were then kept superimposed on the target, using the pilot's hand controller. Weapons release at the correct moment was automatic. After weapons release a 'Break Away' indication showed in the HUD and the INAS could be switched back to 'Normal' to generate new steering signals.

An offset target facility could be called up, using a prominent feature such as a bridge or tall building in the target area. Initially an 'attack' was aimed at this offset point and the target bar in the HUD was held on it while the pilot switched in the known offset bearings and range to the true target. As with the more direct method, the pilot would usually 'pop up' or 'unmask' to get a better view of the target during the final run, the height and timing of the 'unmask' relating to the types of weapons being used and their related delivery profile, and the intensity of any anti-aircraft defences.

Guns, rockets or unplanned manual bomb release were all made possible as armament options by switching to 'Strike Manual' mode. This used depressed sight-line (DSL) techniques whereby an aiming deflection mark appeared in the HUD. This had to be kept visually superimposed on the target, with weapon release trig-

HUD symbology associated with the various stages of a mission.

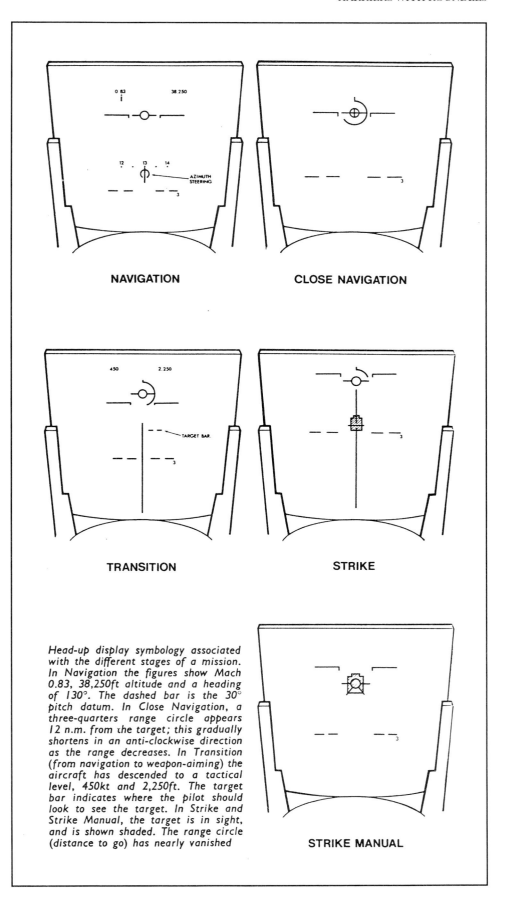

NAVIGATION

CLOSE NAVIGATION

TRANSITION

STRIKE

STRIKE MANUAL

Head-up display symbology associated with the different stages of a mission. In Navigation the figures show Mach 0.83, 38,250ft altitude and a heading of 130°. The dashed bar is the 30° pitch datum. In Close Navigation, a three-quarters range circle appears 12 n.m. from the target; this gradually shortens in an anti-clockwise direction as the range decreases. In Transition (from navigation to weapon-aiming) the aircraft has descended to a tactical level, 450kt and 2,250ft. The target bar indicates where the pilot should look to see the target. In Strike and Strike Manual, the target is in sight, and is shown shaded. The range circle (distance to go) has nearly vanished

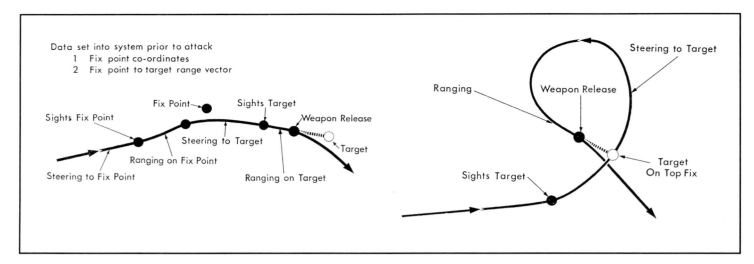

Data set into system prior to attack
1 Fix point co-ordinates
2 Fix point to target range vector

Plan views of Harrier attack missions: the precise local fix attack (left) and the target of opportunity attack (right).

gered manually at a predetermined range to target. For the seldom-used air-to-air gunnery option the Smiths HUD reverted to the standard gyro-type gunsight, computing a lead angle for a stern attack.

Ballistic information on the chosen weapon was supplied to the weapons-aiming computer via a ballistics box. Each weapon type—guns, 'iron' bombs, rock-

ets and cluster bomb units (CBUs)—had known ballistic characteristics which were stored in small 'plugs'. These were inserted in the box when the warload was in place, one for guns (a fixed plug) and a combination of the three others.[7]

In its original configuration for the Harrier GR.1, Ferranti's FE.451 accounted for about ten per cent of the total cost of the aircraft. Its effectiveness in allowing accuracy to within 1nm per hour of flying time to target (without updates), and then giving the pilot the chance to make an accurate single-pass attack, was considered to be worth the expense.

Throughout his attack a Harrier GR.1/3 pilot relied on top cover to keep off the

GR.1A XW922/49 from No 233 OCU at the nozzle-stop position in 1976. The previous year a pilot was killed when he was accidentally ejected through the canopy while this aircraft was parked at RNAS Yeovilton. It was damaged again in a landing accident at Wittering and written off. (Authors)

fighters, plus his own speed, low altitude and the small size of the aircraft. If his RWR indicated an imminent fighter interception he could switch his HUD to air-to-air mode in the hope of bringing guns to bear on a hostile aircraft. Near to the target, however, he would be more likely to try and maintain his attack, using evasive tactics to deter the fighter. In the later GR.3 variant the Laser Rangefinder and Marked-Target Seeker (LRMTS) could be used in two modes to assist in weapons aiming. Once its protective 'eyelids' were

retracted, the nose-mounted laser could be used to give a range measurement to a visually identified target. Accuracy would be improved considerably by the system's inherent stabilisation against vibration, and angular movement by the aircraft, helping the ballistics system fine-tune its automatic weapons release computations. Preferably, a target would be 'ground-lased' by a FAC (usually an RAF ground attack pilot seconded to a tour with the Army, or forward emplaced reconnaissance elements of the SAS). His job was to guide the pilot on his last lap to the target and then illuminate it once the Harrier's LRMTS was able to pick up the 'laser spot' at a little over five miles' range. The rest of the attack was then mainly automatic, with LRMTS passing steering data to the pilot's HUD. Flying at around 100ft AGL or less, and at speeds over 500kt, a Harrier GR.3 pilot appreciated all the 'automation' he could get in those few blurred seconds before weapons release. Trying to acquire a target visually, and avoid the threats (principally the ground), in those conditions took piloting skills to the limit.

Assuming that the pilot survived the opposition and found his way back to his base or camouflaged FOB, he would then begin 'approach and landing' procedures. Landing gear was lowered at 240kt, giving four green lights when locked down. For a short landing, nozzles were swung to the 40-degree mark, flaps lowered and fuel booster pumps confirmed 'On'. Checks were made for 'brakes off', harness tight and adequate RCS pressure. The aim was to try and land the aircraft squarely on all four undercarriage units, whereupon the nozzles were swung to the braking stop position (9 degrees forward), reducing speed to 50kt, at which point nozzles were set aft, in order to avoid FOD, and wheel brakes used. After taxying to his parking position the pilot shut down

[7]USMC AV-8As had different plugs designed to allow for the ballistics of USN weaponry, such as the Douglas-designed Mk 80 series bombs, 2.75in and Zuni 4in rockets and Rockeye II CBUs. The ingenious plugs were a British invention. In contrast, contemporary aircraft of American origin used a 'dial-a-bomb' system, which necessitated using a large analogue computer.

the HP fuel cock to 'switch off' the Pegasus.

A hover/vertical landing had to be done with no more than 2,000lb of fuel aboard and into the wind, using the wind-vane to judge the direction in which the nose had to be pointed. To avoid the dangerous yaw phenomenon it was necessary to prevent the Harrier from drifting laterally. If a drift did develop the occupant would feel a rapid vibration through his boot-sole from the rudder pedal on the side corresponding to the direction of drift. Urgent application of rudder was then needed to restore equilibrium.

In the approach to a vertical landing the nozzles swung to the 'hover stop' position, then to 'braking stop'. At high power the Harrier was transferred to the hover at around 70ft AGL. Most pilots preferred to alight on an FOB landing pad by approaching from the side and slightly to the rear, moving diagonally over the landing position. Throttle setting was then slowly reduced to allow the aircraft to settle into ground effect, with a burst of extra power to cushion the last few feet of descent.

Details of the throttle control box.

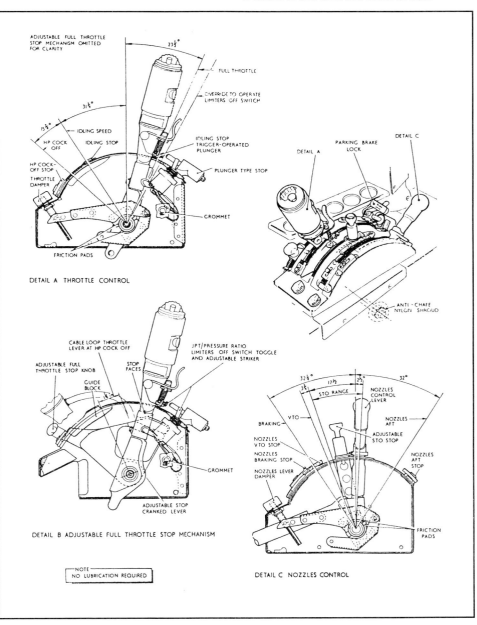

GR.1A, GR.3

As the Harrier GR.1 became an accepted piece of 'kit' a number of improvements to the breed were instigated. The first, quite small but important update was the introduction of the interim Pegasus 10 Mk 102 with a thrust increase to 20,500lb, allowing an extra 1,000lb in take-off weight. This engine was retrofitted to 41 Harriers as their Pegasus 6 Mk 101s became due for change, and the aircraft were re-designated GR.1A. One of the early Pegasus 10-equipped aircraft (XV739, the second production GR.1) was used to notch up a series of world records for the Class H (Vertical Take-off Aircraft) Category at RAF Boscombe Down on 5 January 1971. The times achieved were 1min 44.7sec to 9,000m and 2min 22.7sec to 12,000m (maximum altitude 14,000m/47,447ft). New records for the 3,000, 6,000 and 9,000m heights were set by a GR.3 with the Pegasus 11-21 in 1987, but the 12,000m climb record remained unbeaten until the 1989 attempt in a Harrier GR.5.

A further 1,000lb growth in engine thrust led to the Pegasus 11 Mk 103, which was installed in 40 new-build Harrier GR.3s. It was basically the same engine as the F402-RR-402 for the AV-8A. From 1973 onwards it also became available for RAF recruits, and it was specified for the twelve Harriers ordered in 1974, the first of which (XZ128) flew on 9 January 1976. A re-bladed fan to increase mass airflow to 432lb/hr, improved combustion and water-injection cooling of the HP turbine blades made the thrust increase possible up to 30°C ambient conditions. HP compressor blades were also given a coating known as Cocraly to increase fatigue life, and service 'life' was increased to 600hr. Cocraly was later replaced by a system of spanwise cooling holes in each blade. Rolls-Royce test pilot Tom Frost flew the first Pegasus 11 (No 922, Build 23) in test-bed Harrier XV738 on 19 February 1971. As Rolls-Royce Flight Test Engineer Alan Baxter related, 'a number of flights around this time were abandoned before take-off, one being because the pilot's parachute was found to be soaked with rain. Perhaps the most amusing reason, for everyone ex-

Left, upper: The LRMTS installation significantly altered the Harrier's capability—and its appearance. A No 3 Squadron example, still bearing Type D underwing roundels, hides under its green net . (BAe via R. L. Ward)

Left, lower: All-over 'wraparound' camouflage had appeared on many RAFG Harriers by 1978. The idea was to make the aircraft less visible to enemy fighters when banking and turning over a European landscape. XV758/V received Cat-4 damage when its pilot ejected at 30ft over Wildenrath's runway after a sudden loss of power on 20 October 1974. It was rebuilt at Kingston and returned to No 3 Squadron. (R. L. Ward)

Right, upper: When the Harrier entered service with No IV Squadron in 1970, Sir Christopher Foxley-Morris, C-in-C RAFG, described it as 'the most valuable weapon any Commander in Europe could have'. This GR.3, with Vinten camera pod, displays the red two-letter codes introduced in July 1980 to the RAFG Harrier Force. No 3 Squadron had codes in the AA–AZ range. (Authors' collection)

Right, lower: Churning up the rain on a wetter than average Greenham Common runway is No 233 OCU's GR.3 XV748/B on 31 May 31 1980. No 233's codes changed from two figures to a single letter in spring 1977, and from blue to white in spring 1983. In March 1989 the letter was prefixed by a '3' and XV748 became '3D'; GR.5s had codes beginning with '5' and GR7s with '7', to distinguish the different Harrier variants in use at Wittering. (R. L. Ward)

HARRIER FLIGHT TEST-BEDS IN USE AT ROLLS-ROYCE PATCHWAY

Aircraft	Serial no	First used	Last used	Remarks
Kestrel F(GA).1	XS693	23/02/67	21/09/67	Crashed 21/09/67
Harrier GR.1	XV738	19/04/68	09/11/72	First production GR.1
Harrier DB	XV276	04/12/72	29/03/73	Crashed Dunsfold 10/04/73
Harrier DB	XV281	02/04/75	30/09/87	Several visits to Rolls-Royce
Harrier DB	XV277	14/11/78	29/11/88	Several visits to Rolls-Royce
Harrier GR.3	XW917	18/02/83	28/02/83	
Harrier GR.3	XZ991	28/02/83	19/12/83	
Harrier DB	XV278	25/04/85	26/09/85	No record of flying
Sea Harrier FRS.1	XZ459	16/11/88	06/12/88	
Harrier GR.5	ZD402	28/03/89	22/08/89	
Harrier GR.5A	ZD466	20/01/90	25/07/91	

Including the Valiant FTB (with Pegasus 3), the above aircraft completed a total of 1,082hr of Pegasus test flying in over 1,200 flights. Information by courtesy of Alan Baxter.

cept Tom Frost, was the attempt to achieve Flight 316. Before the engine was started Frost was stung by a bee and was compelled to abandon the aircraft. What with oxygen mask, flying kit, gloves and so on it is surprising that the bee found any exposed skin to sting!' Despite its extra thrust the Mk 103 'Peggie' was still remarkably economical. Fuel consumption at full throttle was a mere 220lb per minute. In the same flight regime an F-4 Phantom used 1,200lb a minute!

Several other modifications to the Harrier took place at the GR.3 update juncture. A 12kVA alternator replaced the two previous 4kVA units and a more powerful Lucas Mk 2 APU generated 6kVA with a small gas turbine. The extra 'juice' was needed to power the most important innovation for the GR.3, Ferranti's Type 106 LRMTS, similar to the equipment used in the SEPECAT Jaguar GR.1. A new 'bottle nose' extension housed an active laser and receiver, linked to the aircraft's nav-attack avionics, this nasal extension also housing the 70mm F95 camera in a curious 'rhino's-eye' location. The laser was stabilised through a full 360 degrees of roll and +/−25 degrees of pitch. It could be directed as a pencil beam within a 20-degree cone ahead of the jet, emitting laser pulses which were adjustable between two and four per second, permitting two different aircraft to engage the same target in a scissors attack without confusing each other's receivers or allowing the enemy to jam the system. A ground target had to be laser-marked by a ground-based Primary FAC (PFAC): LRMTS then searched for and detected the 'spot', as described earlier, supplying precise slant-range data, closure speed and attack angles to the HUD and ballistics computer. A small green 'T' appeared in the HUD to indicate an LRMTS lock-on. After extensive tests in an RAE Canberra the equipment was installed in the 207th Harrier, XZ128 and the rest of the batch ordered in 1974, and grafted on to all other emerging GR.3s by 1979.

Another vital upgrade to several RAF types, including the Harrier at that time, was the addition of an RWR—Marconi's ARI.18223 system. Two passive aerials, one forward-facing near the top of the fin (giving an 8 per cent increase in fin area), the other on the tailboom tip, passed warnings on hostile RF-spectrum threats (such as fighter, SAM and triple-A radars) to the pilot's cockpit display. A 'dialling tone' audio-warning also sounded in the pilot's headset. Each antenna covered a 180-degree arc.

Seventeen years after its first flight the Pegasus had grown into a reliable, durable powerplant. The original 1960 engine had a mere one-hour life before a major overhaul became due, whereas by the late 1970s the RAF stipulated a 700hr TBO (time between overhauls). In the three-month period up to 31 October 1976 the RAF had to pull out only three engines for unplanned major maintenance, usually due to FOD. However, wear and tear on the engines was considerable. In VTOL or STOVL modes take-off thrust was used twice in each sortie rather than once for take-off as in a conventional jet, shortening 'hot-end' life. Yet reliability steadily improved. By 1980 Rolls-Royce had records of over twenty engines which had exceeded 2,000hr service lives.

In the early 1980s some Pegasus 103s began to exhibit deterioration in surge margins. Two RAFG Harrier GR.3s were flown to Rolls-Royce Filton for tests. Both arrived from their German forest FOBs in an extremely dirty state and had to be cleaned before testing could begin. Alan Baxter remembered that the No 3 Squadron pilot who eventually collected XW917

Squadron Leader C. R. Loader's No IV Squadron GR.3 with specially marked tail in 1989 to celebrate the unit's 75th anniversary. Coloured tails were tested on a variety of RAFG types in the late 1980s as an anti-collision measure. (Via R. L. Ward)

Right, upper: Three from Three. No 3 Squadron's insignia, a cockatrice on a Stonehenge slab, appeared on its Canberra B(I).8s but the unit has a lineage which dates back to July 1912 and includes a distinguished history on many types including Snipes, Bulldogs, Hurricanes, Typhoons and Hunters. (BAe)

Right, lower: Towards the end of the GR.3 era at Wittering, a No 233 OCU Harrier shows off its SNEB rocket pod. Used with great effect during Operation 'Corporate', this weapon was withdrawn from use in all spheres of operation except Belize by the late 1980s. (Andy Evans)

'was suitably impressed with the pristine condition of his machine and hinted that there was a job for us cleaning the other Harriers if we were interested'. Test pilot John Fawcett carried out most of the test flights on XW917 and XZ991. 'The surge boundary involved pulling the aircraft nose up at 40,000ft to increase incidence until the engine popped or stalled, and noting the angle of incidence when this happened. This was repeated on the next run by pushing the nose down. The engine speed was then increased and the "push and pull" tests were repeated until the maximum allowable engine speed was reached. At the end of 1983 around 550 surges had been plotted and on about 10 per cent of these I had to shut the engine down to prevent over-temperature and "glide" down to 20,000ft to relight it before continuing. The Harrier is not the world's best glider as its vertical speed in a glide with engine off is about 60mph.'

BELIZE—THE EIGHTEEN-YEAR TEMPORARY DETACHMENT

The Harrier Force's longest overseas commitment was its detachment to the former British colony of Belize. Living under persistent threat of invasion from Guatemala since 1948, the newly independent country came under renewed pressure in October 1975 after the breakdown of talks between Britain and Guatemala. A garrison of 1,000 British troops was established, reinforced by six Harrier GR.1As of No 1(F) Squadron. This sextet was flown out from Wittering under the flag-waving Operation 'Nucha' via Goose Bay,

Canada, and Nassau in the Bahamas between 6 and 8 November. The use of US bases for staging was complicated by the US Government's support for the right-wing Guatemalan government, while America's least favourite General, Fidel Castro, had declared support for the government of Belize. Wittering's initial deployment deterred the Guatemalan forces from making a border incursion. At the same time, useful training routines were established, although the crews involved were not sorry to leave the insects, sticky heat and very basic living conditions. In

April 1976 the jets were dismantled and flown home in RAF Belfast 'Dragmasters'. One Harrier had been lost in a brief air combat with an eagle. Its pilot, Flight Lieutenant Scott, ejected after an uncontrollable engine surge at 1,000ft.

A second phase of Guatemalan posturing and troop build-ups was met by a renewed increase in the British garrison during July 1977, including Harriers from all three front-line units. Known as the Strike Command Det, the quartet of Harriers was flown and maintained on a rota basis, drawing personnel from all areas of

51

No 1417 Flight's sailfish emblem painted on GR.3 ZD669, which was being prepared for gate-guard duties at Belize International Airport when this photograph was taken. Squadron Leader John Ferguson was the unit's first CO in 1980 and its last in 1993. (Via R. L. Ward)

the Harrier community. Before taking their first share of the duty, No 1 Squadron put in some ACM (air combat manoeuvring) practice in case the 'Guats' decided to try their luck with their air force of ten Cessna A-37Bs. From 28 March 1978 No 1 passed the baton to No 233 OCU. As the need to maintain the British presence continued, it was decided to create No 1417 Flight to operate the four Harriers, beginning in March 1981.

Conditions improved a little. In temperatures which often exceeded 90° F (ruling out VTO as a practical tactic), the 22 engineers lived in air-conditioned Portakabins in a defended enclosure while a team of second-line service engineers operated from an old shirt factory. Perma-

Harrier T.4A XW269/BD of the SAOEU at Boscombe Down departs IAT '93 as 'Gauntlet 45'. The aircraft has the modified nose fairing used to test the Nightbird FLIR unit. (Authors)

nent buildings were erected in 1986. Heavy servicing was done with the help of the Royal Engineers' mobile cranes which could lift a Harrier's wing off with tanks and pylons in place, for engine work. The aircraft were kept at 20 minutes' readiness in two hides later known as Foxy Golf and Charlie Delta, each side of the runway at Belize International Airport.

They were tasked with air defence, reconnaissance and CAS, with over thirty forward strips available for the latter type of sortie. Most aircraft used in Belize had the Phase 6 modifications, enabling them to carry AIM-9G Sidewinders for anti-air operations. SNEB rockets were used for air-to-ground practice on the range at New River Lagoon, where old Land Rov-

ers and oil drums were regularly deluged with practice bombs, rockets and 30mm shells. Pilots flew regularly, making up to ten sorties a day with the four aircraft. Short-lift wet take-offs were standard practice, with a 15sec burst of water injection before the nozzles swung to the rear on lift-off to prevent JPT hitting the limits at maximum thrust.

Early morning take-offs were favoured, before the temperature rose. The climate also brought the recurrent threat of hurricanes, and 330gal ferry tanks were kept in readiness in case the aircraft had to decamp to the Bahamas or Jamaica to avoid a 'twister'. Excessive humidity also caused constant problems. Electronics suffered most, but condensation built up in the airframe despite extra drainage holes. After two or three days panels had to be removed from the lower surfaces of the fuselage to drain off several pints of warm water. Corrosion-prone surfaces received regular spraying with WD-40 de-watering agent and Pegasus compressors were hosed out at the end of the day's flying. Wing tanks tended to leak fuel, but the heat prevented a sealer used in repairing them from bonding properly. As a crude solution, spare wings were sometimes 'trucked in' aboard the C-130K Hercules shuttle.

Despite the environmental problems a Belize posting gave Harrier pilots the chance to fly with few restrictions over an area the size of Wales in constantly good visibility. There was plenty of opportunity for low-flying and ACM practice—though there were never any serious violations of Belize airspace.

As No 1417 Flight's duty continued into the 1990s, tension with Guatemala gradually receded to the point where a Harrier appeared at one of that country's air shows. Demonstrations had been given previously in several other South American countries. Harrier GR.3s and the aircrew to fly them became ever more scarce as the variant was gradually supplanted in RAF service by the GR.5. A small pool of pilots was kept current by No 233 OCU/20 Squadron at Wittering. Increasingly, they were pilots who enjoyed the Belize detachment as an option since the length of the tour increased from the origi-

nal three months to a demanding eighteen-month stint. In February 1993 the Ministry of Defence decided that Belize's political condition had relaxed sufficiently to allow No 1417 Flight to withdraw. Three Harriers, led by Squadron Leader John Finlayson (No 1417's first CO in 1980 and last in 1993), flew back to Wittering on 8 July via Key West, Florida, and Goose Bay. The return of ZD667/C, ZD670/F and XZ971/G (still with its 'fin art' nickname 'Hod Carrier'), marked the end of the lengthy detachment. A fourth Harrier, ZD669, was left at Belize

Another Harrier T.4A sortie gets started as the crew prepare to settle into this No 233 OCU jet. (Andy Evans)

Airport as a gate guard. In order to reassure those local Belizeans who were concerned at the withdrawal of the British presence, a quartet of Harrier GR.7s from No IV Squadron was despatched to Belize on 6 September 1993 and stayed there until the end of the month. The logistics for mounting such a fast-reaction deployment in case of an emergency remain in place.

3. 'It Changes Everything'

Reflecting on the US Marine Corps' long, bloody immersion in the South-East Asian conflict Lieutenant-Colonel Drax Williams stated simply: 'The Marine Corps bought the Harrier because of its experiences in Vietnam'. Major-General Keith McCutcheon, reviewing the same experience in 1971, looked forward to having an aircraft which would 'permit operations from more sites, improve response time in CAS by reducing the time taken to request support (there will be fewer echelons of command to go through), and it can be staged closer to the action, thus cutting flight time'. Williams felt similarly, believing that CAS had to be delivered within 30 minutes of a call from a FAC to be of any real use. An aircraft which could 'ground-loiter' close to the battle line would ideally fulfil this need.

Of the twenty-three aircraft types operated by the USMC in Vietnam, only the A-4 Skyhawk, F-8 Crusader and F-4 Phantom had been employed for CAS, all from the crowded in-theatre main bases at Da Nang and Chu Lai (although the latter originated as a SATS forward base area), with a facility in Nam Phong, Thailand, opening up late in the war. Accu-

racy in the CAS role depended largely on the bombing skill level of the pilot, his rapport with a FAC, and the time taken to haul ordnance to the target.[1] The Marines perceived a clear need for an aircraft which would enable much higher mission frequencies, shorter reaction times and precise, high-speed weapons lay-down. In the words of Lieutenant-Colonel (later Lieutenant-General) Harry Blot, an early champion of the Harrier, 'The only reason the Marines own airplanes is to support the guy with the rifle, and everything is wrapped around that mission.'

One possibility was the helicopter, and the USMC had been among the first to integrate vertical replenishment and reinforcement into a beach-head assault strategy from the late 1940s. In 1957 the Marines' Commandant, General Randolph Pate, recommended to the CNO (Chief of Naval Operations) that 'obtaining STOL/VTOL capability is vital to Marine aviation'. He was referring to the whole spectrum of aviation, not just helicopters. His interest was in having a self-contained CAS force available to an expeditionary brigade at all times. Memories of Second World War battles in the

South Pacific where the 'guy with the rifle' sometimes had to rely on USN air support and did not always get it in time were still fresh.

In the mid-1960s there was the vague possibility of a USMC version of the Lockheed AH-56A Cheyenne, but this complex attack helicopter proved costly and technically unfeasible. Of far more interest was a V/STOL jet fighter-bomber. The Marines thus could have written an operational requirement for the Harrier long before it took shape at Kingston.

Ironically, it was the US Army which first expressed an interest in the P.1127 as a replacement for their twin-turboprop OV-1 Mohawk battlefield surveillance aircraft. HSA and Northrop had just signed an agreement to explore the possibilities of an Army variant when interservice power games transferred all fixed-wing Army flying to the USAF's domain. American participation in the Kestrel Tripartite Evaluation Squadron (TES) had not included USMC personnel, but the Kestrels which were returned to the USA were flown by Marine pilots at times. The very favourable USAF/USN reports on the evaluation also increased Marine interest. After the completion of the TES programme the three US-owned aircraft, together with West Germany's unwanted trio, were shipped to the United States in 1966 for extended tests. Known initially as VZ-12s, then as V-6s, they were even-

After use by the Tripartite Evaluation Squadron, Kestrel XS692 (as 64-18266) was used for a series of US trials. Sea trials were carried out on USS *Raleigh* (LPD-1) and on the carrier USS *Independence* (CVA-62). The Kestrel was then used as a spares source for the two NASA XV-6As. (Via R. L. Ward)

AV-8A BuNo 158387, the fourth aircraft, in the markings of the first USMC Harrier squadron, VMA-513. Training under Lieutenant-Colonel C. M. 'Bud' Baker at 'Hoot's Half Acre', MCAS Beaufort, as part of MAG-32, the unit was formed on 15 April 1971. Support in the early days came from a seventeen-man team from the British aircraft industry, including a substantial delegation from Ferranti. (Via R .L. Ward)

area. The USAF quota of Tri-Service Testing was conducted at Eglin AFB, Florida, in July 1966, and the Kestrels were then divided up among several agencies, including the Flight Test Center at Edwards AFB, California, and NASA, who took two examples (64-18263 and 18267). NASA eventually took on 18265 and 18266 as 'spare parts lockers' for cannibalisation too. The Kestrels continued to provide useful data until their retirement in 1974, none more so than the NASA examples which were to provide vital development work for the USMC Harrier combat 'textbook'.

In May 1966 news of these trials still had not gone far beyond the immediate circle of the Tri-Service team. As Lieutenant-General Tom Miller (who was then a USMC test pilot and Colonel), told the authors, 'The Marine Corps had little knowledge of the XV-6A trials or the program in the USA after the trials in England. Data available to the Corps indicated that considerable improvement in thrust-to-weight would be required before it could perform military missions. Although the Marine Corps followed the extended trials in the USA they provided little data. It was the USMC's opinion that these trials were little more than limited research efforts for vertical flight control. General McCutcheon and his staff became interested when the Harrier data became available. A movie provided by the British Embassy (Captain John Glendenning RN) described the most realistic improvements of the Harrier. After seeing the Harrier

tually designated XV-6A and given the serials 64-18262 to 18267. At first they were allocated Army ground support tests at Fort Campbell, then transferred to the NATC, Patuxent River, in Maryland. In May 1966 they performed 'carrier' trials on NATC's marked-out 'decks', following up with the real thing aboard USS *Independence*. For these preliminary trials the pilots were all ex-TES crew, including Colonel Barkhorn (WGAF) and Major J. Johnston from the US Army. A parallel 'small deck' trial was conducted on USS *Raleigh* (LPD-1) by XV-6A 64-18266.[2]

The Kestrel's sea trials were most impressive. Apart from problems with inadequate windscreen rain removal, and the obvious lack of equipment to conduct night or IFR (Instrument Flight Rules) operations with these very basic machines, the pilots learned a great deal. New deck-operating skills were absorbed, such as avoiding hot gases from ships' exhaust stacks or from other aircraft on deck while in the hover. The *Raleigh* trials were also successful and it was envisaged that four such aircraft could comfortably operate from the vessel's 85 by 200ft rear deck

[1] In those days these three aircraft employed strictly manual dive-bombing and rocketry delivery methods coupled with dead-reckoning navigation using only rudimentary radio aids.
[2] Aboard ship for both sets of sea-trials were Pegasus Chief Engineer John Dale—and his wife Joan.

movie and looking over the performance data, I felt that there was considerable potential for such an aircraft to replace the A-4 as the USMC's light attack aircraft.'

The success of the XV-6A's sea trials created a much wider interest in the type throughout the US defence world. Northrop was given a $330,000 contract to continue testing through 1967 and the results were keenly observed by Major-General McCutcheon. His decision to send a Marine delegation to the 1968 SBAC show at Farnborough to glean more from Hawker Siddeley was therefore the culmination of a long period of developing interest. It also followed directly from a 1965 USMC study of long-ranging air power requirements: this, too, placed a heavy emphasis on V/STOL. The sincerity of the visiting team's interest was immediately apparent to the British Ministry officials and flight trials for the team's two pilots, Colonel Tom Miller and Lieutenant-Colonel Bud Baker, were quickly arranged at Dunsfold. Both men were experienced test pilots. Tom Miller, the first American to fly the Harrier, had estab-

lished a 500km closed-circuit world speed record in F4H-1 Phantom BuNo 145311 on 5 September 1960, spending almost 25 minutes in full afterburner!

At the time Dunsfold had no two-seat Harrier or simulator. The 'house rules' demanded that new converts should begin their experience of Harrier with a taxy session—'a proper one where you taxy around, shut down, get out and talk about it,' as John Farley recalled. 'Many experienced pilots were very angry that we made them do the taxy sessions—before they did them. When they got back they were never other than pleased to have done them. We set the sessions up to teach them one very important lesson: however much experience they had of high-powered jets, the Harrier had a higher thrust/weight ratio. After an initial taxi around to get used to the toe brakes and nosewheel steering, pilots were allowed to line up on the runway, run through the checklist and be ready to go. The instructions were then to let the brakes off and open the throttle at 50kt, close the throttle, put the brakes on and stop, then taxy back and shut down.

Above: VMA-231 became the USMC's primary deployable Harrier unit. AV-8A BuNo 158396 is seen here with a pair of Zuni pods. (BAe)

Right: Toned-down markings on AV-8A BuNo 158706/WH 03 of VMA-542. This Harrier was later to join the AV-8C CILOP line. (BAe)

The best guys usually got the throttle back at 60–65kt, the worst at 120kt.' With acceleration which took the aircraft from 0 to 70kt in 2.3 seconds, most pilots were left way behind mentally. Their reactions were geared to a far less dynamic ride. However, getting left behind by the aircraft in a safe, taxying environment was far preferable to having it happen on the first conventional take-off.

Among the slowest to 'get the throttle off' was Bud Baker, a very experienced Phantom pilot. Having initially objected to the taxy session, he bowed to pressure from team leader Brigadier-General Thompson and set off down the runway for his 50kt run. 'He was just shattered by the rate of acceleration,' John Farley remembers, 'so he just sat there and didn't close the throttle. When he finally did (at 120kt) he was back in his Phantom, where you put on the brakes but also pull the stick back hard to enhance the coefficient of friction between the mainwheel tyres and runway. Baker was going so fast that when he pulled back on the stick the nose lifted off and, because he pulled at an angle, the Harrier rolled to the right, leaving showers of sparks as it ground off the tip of the right tailplane. The nose then fell back and the aircraft stopped. Baker came back with eyes like organ stops, but he then went on to do a brilliant eight-flight evaluation of the Harrier. This convinced the USMC that they had to send a full NPE (Naval Preliminary Evaluation) team of four USN pilots across from Patuxent River, in January 1969.' Two years later Bud Baker was in charge of the first USMC Harrier squadron.

Tom Miller, who was the first of the two pilots to take the Harrier aloft, was also impressed by its acceleration: 'As an early test pilot on the A-4 Skyhawk program I had become impressed by the ever greater acceleration of the Harrier. I recognized that a pilot had to be careful because the aircraft reacted so fast that it would be easy for the pilot to get behind in control, which would be vary dangerous.'

USAF interest in the Harrier was also spurred by the XV-6A tests. Not to be outdone, they also sent two pilots to check out the Harrier at Dunsfold. On 27 January 1969 one of them, Major Charles Rosberg, appeared to have lost sight of the crucial yaw vane, mounted ahead of the windshield to warn the pilot of sideslip. He took off vertically with the sun ahead of him and may have been affected by glare. The aircraft (XV743) began to sideslip, gradually entered an unrecoverable roll and crashed, killing him. It was the first fatality in the programme. To prevent similar accidents Harriers were fitted with rudder pedal shakers, yaw autostabilisation in the RCS and a sideslip accelerometer indicator in the HUD. Rosberg's accident also illustrated how small relaxations in safety procedures can lead to tragic consequences. Because he intended to stay within the vicinity of the airfield Rosberg chose not to wear a lifejacket. He clipped his oxygen hose to a D-ring sewn into his flying overall—a D-ring designed to do no more than keep an oxygen mask tube tidy inside a non-ejector seat cockpit. His lifejacket would have provided a much sturdier D-ring. On separating from his seat as the Harrier rolled at 50ft and 90kt, the D-ring ripped free from his overall, leaving him connected to the seat via the oxygen hose system. This elastic system eventually broke and catapulted a metal fitting back into his throat, causing a potentially fatal injury.[3]

Armed with the NPE's conclusions that the Harrier could offer useful range and payload together with its unique V/STOL characteristics, General McCutcheon pushed ahead with its plan, which now extended to provide the USMC with an all-V/STOL air element by the end of the 1970s. The first stage was to propose an outright purchase of 114 Harriers, with no 'trial' batch, to equip four 20-aircraft units, plus an attrition quota. (In due course the extra unit price of the eight TAV-8A trainers and the cost of modifying the single-seaters meant a reduction of four aircraft to keep within the $474.4 million budget.) The Marine Corps' commitment to the Harrier was such that they accepted the reallocation of FY 1970 funds previously earmarked to enable two F-4B units (VMFA-513 and VMFA-542) to upgrade to the F-4J. Instead, the money, equivalent to seventeen Phantoms, was used to finance the first dozen Harriers. Both Phantom squadrons were disestablished in June 1970 and designated as the first two Harrier units.

The prospect of a substantial sale to the United States was of great importance to HSA, who initially had not seen the Americans as potential customers. Although it was realised that the amphibious assault role, with V/STOL CAS, was a USMC speciality, unlikely to be duplicated by other nations, the USMC endorsement of Harrier's combat capability was an encouragement to wider foreign sales. For the Marines, the Harrier

[3]Lecture to Survival and Flight Equipment Association (SAFE) on 21 September 1983, by J. F. Farley.

was thought to present no serious transition problems for A-4 Skyhawk crew. In many respects, as a 'conventional' light attacker it resembled the Skyhawk, but offered better acceleration and performance at altitude. In both aircraft, the pilot was positioned well forward, looked back and/or down into a large pair of intakes and couldn't see much behind him.

There were some reservations about the forward-site maintenance requirements for removing the Harrier's wing for engine access, and about the seat harness. Onboard self-starting was seen as a real advantage. Above all, the prospect of flying CAS straight from the deck of an LPH and then moving ashore to a very basic forward site to continue the fight was extremely appealing. While the US Navy replaced its Skyhawks with the A-7 Corsair II, the Marines, for once, chose not to follow suit and put their faith in the Harrier early in 1969.

AV-8A and TAV-8A airframes on the HSA Kingston production line. (BAe)

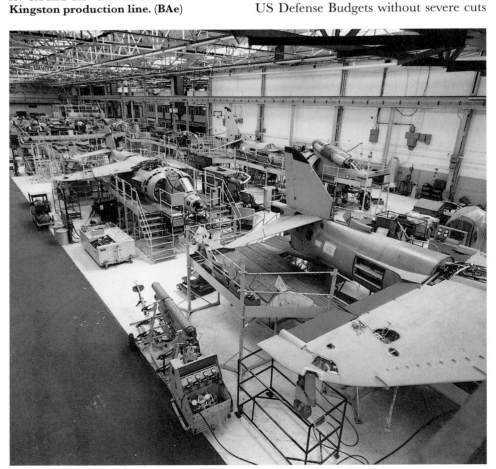

General McCutcheon moved very quickly to get his first twelve Harriers slotted into the FY 1970 budget. The question of longer-term funding was more challenging. Although he had ridden down most of the objections to buying a foreign aircraft, McCutcheon was obliged to investigate the prospects for licence-building the Harriers in the US. Partly, this was to satisfy those who felt that key spares and attrition replacements in case of war could only be obtained reliably from the home market. A fifteen-year agreement was therefore signed in 1969 between HSA and McDonnell-Douglas, chief suppliers of combat aircraft to the USMC; Northrop's production rights had lapsed at this time. The deal gave McAir exclusive rights over Harrier in the USA, transfer of VTOL data to the company, and licence production rights. It soon became clear that major one-off funding would be needed to establish production at St Louis, and that this could not be found easily under the year-on-year funding system for US Defense Budgets without severe cuts

AV-8A PAYLOAD/RANGE PERFORMANCE

TO roll (ft)	Warload (lb)*	Radius (nm)
VTO	3,000	50
600	5,000	125
1,500	8,000	222
1,000	3,000	360

*Ordnance, not fuel

to other USMC programmes. The Corps wanted their jets quickly without the expense of starting up a limited production line. Congress therefore agreed to a straight purchase of HSA-produced GR.1 aircraft, to be known in the USA as the McDonnell-Douglas AV-8A (or Harrier Mk 50 at Kingston). The decision was a surprise to Hawkers: as John Fozard remarked, 'To our astonishment, against all the odds and despite the advice and counsels we had been given in 1969, the total USMC procurement was in England.'

MODIFICATIONS

Modifications to the GR.1 for USMC service were inevitable, but quite minimal. The basic airframe and engine were retained, including their magnesium components (later to be replaced by less corrosion-prone alloys in the Royal Navy's seagoing variant). The Marines settled for frequent repainting of these items during salt-water deployments. Revised IFF gear was installed and the altimeter and HUD was recalibrated in inches of mercury rather than millibars. American radios were installed: a Magnavox UHF/VHF homing set and a Sylvania VHF/Tactical UHF set whose tall blade antenna became a distinctive feature on the aircraft's spine. Despite their preference for Martin-Baker seats in the Phantom, the USMC opted to retrofit the lighter Stencel SEU-3A (later SIIIS-3) seat. Ostensibly this was because it offered quicker parachute deployment at low altitude, but it was also an easy way of introducing some US-built equipment into the AV-8A. Stencels replaced the Martin-Baker Mk 9a in the final production batch (BuNos 159366 and up) and were retrofitted to surviving earlier examples in 1977–78. G. W. 'Johnnie' Johnson felt that 'the USMC had the Stencel for commonality, but were said to prefer Martin-Baker. The Stencel was regarded as less likely to get you out at low level in the hover and it was suspected that a certain amount of limb flailing would occur during high-speed ejection.'

More sweeping changes were made in mid-production to the aircraft's avionics under the same Phase I modification programme which included the seat. The Marines wanted a nav-attack system which was optimised for short-range dive-attack CAS sorties. They decided that this could be achieved with a more basic avionics fit than the RAF's European scenario demanded. When it was originally ordered the terms of the Congressional approval for the Harrier purchase were that it should be an 'off the shelf' item, and the substitution of a different system would have contravened that principle. Once the aircraft was established in service, changes could be made to increase its suitability for the Marine mission, where multi-pass in CAS in support of TICs (troops in contact with the enemy) would probably be done without the availability of exact co-ordinates at the mission planning stage. In particular, the time taken to align the FE.541 inertial system was seen as a handicap to CAS reaction time, with little compensating advantage. Moreover, the moving map display was hardly used in short-range, single-target missions and it was replaced by tacan. Ferranti's FE.541, in-

Right, top: VMA-542's *Flying Tiger* **patch decorates the tail of AV-8A BuNo 158948. Delivered to the Marines on 2 February 1973, it crashed on landing at Beaufort eighteen months later. It is seen here landing at MCAS El Toro in May 1973. (Frank Mormillo)**

Right, centre: A final windshield polish for a bombed-up VMA-513 Harrier at the Twenty-Nine Palms Expeditionary airfield, where the Marines were practising forward-deployed combined forces exercises. The airfield became operational in 1976. (Frank Mormillo)

Right, bottom: An impressive 'furball' of condensation surrounds an AV-8A pulling g over MCAS El Toro in May 1983. (Frank Mormillo)

The AV-8A cockpit, with seat and stick removed. Essentially similar to that of the Harrier GR.1, it lacks the Ferranti moving-map display, replaced by a standard gyro compass on the centre panel, with throttle and nozzle levers on the left side console. Fuel and engine dials are on the right front panel, with communications buttons on the pilot's right side. (BAe)

stalled in the first 60 aircraft, was removed and deleted from later batches. In its place a Smiths Industries' interface/weapons aiming computer (I/WAC), without navigation capacity, was slaved to the HUD, providing attack ballistics solutions with CCIP (continuously computed impact point), lead-angle computing for the 30mm guns and a roll-stabilised sightline for ground attack. Known as the Baseline Systems, this equipment was trialled in BuNo 158977 (the 60th AV-8A), installed in subsequent aircraft and retrofitted to the fleet from 1974 onwards.

A final minor but important change was the wiring of the outboard pylons for AIM-9 Sidewinders. This made the two pylons a permanent fixture and reflected the AV-8A's need to defend its own airspace over the CAS area rather than wait for dedicated 'CAP-ers' to show up. Right at the end of production it was decided to delete the RAT from the final aircraft (BuNo 159385) and retrospectively from previous examples. (The RAF made a

similar move with their GR.3 fleet.) A minor electrical modification also gave automatic 'safe' status to all weapons stations at touchdown via a 'weight on wheels' switch on the undercarriage.

There was some dissatisfaction with the 30mm Aden gun. Although it was found to have a good anti-armour punch it did not use a standard type of US ammunition. Tom Miller explained: 'Although considered better than any US 30mm cannon, the gun was not designed for operations aboard ships at sea. It had no protection from high RF voltages generated by radars aboard ship. Also, the fact that the gun could not be armed and de-armed by the pilot was thought to make it dangerous in the confined spaces aboard ships.' Cost limits ruled out a change of weapon. As early as 1972 studies began of a 'basic' AV-8A with INAS replaced by tacan, the Hughes Angle-Rate Bombing System (ARBS) and a laser target designator to be used with Maverick missiles. In 1972 it was also expected that the AV-

8A would regularly use laser-guided bombs (LGBs)—and VMA-513 trained with LGBs in the Philippines in 1973–74. In practice, all these proposals were held over for true second-generation Harriers.

Service introduction of the AV-8A progressed rapidly, spurred on by General McCutcheon and by the CNO, Admiral Elmo Zumwalt, who had visions of a Harrier derivative aboard the 15,000-ton Sea Control Ships which he was promoting in the early 1970s as a more numerous alternative to big carriers. Following the first flight on 20 November 1970 of the No 1 AV-8A (BuNo 158384), BIS trials by the first four aircraft were completed at NATC Patuxent River by March 1971. During the next stage of trials Mike Ripley became the first AV-8A casualty when he suffered 'target fixation' during a dive-attack with guns against a float target. BuNo 158386 crashed into Chesapeake Bay and he was killed. One of the Harriers set a new serviceability record, flying a total of 20hr 20min out of a 40hr day and night period. Six pilots took turns in the jet, flying a total of seventeen sorties. 'Surge' operations of this kind quickly became standard practice for Harrier operators as they discovered just how hard they could fly the aircraft. BIS trials included deck sessions aboard the LPH USS *Guadalcanal* and LPD USS *Coronado*, clearing the AV-8A for the first time to operate from vessels smaller than an attack carrier.

In August 1970, following the four-month NATC trials, a joint USN/USMC programme called Project 'Battle Cry' was initiated to establish operational procedures for the AV-8A and to evaluate the long-term possibilities of V/STOL. Lieutenant-General Harry Blot told the authors: 'Everyone was surprised at how well the little subsonic airplane performed. It clearly demonstrated the value of thrust vectoring combined with tactics.' Shipboard compatibility was evaluated, weapons delivery procedures were written into the AV-8A Tactical Manual and pilots continued to learn the subtleties of Harrier flying. Quite minor and unexpected facets were discovered. For example, it was found that the bolt-on refuelling probe, more often used by the Marines than by the RAF, acted as a lifting surface. While this presented no difficulties in normal flight, at high AOA the effect could induce a sharp yaw and roll to the left.

By April 1971 ten of the first production batch proudly wore the insignia of VMA-513 at MCAS, Beaufort. A month later the unit was declared operational, only twenty months after the first RAF Harrier GR.1 squadron. Production of 102 AV-8As continued until the end of January 1976. BuNo 159377 was the last

BuNo 158965, assigned to the CO of VMA-513, makes a vertical landing at MCAS El Toro in 1978. Although its paint scheme and markings are 'lo-viz', the aircraft retains the original star and bar colours. The unit's WF Modex appeared under the right wing of the earliest AV-8As. (Frank Mormillo)

to be flown out of RAF Mildenhall in the C-5A transport, the standard delivery procedure (though C-141s were also used). By that stage there were three operational squadrons, VMA-513, VMA-542 and VMA-231, with a training unit, VMAT-203. The training version of the AV-8A, however, had only just entered service. Fighting constantly against tight budgets and continued Senate opposition to a foreign purchase, the Marines managed to preserve their single-seat order partly by delaying the purchase of eight TAV-8As until all 102 had been delivered. Before that, the first complement of Marine 'AV8-tors' followed the RAF example and trained on single-seaters. Like the British teams they assembled a nucleus of high-time jet pilots, led by a select few (including Bud Baker) who had been initiated by the highly experienced Dunsfold pilots. Major Jacob 'Bud' Iles USMC was posted to the Harrier HCU at RAF Wittering in November 1970 to be trained as an instructor. He was joined by Captain 'Speedy' Gonzales who was there to receive familiarization training as a Maintenance Officer for the Beaufort operation. Baker's VMA-513 *Flying Nightmares*, up

and running by April 1971, trained VMA-542 *Flying Tigers* by the following November, using the last of the FY 1971 aircraft. They in turn passed on their knowledge to VMA-231 *Ace of Spades*, who were on-line by July 1973, commanded by Lieutenant-Colonel Rocky Nelson. MCAS Beaufort had three gun squadrons but only two years of Harrier experience to share around. A similar syllabus to the RAF's was used, consisting of helicopter-based introductory V/STOL flying followed by solo STOL/conventional Harrier flights. Vertical 'press-ups' usually began on the fifth flight, with a ground instructor monitoring progress via a radio link. Pilots learned that the AV-8A was relatively easy to fly but needed constant control inputs, particularly in the 40–100kt range where stability was reduced and manoeuvrability consequently more rapid. As one VMA-513 pilot put it, 'It's a sports car of a plane. The others almost fly themselves; Harrier leaves the pilot something to do.'

VIFF

The *Flying Nightmares* attained Phase II combat readiness just under two years from receipt of their first jet, with all pi-

Lieutenant-Colonel Harry Blot (right) championed the AV-8A in USMC circles and developed VIFF tactics. He is pictured here with test pilot John Fawcett AFC (in flight suit) and Peter Calder (dark suit), who became Pegasus 11-61 Project Manager. (Via John Fawcett)

lots qualified to deliver every store cleared for the AV-8A except the AIM-9G Sidewinder. Weapons trials were conducted at China Lake by VMA-513 personnel, clearing the type for Zuni rockets, LAU-69/2.75in FFAR, Mk 81, Mk 76 and Mk 77 bombs and CBU/APAM. Sidewinder trials followed and pilots began to explore the aircraft's air-to-air envelope in 1971–72.

It was at this time that the VIFF (thrust vectoring in forward flight) 'speciality' began to emerge. Although some earlier experiments with in-flight nozzle vectoring had been done by RAF and HSA pilots, the Marines began to realise that VIFF could give Harrier real advantages in the air-to-air situations which they envisaged for it. NASA had begun VIFF trials at Wallops Station, Virginia, in January 1970, using XV-6A 64-18263 (NASA 521). The Kestrel, in metal finish, had a 'barber's pole' nose boom and a large gun-camera bulge beneath its nose. Testing gradually advanced to the point where unrestricted VIFF-ing was allowed above 10,000ft at speeds of up to Mach 0.9 with 80–90 per cent thrust. 'Wind-up' turn techniques were developed, using nozzle angles up to 30 degrees to tighten turns in

the 200–450kt regime. In level flight the same procedure produced a marked nose-up pitch angle which needed trimming out. In general, the programme identified distinct improvements in sustained turn rate below Mach 0.72 and 'eye-watering' increases in deceleration and acceleration with large nozzle deflections. In combat, VIFF was seen as a way of giving AV-8A pilots a far better chance of survival against more capable fighters, and a real opportunity to fight back. In 1971 the NASA Kestrels were flown against T-38As and used VIFF to score a convincing lead in ACM, albeit with some excess strain on the nozzles. Early in 1972 VMA-513 pilots at Point Mugu took on F-4 Phantoms and a nimble F-86 Sabre. These trials, extended to China Lake in October 1972, confirmed that AV-8A pilots tended to lose to the Phantom in conventional ACM, when inside the F-4's minimum AIM-7 Sparrow range as well as in BVR (beyond visual range) situations. With VIFF, though, the AV-8A won on virtually every occasion. F-4 pilots were also surprised to find that the AV-8A could out-accelerate them in a climb and leave them behind in the lo-lo cruise speed range for CAS too. In March 1976 a clean AV-8A flew time-

to-climb to 30,000ft against a clean F-4J and beat it by 13 seconds.

The first USMC VIFF trials were led by Lieutenant-Colonel Harry Blot, USMC Harrier Project Officer, who chose to begin at the upper end of the performance range. He slammed the nozzles to the braking-stop position at around 500kt, producing 'alarming' deceleration. Methodical on-site analysis of the results was impeded by having his nose mashed into the HUD and the control column virtually inserted into his lower abdomen. Until that time, Blot's preference had been for a rather loose seat-belt adjustment so that he could keep a good look-out behind him. Despite this challenging experience he decided that VIFF at such extremes of flight imposed no undue strains upon the airframe or engine and would be useful to outwit an opponent in the AV-8A's six o'clock. His previously rather pessimistic view of the Harrier's chances against fighters was drastically improved. Blot stayed in the Harrier business, commanding VMA-231 and leading their deployment on board USS *Nassau* for their September 1982 participation in NATO's 'Northern Wedding'/'Bold Guard' exercise.

The 1972 China Lake trials, which drew in a wide selection of US fighter types anxious to try their skills against the Harrier, concluded that there was 'no known tactical aircraft' which could 're-main behind the AV-8A if the latter's pilot does not desire it to do so'. A parallel series of tests was run by British and US pilots at RAF Valley, using the Aberporth missile range. Harriers duelled with a Hunter, an RAF Phantom and a Lightning F.6. They also practised limited VIFF-ing to disorientate ground fire in attack routines. Throughout 1972 techniques for tackling all known fighter types, including Soviet models, were formalised and the Harrier's reputation as an unkillable dogfighter grew apace. Most popular was sudden deceleration, forcing the pursuit aircraft to overshoot and enter the Harrier's missile or gun envelope. In a vertical climb pursuit the Harrier pilot could use nozzle deflection to flip into a square turn and get behind his adversary on the downward leg of the spiral. A variety of defensive breaks was developed, allowing the AV-8A to VIFF into a tightened turn and reverse the situation against a fighter on its tail. Even if a Harrier pilot could not get on his opponent's tail, he could very often run an afterburning adversary out of fuel as it blasted away at full power, trying to stay in the fight.

The manufacturers improved the situation further by strengthening the nozzle system and adding a screw-in turbine temperature control fuse (combat 'plug') to the engine. This allowed the pilot to squeeze extra power from the Pegasus for up to two minutes—the average length of a dogfight. Rolls-Royce also modified the third-stage stator to facilitate rapid changes of power setting. Any long-term effects on engine life from this power boost were unknown, but there was concern at Rolls-Royce that reliability might be reduced. When Harry Blot received his first combat plug it came with the message: 'Personal. For Harry Blot only. Do not reveal source. If the aeroplane crashes while plug is installed and you get thrown clear, climb back in the fireball!' Despite this dire warning the plug turned the Harrier from 'being good to being great' in Blot's estimation. 'The raw power allowed you to pitch vertically high enough to make the pilot of a low wing-loaded airplane commit himself to a turn direction, thus enabling you to flip back at him, accelerate to gun range before he could escape, and get in a good shot. No longer was it necessary to look into the cockpit to check [engine] gauges. You could concentrate on the target.' For John Farley, VIFF was 'a pure bonus, something we were never looking for at the outset'. Ralph Hooper recalled that the 'combat plug' allowed an increase of 35° in TET (turbine entry temperature). It was to be combat proven a decade later by the Royal Navy's Sea Harriers in the Falklands conflict

VIFF combat techniques were established, allowing pilots to use it without speed or power restriction above 15,000ft. Below 10,000ft the upper speed limit was 300kt. In the same period the RAF pegged the upper limit to VIFF at 300kt, with power settings below 80 per cent. At lower speeds VIFF could be used to cause a sudden change of aircraft attitude which would cause an opponent to stall if he attempted to follow. Sudden increases of 1g in a turn could be made by flipping the nozzles down 20 degrees. Alternatively, VIFF could be used simply to disorientate a hostile fighter pilot by presenting him with a totally unpredictable manoeuvring pattern.

The downside of VIFF also became obvious in trials. Suddenly ditching the majority of a Harrier's forward energy through drastic deceleration would certainly disconcert a tail-chasing enemy, but it could also leave the jet as cold meat for his wingman. Typically, hauling the nozzle lever to the braking stop (17 degrees forward position) at around 600kt would reduce forward airspeed by 200kt in 25 seconds. It would then take over 45 seconds with nozzles fully aft to regain 500kt straight and level. More subtle vectoring could be used without a marked speed penalty. For example, a 15-degree nozzle deflection converted up to a quarter of the engine's thrust into lift for only 3 per cent of forward speed loss. The resultant manoeuvre would yank the Harrier out of an attacker's gun/missile tracking solution at short range.

These new combat techniques were fed into the syllabus at Beaufort and developed further by the first generation of squadron pilots. In most cases those personnel were particularly able second-tourists who brought ample experience, and an element of restraint, to their flying. The result was an excellent safety record with only three serious accidents in the first four years of squadron operations. From 1975 onwards there was a severe downturn, with eight crashes and four fatalities in 1977, the worst year. In the main this was a result of policy changes which admitted trainee pilots from a much broader spectrum of naval aviation, including 'new guys'

straight from basic training.[4] Because of the delay in obtaining the batch of TAV-8As, from FY 74 to FY 75, first-tourists were trained on single-seaters. VMAT-203 also continued to provide basic induction training on TA-4J Skyhawks and did not begin to receive AV-8As until April 1975, and the first TAV-8As in October of that year. Attrition began to decrease once the full complement of trainers was worked into the syllabus. Over the first ten years of operations AV-8A losses were less than the RAF's (28 against 36), but the far more demanding low-level European flying environment accounted for most of the difference. RAF losses were rather more evenly divided, with a peak of eight in 1972, of which four were attributed to pilot error. This was very similar to the USMC's 1977 record.

Although much was made of the AV-8A having a worse safety record than other USN/USMC jets (often for political reasons), the figures applied only to the training programme. In other areas the record was exemplary. In its first ten years of operations from USN/USMC ships, AV-8As flew over 10,000 sorties in all kinds of weather conditions without loss or serious incident. The overall attrition rate was certainly higher than that of the Marines' A-4 or F-4 over a similar period, though significantly less than the 'hot' F-8 Cru-

---

[4]General Tom Miller (the first Marine to fly Harrier) took full responsibility for the accident rate and admitted a mistake in training policy which had 'promoted out' experienced Harrier leaders. Furthermore, as he told the authors, 'The Marine Corps attempted to allow pilots from other types of aircraft communities to transition into the AV-8A. This was a mistake because once pilots become accustomed to aircraft with less pilot workload requirements it is difficult to transition them back to a high-workload aircraft. Aircraft with less performance like the A-6 Intruder, OV-10, KC-130 or helicopters have significantly less pilot workload. The A-4 Skyhawk and F-4 Phantom (because of its high performance) pilots were better candidates for AV-8A transition. As a result of the rise in accident rates the USMC changed its policy and slowed down transitions from the less desirable aircraft communities. We also found that newly graduated pilots who had flown the A-4 in flight school were very good candidates for AV-8A transition. There was definitely an improvement in the safety of training when the TAV-8A came along.'

An AV-8C with Snakeye bombs aboard and modified LIDs on its gun pods heads for the range from MCAS Yuma in December 1982. (Frank Mormillo)

sader's in USMC service. Figures were also influenced by the fact that a greater proportion of each 1,000hrs of flying, the yardstick for safety statistics, was spent in the AV-8A's case in take-off and landing, due to the brevity of an average CAS sortie. Clearly, safety is more likely to suffer in these portions of the mission, always more hazard-prone for any aircraft than straight-and-level flight. In 1971–82 half the accidents were put down to pilot error, and half of those occurred in situations relating to take-off or recovery. The 'bad luck' batch were FY 73 aircraft, of which 13 out of 30 were struck off, including six consecutive aircraft (BuNos 158852–158957 inclusive).

In late 1975 VMAT-203 *Hawks* had eleven AV-8As on strength, gradually reducing these to eight as the TAV-8As began to arrive. Pilots began their training with six hours in the right seat of a CH-46 Sea Knight to adjust to the unfamiliarity of vertical flight, followed by fourteen hours of AV-8A tuition. The full 60-week course included 171 sorties in all. Training was provided on the three types of site from which the Marines could operate

Harriers: the 'main base' site (Beaufort), a 'facility base' nearby, providing an 800ft strip for STOL with basic support facilities, and a 'forward site'. For the last, roads or firm ground could be used. The RAF and USMC shared a common test for firm ground. A jeep-class vehicle was driven over the intended operating area at 30–40mph. If the driver was still in his vehicle and relatively intact at the other end, the surface was declared suitable for Harriers! Alternatively, a 72 by 72ft AM-2 aluminium mat or a self-hardening resin 'pancake' could support VTOL sorties with up to four 500lb bombs and 2,000lb of fuel aboard; with a short STOL strip of 800ft the warload increased to 4,000lb plus 5,000lb of fuel. Forward sites of this kind would appear on the real battlefield about 20 miles behind the FEBA, closer by about 50 miles than a typical RAF/European scenario FOB. Refuelling was by helicopter-delivered bladder tank.[5]

Pilots on 'ground loiter' at a forward site stayed in their cockpits awaiting a 'frag' order on the radio and keeping the Harriers' systems on-line with the aircraft's internal ground turbine. Within three minutes of a 'take-off' order the pilot could be en route to his target. Ideally, an advancing force of 'grunts' would push the FEBA forward rapidly and new FOLs could be established nearer the action.

Previously used FOLs could then be made up to 'facility' standard if necessary.

AT SEA

From the earliest stages of its service career the Marines sought to establish a wider seaborne role for their new combat type. Although the Navy's Sea Control Ship (SCS) concept stalled in the mid-1970s, VMA-513 were given the task of proving the V/STOL side of the project through two deployments on board USS *Guam* (LPH-9), regarded as an interim SCS. The first, in January 1972, took place over ten days in North Atlantic weather so severe that the ship's helicopter force was grounded for much of the time. Despite this, a trio of *Flying Nightmares* managed to complete over 170 sorties. This was the first of many occasions on which Harriers continued to operate in weather and sea conditions which closed down fly-

[5]On 'facility' sites the replenishment process would have been eased by a larger V/STOL supply aircraft. Following the RAF's unsuccessful attempt to acquire such a V/STOL transport, the Marines issued a requirement for a similar type in 1975. Rockwell's proposed NA-382 would have used a C-130 fuselage and a thrust augmentor wing (TAW), mixing the thrust from four GE F101-GE-100 engines with ambient air to provide enough energy for VTOL. It never advanced beyond the preliminary design phase.

ing on the larger CVA/CV ships. The squadron, under Lieutenant-Colonel Robert O'Dare, made a second 'blue water' deployment on *Guam* for her 1974–75 Mediterranean cruise, with diversionary sorties from other, smaller decks as well. Although the SCS idea was substantially proven by this experience, its proponent Admiral Zumwalt had retired and the 'big carrier' league reasserted itself in Navy planning.

VMA-231 established their role as the primary deployable squadron with a detachment at Roosevelt Roads, Puerto Rico, in January 1975. The squadron regularly visited European waters to take part in 'Northern Wedding'/'Bold Guard' exercises in the early 1980s. It shared a Mediterranean cruise on USS *Nassau* (LHA-4) with VMA-542 in 1981 and returned to the Mediterranean in 1983 on USS *Tarawa* (LHA-1) as part of the UN peacekeeping force off Lebanon. The 'Aces' then transferred to USS *Inchon*

Armed with gun pods and 500lb bombs, a division of AV-8As, with pilots aboard, awaits the start-up signal at Twenty-Nine Palms. (Frank Mormillo)

(LPH-12) under Lieutenant-Colonel Robertson for further NATO exercises in the North Atlantic in the winter of 1983—their last stint in the AV-8A.

Perhaps the most interesting, and certainly the most publicised, AV-8A deployment was also made by VMA-231, from September 1976 to April 1977. This was designed to demonstrate how a complete Harrier detachment of fourteen aircraft could be integrated into a normal Sixth Fleet Carrier Air Wing (in this case CVW-19) aboard USS *Franklin D. Roosevelt* (CV-42). Operating alongside the F-4N Phantoms of VF-111 and VF-51 and three A-7B Corsair II outfits, the 'Aces' replaced the Wing's A-6 Intruder squadron. Eighteen pilots amassed 2,000hrs' flying time, including 400hrs at night. Their flying was scheduled in between the launch and recovery cycles of the catapult-launched types. Normally they joined A-7 elements in strike packages with F-4N top cover. Above all, the exercise showed the Harrier's flexibility and reliability in rapid deployment. Thirteen 'Aces' flew from 'Rosie''s deck to USS *Guam* (LPH-9), passing through the Suez Canal on her deck (the only fixed-wing jet to have done this

at the time). Off the coast of Kenya the squadron overflew Nairobi for Kenya's Independence Anniversary on 12 December 1976. Returning to *Guam*, the Harriers then sailed back to the Mediterranean and re-joined USS *Franklin D. Roosevelt*, completing a 5,000-mile trip with fully serviceable aircraft throughout. Two pilots, Captain John Demsey and Captain John Lizzo, chose to make their landing approach and touchdown over the 'Rosie''s bow. Sadly, photographic evidence of the expressions on the Phantom pilots' faces is not available!

High sortie rates and intensive utilization were the keynotes of this and all subsequent deployments. Supporting development work for these techniques continued in the United States and at the Rolls-Royce Flight Test Centre in Bristol as part of the Pegasus programme. At the beginning of 1973 the first production Harrier (XV738) was employed to simulate the highest possible RAF/USMC utilization rate. With a team of four pilots headed by Harry Pollitt taking turns in the saddle, the long-suffering jet was flown for seventeen out of nineteen consecutive days, averaging twenty take-offs and landings daily for

a total of 348. Two-thirds of them were VTOL. XV738 survived the experience (although the local neighbourhood was less happy). It went on to serve with all of the RAF's operational Harrier units and gave 'posthumous' service as instructional airframe 9074M at RAF Halton, Buckinghamshire.

Shipborne testing established a minimum VTOL deck area requirement of 60 by 60 ft, with a load-bearing strength of 20,000lb. This opened up a huge range of vessels in addition to the LPH/LHA/CV 'sea bases' normally in use. Suitable 'decks' ranged from Deck Landing Ships (LSD) at 13,700 tons, up to fast Combat Support Ships such as USS *Sacramento* (AOE-1) at 52,500 tons. Basically any ship with a helicopter deck, including *Spruance* class destroyers, could take an AV-8A for a diversionary landing or even as an emergency point-defence fighter. Between 1971 and 1978 eighteen decks were regularly used for AV-8A movements, the largest being that of USS *Eisenhower* (CVN-69). Deployments took the squadrons to a variety of foreign bases. VMA-231 flew six aircraft from USS *Iwo Jima* (LPH-2) to RNAS Yeovilton in October 1980 for a week of joint operations with 899 NAS (Naval Air Squadron) Royal Navy. They had participated in NATO's 'Teamwork 80' off Norway earlier that month on USS *Saipan* before transferring to *Iwo Jima*. The sextet also spent a day at BAe Filton, giving the Pegasus workers a rare view of their products under US insignia. VMA-231 had previously demonstrated its ability to operate from NATO bases during the October 1978 'Northern Wedding'/ 'Bold Guard', which included joint operations with Wittering-based RAF Harriers.

By far the most regular demand on the squadrons was the rota of six-month detachments at Kadena under the Unit Deployment Program. The three squadrons in turn provided up to two-thirds of their complement each time to maintain the Marine presence there. Once again, VMA-513 was first to take up position, previously occupied by A-4 Dets from Marine units. Kadena visits provided opportunities for live-firing in the Philippines, ACM with 18 TFW F-15 Eagles and CAS

practice in support of the Marines' 3rd Division.

At Cherry Point, North Carolina, and its satellite airfields, training techniques were continuously refined. VMA-542 moved to the base from Beaufort in June 1974 to join MAG-20. In 1976 the other two squadrons also made the move and the MAG's designation changed to MAG-32. The aggregation of all USMC Harrier squadrons (including VMAT-203) on one base was temporary: VMA-513 moved once again, to Yuma, Arizona, in April 1983. Cherry Point supplied 'facility' experience at Bluebird and Bogue Field, North Carolina. Regular turnaround times of 30 minutes were normal, compared to 45 minutes for an A-4M 'Scooter' or an hour for the more complex Phantom. 'Buddy-bombing' was practised, with pairs of AV-8As flying off the navigation and bombing commands of an A-6 Intruder.

The learning curve advanced in smaller ways too. One pilot returned to base with a 2,500lb fuel reserve which he considered too great for safe vertical landing in the prevailing ambient temperature. Rather than making an emergency short landing (he claimed that this had not been covered in training), he proceeded to make five approaches. On the sixth he got a low fuel 'flasher' warning for his left fuel tank, closely followed by the right flasher. These indicated 250lb of fuel remaining in each tank, but the hapless pilot didn't realise that only 150lb of that fuel could actually be used from each tank. He continued to aim for a vertical landing, switching to a short landing when the fuel booster pump warnings came on to show only 9psi in

USMC AV-8As were often flown without gun pods aboard. This *Flying Nightmares* Harrier is seen at speed over El Toro in May 1978. (Frank Mormillo)

the system. As the engine began to call it a day at 100ft he ejected, landing in time to watch his Harrier skid to a halt on the runway. To compound the 'Keystone' flavour of the incident, a fire truck on its way to the scene lost control, overturned and skidded on its side towards the spark-showering Harrier. Both vehicles ground to a halt about a foot apart, but no one was injured.

VARIATIONS

By far the most significant addition to the training programme was, of course, the TAV-8A—originally known as the AV-8B. The eight copies purchased for VMAT-203 were the hardest-worked Harriers of all. HSA wanted the Marines to have more, and did their best to extend the order. Essentially similar to the RAF T.2 variant, the two-seater had full dual controls and instruments together with the equipment changes of the AV-8A including the Baseline system. A certain amount of airframe reinforcement was needed to enable it to perform the full ACM envelope of the AV-8A, though missiles were not carried. Electro-luminescent 'formation' strip-lights were attached to the nose and fin, as on later batches of AV-8As. An additional USMC requirement was for the aircraft to perform the Airborne Tactical Air Commander combat role. A full suite of TAC VHF and UHF radios was installed to provide the necessary communication facilities, although the role was never performed 'for real'. After brief BIS trials and 'Carquals' (again, never followed-up in service use) on board *Franklin D. Roosevelt*, the TAV-8A arrived at Cherry Point in October 1975 and continued in service until November 1987.

A second variation on the basic AV-8A was the AV-8C, introduced as a CILOP (Conversion In Lieu Of Procurement) rebuild for part of the existing fleet of A models. The programme was partly a response to perceived deficiencies in the AV-8A as it entered its second decade of service. To some extent, too, it reflected the need for an interim Harrier while the Advanced Harrier programme became established, and it incorporated a few of the results of that programme's research. A major shortcoming in the AV-8A for the 1980s was the lack of ECM equipment. In an increasingly sophisticated electronic environment the AV-8A was seen (in a USMC report curiously titled Operation 'Frosty Nozzle') to lack secure voice communications, RWR gear and internal ECM (electronic countermeasures). A three-phase programme was set in train in June 1978 to develop and verify modification kits for sixty aircraft. After McAir tests of the updates in two AV-8As (BuNos 158384 and 158387), a third (158706) was

Standard RAF-style camouflage combined with high-visibility US insignia on the AV-8A as originally supplied to the Marines. (Frank Mormillo)

used to demonstrate service installation of the kit. Modification by Naval Air Rework Facility Cherry Point, in collaboration with McAir, was then scheduled for a six-year period from 1981. In fact, only 47 aircraft received CILOP in a little under half that time. By 1983 continuing attrition had caused squadron establishments to be reduced from 20 to 15 aircraft each, and the definitive AV-8B 'Advanced Harrier' was beginning to enter service.

An extensive range of equipment updates was involved in the CILOP. A few had already been incorporated in the final AV-8A batch: formation lights (Mod 1011), a CCIP modification to the HUD, improved hydraulic filtration (ECP 0008R2) and the Stencel SIIIS.3 seat (Mod 613R8). To these were added KY-28/TSEC secure voice radio, ALE-39 countermeasures dispensers, ALR-45F/APR-43 RWR (later updated to the ALR-67), ARC-159 UHF radio and remote indicator and provision for the ALQ-126C DECM pod (also later 'revisited' by the manufacturers) on the centreline. Most of this equipment was housed in the rear fuselage bay with antennas in the rear fuselage cone, in the wingtips and on the spine (omni antenna) and lower nose (APR-43 array). An onboard oxygen generating system (OBOGS) was included to free the aircraft from dependence on LOX (liquid oxygen).

Aerodynamic improvements were effected via a spin-off from YAV-8B development: extended strakes or lift improvement devices (LIDs) were attached to the gun pods and a retractable cross-dam could be extended to 'block off' the gap between the front ends of the pods with the landing gear extended. These changes enhanced engine lift in ground effect and reduced exhaust ingestion into the intakes. At the same time, various items of equipment were deleted, amongst them the RAT, F95 oblique camera, sound recorder, fire extinguisher system, ARC-150 radio and several now redundant cockpit instruments. The result of all the updates was a significantly more capable Harrier with a net weight increase of only 197lb. As a bonus, NARF took the opportunity to inspect and 're-life' each airframe with structural strengthening, which cleared the AV-8C for a 4,000hr fatigue life.

AV-8C BuNo 158384, the first of the development aircraft, flew on 5 May 1979 in a dashing red, white and blue paint scheme similar to the YAV-8B's. Pax River tests followed, with sea trials aboard USS *Saipan* (LHA-2) in October. Sadly, '384's career ended on 5 September 1980 when it lost power on take-off from USS *Tarawa*. Its pilot managed to eject 25ft above the sea as the Harrier splashed in at 90kt. Production examples began to reach the squadrons in 1983, operating alongside A models until transition to the AV-8B began in 1984–85. The majority served with VMA-513, which had completely re-equipped with AV-8Cs when it disestablished, following a final six-aircraft deployment to USS *Tarawa* (LHA-1) for Exercise 'Valiant Usher' in 1986. VMA-542 still had a majority of AV-8As when it converted in the same year. Several of the aircraft were used by VMA-203 for conversion training until mid-1985, when first-generation Harrier instruction ended. When they headed for AMARC (Air Matériel and Reclamation Center) in 1986–87 the AV-8C's low airframe hours would have made them an attractive buy to a small navy. They and their predecessors had vindicated beyond doubt the wisdom of the Marine Corps' operating procedures which wrote the book for the next, much more numerous generation of Harriers.

4. Sea Jets

In the mid-1990s the sight of a Sea Harrier suspended briefly above a pitching carrier deck, before making solid contact with sheet steel, seems so normal that it is hard to believe the concept took so long to be accepted. Hawker Siddeley stressed the virtues of VTOL at sea from the earliest days of the P.1127 in study documents and promotions. In 1959, when the Government first agreed to limited funding of P.1127 under Experimental Requirement ER.204D (followed by OR.345) there was little interest from the Royal Navy. Their carriers were populated by the heavyweight strike survivors of the 1957 Defence Review, the Buccaneer and the Sea Vixen. A jet/rocket powered interceptor, the SR.177N, had been in prospect to replace their Scimitar fighter, but that was axed in 1957. This left a gap in naval procurement policy but the subsonic, short-range P.1127 did not appear to offer immediate answers. However, the prospect of a supersonic P.1154 derivative, proposed in 1962, haggled over for two years and cancelled in February 1964 in favour of the F-4K (FG.1) Phantom, did at least expose naval thinkers to the potential benefit of V/STOL. Even so, the entirely convincing demonstrations by a P.1127 on

Watched by a fair proportion of HMS *Ark Royal*'s crew, a No 1 Squadron Harrier settles beside the Air Group's Phantoms and Buccaneers in March 1970. (BAe)

One of Hawker's P.1154(RN) proposals with a two-man crew, inboard undercarriage fairings and Phantom-like intakes.

board *Ark Royal* in 1963 were seen merely as further justification for the 'real' P.1154 option at the time. In 1966 the cancellation of the Navy's next big carrier, CVA-01, radically altered the situation.

CVA-01 would have been the first of five ships, the largest and most costly ever produced in Britain. Initially a whole new generation of aircraft were proposed for this fleet, including the swing-wing Vickers Type 583 attack fighter and a new ASW aircraft with twin fore-and-aft radomes. In 1962 the P.1154 killed off Vickers' Type 583, but it may also have helped to kill CVA-01. Although the Navy rejected the proposed supersonic VTOL type because of impracticalities in its conception, there was also an element of self-preservation involved. The 'big carrier' admirals saw the P.1154 as a threat to the catapult-and-landing-wire traditions of carrier aviation and as justification for smaller, less capable ships with a token air component. This explained the Navy's preference for the 'conventional' Phantom from 1964 on-

wards rather than having 'commonality' thrust upon them in the form of a joint RAF/RN P.1154 design. But the damage was done. Cash-conscious ministers had learned from the P.1154 debate that V/STOL could save the massive expense of big decks and this, together with Britain's shrinking global defence commitment, undoubtedly contributed to the death of CVA-01.

Although HMS *Ark Royal* was refitted for Phantoms and reprieved until 1979, the loss of CVA-01 effectively removed the Royal Navy from the carrier 'big league'. HMS *Eagle* and HMS *Victorious* were withdrawn and the smaller carriers were scrapped or converted into helicopter assault ships, including HMS *Hermes*. It was a rapid reversal of fortunes for a force which, at the beginning of the 1960s, had the world's second largest carrier fleet. The loss of its fixed-wing carriers, following the withdrawal of HMS *Ark Royal*, left the RN with no air defence and without fixed-wing capability for the first time since 1911. Government policy therefore passed the 'air defence at sea' task to the RAF, an idea which lacked credibility from the outset despite the RN's new NATO-centred role. Admirals began to wonder about life spent

under an umbrella of USN air power, or the prospect of having their operational radius restricted to the effective range of an RAF Lightning! Other naval planners pressed ahead with the new generation of 'through-deck cruisers'.

Planned towards the end of the 1960s, these 18,860-ton vessels were intended to carry an ASW (anti-submarine warfare) helicopter Air Wing, with an added commando-carrying capability from 1977—the year in which the first of the ships, HMS *Invincible* was launched. Ironically, their original function was to escort CVA-01 class carriers, providing the ASW screen for the big carrier which would have operated all the fighter and strike jets. Instead, the *Invincible* class ship became the centre of the force, but without fixed-wing aircraft (in its original version). By 1969, when designs began to firm up at MoD(PE) Bath, the ship resembled the USN's *Iwo Jima* class LPH vessels which were at that time beginning to operate AV-8A Harriers alongside their ASW complement.

Throughout the Royal Navy's period of uncertainty HSA continued with a policy of demonstrating the P.1127, and later the Harrier, on naval decks whenever

possible. The 3 February 1963 'hop' was the first deck landing by a fixed-wing VTOL aircraft. Bill Bedford (in XP831) made a decelerating transition over the stern of HMS *Ark Royal* as she lay in Lyme Bay, Dorset. 'The island superstructure provided a good height reference and no difficulty was experienced in accurately positioning the aircraft,' Bedford reported. He then made an immediate VTO and landing, followed by a succession of short take-offs and transitioning approaches from all angles while a large proportion of 'Ark''s crew occupied every vantage point on the ship. Bedford and Hugh Merewether practised taxying, parking the jet on the decklift and avoiding the ingestion of funnel gases into the Pegasus while hovering. Finally the P.1127 returned to Dunsfold, lifting off at 80kt into a 30kt wind in less than a third of the deck-

length. It left only a few blisters in the deck paint to mark its visit, but a lasting impression was made on the representatives of the RAF, USN, Royal Australian Navy and Ministry of Aviation who had been invited along.

After a gap of several years surrounding the protracted cancellation of the P.1154, shipborne trials recommenced on HMS *Bulwark* on 18 June 1966. Bill Bedford brought P.1127 XP984 over the ship with a sonic bang, made a vertical landing and then conducted twelve test flights over the ensuing two days. To follow up, an armed Harrier GR.1 (XV758, from No 3 Squadron) flew from the same ship in September 1969. These trials were the first to explore the possibility of using seaborne Harriers to support an amphibious assault from this commando carrier. They also echoed the successful sea trials of the XV-

6A on USN assault ships. Also in 1969, a Harrier joined the 12,000-ton cruiser HMS *Blake*, operating from the 'sulphur-filled turbulence of her helicopter flight deck'. A Royal Navy diarist recorded that 'the influential observers could not fail to be impressed by the remarkable aircraft and its apparent ease of operation with *Blake*'.

Official sea trials for the Harrier took place on board HMS *Eagle* over two weeks in March 1970, two years before the ship was laid up for spares and a year after the scrapping of HMS *Victorious*. The intention was to explore the possible deployment of RAF Harriers aboard the two remaining large carriers, *Eagle* and *Ark Royal*. Harrier was given full Service Release for deck operations by RAF crew, the first clearance of its kind in the world. Two GR.1s were flown by day and night, pi-

Left: John Farley takes XZ450 aloft on one of its early test flights. He demonstrated it at SBAC Farnborough less than a month after its first flight in August 1978 and it was the first Sea Harrier to make a deck landing—on HMS *Hermes* three months later. (BAe)

Right, upper: Sea Harrier FRS.1 XZ451, with the personal markings of 899 NAS's boss, Lieutenant-Commander 'Sharkey' Ward, prepares to take off at RNAS Yeovilton, 2 August 1980. As CO of 801 NAS, Ward flew XZ451 again in the Falklands, shooting down a C-130E and a Pucará. It was also used by Lieutenant Curtis to destroy Canberra B-110 in that conflict. XZ451 was lost during ACT off Sardinia in 1989. Lieutenant Michael Auckland ejected, but seven years later he was killed in the crash of a Harrier T.4N near Yeovilton. (Authors)

Right, lower: 800 NAS's attractive red tail insignia enhances the glossy Extra Dark Sea Grey paintwork on XZ460 in August 1980. This Sea Harrier, flown by Lieutenant-Commander Batt, bombed the Argentine intelligence-gathering trawler *Narwal*. It survived until May 1990, when it crashed into the Mediterranean during Exercise 'Dragon Hammer'. (Authors)

loted by John Farley and two RAF pilots from Boscombe Down, Squadron Leader Graham Williams and Wing Commander Ian Keppie, neither of whom had previously flown from a ship. Particular attention was paid to the problems of aligning the FE.541 INAS on ship and to STO take-offs in various load configurations and wind conditions. 849 NAS's resident Gannet AEW aircraft were disembarked to accommodate a squad of Harrier technicians and the ship was swamped with carefully selected guests from the USN and USMC plus a large cast of Rolls-Royce and HSA directors, ETPS (Empire Test Pilots' School) staff and 'men from the Ministry'.

Meanwhile HMS *Ark Royal* was on her sixth commission (marked by a 420lb commissioning cake, the heaviest ever). She was visited by a GR.1 for preliminary deck trials as a prelude to No 1 Squadron's detachment to the ship the following year. Four Harriers joined ship for ten days in April 1971, led by No 1 Squadron's boss

Wing Commander Ken Hayr. Once again the 'goofers' were out on the ship's island for the arrival, and nearly had their day ruined. Hayr's aircraft made a short, rather than vertical landing, but a little fast. With brakes locked the aircraft skidded on the painted, wet deck, headed resolutely for the island but stopped safely. Despite this slightly undignified entry by the 'crabs', they impressed 'Ark''s crew by recovering a Harrier aboard in weather which had caused the ship's Buccaneers and Phantoms to divert ashore. There is little doubt that the case for a seaborne Harrier derivative was considerably strengthened by the whole exercise. Once again, there was a sizable entourage of influential observers. 'Ark Airways' helicopters handled over 300 arrivals and departures, including that of Peter Firth, Undersecretary for Defence, and representatives from the USN

and (significantly) Argentina. HSA gave the crew of *Ark Royal* a 'well done' gesture at the end of the trials—a free can of beer for every man aboard. No 1 Squadron returned to the ship in September 1976 to complete its sea performance trials.

Carrier visits became more frequent in the 1970s. HMS *Bulwark* took aboard a No 1 Squadron detachment off Akrotiri in May 1973. In December of that year the inhabitants of the ship's '2 Alpha' messdeck had their crockery rattled by the blast of G-VTOL's exhaust as it did a STO off the bow. Following the USMC's example, operations from smaller vessels were also practised. Visitors to the Chatham Warship Day in September 1977 would have witnessed one of these—a GR.1 VTOL session from the Fleet Auxiliary *Stromness*. Probably the smallest area used was the 55 by 85ft landing platform

of HMS *Green Rover* (11,520 tons) in September 1971. In 1975–76 Harriers flew from the 9,000-ton HMS *Engadine*, from HMS *Fearless* and in April 1976 from the larger and more appropriate HMS *Hermes*. Added to this were the XV-6A and AV-8A operations from fourteen different ships by February 1977, and the HSA sales effort in other countries. Beginning in October 1967 with a landing on the 6,500-ton Italian *Andrea Doria* and progressing in September 1969 to Argentina's only carrier, *25 de Mayo*, HSA pilots made demonstrations on Indian, Spanish, Brazilian and French vessels, confirming the Harrier's versatility in an assortment of nautical environments.

By 1972 wiser councils had prevailed in the debate over Britain's air defence at sea. The Harrier's various sea trials, and the important development work by the USMC, had altered the Royal Navy's perception of the aircraft. In particular, the Marines' air defence requirement caused them to explore the aircraft's air-to-air potential much more closely than was necessary for its RAF tasking. Defence chiefs began to see that it could provide credible defence for a 'through-deck cruiser' at low cost, at least against hostile reconnaissance

Left, upper: Lieutenant-Commander Rod Frederiksen in XZ458, which bears his name beneath the windshield. He was the second RN pilot to fly the Sea Harrier and he took command of 800 NAS several years after this photograph was taken. (Authors)

Left, lower: The Sea Harrier FRS.1 cockpit. At the upper right of the front panel is the Blue Fox radar display, with the RWR panel (white circle) below and to the right. (BAe)

Right, upper: 800 NAS CO Lieutenant-Commander Tim Gedge had XZ454 as his personal aircraft. Its career was short-lived. Less than a year after delivery it became the first Sea Harrier casualty when it hit HMS *Invincible*'s ski-jump during a fly-past, lost stability and crashed. (Via R. L. Ward)

Right, lower: Every inch a fighter, XZ454 shows off its twin AIM-9G missiles, Aden gun pods and 100gal combat tanks. Under the nose is the rectangular Decca Type 72 doppler radar. (Via R. L. Ward)

flights. RAF opposition continued, partly because the reintroduction of RN fixed-wing self-defence was seen as a threat to their embryonic Tornado ADV. This was intended to provide a better deterrent (in RAF eyes) against the USSR's supersonic bombers with stand-off missiles, and was specifically designed for prolonged CAP duties to protect sea lanes as well as for sector defence of cities and military facilities.[1] No 1 Squadron's early 1970s sea trials were partly designed to show that the RAF could put Harriers aboard ships quite rapidly to counter an air defence threat. In RAF thinking, this obviated a requirement for a naval version under RN control. Clearly, there were major practical problems. Among these was No 1 Squadron's role as the forward-deployed Harrier unit worldwide. Even Harriers could not be in three places at once!

All of No 1 Squadron's aircraft were cleared in 1971 for naval modifications

which included undercarriage tie-down rings and an alteration to the nosewheel steering circuit. This caused it to engage when the anti-skid brakes were off, preventing the nosewheel from castoring around on a heaving deck. However, there was no funding for Sidewinder capability, severely limiting the 'land Harrier's' sea-defence credibility. RAF training philosophy dedicated less than 10 per cent of the Harrier role to air-to-air, whereas the RN needed at least half this function, the rest being split between attack and reconnaissance. In addition, the Admiralty saw that the Harrier's lack of radar was a major constraint on its use for air defence.

In 1972, the same year that HMS *Invincible* (CAH-01, later R-05) was laid down, HSA was awarded a study contract for a Naval Harrier based on the company's very tentative P.1184 Maritime Harrier proposal of 1969. The Admiralty anticipated up to six aircraft plus about ten

Above: Lieutenant-Commander Robin Kent settles on to HMS *Invincible*'s deck in XZ454, the first Sea Harrier to land aboard. 'Sharkey' Ward waits his turn above, in an 899 NAS aircraft. (Via R. L. Ward)

Right, upper: Harrier sea trials continued throughout the 1970s. This No 1 Squadron GR.1A is landing on *Ark Royal* in October 1975 as the ship passed through the English Channel. (Via R. L. Ward)

Right, lower: 801 NAS had just two aircraft on strength, including XZ493/001N, when it was commissioned in 1981 with 'Sharkey' Ward as CO. XZ493 made the inaugural ski-jump at Yeovilton that day. The aircraft's long service career ended in December 1994 over the Adriatic after loss of yaw control. (Via R. L. Ward)

---

[1] In contrast to their previous indigenously produced point interceptors, the Hunter and Lightning, which were always short on range.

Sea Kings in each of the Air Groups on the three projected *Invincible* class ships. To accommodate this change of role *Invincible* herself went through a series of designation changes—through-deck cruiser, command cruiser and eventually ASW carrier when the forbidden allusion to her aircraft-carrying function could once again be permitted.

'MINIMUM CHANGE'

At a time of great pressure on defence budgets because of rampant world inflation, the design work for the Naval Harrier had to be based on a 'minimum change' principle. Major redesign would, in any case, have been physically limited by the location of the Pegasus and the consequent need to preserve the CG. In the Naval Harrier this is slightly further forward than the GR.3's, and the addition of radar in the nose meant placing a large proportion of its allied avionics in the rear fuselage to maintain the CG as far as possible. Radar was the only major addition to the basic GR.3, used for air-to-air combat and ground mapping. To avoid the cost of developing a purpose-built radar it was decided to modify Ferranti's ARI.5979

Seaspray search and monopulse tracking radar, used in the Navy's Lynx helicopters. The set was optimised for the air-to-air role. Its sea-search ability was retained for the new variant's low altitude reconnaissance role, and a limited attack function was incorporated. The aircraft's FRS.1 (Fighter, Reconnaissance, Strike) designator reflected these tasks, with 'Strike' implying nuclear anti-shipping attacks if required.

At Kingston, Dr Fozard was put in charge of the design, which was firm by the end of 1973 when it seemed that a production order was imminent. However, a long period of industrial unrest and two General Elections in 1974 caused considerable delays to that decision. HSA considered the programme to be very much at risk under a new Labour Government, which might well have seen it as an easy target for cancellation. Finally, on 15 May 1975, Defence Secretary Roy Mason announced an order for 24 Sea Harriers (the name eventually selected over the more obvious 'Osprey'). This was thought sufficient to provide small squadrons of five aircraft for the three ASW cruisers ordered at the same time. To provide training,

XZ451, in 801 NAS's 1983-style markings, approaches HMS *Invincible*. The Squadron's CO, Lieutenant-Commander A. R. W. Ogilvy (whose name appears on the aircraft's nose), flew with 800 NAS during Operation 'Corporate', having prepared to take over 801 NAS from Lieutenant-Commander Ward when hostilities commenced. He finally got his chance when 'Sharkey' Ward handed over the Squadron to him on windswept Port Stanley airfield in July 1982. (Via R. L. Ward)

Mason's accountants allowed for two RN Hunter T.8s to be converted for radar training and a single Harrier T.2 for VTOL initiation. A further ten FRS.1s and four T.4 aircraft were added in 1978.

Although pilots of later, more potent Sea Harrier variants now regard the FRS.1 radar as something of a 'Mickey Mouse' installation, it packed a great deal into a small space. Building on Ferranti's experience in designing compact radars for the TSR.2 and BAC Lightning, the Blue Fox pulse-modulated I-band radar offered several modes:
Search and Detection, with a B-type scan for air-to-air and air-to-sea. Two pulse widths and single- or two-bar scan were select-

able. A frequency-agility mode gave limited ability to defeat jamming and clutter, with auto-tracking of jamming targets being possible. This would be used for reconnaissance and acquiring targets.

Lock-on Track, for actual attack, furnishing target range and angle steering inputs to the HUD/WAC, for gun and air-to-air missile attacks.

Boresight, for ranging data to assist engaging targets of opportunity using an aiming point displayed in the HUD.

Navigation, the antenna ground-stabilized by NAVHARS (Navigation, Heading and Attitude Reference System), sweeping in a PPI ground-mapping mode.

Blue Fox also gave an I-band transponder IFF function and quick-fix maintenance with its nine LRUs (line replaceable units) mounted in the aircraft's nose. MTBF (mean time between failure) times of 300-plus hours were designed in. The entire radar nose folded back, reducing aircraft length by 5.3ft for easier deck handling. Radar information was passed to the Sea Harrier's HUD/WAC (head-up display/weapons aiming computer). Using a Smiths HUD with a larger lens and reflector plate than the GR.3's and a 20Kb digital computer rather than the analogue type in earlier Harriers, this system provided the pilot with a full range of attitude, heading, altitude, Mach, AOA and side-force indications. Navaids, tacan and MADGE (Microwave Aircraft Digital Guidance Equipment) data could also be called up. In air-to-surface modes the HUD displayed CCIP and DSL release data and air-to-air symbology for missile and gun attacks.

In place of the GR.3's INAS, which had proved too difficult to align on an unstable ship's deck, the Sea Harrier carried Ferranti's NAVHARS. It was coupled to a Decca Type 72 doppler radar (the yellowish panel under the nose), interfaced via a second 8Kb computer to provide accurate grid references. Although not inertial in operation, the system gave accuracy comparable to the GR.3 INAS. Its twin-gyro platform derived from the Tornado GR.1 model and could be aligned in 2–3 minutes. Moving-map equipment was deleted, in accordance with the air-

craft's predominantly over-water mission; a nine-waypoint memory within NAV-HARS, which could be updated via tacan or radar, was used instead. Communications equipment included a UHF/VHF PTR.377 radio with VHF standby. Passive ECM consisted of RWR receivers in the fin leading edge and on the tip of the tailboom. The fin installation added extra area to compensate for the slight increase in side area at the front of the aircraft. All new electronics were required to be self-checking without external test equipment.

Installation of the radar and other equipment in the nose necessitated a total revision of the aircraft's 'front half'. An enlarged mock-up nose was flight-tested in the second DB GR.1 (XV277, later to end its days at Yeovilton's AMG in 1974. However, to improve pilot visibility and to provide more equipment space the entire cockpit was raised 10in (25.5cm) and covered by a new bubble canopy. The change meant improved vertical display space for the cockpit panels as well as increased equipment room under the cockpit floor. The Decca Type 72 navaid was the main addition in this area. BAe (HSA) took the opportunity to sort out the random mess which the GR.3 cockpit had become and

modernised the whole 'office'. Instruments were simplified and arranged more logically. In the GR.3 even the bottom of the windscreen area had become cluttered with various instruments, causing pilots to crank their seats up as high as possible to see forward. In so doing it was quite possible to raise the line of sight well above the HUD 'porthole', causing some interesting contortions. Sea Harrier's enlarged HUD, improved RWR information display and radar altimeter made life easier although the cockpit was still only fractionally wider than the cramped office of the P.1127 with the HUD only 8 or 9in in front of the pilot's nose. A basic autopilot was installed as well.

At the centre of the Sea Harrier was the 21,500lb Pegasus 104, 'navalised' by the replacement of two magnesium-based compressor casing components with aluminium parts to alleviate salt corrosion. Similarly, seven magnesium airframe parts were replaced, adding 60lb of weight, though the total weight penalty in producing Sea Harrier out of GR.3 was only around 100lb. As part of the anti-corro-

Sea Harrier 003 of 801 NAS is securely chained to HMS *Invincible*'s deck. (Via R. L. Ward)

sion treatment, many other internal components were coated with Sermetel-W, and RAF Harriers used in Belize were also given this treatment. Increased electrical requirements for the radar and other new systems required a bigger accessory-drive gearbox and a 12kVA generator. Funding was not available for airframe changes aft of the cockpit, so the GR.3 intake was used. It could handle the Pegasus 104's mass airflow requirements, but a more powerful engine such as the Pegasus 11-35 with 5 per cent greater airflow would probably have needed the bigger AV-8B-type inlet. Consideration was also given to increasing hover uplift slightly by fitting cushion air devices (CADS) to the gun pods. These would have been smaller versions of the LIDs used on AV-8B. BAe also proposed LERX (leading-edge root extensions), which they were testing in 1977, to improve turning performance.

Other airframe modifications included a strengthened tailplane with increased positive travel for STO command, a slightly longer tailboom, tie-down lugs on the undercarriage and an independent braking system to increase the pilot's peace of mind on deck. Revised LOX and air-conditioning systems were installed and hydraulics were modified. An MB Mk 10 zero-zero ejection seat replaced the Mk 9 of the GR.3, giving full parachute deployment within 1.5 seconds of initiation of ejection at low level and low speed.

A small but important change to the RCS gave increased speed of reaction in the turbulent conditions which could be experienced on deck. Although the RCS retained the same power as the GR.3's it was possible to obtain full RCV thrust in any direction with only half the movement of the control column. Tests by John Farley were largely responsible for this improvement, which radically altered the control 'feel' of the aircraft in the hover. He argued that effective control, and therefore the stability of the aircraft, re-

899 NAS Sea Harriers in their hangar at Yeovilton. At the rear left is one of the T.4 aircraft (XZ455/Q) shared with RAF Wittering but in RAF markings. (Via Simon Hargreaves)

quired very rapid control inputs with a minimum of physical movement by the pilot. In several cases uncommanded rolls during VTOL had occurred because pilots were fractionally slow to correct an asymmetric situation. In 'ground effect' (the first 1–2ft from wheels clear of the deck), with only 7 degrees of bank, the Harrier's instability would be such that application of full RCS would be insufficient to recover the aircraft. The cause is the spread of jet efflux beneath the aircraft. In a slight asymmetric attitude, with one wing only a foot closer to the ground than the other, greater suction is created under the wing which is lower, pulling it further down into an irretrievable roll. Several Harrier and AV-8A losses were attributable to this phenomenon. Managing the situation was inevitably a 'seat of the pants' affair. (In training new pilots John Farley always insisted that they focused on the horizon and/or view ahead in VTOL to keep 'wings level', rather than looking down at instruments and 'losing it'.) Increasing the airflow through the RCS would have meant bleeding off too much basic engine thrust, so the emphasis had to be on employing the available power more quickly.

On the Harrier GR.1/3 full RCS power was obtained at 80 per cent aileron deflection on either wing and Farley wanted to halve that. Kingston and RAE Bedford felt that this would result in over-control, basing their judgement upon the only available published criteria on stick forces and RCV power, derived from the NASA hovering simulator. Farley doubted that this simulator was representative of actual VTOL flight, having 'flown' it a few years previously. The device provided 'the best motion base available to the aeronautical world' for the purpose, as it gave an enormous amount of heave and sway—up to 20 or 30ft (6–9m)—in each of its axes of movement. It was situated in a hangar, but for a 'real world' forward view 'You opened the hangar doors and "hovered" in the car park outside,' as John Farley recalled. After an initial check ride he asked if he could 'fly' it with the hangar doors shut, but NASA technicians felt that the close-up view of the doors whizzing

to and fro would be too disorientating. Eventually his request was granted and NASA got 'very excited' by his ability to control the simulator successfully in those conditions, particularly when he announced that he had 'flown' most of the session with his eyes closed. In fact, during his 'car park' ride (eyes open) he had taught himself all the various noises made by the simulator in each of its axes of movement. He 'flew' using those sounds for guidance rather than normal piloting skills. His real point to NASA was that all the published data from the device could have been tainted by the fact that the researchers did not know how many previous occupants had been 'unconsciously listening to it and using those cues as well as their ordinary skills'. NASA's evidence was therefore not fully representative of the real VTOL scenario and of dubious use in proving the Sea Harrier RCS issue.

Years later John Farley appeared at Kingston bearing a schematic diagram of G-VTOL's control system and asked the designers to halve the length of one of the rear cockpit control rods in order to double the sensitivity of the pilot's control column for RCS operation. When told that the modifications could take weeks to design and produce he replied that he wanted to try it that afternoon. There was another solution: 'I'm flying a single-seater later today. I'll try it in that by holding the control column with my hand half-way down it, thereby doubling control sensitivity.' In practice this meant moving his hand half the distance to achieve the same effect as a normal stick input. He and the other Dunsfold pilots tried the technique in instrumented Harriers and reported easier and more precise control in the hover, and no over-control. The modified control rods were incorporated into the Sea Harrier before it flew. A corresponding increase in stick forces was added to the system, resulting in an extremely stable aircraft in the VTOL situation and a more stable aircraft in the hover.

Farley's main recollection of the first flight of XZ450, the Sea Harrier 'prototype', on 20 August 1978 was that the revised RCS 'feel' was demonstrated very effectively. At the end of the first-ever Sea

Harrier sortie, in which he had made three VTOs, an STO and various hovers and transitions for 35 minutes, his official verdict was that the flight was 'uneventful'. In fact, as he entered the final hover he was able to trim the aircraft so accurately that he took his hands off the stick. He then whipped out a small camera and snapped an unsuspecting BAe representative on the ground. 'The idea of letting go of the controls in the hover, however briefly, was unthinkable with the ordinary Harriers. In the Sea Harrier you could feel the centre position of the stick much more precisely and trim the aircraft so that it stayed in that position and only drifted into instability very slowly.'

Two other small additions were tested in the early days of Sea Harrier, although one of these, the hold-back device, was not adopted for production. It consisted of a small metal restraint rod similar to the one attached between the rear end of the FG.1 Phantom and the carrier for catapult launch. For the Phantom, the restraint was designed to snap under the force of the catapult stroke. The Sea Harrier version, attached to the main undercarriage, held the aircraft back under full power also but it was released via a button on top of the nozzle lever when the pilot was confident of his engine acceleration times and power settings. Usually, pushing the throttle to the stops could only be done with a 300yd ground-run and a stopwatch as the brakes would not hold the jet beyond 50 per cent power. In 1978–79 it was not always possible to attain precisely repeatable engine acceleration times, and there was the chance of a lack of peak power on launch and a dive into the drink. Using the hold-back a pilot could see his actual maximum rpm on a gauge for reassurance. However, fitting the bar took a few precious seconds before launch and by the time the Sea Harrier was with the squadrons the Pegasus 104, with improved hydro-mechanics, reliably produced repeatable acceleration times.

The second minor modification was the so-called 'nozzle nudger', a speed trim system operated via the air brake switch on the throttle control. It gave the pilot an 11-degree change of nozzle direction from datum in either direction without having to take his hand off the throttle. Precise forward or rearward speed control was possible through small nozzle movements on final approach to vertical landing without having to alter the aircraft's attitude. Initial tests of the 'nozzle inching system' (as BAe called it) were done at Bedford and Farnborough using P.1127 XP984 in 1968 and XV472 in May 1971, and aboard HMS *Hermes* with G-VTOL in February 1977.

The Sea Harrier's primary air-defence role required pylon and wiring changes to accommodate two AIM-9 Sidewinders on LAU-7A/5 launchers. In defining this role BAe drew upon USMC experience with the AV-8A. Unlike the RAF, the Marines had always emphasized air combat and developed special tactics, including VIFFing. Although the latter was not foreseen as having a big part in Sea Harrier training, it was allowed for, though no engineering changes to the Pegasus or its nozzles were considered necessary. As part of the armament package the inboard pylons had stronger ejector release units for the carriage of Martel or Sea Eagle anti-shipping missiles. In fact, the Sea Harrier was the only variant of the family to have fixed inboard pylons. This was to ensure adequate electrical integrity for the complex fusing required for nuclear weapons, which would be carried on these pylons. Two types were available, the British WE.177, and American Mk/B-57 nuclear depth charge. Control of these weapons was accomplished via a small panel at the base of the central instrument console.

SKI-JUMP

The aircraft's lengthy gestation period (five years from provisional go-ahead to first flight) gave BAe time to finalize the design in detail well before the production order was firmed up. For this reason, and to reduce cost, all 24 of the initial batch of Sea Harriers were considered to be production aircraft, with no prototypes. However, the first few copies did the development work and service trials. After XZ450's first flight and its first carrier landing on HMS *Hermes* on 13 November 1978, with Mike Snelling at the controls, the next three off the line undertook different aspects of the programme. XZ438 performed basic handling and performance trials at Dunsfold. XZ439 went to Boscombe Down for stores trials (and later tested the twin-Sidewinder installation at Aberporth in April 1982). XZ440 performed various tests at Dunsfold, at Boscombe Down and for Rolls-Royce at Filton, as well as Sidewinder trials. All three eventually appeared in RN squadron service, as did XZ450. During the same five-year period BAe and the MoD also had the opportunity to plan the aircraft's complete operational scenario in detail. A vital part of this was the ski-jump concept.

The idea of using a ramp to impart upward velocity to a deck-based aircraft's launch trajectory was not entirely new. HMS *Furious* had a ramp fitted to the end of her rather limited flight deck in August 1944 to enable heavily laden Fairey Barracuda torpedo bombers to take off and attack the *Tirpitz*. The advent of V/STOL meant that the concept could be used much more efficiently. Lieutenant-Commander Douglas Taylor RN gave the idea very detailed consideration in his MPhil thesis at Southampton University, presented to the Royal Navy in 1973. His findings were developed at Kingston using computer models, followed up by MoD simulator studies in 1975. In simple terms they suggested that the Harrier, on a flat deck-run, could double its fuel and armament load with a rolling take-off, adding 6lb payload for every foot it rolled, and 66lb for every knot of wind-over-deck. With a ski-jump, Taylor predicted up to 60 per cent less deck-length would be required, while payload could be increased by 30 per cent. He calculated that the aircraft should reach transition point at the top of its trajectory, some 15 seconds from 'wheels rolling'. Obviously these ball-park figures depended upon the selection of the optimum ramp angle, and the only way to establish that was to build a ramp.

In 1976 HSA designed an adjustable ramp using components from British Steel and it was erected at RAE Bedford. Once again John Farley's influence helped to move forward this crucial stage in Sea Harrier evolution, because he was determined that the ramp should be built at Bedford. John Fozard and others at Kingston wanted the ramp at Dunsfold where they could have easy access to it. Since meeting Lieutenant-Commander Taylor, John Farley was determined that the RN should have the ski-jump in time for Sea Harrier's service entry. He had received detailed briefings on the logic of the ski-jump from T. S. R. Jordan at BAe. Based on his own shipborne experience with earlier Harriers, he judged that the ramp could 'answer all the shipborne Harrier problems which we had sensed since

1972'. One of these was the carrier's tendency to 'dwell' in certain sea-states, pausing with its bow up or down about once in every five or six cycles of rising and falling with the waves. Much of the early Harrier testing at sea had been aimed at working out exact weights and velocities to prevent any chance of the aircraft flying directly into the sea if launched during a 'dwell' point. With a briefly sustained downward deck angle there was every chance of this occurring. Even a modest increase in exit angle from the deck would reduce the risk greatly. Deck landing in

heavy seas was not a problem: the aircraft could touch down amidships where the ship's pitching motion was less apparent.

Another difficulty was the impaired handling characteristics of the aircraft over the bow. At relatively low forward velocity (around 90kt) the Harrier encountered a stream of air rushing up and over the forward edge of the flight deck. This immediately increased the Harrier's AOA, producing an unstable aircraft. In early flat-deck launches Harrier pilots had been accustomed to counteracting this effect by applying full forward stick for one or two seconds, an unnatural action at the point where the aircraft was attempting to gain altitude and speed. A third risk had been the possibility of engine or nozzle-control failure at the point of launch. In that situation the pilot would have a couple of seconds to recognise the problem, react to it and eject—i.e. with nowhere near enough time to stand a chance of survival. Once again, a calculated upward trajectory from a ramp created those few extra seconds.

The exit angle of the ramp therefore had to be calculated to exceed any likely 'bow-down' angle of the ship, and in so doing it permitted STOL take-offs in virtually any sea conditions. In all, the 'something for nothing' advantages of the ski-jump were so compelling that John Farley was keen to speed up the decision-making machinery at the MoD. His approach was to win over the decision-makers by siting the ramp at Bedford (where he had worked as a test pilot for three years) so that its success would be visible to as many of the resident MoD procurement personnel as possible. He judged that they would therefore feel involved in its success and accelerate the incorporation of a ski-jump in HMS *Invincible* before it was launched.

The Bedford ramp was christened on 5 August 1977 when John Farley took off in the sixth pre-production Harrier (XV281). It was set at a 6-degree exit angle. In the first intensive series of 116 launches, completed in September that year using XV281 and two-seater

With its yellow primer replaced by smart RN grey and white, XZ450 leaps from RAE Bedford's ski-jump. (Via R. L. Ward)

XW175, ramp angles were stepped-up to 12 degrees. Subsequent tests performed through June 1979 took the ramp progressively up to its maximum 20 degrees during another 251 launches. The aircraft's wheels were leaving the upper edge of the steel structure at speeds as low as 42kt, less than a third of the normal STO lift-off speed on a runway. At the higher angles the undercarriage sustained greater punishment, although take-off runs could be effectively halved compared with the 6-degree angle, or warloads increased up to 3,000lb. Bedford's ramp was tried by a wide variety of pilots and the reaction was always positive. On a fixed-price contract HMS *Invincible* was modified to take a ramp giving a 7-degree angle over a 90ft deck-run (an effective rise of 6.5ft). This shallow angle was dictated by the position of the ship's main defence, a twin-arm Sea Dart missile launcher, on the foredeck. A higher ramp angle would have impeded the 'view' of this launcher, which could not be relocated. The flight deck of *Invincible* was angled slightly to the left for the same reason.

HMS *Illustrious* (R-06), second of the class, had the same fit, while the new *Ark Royal* (R-07), which was not commissioned until 1985, was redesigned for the optimum 12-degree ramp. This was also nearly 40ft longer and enabled Sea Harriers to launch with their full fuel and weapons load. HMS *Invincible* had the 12-degree ramp retrofitted during her first major refit in 1986, and a main armament redesign, and HMS *Illustrious* was similarly refitted in the early 1990s. HMS *Hermes* was the first ship to be given the 12-degree version. Without missile launchers at her bow, and limited only by the need for an adequate view from the bridge, the carrier had a full 150ft run installed during her 1979 refit, giving an effective 15ft vertical 'lift'. Prior to this the ski-jump was demonstrated to a much wider audience in September 1978. Fairey Engineering built a 15-degree ramp at Farnborough in

time for the SBAC show and John Farley astonished the crowds with his daily ramp-runs in Sea Harrier XZ450 only two weeks after its first flight.

ROLE REFINEMENT

Sea Harrier testing progressed smoothly despite some delays with the installation of test equipment. The first eight aircraft were constructed at Kingston; XZ455 was the first to be built at Brough, and subsequent aircraft were assembled there and finished at Kingston until the closure of the latter facility. As the Navy began to work towards defining the new aircraft's role there was a good deal of resistance within the service from those who saw it as a poor substitute for their previous Phantoms and Buccaneers. In a relatively brief time entirely new operational techniques had to be devised for a completely new type of aircraft whose effect on naval aviation was to be far more profound than Sea Harrier's heavyweight forebears.

In this striking Neil Mercer photograph of two 801 NAS Sea Harriers, Lieutenant-Commander Don Sigorney keeps a wary eye on the Hercules photo-ship. (Via Simon Hargreaves)

An early indication of the Navy's intentions came from Vice-Admiral Sir Desmond Cassidi shortly after the launch of HMS *Illustrious* in May 1977. He described the Sea Harrier as 'a quick reaction weapons system which, in its fighter role, will be aimed against the enemy long-range reconnaissance and missile direction aircraft, the harbingers of attack'. In practice the RN required that response time to be about two minutes from alarm bell to lift-off, with interception over a 400nm

radius, including air combat for three minutes. In support of the Air Wing's dominant Sea King complement, the Sea Harriers could be tasked with high-speed dropping of a sonobuoy screen against submarines, or torpedo attacks on incursive vessels. This was actually a very much underplayed vision of the aircraft's true capability as it was to be seen within five years.

Much of the responsibility for role refinement and development fell to the Sea

Harrier IFTU (Intensive Flight Trials Unit) at RNAS Yeovilton. It began operations on 26 June 1979 with a single aircraft (XZ451, delivered on 18 June) and backed up by a borrowed RAF T.2A (XW927). A second FRS.1 (XZ452) was made available in October, enabling sea trials to take place on HMS *Hermes* using five Sea Harriers and G-VTOL. A slow delivery rate caused by industrial action meant that three aircraft had to be borrowed from the A&AEE and Dunsfold for the nine-day 'carquals', during which 40 sorties were flown. The verdict was one of unqualified success. By the end of the year IFTU had six aircraft and changed itself into 700A NAS (following its commissioning on 19 September 1979), and eventually to 899 NAS at the end of March 1980. Introducing the first full squadron to the public was the job of Flight Lieutenant Ian 'Morts' Mortimer, chosen to fly the 1980 air display circuit, despite being an RAF officer!

899 NAS had a lengthy operational history. Formed in 1942, it saw action in the Mediterranean, flew Sea Hawks during the Suez Campaign and operated the weighty Sea Vixen at the time of the Rhodesian Crisis of 1965. Having closed down and disbanded in January 1972, the 'Bunch with the Punch' (after their winged-fist tail logo) became the Sea Harrier training unit. At their helm was Lieutenant-Commander Nigel Ward, who had flown Sea Vixens and completed two tours with 892 NAS on FG.1 Phantoms before being posted to the MoD as 'Sea Harrier Desk Officer' in 1976. After three years' involvement in its pre-service development, 'Sharkey' Ward oversaw the aircraft's naval introduction as boss of IFTU/700A Squadron and then 899 (Headquarters) Squadron. Unlike some former FG.1 flyers, Ward felt that his experience on the afterburning monster enabled him better to appreciate the advantages of the Sea Harrier. For example, the training syllabus of 767 NAS (Phantom) had required pilots to make at least fifty simulated shore-based 'deck landings' in order to acquire the skill of hitting glidepath approach speeds within a couple of knots of the optimum for placing

800 NAS aircraft head for the range, armed with practice bomb dispensers and 30mm guns. Keeping station is one of three Hunter T.8M conversions used to provide aircrew with Blue Fox radar training. (Via Simon Hargreaves)

the F-4 on *Ark Royal*'s limited deck. Deck handling the big jets took huge quantities of equipment and people, an exact into-the-wind carrier heading and a precisely orchestrated cycle of catapult launch and wire recovery which admitted no minor mishaps. The Sea Harrier suffered none of these constraints. It could be launched with a tail wind. Rather than relying on deck-tractors and starting 'huffers', it could 'spot' itself accurately on deck using its nozzles to taxy back into position and use its APU to start-up its Pegasus. Although the Phantom's twin engines produced twice the thrust of a Pegasus, its fuel requirements were far greater—1,450lb from engine start through acceleration to climbing speed, against 400lb for the Harrier. Moreover, there was no need for a large minimum fuel reserve for landing (2,500lb in the F-4) as the Sea Harrier

would not experience arresting wire 'bolters' and 'go-around' repeat circuits. Approaches in darkness or fog, a nightmare for conventional carrier landings, could now be made in safety at virtually zero forward speed, giving the pilot complete control over his choice of landing spot. USMC experience had shown that it was possible to recover up to four Harriers virtually simultaneously on an *Invincible*-size 'boat'. Another important legacy of Ward's days as Senior Pilot with 892 NAS was his understanding of air-to-air fighting in the kerosene-thirsty FG.1. American practice had been to use afterburner to gain the advantage in ACM in the knowledge that tankers would be around to replenish the fighter's rapidly depleted fuel. Lacking tanker support, Ward's training philosophy was to emphasize the possibilities of non-afterburner

fighting, using manoeuvring tactics to defeat the enemy or cause him to run low on fuel. His 'low and slow' experience was very useful in training the first generation of Sea Harrier crew (including several other ex-892 men). Ward was determined to show that the Sea Harrier was a credible air-fighting machine, not just a watchdog to see off nosey reconnaissance types.

As a fighter, the Sea Harrier had the advantage of small size and smokeless exhaust, making it hard to see. The location of the engine exhausts meant that pilots could shield their IR signature from heat-seeking missiles by deflecting the nozzles away or by turning so that the high wing covered the nozzles from the missiles' view. Excellent low-speed handling was combined with virtually spin-proof departure characteristics. With nozzles fully aft the aircraft quickly recovered from an unstable flight condition. Its low fuel consumption (100lb for a VTO, 200lb/min 'low and fast') gave it a huge potential advantage over afterburning jets like the F-4 which drank gas at up to 1,800lb/min. The Marine Corps had already shown how the Harrier could kill off the majority of other US fighters despite having an inferior top speed and turn rate to some of them. Several early Sea Harrier recruits gained AV-8A experience via exchange postings.

700A, and later 899, NAS wasted no time in arranging some DCM with the specialists in that art, the F-5E pilots of the 527th TFTAS, USAFE, who were then stationed at RAF Alconbury. Three 700A pilots, who all made good use of the experience in the South Atlantic conflict soon afterwards, scored an aggregate 27:10 against the nimble, supersonic F-5E, fighting usually to the Aggressor's rules. Determined to even the score, a posse of Bitburg's 36th TFW F-15 Eagles, 'USAFE's best', visited IFTU/700A and lost by a ratio of 7:1. To the RAF's embarrassment its Phantoms suffered 'losses' of 25:1 to the new Navy jets! Those figures were even more remarkable because the Sea Harriers at the time were carrying ballast in place of their delayed Blue Fox radars and they had not received their new Smiths HUDs either. The first of these arrived for testing towards the end of 1979, but production radar sets only began to appear in November 1980, when 899 NAS had already begun training in earnest. A continued shortage of fully equipped aircraft persisted for another six months, although NAVHARS and the ECM gear were up and running much sooner.

SHIPBOARD TECHNIQUES

The Sea Harrier's work-up period was a time to rehearse safe, practical carrier operational techniques, following on from work done by HSA/BAe test pilots and the A&AEE from 1972. The earliest tests showed that VTO from the deck gave the fastest reaction times, partly because the ship could avoid having to turn into the wind. STO/VL was soon established as the standard technique for optimum mission load. CAP requirements for the FRS.1 were 45 minutes on station at 100 miles' radius with two Sidewinders, gun pods and a pair of 100gal tanks—far more than the design VTO load. Other missions, such as anti-shipping with guns and two Sea Eagles over a 280nm radius, or recce with two 100gal tanks and a 900nm hi-lo-hi range clearly required an STO start. It was established that stream take-offs could be used to get several aircraft aloft quickly with a 100ft gap between them on the take-off 'tramlines'. Crosswind limits up to 20kt were possible. There were no problems with deck erosion nor risk to deck personnel from downward jet blast outside the immediate launch path.

Engine checks were done with nozzles aft, up to a maximum 55 per cent power which the brakes would hold. Nozzles would then be set at the predetermined angle for lift off at the bow and visually checked by an FDO. When the 'traffic lights' attached to the Flyco's position on the left of the bridge turned green, the FDO waved his green flag in a circular motion. With nozzles swung back to 8 degrees and tailplane angle checked, the pilot then began his run, slamming the nozzles to the previously calculated lift-off 'stop' position again as the aircraft, at full power, reached the upper limit of the ski-jump. The launch trajectory impetus gave an initial climb rate of 1,000ft/min, falling off steadily until the Pegasus began to provide the sole motive force at around 130kt. Leaving the ski-jump was compared by one pilot to taking a car over a hump-backed bridge 'fast enough to worry your passenger'. At take-off the aircraft generates around 16,000lb of 'jet' lift and 5,000lb of 'wing' lift. At about 130kt the nozzles would go fully aft and the Sea Harrier would then be straight and level at 165kt in a few seconds. In order to prevent over-controlling the aircraft on launch it is ideally flown 'hands off'. Pilots were at first offered a cable device to set the control column at the required position, though this was seldom used.[2]

Another equally simple device of far more lasting use to Sea Harrier pilots on launch are the painted 'tramlines' on the carriers' decks. This innovation arose out of John Farley's sales promotion for the Indian Navy in July 1972. Flying G-VTOL from the Indian carrier *Vikrant* (ex-HMS *Hercules*), he had been used to a single deck centre-line marking and asked the crew to paint one for him. A two-foot wide white line, slightly offset to port, duly appeared, but in rather slippery gloss paint. To prevent a loss of directional stability through the nosewheel slipping on the line Farley decided to run slightly to the left of the line, but he then risked hitting the ship's catapult shuttle with his outrigger. He therefore decided for a take-off between the 'Harrier' line and a second line seven feet to its left. In practice this arrangement worked much better than a single line. In all but the calmest seas the lateral velocity of the deck, particularly at the bow, makes it very difficult to keep a moving aircraft to a straight line. As John Farley described it to the authors, 'It's as if the runway was being moved from side to side as the aircraft takes off.' Having two lines was much less disconcerting for the pilot and still pointed the aircraft the right way, so he asked if HMS *Invincible*, then under construction, could have the 'tramlines' incorporated. It turned out that the yard had already laid a single line marked by rearward-facing lights for night ops. Despite the expense and delay they were persuaded to remove this and replace it with two, bordering a 48ft black 'path', but also using two lines of lights which faced forward and aft so that aircraft could approach over the bow if need be. This quite basic improvement has made life much easier for hundreds of Sea Harrier aircrew and it is something in which John Farley takes great pride.

Carrier landings with the Sea Harrier were even more straightforward. In place of the tough challenges of the arresting hook and 'third wire', a pilot had only to achieve a hover point about 100ft above

---

[2] Refer to Appendices.

The camera of Neil Mercer captures the Sea Harrier's sinister grace in this close-up. (Via Simon Hargreaves)

nation had proved itself capable of bringing aircraft aboard in virtually zero visibility, with fog and darkness on several occasions.

The Sea Harrier's Phase I update programme in 1987–88 included the installation of an even more effective 'blind' landing system—MEL's MADGE. The great advantage of this system is that it does not give away the ship's position to reconnaissance aircraft or satellites because neither the ship's Type 1006 radar nor the aircraft's transponder is employed, making the whole recovery process both extremely accurate and 'invisible'. MADGE has proved to be a good piece of kit and it is much used by the Sea Harrier community. Phase I also included the nozzle-inching speed-trim button (described earlier), Sea Eagle missile capability, improved power supply and a TV recording system slaved to the HUD to store imagery from training sorties or for combat analysis. Clearance for the twin-Sidewinder launchers and 228gal drop tanks had already been given during the Falklands period. However, full clearance for water injection on STO or VTO from carriers was allowed in Phase I also. As Falklands veteran Rod Frederiksen pointed out to the authors, the first generation of Sea Harrier pilots tended to work on a certain amount of RAF folklore which included the belief that water injection was not entirely reliable at first. 'Also, there was no clearance and no data to begin with. The Navy always tended to use it in the hover for vertical landing but after clearance was given it was used for STO too, with about 20 gallons for take-off and the other 30 for vertical landing.' The demineralised water supply on all Harriers is filled, often by hand-pump, via a receptacle on the fuselage spine level with the trailing edge. It became a very reliable system, giving 1,000lb of thrust in half a second. Consideration was given to a pump modification which would have allowed half the flow rate for double the standard 90sec 'water time'. This could

deck height and 30ft to the left of the deck edge. This followed a conventional approach, with nozzles lowered at the end of the downwind leg to begin deceleration on the crosswind section. Having reached his hover point, the pilot had an excellent view of the deck for his vertical landing. Night and bad-weather approaches could be accomplished using a Pilot Interpreted Approach (PIA) or Carrier Controlled Approach (CCA). For the former, pilots could use a 3-degree glidescope from 1,000ft and three miles astern, reducing to 200ft. Range and altitude data are presented on the pilot's

HUD, using the ship's returns from the Sea Harrier's radar. In a CCA the pilot corrects his glidepath through a conventional radio talk-down using the ship's radar. At a little under a mile a shallower glidepath is held using HAPI (Harrier Approach Path Indicator). Invented by scientists at RAE Bedford and the Admiralty, this variation on the traditional carrier landing optical devices used a pattern of red and white lights on the left edge of the rear deck and a second pattern on the rear of the island. A further arrangement of lights on the island gave the pilot a height reference for his final let-down. This combibe useful in a prolonged hover-before-landing in poor visibility or in high ambient temperatures. Only the export Sea Harrier batch for the Indian Navy actually had this modification, to cope with their hotter climate. Basically, water injection cools the Pegasus's exhaust gases, enabling higher engine rpm while reducing temperature-induced fatigue.

TRAINING
Basing the Sea Harrier training syllabus, inevitably, on the ten years of experience at RAF Wittering carried the bonus of an excellent safety record. Cynics who had observed the USMC AV-8A accident record expected problems with Sea Harrier. In fact, the acquired wisdom of RAF and USMC Harrier personnel helped 700A, 899 and then 801 NASs under 'Sharkey' Ward's leadership to avoid any serious mishaps. Ward attributed this partly to the loan of one of Wittering's best QFIs, Bertie Penfold, who enforced rigorous safety standards.[3]

A vital component in the training scheme was the trio of Hunter T.8M radar trainers, allowed for in the funding of the original 1975 Sea Harrier order, rather than a purpose-built two-seat radar-equipped Sea Harrier. BAe Brough initially converted two of FRADU's nine surviving T.8s to T.8M standard in 1979–80. They were given the full Blue Fox installation in new radomes, the new HUD and most of the related avionics. XL580, which had been the first RN T.8 in 1958, was used for Dunsfold tests and XL602 went to Holme-on-Spalding Moor and then the Royal Signals and Radar Establishment at Bedford. Later XL603 was added and all three moved to Yeovilton to provide radar and weapons training. Products of virtually the same design team, the Hunter and Harrier had very similar handling characteristics in conventional flight. Harrier's VTOL aspects could be learned on Wittering's two-seaters and then on the single T.4 allowed for in the Navy's original budget allocation (XW927, detached to 899 NAS from July 1979 to October 1983).[4] One Hunter T.8M passed to Dunsfold in 1990 for MoD(PE) use. The other two aircraft were withdrawn in Oc-

Sea Harrier FRS.1 ZD614 in 801 NAS's 1992 markings, under tow at Yeovilton. (Authors)

tober 1993, stored at Shawbury and auctioned at Sotheby's with other RN Hunters in November 1994. 'Lot 189', XL580, was sold to the FAA Museum, appropriately because it had been the Flag Officer (Flying Training) 'flagship' in 1962 at Yeovilton.

Training Sea Harrier pilots was a complex procedure in 1981, involving over 460 hours in up to six different aircraft types in 2½ years. 'Old hand' Phantom or Buccaneer pilots passed with a couple of weeks' refresher training on a Yeovilton Standards Flight Hunter before 'going vertical' at Wittering. New boys went through the standard RAF courses—21 weeks on Leeming's Bulldogs, 44 weeks at Cranwell on 'JPs' and then 85 hours' fast-jet time on Hawks at Valley, with a 50hr tactical Hawk follow-up at Brawdy. Wittering then gave them thirteen weeks' Harrier conversion (CONVEX), handing over to 899 NAS for their 90hr Sea Harrier syllabus. Wittering's share of the *ab initio* training continued until 1 January 1989, when No 233 OCU passed the job to 899 NAS, who by then had received several RAF T.4As (including XZ147, XZ445 and XZ455). These were kept in RAF colours and markings to simplify spares commonality, including access panels. 233 OCU unit markings were retained too. By 1989 the 899 NAS course had been refined to include 28 hours in the T.4A, an eight-hour radar course aboard Hunter T.8Ms, eleven hours on navalised Harrier T.4Ns (three of which, serialled ZB604–606, were ordered in the spring

of 1979 and delivered between September 1983 and January 1984, equipped with Pegasus Mk 104s and without the RAF's LRMTS nasal trademark) and, finally, 72 hours in Sea Harrier FRS.1s. NAVHARS training for the first batch of pilots was done at BAe Hatfield on a very basic simulator, and Wittering's GR.3 'sim' was also extensively employed. Yeovilton's own Sea Harrier simulator was 'born by Caesarean section out of necessity by crisis' in 1982 after four years of development by Link-Miles. Its first simulated scenarios were visual representations of the Mirage, Pucará and A-4 Skyhawk, showing their pick-up ranges on radar in various sea states. After the Falklands engagements to which this training related, it became normal for students to have at least 40 'sim sorties', and in 1983 the six-axis machine was regularly running 10–11 hours daily with practice in everything from flight emergencies to teaching how to grapple with the enemy in multiple air-to-air engagements.

Having established a service regime for the Sea Harrier, Yeovilton was ready to commission the first operational Squad-

---

[3] The first Sea Harrier loss was an 800 NAS aircraft which struck *Invincible*'s ski-jump with its outrigger while making a slow flypast for BBC TV cameras and went into the sea.
[4] XZ445 was the T.4 actually allowed for in the RN funding, but it remained at Wittering until late 1987.

ron, 800 NAS. The oldest FAA unit, 800 had been formed in 1933 from 402 and 404 Fleet Fighter Units. After distinguished Second World War service it flew the Supermarine Attacker, the first RN jet, in 1951, and the Buccaneer S.2 from HMS *Eagle* until 1972. The Squadron recommissioned on 23 April 1981 at Yeovilton under Lieutenant-Commander Tim Gedge (ex-892 NAS, who later took over nominal command of 809 NAS during the Falklands campaign, although he actually flew as a member of 801 NAS during that conflict). 800 NAS deployed several aircraft on HMS *Invincible* for work-up trials in 1980 (Lieutenant-Commander Robin Kent had the honour of making the first landing). Visits were made to Norway and Gibraltar, although the Squadron was restricted to VTOL deck operations for this cruise. After the next stage of CA release in November 1980 a combined force of eight aircraft from 899 NAS, the A&AEE and BAe Dunsfold undertook the world's first Harrier ski-jump sea-trials, on board HMS *Invincible*. The 899 NAS quartet amassed over 60 sorties in a five-day period. 800 NAS then changed its 'N' tail letter, used on *Invincible*, for 'H-for-*Hermes*', embarking on the

older ship in 1981 with the statutory five aircraft as they became available through the Sea Harrier Support Unit (SHSU). Their place on *Invincible* was occupied by 801 NAS, commissioned on 28 January 1981 with 'Sharkey' Ward as boss. He read the commissioning warrant to the assembled unit in front of XZ496, one of the two aircraft which his squadron owned at the time. One the same day Yeovilton's own ski-jump was opened by Lady Eberle, wife of the C-in-C Fleet, and inaugurated by 801's other Sea Harrier, XZ493/001N. The structure was built by BAe inside twelve months for £500,000. Part of the cost was involved in its 96 by 18 m concrete ramp which had to be adjustable hydraulically between 7 and 15 degrees to allow for the two types of carrier ramp then in use!

Established in 1933, a few months after 800 NAS, 801 had a proud record of service in the Second World War and Korea. In October 1965 it has been the Navy's first Buccaneer S.2 squadron. The unit's intensive work-up at sea from May 1981 included North Atlantic training with USN units. Participation in NATO Exercise 'Alloy Express' off Norway took place on a full deployment from June to

late September with a naval force including USS *Nimitz*. There was some extremely valuable flying at night and in appalling weather over bone-chilling seas. At the time, Sea Harrier crews thought that their operational role might be quite brief. Despite the aircraft's proven success, many at Whitehall still saw it as an expendable luxury. Persistent defence cuts had scheduled the recently acquired HMS *Invincible* for sale to Australia in 1982, along with a batch of Sea Harriers, and the myth of RAF air defence for the Fleet at sea was reasserting itself. While 801 NAS fought the elements over the North Sea, operating in conditions which often kept all other aircraft chained to the deck, including the complement aboard *Nimitz*, neither they nor the budget-conscious politicians could have realized for one moment how vital that training would be in a few short months.

New lamps for old. Sea Harrier F/A.2 ZD615, the third conversion, poses alongside ZA175, which became the twenty-third Sea Harrier to be updated to F/A.2 standard. Differences in nose profiles and camouflage shades are clearly visible. (BAe via Simon Hargreaves)

5. Harrier Warriors

At a distance of almost fourteen years the 75-day Falklands conflict of 1982 still provides the most conspicuous example of the success of the Harrier concept. Amidst the continuing controversy about aspects of that war, the achievement of the Task Force Sea Harriers and No 1(F) Squadron Harrier GR.3s remains undiminished by time and historians' reinterpretation of events. In the post-war period the only real 'down side' to that victory was probably the disappointment that BAe did not land a few hundred Sea Harrier orders after such well-publicised success. Certainly there was interest in the product in the wake of war, particularly from Italy and China, but at the time of writing the Indian Navy is still the sole export customer. When Roy Mason ordered the first batch of RN Sea Harriers he told Parliament that 'a great amount of interest in Sea Harrier has been shown by overseas navies'. In retrospect that might seem to have been a way of helping to justify the order during a period of austerity, but the fact that the interest shown by several countries failed to be converted into orders was usually due to political factors rather than a reflection on the unique capability of the aircraft. Sales pressure from McDonnell-Douglas was also a factor. They would have preferred the all-British Sea Harrier to have been strangled at birth, and the Harrier derivatives which did eventually appear on the decks of Spanish and Italian carriers were to be AV-8s rather than Sea Harriers.

For the Royal Navy, 'Corporate' proved beyond question the wisdom of having Harriers on decks to those in Britain (and the United States) who were still doubters. The myth of all-RAF air defence for the Fleet was dealt a severe, if not mortal, blow. 'Corporate' ensured the retention of the British carrier force, including HMS *Invincible*, and the development of a more capable Sea Harrier variant, thereby guaranteeing the aircraft's place in the RN's hardware budget for many more years. That was by no means a certainty in 1981. In the USA, confidence in the Harrier also increased and political opposition to the AV-8B was reduced by the spectacular success of the VTOL jet's first combat test.

In broad terms, the Sea Harrier's contribution to the retaking of the Falkland Islands from Argentina can be viewed in a number of ways. Statistically, 28 out of the 30 Sea Harriers built by April 1982 (including XZ454, written off on 15 February 1980) were eventually deployed to the South Atlantic. Two were lost to enemy action, none to hostile air action. Oddly, the Sea Harriers' 'score' against the Argentine Navy and Air Force is still uncertain. 'Final totals' have varied between 20 and 27 losses; the most plausible figure is 23 destroyed. Other bald statistics reveal that the aircraft's operational record for April–June 1982 included 2,197 sorties (2,000 operational) in 2,514 flying hours. In practical terms those figures translate into an unprecedentedly high availability rate approaching 96 per cent, and up to three sorties per day, sometimes in appalling weather conditions, for each of the aircraft on the two carriers. The Sea Harrier did better than anyone, except for those closely associated with it, imagined it could.

The slogan 'Mission Impossible Without V/STOL' appeared in post-war BAe commercials and it contained far more truth than the average advertisement. Apart from a small number of complex and hugely expensive raids by the small RAF Vulcan force, there was no other way in which British air power could have been employed effectively. In the words of Admiral Sir Henry Leach, First Sea Lord at the time, 'Without Sea Harrier there could have been no Task Force.' A rather less serious maxim was current in the Sea Harrier community in 1983: 'Never was so much achieved by so few and such old fighter pilots.' The handful of RN and RAF pilots who fought from the carriers included some of the senior instructors and pilots from Yeovilton, Wittering and Gütersloh. Their experience, and tough, realistic training, was as vital a weapon as the Harrier itself.

In 1995 only one of that group is still flying with an operational Sea Harrier squadron, Lieutenant-Commander Simon Hargreaves, boss of 899 (HQ) Naval Air Squadron at the time of writing. One of the younger members of 800 NAS in 1982, he recalled his time on HMS *Hermes* phlegmatically: 'Perhaps time dulls the memory, but it all seems pretty routine now. It was much easier flying than being a sailor on one of those ships!' As for the hostile climate, 'the weather was either gin-clear perfect or so obviously dreadful that you couldn't fly. Unpredictable fog was the biggest limitation.'

When Task Force 317 departed from Portsmouth on 5 April 1982, public confidence in its ability to do the job was obvious, but there were doubts too. Cynics questioned the wisdom of sending a handful of untried 'Jump Jets', barely out of their operational work-up, to oppose supersonic Mirages and Exocet-firing Super Etendards. The national press carried diagrams of Harriers 'VIFF-ing' frantically to avoid these threats. (In reality, the technique was never employed in combat there because it was always the Sea Harriers who were in pursuit.) It was known that the shoals of old but capable Argentinian Skyhawks had access to flight-refuelling, theoretically increasing the number of directions from which they could fly attack profiles against the Fleet, although it later became clear that this was provided by just two overworked KC-130H tankers. Once again, the familiar jibes about the Harrier's 'short range' were trotted out too, based only on misunderstood 'VTOL with maximum warload' figures. Even the 1969-model Harrier GR.1 could fly 1,800 miles in ferry configuration, 200 miles further than a Trident airliner of that period. At the other end of the story, it has recently been shown that the Harrier GR.7 has a longer unrefuelled range than a Tornado GR.1. The Sea Harrier, with a ski-jump STO, could operate from carriers at a sufficient distance from the Falklands for Admiral Woodward to feel relatively safe from Argentinian attack, and still offer a useful combat air patrol (CAP)-plus-attack role. If there was a 'short-range' criticism of Sea Harrier it applied to its

weapons rather than to the aircraft. Lacking a BVR missile, it always had to engage targets well within the eleven-mile maximum range of its AIM-9 Sidewinder, or gun-fight at a few hundred feet.

Conservative estimates placed the Sea Harriers at a severe numerical disadvantage against Argentina's combat aircraft, which were thought to be anywhere between 120 and 230 in number. Losses of only one Sea Harrier daily would have reduced the original force of twenty to a token element within two weeks. Post-war calculations by the Argentinians showed that their actual total of serviceable Skyhawk, Canberra, Pucará and Mirage/Dagger aircraft was 82 in *Fuerza Aérea Argentina* (FAA) service plus five Super Etendards and eight Skyhawks with the Navy's *Comando Aviacion Naval Argentina* (CANA).

To other doubters the problem was simply the lack of 'proper' aircraft carriers. Instead of a traditional Air Wing with BVR missile-firing fighters operating under the own AEW umbrella and supporting long-range heavy strike aircraft, it ap-

peared to some observers that a couple of 'helicopter ships', hastily overstocked with the RN's entire supply of fixed-wing combat aircraft, were being sent. Even worse, one of those vessels had to complete the first leg of its 'dash' to the South Atlantic at 15kt because of a damaged gearbox!

Fortunately the Sea Harrier community were well aware of the true capability of their aircraft and they approached the unexpected challenge with a rapid but intensively organised effort. The first problem was to muster enough pilots and aircraft. When the FONAC/MoD order to 'mobilise for sea immediately' was telephoned to Squadron commanders at 0400 on Friday 2 April, 800 NAS had re-

XZ496/27 is positioned on HMS *Hermes'* deck after a CAP sortie over the Falklands. Lieutenant-Commander Mike Blissett shot down an A-4C Skyhawk with a Sidewinder from this Sea Harrier and damaged a second with its guns. It returned to the area with 809 NAS in August 1982, sprayed in Medium Sea Grey and named *Mrs Robinson*. (Via R. L. Ward)

XZ498/005 of 801 NAS approaches HMS _Invincible_. In the nearer aircraft, Lieutenant Steve Thomas waits on cockpit alert for a CAP launch. Steve Thomas DSC, who was often 'Sharkey' Ward's wingman, shot down two Argentinian Daggers and a Mirage, becoming the only pilot in the conflict to destroy three fast jets. (Via R. L. Ward)

4 April Taylor Scott took XZ450, with the Sea Eagle panel still in place, and landed on _Hermes_ while she was still in dock. Of the other three development batch (DB) aircraft, MoD(PE) only managed to hang on to XZ440 for development work on a whole range of Falklands war 'mods'. XZ438, XZ439 and XZ497 spent much of the war period with 899 NAS to provide a small nucleus of training aircraft, although XZ438 was shared with the A&AEE and crashed while testing 330gal ferry tank configurations on Yeovilton's ski-jump. Sea Harriers were in very short supply!

Invincible took aboard four aircraft above her peacetime complement and as much support equipment as she could carry. Among the smaller items of 'stores' was a silver toast rack, a souvenir from the battle-cruiser HMS _Invincible_ which had taken part in the 1914 Battle of the Falklands. There were still deficiencies, however, mainly in completing the full range of weaponry trials. On the voyage south, several members of 801 NAS did their first live firings of 2in rocket projectiles (400 were fired in two days), live AIM-9G and night-dropped Lepus flares. New software for loft-bombing profiles using live 1,000lb (450kg) bombs was tested as well. Ground attack work had not been a priority in training the newer pilots, so a crash course in 'sea attack' and anti-shipping occupied some of the time en route to Ascension Island. Several of 800 NAS's pilots had to do their deck qualification flights too.

cently disembarked from HMS _Hermes_ and was about to go on Easter leave that day. 801 NAS had already dispersed. _Hermes_ was under heavy scaffolding for post-cruise maintenance at Portsmouth and HMS _Invincible_ was berthed there too without an Air Group. By 1600 the same day Lieutenant-Commander Auld was aboard _Hermes_ with five aircraft, plus three and their pilots borrowed from 899 NAS. Three more arrived during a weekend of frantic replenishment of the 'boat' and _Hermes_ was ready to sail on Monday 5 April. Their twelfth aircraft, flown by Bertie Penfold, caught up in the Bay of Biscay.

Having received his 0400 call, Lieutenant-Commander Ward issued call-out notices to all his pilots and drove 150 miles to Yeovilton. Within two days he had re-assembled his squadron and embarked four 801 NAS aircraft, plus four from 899

NAS, aboard HMS _Invincible_. 899 also supplied five pilots. _Invincible_, too, was ready to sail on 5 April. Among 800 NAS's extra Sea Harriers were two (ZA192 and ZA193) fresh from the stored attrition batch of seven held at RAF St Athan, and XZ450, the first Sea Harrier to fly. It was one of four in use with MoD(PE) and the sole development aircraft for the Sea Eagle anti-shipping missile. It had the only full-production model control unit for that weapon. John Farley had been test-flying the aircraft with a heavy load of Sea Eagles, guns and AIM-9s: 'Half way through the debriefing fellow test pilot Taylor Scott (the only RN Reserve Pilot with Sea Harrier qualification) burst in and said "There's a war on. I've got to get back to the Navy. I'm off!" That evening the call came that the Navy wanted as many Sea Harriers as possible got ready for them, and they were told that the aircraft would take a while to be properly prepared.' Undeterred, Yeovilton sent a helicopter full of aircrew to Dunsfold to collect 'their' aircraft. They were met by John Farley, who had been alerted 'after hours' by works police and told again that the Sea Harriers were not yet ready for embarkation and BAe personnel would fly them to catch up with the Task Force. On Sunday

Also missing from the two carriers' stores were the all-aspect AIM-9L Sidewinders and their associated HUD software, replacing the 'Golf' model used previously. AIM-9 'Limas' were on the RN inventory but they only became available when the Task Force reached Ascension Island. Although great emphasis has often been given to the AIM-9L variant's role in the war there were actually very few occasions on which its all-aspect capability was a deciding factor for the 26 examples which were launched in combat. Simon Hargreaves reckons that 'for virtually all the kills a Golf [AIM-9G] would have done the job just as well. Most of them were "dead six" [tail-chase] shots at

Left, upper: HMS *Hermes'* relatively confined deck space exacerbated the sense of organized chaos in which any carrier deck-crew has to work. (BAe)

Left, lower: Sea Harriers lined up on HMS *Hermes'* deck as she departs from Portsmouth on 5 April 1982. In the foreground is one of the two uncoded FRS.1s straight from storage at St Athan; to its left is ZA191 (ex 899 NAS), which was used in successful attacks on the Argentinian ships *Narwal* and *Bahía Buen Sucesco*, an A.109A helicopter and a Pucará. (Royal Navy)

899 Squadron course unfinished. He had been seconded from No 3 Squadron RAF with 800 hours on the Harrier GR.3 and made his first-ever deck landing (in XZ450) the day after he joined 800 NAS. There would be several other 'crabs' who saw an aircraft carrier for the first time while landing on its deck. Morgan went on to fly 50 sorties, shot down two A-4s and a Pucará, bombed an Islander aircraft and shared two other helicopter kills. He also bombed the intelligence-gathering trawler *Narwal* which shadowed the Task Force on its approach to the Falklands. Top 'scorer' in the conflict, he was one of five Sea Harrier pilots to be awarded the DSC. 800 Squadron's AWI was Lieutenant-Commander Tony Ogilvy, Ward's scheduled successor as CO. 899 NAS's CO, Lieutenant-Commander N. W. Thomas, became their Chief Tactical Instructor while his squadron, back at Yeovilton continued to support the front-line units despite being stripped of most of its aircraft, pilots and maintainers. Also aboard was Flight Lieutenant Bertie Penfold, who had been a vital figure in 899's training programme.

Cosmetic changes to the aircraft also appeared during the voyage. 801's aircraft were tastefully spray-painted by an Air Engineer Team in *Invincible's* air-conditioned hangar. Their white undersides and squadron insignia were obliterated with Extra Dark Sea Grey. Lacking the luxury of air-conditioning, *Hermes'* maintainers applied a similar scheme with three-inch paintbrushes. Red/blue roundels and low-visibility codes were applied. This scheme contributed to the rueful nickname '*La*

about a mile; nothing clever about them. But the most impressive thing was the reliability of the AIM-9L compared with the Pk [probability of a kill] of the older kit. Virtually everything that was shot was a kill.' The psychological impact of the AIM-9L was also important. Argentinian pilots had the accurate impression that there was no escape from the missile once it left the rail, particularly head on, and they avoided confronting Sea Harriers. The possibility that VIFF might be used was also a deterrent.

As *en route* training progressed the two fighter squadrons were able to employ another major asset, the experience of the 'older, bolder' pilots. 801 NAS included

three Air Warfare Instructors (AWIs) instead of the usual one or two, Lieutenant-Commander John Eyton-Jones, Flight Lieutenant Ian 'Morts' Mortimer (one of first 700A Squadron pilots), and the CO 'Sharkey' Ward. Lieutenant Alan Curtis, who had flown RNZAF Skyhawks and RAAF Mirage IIIs on exchange, was a useful source of data on the opposition to add to the gleanings from *Jane's All The World's Aircraft* and memories of ACM with French Mirages. Only one 801 pilot, Lieutenant Mike 'Soapy' Watson, was a 'new boy' from 899 NAS.

800 NAS also had a fresh trainee, Flight Lieutenant Dave 'Moggie' Morgan, who was rushed off to war with a third of his

Left, upper: During the Falklands conflict, post-CAP recovery proved possible in sea states and weather which would have stopped conventional deck operations. Here *Hermes* accepts an 800 NAS jet with its missiles still in place. Vertical landing with a 'hung bomb' under one wing was not possible: an aircraft in that configuration had to make landfall or be abandoned. (BAe via R. L. Ward)

Left, lower: Sea Harrier XZ440 replaced XZ450 as the A&AEE's Sea Eagle test aircraft when '450 fell to Argentinian AAA. At the time of writing it was one of the last FRS.1s to remain in store awaiting conversion to F/A.2 standard. (BAe)

Muerta Negra' (The Black Death) used later by Argentinian pilots. As camouflage at low level the all-over grey worked extremely well, though 800's paint jobs took the wear better than 801's because of the generous method of application—a source of humour to the *Invincible* squadron.

Training and VERTREP (vertical replenishment) sorties were completed by the time the carriers made their two-day stopover at Ascension Island. Departure from there was precipitated by a major alert when a large whale was initially mistaken for one of Argentina's two submarines. Two days later the Sea Harrier units were declared fully operational and two-

aircraft deck alerts were mounted, with a second pair on Alert Five (five minutes' warning). Several low overflights by Soviet Tu-20 'Bear-D's occurred despite warnings from London. On 21 April the first overflight by an Argentinian *Grupo 1* Boeing 707 took place. Simon Hargreaves was on the 1130Z deck alert with XZ460. He intercepted the intruder and after a mutual photo session warned it off with some vigorous wing-waggling. The *Fuerza Aérea Argentina*'s three 707s (which had been regular visitors to Stansted Airport to collect military stores up to the end of March 1982), had no reconnaissance gear but they located the Task Force repeatedly by calculated guesswork and seriously com-

promised its security. As Britain and Argentina had not commenced hostilities the so-called 'Burglar' was not attacked and its flights continued with Sea Harrier interceptions up to 120 miles from the Fleet. On its next appearance the Burglar was seriously boxed in by Lieutenant-Commanders Broadwater and Eyton-Jones, with Flight Lieutenant Barton—a show of strength which Task Force commander Admiral Woodward considered 'well over the top'. After an overflight of South Georgia on 24 April Argentina was warned via Swiss diplomatic channels that any further 707 flights would be terminated by Sea Harriers. The Burglar tactfully withdrew, only to reappear on three occasions later in May and June.

In this opening phase of the action Sea Harrier demonstrated its original 'brochure' profile as an interceptor of unwanted snoopers. On 23 April it went further and prevented a 'KAL 007' incident which could have undermined the entire operation. A large aircraft was tracked on radar heading straight for the Task Force. As it approached the ships' Sea Dart missile envelope, Admiral Woodward decided to order 'Weapons Tight' and sent the deck alert Sea Harrier for a final check before activating the defences. The news came back that the 'intruder' was an innocent Brazilian airliner! In case anyone had any doubts as to the efficiency of the Sea Dart in those circumstances, it was demonstrated on 7 June when a *Grupo 1* photographic Learjet was hit by a missile from HMS *Exeter*. With its tail blown off, the jet tumbled 40,000ft to the sea with five crew still on board.

HOSTILITIES BEGIN

A mutual declaration of Total Exclusion Zones (TEZ) by the two sides on 30 April signalled the outset of combat as the carrier force took up position less than 100 miles north-east of Port Stanley, well inside the Argentinian 200-mile TEZ. Usually that distance was more like 150 miles, so that Sea Harriers were never less than twenty minutes' flying time from their CAP positions. Following the first 'Black Buck' Vulcan B.2 raid early on 1 May, the second phase of Sea Harrier operations began. At 1048Z Lieutenant-Commander Auld in XZ494 led nine 'Sea Jets' from *Hermes* to attack Port Stanley airfield, the principal target on the Falklands. This attack had been planned for some time: CBUs were air-tested on 28 April and a

simulated attack on Wideawake had been planned in great detail as a training exercise earlier in the month. Although Port Stanley's runway was based on solid rock it was hoped that it could be damaged sufficiently to deny its use to hostile aircraft. In Simon Hargreaves' estimation a direct hit from a 1,000lb bomb from 18,000ft would have put 'a whopping great crater in it'.

Auld led Black Section of four aircraft each carrying three BL.755 CBUs, while Penfold's XZ455 had 1,000lb DA (direct action) bombs. Red Section, led by Lieutenant-Commander Ogilvy (XZ500), broke away to attack from the north. Three miles from the airfield they pulled up and each lofted three 1,000lb VT (variable time fuse) airburst bombs at Argentine AAA positions. Bertie Penfold, whose aircraft had suffered a NAVHARS failure just before launch, hit the runway, causing surface damage. Auld's section went for parked aircraft and airfield facilities, approaching the target at altitudes below 50ft in some cases and pulling up to drop from 150ft. Dave Morgan, who destroyed the Governor's BN Islander with CBU, sustained the only damage despite vigorous AAA and Tigercat missile reaction from the ground. Having broken the lock of a Skyguard tracking radar by using his only countermeasure, a one-off chaff 'dump'

from the air brake well, Morgan's ZA192 took a hit in the fin from a Rheinmetall Rh 202 gun. Its electrical rudder trim was knocked out, making the rudder vibrate severely at more than 500kt. Morgan recovered safely and the fist-sized hole was quickly patched by MARTSU personnel.

Hermes' other three aircraft, led by Rod Frederiksen in ZA191, followed the Port Stanley attackers off her deck and flew around the north coast of East Falkland, down Grantham Sound and towards Goose Green airfield at around 30ft altitude. Two jets had CBU; XZ457 had DA bombs. A Pucará was destroyed with a 'Delta Hotel' from a CBU and two others heavily damaged. While 800 NAS put in their maximum effort involving every Sea Harrier aboard, 801 provided two four-ship CAPs to give the attackers continuous cover. Launching before the Sea Harrier bombers, the first CAP was vectored on to '*Toro*' Flight, a pair of *Grupo 6* Daggers. The two pairs of fighters circled before approaching each other head-on, passing with 5,000ft vertical separation. As they closed, the Daggers released their wing tanks at nine miles' range and their centreline tanks at closer quarters, streaming fuel vapour as they fell. Sea Harrier pilots Robin Kent and Brian Haigh considered briefly that these objects might be Matra R.530 missiles. In fact, *Hermes* apparently received urgent reports that the aircraft were actually Super Etendards. It was therefore assumed that the 'missiles' could be AM.39 Exocets and all ships in the Task Force promptly turned their sterns to the supposed threat and started pumping out chaff. Having passed through the CAP the two Argentinians, still carrying the Shafrir missiles which they never fired, looked at their fuel gauges and headed for home rather than allow the British jets to turn in behind them.

Having returned safely from their attacks, 800 NAS aircraft were turned around and re-armed for CAP. Bertie Penfold (still in XZ455) launched again with Martin Hale that afternoon to intercept another pair of Daggers. While Hale was busy avoiding one of the very few deliberate attempts to engage a Sea Harrier in combat—a Shafrir launched from

By May 1979 over 500 launches had been made from RAE Bedford's ski-jump: Mike Snelling is seen here doing the 500th in GR.3 XZ136, from a 20-degree ramp angle. The experience made No 1 Squadron's preparations for operating from HMS *Hermes* quite straightforward. Most pilots felt confident after a single 'jump'. (Via R. L. Ward)

the Dagger flown by José Ardiles—Penfold closed to within three miles astern of the Dagger, fired an AIM-9L and blew the aircraft apart. The spectacular destruction of the Argentinian aircraft and its pilot, a well-known personality in Argentina, so disturbed Bertie Penfold that he was taken off combat duties shortly afterwards and returned to the United Kingdom. There were several other near-engagements earlier in the day but in all cases the *Fuerza Aérea Argentina* aircraft drew away from combat when Sea Harriers attempted to engage them. A final effort was made at 2047Z by three low-flying *Grupo 2* Canberra B.62s which were detected by *Invincible*'s Fighter Director and intercepted by ex-Vulcan pilot Lieutenant Alan Curtis and Lieutenant-Commander Broadwater (ZA175). Canberra B-110 was hit by an AIM-9L from Curtis's XZ451 and an engine caught fire. The crew baled out but were never found and their aircraft crashed seconds before Curtis's second 'Winder contacted it. Broadwater scored a hit on a second aircraft, causing only slight damage.

The opening bout of hostilities gave the RN pilots a chance to reflect on the opposition. Argentina's 37 IAI Daggers (bought from the IDF/AF as Neshers—Atar 9C-engined Mirage 5 derivatives) were all with *Grupo 6 de Caza* based at Santa

Cruz and Rio Grande, Tierra del Fuego, both around 400nm from Port Stanley. They could not be flight-refuelled, they lacked ECM and they relied on two outdated Shafrir missiles for fighter duties or two 500lb bombs in the attack role. Always at the extreme limit of their range, they were restricted to 'there-and-back' flights to the Falklands with a very small combat or loiter margin. Although the use of afterburner gave a useful speed advantage over the Sea Harrier, it could only be used as an emergency 'escape' device because of the penalty in fuel usage, and even then it acted as a magnet for IR-seeking missiles.

Premier Teniente José Ardiles' Shafrir, fired from Dagger C-433 towards Martin Hale's aircraft, was probably the only occasion on which a Dagger seriously threatened a Sea Harrier. The Shafrir locked on to the aircraft, following it from 30,000ft down to 5,000ft as Hale dived to escape, releasing chaff. The Shafrir fell short. Hale had a similar experience on 21 May when one of his AIM-9Ls, fired at a Dagger just beyond the missile's envelope, also fell short. It was one of the very few occasions

on which an AIM-9L failed to connect, and no fault of the missile's!

A very small number of Mirage IIIEAs and IIIDEAs were at first held back in case of RAF Vulcan attacks on mainland targets. With their R.530 or recently-acquired R.550 Magic armament, these eleven *Grupo 8* fighters might have offered some opposition to the Sea Harriers. In fact, their role was very limited. On 1 May a pair attempted to engage a CAP flown by Nigel Ward and Mike Watson. A single R.530 was fired without result in an inconclusive encounter. Later that day another two Mirages were vectored towards an 801 NAS CAP flown by Steve Thomas and Paul Barton. As the first Mirage attempted to line up on Thomas it was shot down by a missile from Barton's XZ452 at a range of one mile. Its pilot, *Premier Teniente* Perona, baled out—the first victim of the Sea Harrier. Steve Thomas thought that he had come under missile attack from one of the Mirages earlier, but this was probably a fuel-streaming drop

Hermes' crowded deck, with Sea Kings, Sea Harriers and weaponry occupying every square inch except for the ski-jump. (Via R. L. Ward)

A pair of 801 NAS Sea Harriers returning to HMS *Invincible* from CAP. In the foreground is XZ495/003, while ZA175/004 awaits its turn. The latter aircraft was used by Lieutenant-Commander 'Sharkey' Ward to shoot down Dagger C-407 on 21 May. (BAe).

tank. He closed on the second Mirage IIIEA in XZ453 and damaged it with a Sidewinder. The Argentine pilot, *Premier Teniente* Garcia Cuerva, attempted to land his crippled aircraft at Port Stanley. With undercarriage down and landing lights on, it was hit twice by Argentinian AAA and crashed, killing Cuerva. It is likely that he had also 'cleaned' his aircraft of missiles and tanks to make the landing on a 4,300ft runway, possibly giving the AAA crews the impression that they were being attacked. As Admiral Woodward put it, 'Bad luck, really, but one less for us to deal with.' Thomas, one of the least experienced pilots with only 200hrs on Harriers, went on to destroy two Daggers, making him the only RN pilot with three fast-jet kills. He was 'Sharkey' Ward's most frequent wingman (although the term was not used in Sea Harrier tactics) and the partnership resulted in a total of five kills.

Grupo 8 realised that they had seriously underestimated the Sea Harrier and its aircrew. Their Mirages reverted to main-

Wing Commander Peter Squire lands the first of six Harrier GR.3s (XZ972) from the ill-fated *Atlantic Conveyor* aboard HMS *Hermes* at 1630Z on 18 May. Three others arrived that day, and two more on 20 May via HMS *Invincible*. This Harrier's combat career lasted only three days: it became the first Harrier casualty, shot down by a Blowpipe missile over Port Howard. (BAe via R. L. Ward)

land air defence, returning briefly to fly decoy and escort missions on 8 and 13 June. Rather than posing a serious threat to the Royal Navy fighters as many had predicted, the Dagger and Mirage force was totally outclassed by the Sea Harrier and its aircrew.

The second day of hostilities gave the Sea Harrier a chance to demonstrate its third design role, sea-search, with considerable effect. On 2 May the Argentine Navy had two groups of warships which appeared to threaten the Task Force. To the south-west was a battle group headed by a 43-year-old *Brooklyn* class cruiser which, as the USS *Phoenix*, had survived Pearl Harbor and gone on to become General MacArthur's Flagship in the Pacific. In Argentine service it was known as ARA *General Belgrano*. It was under close observation by HM submarine *Conqueror* and within hours of being torpedoed and sunk. A second group, centred on the carrier ARA *25 de Mayo* (formerly HMS *Colossus* and then *Karel Doorman* in Dutch service), was in an unknown position somewhere to the north-west. The carrier had received an expensive refit earlier in 1982 to enable her to operate the Super Etendard attack aircraft, but it soon became obvious that this could not, after all, be done effectively. However, the ship's eight A-4Q Skyhawks were considered a major threat, partly because of the difficulty in detecting their approach at low level.

SEA HARRIER FRS.1s WITH TASK FORCE 317, APRIL–JUNE 1982	
800 NAS	
XZ492/23	
XZ460/26	
XZ500/30	
XZ459/25	
XZ496/27	
XZ457/14	899 NAS
XZ494/16	899 NAS
ZA191/18	899 NAS
ZA192/92	
ZA193/93	
XZ450/50	MoD(PE)
XZ455/12	899 NAS
XZ499/99	809 NAS a/c absorbed into main sqn from 18/05
ZA176/76	As XZ499
ZA177/77	As XZ499
ZA194/94	
801 NAS	
XZ493/001	
XZ495/003	
ZA175/004	
XZ495/005	
XZ451/006	899 NAS
XZ458/007	899 NAS
XZ456/008	899 NAS
XZ453/009	899 NAS
ZA174/00	809 NAS a/c absorbed into main sqn from 18/05
XZ491/002	As ZA174
XZ452/007	As ZA174; replaced XZ452
ZA190/009	As ZA174; replaced XZ453

Sea Harrier ZA177 occupied pride of place on HMS *Hermes*' ski-jump when the carrier returned to Portsmouth on 21 July 1982. It had two Mirage silhouettes briefly marked on its nose, although the two aircraft actually shot down by Flight Lieutenant Dave Morgan on 8 June were actually A-4 Skyhawks. (R. L. Ward)

Land-based attackers could be plotted with some success through intelligence reports from SAS/SBS observer teams on the mainland and West Falkland, but the lack of AEW aircraft gave an unexpected sea-skimming aircraft a real chance. It was therefore vital to discover *25 de Mayo*'s position.

At 0312Z on 2 May *Invincible* picked up radar emissions at 55nm from an S-2E Tracker of the *25 de Mayo* ASW squadron which had located several British ships and was probing further. Flight Lieutenant Ian

Mortimer (in XZ451) was scrambled into the night to investigate. He flew north-west for 50 miles in 'radar silence', hoping to pick up hostile emissions on his RWR receiver. With no apparent business forthcoming 'Morts' gave a brief burst of Blue Fox energy and instantly aroused all manner of radar illumination, including a Type 909 Sea Dart tracking radar. This indicated the presence of one of Argentina's two Type 42 destroyers, ARA *Hercules*, at 25 miles from the fighter. He made a rapid strategic withdrawal and then turned back briefly to take another quick radar peek. It revealed five contacts and *25 de Mayo* was assumed to be one of them, albeit another 60 miles further out.

Invincible prepared herself for an attack by the CANA Skyhawks, which was actually being briefed aboard the carrier as Mortimer recovered to his ship. In the end it was never launched. A lack of over-deck wind meant that the A-4Qs could not take off with a useful bomb load. The S-2E Tracker lost the Task Force and later in the day *Belgrano* was sunk. *25 de Mayo* returned to port and took no further part in hostilities, although her aircraft transferred to Rio Grande and flew a small number of missions from there.

The loss of HMS *Sheffield* on 4 May to an Exocet missile fired by a *2 Esc.* Super Etendard was a tragic reminder that the small number of Sea Harriers could only defend the Task Force successfully if they were accurately positioned and employed as the outer rim of an extremely complex defensive structure. Because other elements in that structure went awry the two 'Super Es' of *Capitán* Bedacarratz (in 3-A-202) and *Teniente* Mayora (in 3-A-203) managed to penetrate the CAP and launch two missiles from about 25 miles from *Sheffield*. Although it was known that the CANA Super Etendard unit had only received five missiles, their destructive potential was taken very seriously. It had been conceded from the outset that the loss of either RN carrier would mean the abandonment of the whole Falklands operation. Without·any AEW cover the main defensive strategy rested on the belief that the 'Super Es' would pop-up twice from below the ships' radar detection height to around 200ft in order to check their Agave 'Handbrake' search radar picture of the target area, thereby appearing on the Fleet's radars too. This is exactly what happened on 4 May, but the defensive response was negated by a chain of misfortunes.

Back at Yeovilton on 22 July 1982 were six of *Hermes*' Sea Harriers, including XZ457/14 which destroyed four Argentine aircraft. XZ457 was converted to F/A .2 standard and was seriously damaged by an engine fire on 20 October 1995 as 899 NAS's Senior Pilot, Lieutenant-Commander Bayliss, advanced the throttle for take-off. (Via R. L. Ward)

Assuming that the first 'pop-up' occurred at about 100 miles, the Sea Harrier CAP could reach the intruders in time to forestall a missile launch. Potential target ships could also initiate their own countermeasures, principally chaff. As an Exocet attack was expected as retaliation for the loss of *Belgrano*, Sea Harriers from both carriers maintained visual sea-search out to a 100-mile radius. Radar operators on all vessels were reacting (sometimes over-reacting) to the minutest traces and there was a stream of reported 'contacts' throughout the day. Sadly, the overload led to confusion. Lieutenant-Commander Ward maintains that a CAP which had been vectored towards the actual 'pop-up' location of the Super Etendards, or their SP-2H Neptune radar recce guide, was inadvertently called off. In any event, there was a hole in the CAP line which left three Type 42 destroyers, including *Sheffield*, exposed. They formed a distant radar picket

line, away from the main fleet, and were therefore already vulnerable. One of the three, HMS *Glasgow*, transmitted firm radar evidence of the Super Etendards' approach and Exocet launch; however, these were among many received by the carrier's Anti-Air Warfare Controllers and could not be acted upon quickly enough. *Sheffield* was using her SCOT satellite uplink, blotting out the Etendard contact; *Glasgow* could not lock her Sea Dart radar on to the approaching missiles. *Sheffield*, unaware of the threat until it was too late, did not fire chaff and was hit at 1404Z, the first RN ship to be struck by any form of missile since the Second World War. Ian Mortimer's Sea Harrier was despatched to investigate reports that *Sheffield* had been torpedoed. He reported a hole in the ship's side at Exocet-entry height. *Sheffield* burned out and was abandoned.

An hour after this attack *Hermes* launched a second raid on Goose Green airfield, having already 'CAPped' the second 'Black Buck' Vulcan sortie and flown armed recce to Fox Bay earlier in the day. Lieutenant-Commander Batt (in ZA192) and Lieutenant Nick Taylor were scheduled to drop three CBUs on parked aircraft at Goose Green, while Flight Lieutenant Ted Ball (XZ460) had three 1,000lb DA retard bombs to crater the grass runway. As Taylor's CBU left his Sea Harrier (XZ450) it was hit by one of three GADA-601 Skyguard radar-directed Oerlikon

Above: 'Kill' markings on 'Black 14' (**XZ457**) show the two *Grupo 6* Daggers destroyed by Lieutenant-Commander Andy Auld with two simultaneously launched AIM-9L Sidewinders on 24 May. Below is the stencil for an A-4Q Skyhawk, downed by an AIM-9L on 21 May. A second A-4Q was badly damaged by 30mm fire and its pilot ejected, but this was not confirmed until after the war. (Via R. L. Ward)

Left, upper: Sea Harrier XZ451/006 flew with **801 NAS** from HMS *Invincible* and shot down a Canberra, a C-130E Hercules and a Pucará. On its return to RNAS Yeovilton (and some 'no-hands' taxying!) on 18 September, 006 was temporarily transferred to 800 NAS. (R. L. Ward)

Left, lower: HMS *Hermes*, with RN Sea Harriers and RAF Harriers filling her deck space. (Royal Navy)

Right: One of the replacement Sea Harriers in 809 NAS markings which joined HMS *Hermes* via *Atlantic Conveyor* on 18 May. The 'last two' of the serial—99—were painted on as an 800 NAS-style code, but the aircraft was later coded '255' on joining HMS *Illustrious*. As '99', it downed an A-4B Skyhawk on 8 June and damaged the supply ship *Rio Iguazu* which was strafed by Martin Hale and Rod Frederiksen. (Via Andy Evans)

35mm guns around the airfield. There was a violent explosion and the aircraft hit the ground, slid through a gate and across a road before coming to rest on the airfield. Nick Taylor was killed and his body was later buried by local troops with a funeral service in Spanish. The only consolation to be found in this tragic loss on an already sombre day was that his aircraft, in its demise, did considerable service to the British effort. Although the attack itself did no appreciable damage, XZ450 was perhaps the best Sea Harrier to lose, if there had to be a first loss.

John Farley was working on the AV-8B FSD programme in St Louis at the time, and he saw Argentine video of the crashed jet on CNN. Noticing the still-visible serial, he was saddened that it was 'his' first Sea Harrier and annoyed that it was the only Sea Eagle-equipped aircraft. However, the Argentinians examined the wrecked cockpit, discovered the Sea Ea-

gle panel and assumed that all Sea Harriers were able to launch the powerful anti-shipping weapon. It is very likely that this piece of accidental disinformation was another reason for the complete withdrawal of Argentinian naval units, including *25 de Mayo*, after the sinking of *Belgrano*.

The loss of Nick Taylor marked the end of the second phase of Sea Harrier operations. Admiral Woodward decided that the small number of aircraft could not be risked on low-level attacks, particularly against targets which were of dubious value and well-defended. In its first four days, the Sea Harrier had demonstrated its full potential. On 1 May the initial sorties had shown how the entire complement could be launched on a variety of tasks (when Brian Hanrahan said 'I counted them all out', he meant *all*). Ground attacks had been made with substantial warloads. In the air-to-air arena the two squadrons showed such marked superior-

ity in equipment, tactics and training that *Fuerza Aérea Argentina* pilots considered that further attempts to engage their seriously underestimated opponent were pointless. Ian Mortimer's detection of Task Force 76, with *25 de Mayo*, highlighted the aircraft's sea-search ability and signalled to the opposition that they could not hide. Armed recce flights around the north of the Islands brought back F95 photographs which were the only intelligence images available to the Task Force at the time.

For the rest of the war Sea Harrier bombing was restricted to straight-and-level, or lofted, drops from above the 16,000ft envelope of the Roland missiles which defended Port Stanley. From mid-May onwards aircraft flying to CAP positions regularly lobbed a couple of bombs on to the airfield, using a radar offset IP if bombing above cloud. Although this was not precision bombing, the real purpose, according to Simon Hargreaves, was to

Left, upper: In addition to losing a Sea Harrier overboard from a slippery deck, the Task Force almost lost Harrier XZ997 on 21 May when Flight Lieutenant John Rochfort bounced it on landing, rather too close to the deck edge. *Hermes'* catwalk caught the jet's outrigger wheel and it was hauled back aboard, still with CBU underwing from an armed recce which yielded no targets. (BAe)

Left, lower: Another 809 NAS Sea Harrier, ZA194, back at Yeovilton on 19 July. Its 'kill' marking records the destruction of a *Grupo 6* Dagger by Lieutenant Martin Hale on 23 May over Pebble Island. (Via R. L. Ward)

Right: An 809 NAS FRS.1 arrives on board *Hermes* from *Atlantic Conveyor*. (Via R. L. Ward)

provide 'a good morale-sapping weapon. Every hour or so another couple of bombs would arrive from nowhere.' In total, Sea Harriers deposited 437 bombs (totalling 80 tons), many of them on Port Stanley airfield.

In the campaign as a whole only 1 per cent of scheduled Sea Harrier missions could not be flown. At one stage 800 NAS was launching up to 40 sorties daily. 801 NAS flew 100 sorties in four days following the British landings at San Carlos. On other occasions 150ft cloud bases and visibility below 300yd severely curtailed flying. Between 5 and 8 May 800 NAS made only four sorties, although they would have responded if the enemy had braved the weather. 801 NAS maintained CAP during that period, but lost two aircraft and their pilots as they attempted to follow up a low-level contact sighted near the hulk of HMS *Sheffield*. The two aircraft descended from different headings through thick cloud to very low level. From the last transmissions received it appears that their pilots were several miles closer together than they thought and outside each other's search radar 'vision'. Nothing more was heard or found and it was assumed that they collided and crashed. Two of 801 NAS's most experienced pilots, Lieutenant-Commander John Eyton-Jones and Lieutenant Al Curtis, were lost together with a quarter of 801's Sea Harriers in a million-to-one chance accident.

800 NAS resumed CAP on 9 May. Dave Morgan and Gordon Batt refrained from dropping their 'harassment' bombs on Port Stanley because of unusually thick cloud. On return to 'mother' *Hermes* they located the intelligence trawler *Narwal* on radar and got permission to attack it from the control ship HMS *Coventry*. Although their bombs were fused for a high-altitude drop, the pilots elected to use them for a low 'lob' at the enemy vessel. After a very near miss from Morgan, Batt's bomb from XZ460 penetrated the ship's forecastle and came to rest without exploding. The pair followed up with 30mm fire and were then joined by Martin Hale and Andy George for more strafing passes. The severely damaged vessel was inspected by a Sea King boarding party and put under tow, but it sank the following day. Its crew, all but one of whom survived, were taken aboard *Invincible* but refused to believe that their hosts' ship still existed because the Argentinian Press had repeatedly announced that the carrier had been sunk!

For the next month of the war the Sea Harrier squadrons concentrated on CAP activities and occasional armed recce. One of these, on 16 May, resulted in the destruction of more Argentinian shipping. Simon Hargreaves (XZ494) and Dave Smith (ZA191) did a visual and F95 run over the coast to the south of Goose Green and detected two berthed supply vessels, *Rio Carcarana* and *Bahía Buen Sucero*. The first of these was set on fire by a later flight when Gordon Batt and Andy McHarg bombed and strafed it. Simon Hargreaves and his boss Andy Auld returned to strafe the other ship 45 minutes later, putting it out of action. Hargreaves' ZA191 took a few minor shrapnel wounds in the tail feathers as it pulled off target.

Recce flights became more frequent in the lead-up to the British landings at San Carlos (Operation 'Sutton') as command-

The Fleet Air Arm had no night attack capability. Patrols were usually positioned at 10,000ft, although 801 NAS tended to wait at lower altitude. The aircraft flew 'racetrack' circuits with about a mile's separation, side by side. Carriers launched their CAP pairs at roughly half-hour intervals, alternately, and the lengthy transits to CAP station only allowed about ten minutes on the patrol circuit. Obviously this arrangement tended to leave gaps and could not cope with a large, well-planned assault from several directions. Luckily, this never came.

Constant CAP also placed considerable strains upon the aircrew. By 18 May losses had reduced 801 NAS to nine pilots and six aircraft. 800 NAS were one down. After the first few days of action the Captain of *Hermes*, Lin Middleton (an ex-carrier fighter pilot himself), proposed a US Navy-style CAP rota which would have put each carrier 'on the line' for five days while the other went east for recuperation. His plan was rejected by 'Sandy' Woodward (an ex-submariner) who felt that three two-hour sorties, plus five hours of preparation and debriefing daily, was tolerable for his 'young, tough and fit' pilots. Another solution had to be found and it consisted of the addition of two extra Harrier elements.

From the Sea Harrier's earliest days there was discussion about a third deployable squadron. Originally this was to have been named 802 NAS, equipping the new HMS *Ark Royal* with ten Sea Harriers from a follow-on order. In 1978 Vice-Admiral Cassidi announced that 802 NAS would commission in 1981. Defence Secretary John Nott's 'value for money' package of June 1981 changed all this. *Hermes* was to be withdrawn when HMS *Illustrious* commissioned in 1983 and either *Invincible* or the still-incomplete *Ark Royal* was to be sold or scrapped. Delays in the decision caused the postponement of the June 1981 launch date scheduled for *Ark Royal* (although, post-Falklands, she was finally completed in 1985). An extra Sea Harrier order was not considered necessary for a smaller carrier force, thereby making the formation of a third squadron (should it be required) extremely difficult.

ers tried to construct an accurate impression of enemy assets. Pilots devised their own methods of aiming the fixed F95 camera, the favourite being a grease-pen line on the canopy corresponding to a depressed 20-degree aiming line. Generally, recce missions were based on the standard attack profile. Unlike the GR.3 recce pod, which was unavailable during 'Corporate', the F95 was always aboard and could be switched on very fast if something interesting appeared during a visual recce. Image quality was (and is) usually good, although 801 NAS pilot Lieutenant Charlie Cantan caused some anxiety on the Flag carrier when he brought back a photograph of Port Stanley airfield which appeared to show a line of swept-wing jets near the runway. Closer analysis revealed them to be a trio of MB.339As, but the spectre of land-based Super Etendards took several bombing missions and many more recce sessions to allay.

CAP activity increased after the San Carlos landings began on 20 May as Argentine forces intensified their assault on the new, more vulnerable targets on land and sea. The Exocet threat meant that the carrier force had to be kept at a safe distance. CAPs had to be positioned at the correct distance between the San Carlos landing area and the incoming threat to enable interception in good time, but close enough to the British forces to allow Sea Harriers to turn back and catch any aircraft which might have slipped past. This was particularly important for the first few days after landings began because the British Rapier missile defences took a while to get ashore and set up. Three CAP stations were established: near Pebble Island and to the north and south of the Task Force, which has moved its troop transports and their escorts into San Carlos Water. Two 'Sea Jets' occupied each station on a rota throughout daylight hours.

Lieutenant-Commander Tim Gedge, former CO of 800 NAS, watched the Task Force leave Portsmouth. Later that day he was asked by FONAC to form another front-line Sea Harrier unit. His immediate problem was to locate ten aircraft and pilots to fly them, knowing that the effort to send two squadrons southbound had been something of a barrel-scraping exercise. Furthermore, he was told that the new squadron had to be operational by the end of the month. It was designated 809 NAS rather than 802, reviving the name-plate of a Buccaneer squadron which had decommissioned four years previously. Serious conversion training was out of the question as 899 NAS had virtually decamped to *Hermes* and *Invincible*. MoD(PE) still had three aircraft for trials of new 'Falklands' modifications, such as the twin-Sidewinder launch rail, and there was some reluctance to let them go the same way as the unfortunate XZ450. Five were still in attrition storage at St Athan, two were undergoing maintenance work programmes at Yeovilton's SHSU and one was being pushed through the final stages of construction on the BAe line. The partially complete aircraft for the Indian Navy were strictly out of bounds! St Athan's five were quickly prepared, the first being delivered to SHSU within twenty-four hours. Several arrived without major components for their radar, NAVHARS and HUDs. Inside a week Gedge had acquired eight aircraft and conceded that the other two had to be left behind as the nucleus of a continuation training programme. They all entered intensive maintenance which included a standard Medium Sea Grey/Light Grey (BS.4800) paint scheme suggested by Farnborough's camouflage expert P. J. Barley as the best match for winter weather in the Falklands. It proved less than popular with pilots and was replaced by a darker shade post-war. The last aircraft, ZA194, arrived on 28 April only five days after its first flight.

Aircrew were equally scarce. Lieutenant-Commander Dave Braithwaite and Lieutenant Bill Covington were called back from exchange postings in the United States and Lieutenant-Commander Hugh Slade from one in Australia. Lieutenant-

Commander Al Craig had been on a GR.3 exchange at Wittering and Lieutenant Dave Austin was pulled off Yeovilton's simulator team. Numbers were made up by a couple of RAFG pilots, Flight Lieutenants Steve Brown and John Leeming, chosen because they had previous air-to-air radar intercept experience in RAF Lightnings. They were given some hasty ski-jump practice and DACT, including a few rides in the back of a French Mirage IIIBE, on exchange at Wittering. An indication of the likely method of transit to the war area came when the aircraft were fitted with IFR probes and trial refuelling 'prods' were made with RAF Victors. This was actually the first time Sea Harriers had been flight-refuelled in RN service use. RAF 330gal ferry tanks were trialled but the standard 100gal 'Hunter' tanks were considered more reliable for the long haul to Ascension Island. Their eventual destination there, the container ship *Atlantic Conveyor*, which was to provide a 'lift' from Ascension to the Task Force, left Plymouth on 25 April. Before she weighed anchor Tim Gedge did a trial landing on her newly fitted steel landing pad in XZ438, one of the BAe/MoD(PE) DB aircraft on loan as ground spares for 809's departing octet. All three DB jets received full 809 NAS markings, the new paint job and refuelling probes in case they were needed. A wartime spirit of cooperation continued to work miracles! XV438 was written off on Yeovilton's ski-jump while testing the use of 330gal tanks for carrier take-offs, reducing the DB cohort to two.

On 30 April Lieutenant-Commander Gedge led the first of three 809 NAS sections from Yeovilton. Nine hours' flying time and fourteen Victor 'prods' later they were all safely on Wideawake. A night-stop at a five-star hotel at Banjul in the Gambia was the only *en route* entertainment, but the hotel did hand out well-stocked 'doggy bags' for the rest of the trip. Meanwhile, at Yeovilton the remains of 809/899 squadrons began training the next batch of pilots, including Sub-Lieutenant Alistair McLaren and three more RAF pilots. Lieutenant-Commander Taylor Scott RNR was persuaded away from BAe to become their AWI.

THE GR.3s ARRIVE

Also heading south was the second part of the reinforcement effort. With a very limited number of Sea Harriers and the possibility of punitive attrition, the obvious source of additional, deployable air power was the RAF Harrier GR.3 fleet. Although it lacked radar and air defence missiles, the GR.3 seemed the ideal stopgap in the attack role, and could be cleared to use Sidewinders. No 1(F) Squadron was the RAF's forward deployable Harrier unit. It had been cleared for carrier operations in 1971. The Squadron was therefore not exactly surprised to receive a warning order of likely deployment almost a month before Admiral Woodward reacted to the loss of Nick Taylor by taking Sea Harriers off low-altitude attack. His decision was partly influenced by the knowledge that RAF 'mud-mover' GR.3s were in the pipeline.

Ken Hayr, a former CO of No 1(F), was Assistant Chief of Air Staff at the MoD at the time and he was able to expedite preparations for the GR.3 operation. In addition to the already established 'naval' mods to the jet (deck-lashing shackles on the outriggers and nosewheel steering changes) many more were quickly effected. In the 1970s funding had been unavailable for AIM-9 control wiring in GR.3s, so a system was quickly devised by BAe and Wittering's engineers in three weeks. Redundant wiring in the wings and some home-made switchgear based on Phantom armament components were used. Wittering and BAe assembled and installed an I-band transponder to give the Harriers a friendly signature on ship's radars as they passed through the Task Force's radar barrier. It appeared as a small bulge under the LRMTS nose. Sidewinder wiring allowed the outer pylons to take AIM-9G rounds, bombs or RN-type 2in rocket pods which were considered safer than SNEB pods in the 'electronic environment' aboard ship, where HERO (hazards of electromagnetic interference to ordnance) are always present. However, it was a case of 'AIM-9 or bombs', and a half-hour conversion job was needed to adapt the pylon from one to the other. The first converted GR.3

(XZ989) was ready by 28 April for A&AEE tests. Live AIM-9G firing trials took place at Aberporth on 1 May and eighteen kits were manufactured in all.

There was little that Wing Commander Fitzgerald-Lombard's engineering team could do to remedy the GR.3's nav-attack problems when operating with the Task Force. Its moving map could not be used because map sections for the area were not available from stock and the INAS could not be aligned properly on a moving deck. Whereas NAVHARS could be up and running with all waypoints punched in, within a couple of minutes the fully inertial GR.3's FE.541 required a complete re-think of the alignment procedure if it were to be of any use. Ferranti produced a device known as FINRAE (Ferranti Inertial Rapid Alignment Equipment) based on their FIN.1064 inertial platform. It was a portable unit which evolved out of the 1970s carrier trials when the GR.3's INAS problem was first addressed. FINRAE transmitted basic positional data to the aircraft's FE.541 through plug-in leads. Ferranti assembled two units in a mere eighteen days and they became available for the deployment. Although the system could be made to work reasonably well, and several pilots found it very useful, the majority of GR.3 sorties were flown using old-fashioned compass and stopwatch navigation. Weapons aiming was mostly done with the reversionary DSL weapons aiming sight on the HUD.

No 1(F)'s intended ground-attack/CAS role clearly placed it at risk from anti-air defences on the islands. The Argentinians had flown-in a Westinghouse TPS-43F and a Cardion TPS-44 search radar to detect aircraft in the eastern part of the Falklands and two ELTA radar units on the north coast. A single Roland launcher was operating at Port Stanley, with only eight or ten rounds. All the Port Stanley radars were 'buried' in residential areas for protection and the Task Force had no means of attacking them. More vulnerable were the radar-directed AAA sites. Contraves Skyguard state-of-the-art pulse-doppler radars were extremely effective. Each mobile unit controlled a pair of twin-barrelled 35mm Oerlikon GDF-002 guns,

a combination which destroyed three British aircraft and at least two *Fuerza Aérea Argentina* Skyhawks which strayed into the field of fire. The less sophisticated Super Fledermaus gunlaying radar was also available but suffered from poor reliability. There were also large numbers of optically aimed 20mm weapons. As the Task Force possessed no SEAD assets, two 'Black Buck' Vulcan missions were flown against the Port Stanley radars. Vulcan XM597 initially tested Martel missiles for the job but eventually flew with two, and then four AGM-45A Shrike anti-radar missiles. 'Black Buck 5' on 2 June caused slight damage to a Skyguard antenna but the whole operation was generally ineffective. At Wittering a GR.3 was modified to carry a pair of Shrikes, and a modification kit was flown out to HMS *Hermes*. No 1(F)'s 'Wild Weasel' GR.3 completed its conversion aboard ship just as the war ended and never saw action.

Two other modifications were designed to increase the GR.3 force's protection, though neither of them arrived in the South Atlantic in time to be of general use. 'Blue Eric', named after its inventor, Squadron Leader Eric Annal, was a simple jamming unit fitted in the front of a modified Aden gun pod (Mod No 1504), using components from the Marconi Sky Shadow jamming pod. Production began on 18 April after four days of tests and ten were assembled. Tracor ALE-40(V)4 chaff/flare dispensers were also obtained and two were recessed in each lower rear fuselage of four GR.3s. All Harriers had additional salt-water drain holes drilled and generous internal spraying with PX24 moisture dispersant to keep salt corrosion at bay. Their Mk 103 engines were not corrosion resistant like the Sea Harriers' Mk 104, but no serious difficulties were encountered.

In addition to their practice ski-jump at Yeovilton (one was considered enough by most pilots), No 1's aircrew each live-fired an AIM-9G, flew DCM against RAF Lightnings and Phantoms and put in plenty of lower-than-usual tactical flying in the Welsh hill country. Several pilots flew anti-shipping sorties against Type 42 destroyers in case the Argentinian Navy

chose to reappear. One of the pilots, Squadron Leader Bob Iveson, also passed on his experience of ACM from an exchange posting to an AV-8A squadron in the USA. Although the Harrier pilots had to be prepared to step into the Sea Harrier role to the best of their ability, the only aspect of this preparation which would be of direct use was the low-flying practice.

The flight to Ascension was made via St Mawgan, the first two aircraft departing from there on 3 May with the squadron CO, Wing Commander Peter Squire, in the lead. Two Harriers made it in 9hr 15min (a record distance for VTOL aircraft), the third (Squire's) arriving later after a stop at Banjul caused by tanking shortages *en route*. A second trio on 4 May had an air 'abort' with fuel leaks and the third section also had a Banjul 'overnight' when their tanker ran short in unexpected headwinds. Each GR.3 had two 330gal ferry tanks and empty 100gal combat tanks outboard for use on arrival. Three aircraft were retained at Ascension for the air defence of that crucial staging base until No 29(F) Squadron Phantom FGR.2s could be deployed there on 24 May. Air defence GR.3s had Sidewinder pylons and, as part compensation for their lack of radar, pilots had the use of night vision goggles (NVG)—one of the first operational uses of this kit. They were also given the 'Blue Eric'- and ALE-40-equipped aircraft.

The other six Harriers joined 809 NAS Sea Harriers and an assortment of Wessex and 'Wokka' (Chinook) helicopters aboard *Atlantic Conveyor* on 6 May. They landed on the ship's steel VTOL pad, taxied into tight parking slots in the open hangar between sidewalls made of containers and were then washed and corrosion-treated for the voyage. Finally, they were encased in specially manufactured Driclad rubberized canvas bags. The ship also took aboard a vast array of Harrier spares including a Pegasus 103 and large quantities of CBU and other ordnance. Below decks the ship was fitted out as a workshop for major Harrier servicing and repair, including engine changes. These could not easily be done in the carriers' cramped hangar space and it was fortunate that only one engine change was required during the conflict. An 809 NAS Sea Harrier was perched on the landing pad as air defence for this vulnerable treasury with Tim Gedge and Dave Braithwaite on standby as alert pilots. Because the aircraft would have to VTO in such an emergency, with a subsequent reduction in fuel load, a Victor tanker rota covered most of the voyage. Argentinian 707s still posed a threat of detection and attack. There is little doubt that a 'Burglar' flight would have been swiftly despatched by the 'Shad-Hacker' alert fighter.

Atlantic Conveyor arrived within range of the Task Force on 18 May and four Sea Harriers were flown off to *Hermes*, the other four joining *Invincible* the next day. Their 'Phoenix' squadron insignia were overpainted and side-numbers were applied. 809 NAS's identity was put 'on hold' and its pilots and maintainers were absorbed into 800 NAS and 801 NAS. Lieutenant-Commander Gedge agreed to fly

---

No 1(F) SQUADRON HARRIER GR.3s INVOLVED IN OPERATION 'CORPORATE'

First deployment to Ascension Island 4–6 May (all ex No 233 OCU except ex No IV Sqn XZ947 and XV789)

XV787	Air spare
XW919	Remained at Wideawake for air defence 6–24/05
XZ989	
XZ963	
XZ129*	As XW919
XZ997	
XV789	
XZ972	
XZ988	
XZ132	As XW919

Second deployment, 29–30 May

XZ992	Flown direct from Ascension to *Hermes* 1 and 8 June
XW767*	
XZ133	As XZ992
XV778	As XZ992
XW924*	
XV762*	

*Loaded on *Contender Bezant* for transit to South Atlantic 3–10/06 but not delivered to Sqn until after 14/06. These a/c were equipped with ALE-40 and 'Blue Eric' countermeasures.

---

as regular a 801 NAS pilot with Lieutenant-Commander Ward as his CO. No 1(F)'s GR.3s were transferred to *Hermes* (for several pilots it was their first-ever sight of an aircraft carrier) between 18 and 20 May, five days before *Atlantic Conveyor* was hit by an Exocet. Twelve crew were killed and all but one of the helicopters destroyed, together with all the Harrier support equipment, 600 CBUs and large quantities of bombs and stores.

Life on *Hermes* became even more cramped with fifteen Sea Harriers, six GR.3s and all their associated personnel aboard. Several helicopters had to be transferred to other ships and living space became even more claustrophobic aboard the old 'rust bucket'. But the reinforcements had arrived just in time to cope with the most violent and demanding phase of the war, Operation 'Sutton'. A short work-up period for the RAF contingent gave them an opportunity to start as the Sea Harriers had done—by intercepting the ubiquitous Boeing 707, with Sidewinders underwing. The 'Burglar' was too far out to be reached on that occasion, the only one on which the GR.3s were configured for air defence. For the rest of the war No 1(F)'s briefings contrived to emphasise defensive tactics against the anticipated onslaught of Mirages and Daggers. Without Sidewinders aboard, GR.3 pilots were encouraged to employ VIFF if they encountered opposition at altitude. The idea was to roll the aircraft on its back while turning the nozzles to the hover position and descending as rapidly as possible to an altitude where escape would be possible. (As Frank Robertson, Chief Designer of the Short SC.1 once said, 'Nothing comes down faster than a vertical take-off aircraft upside down!') Since almost all Harrier flying was done 'in the weeds', this tactic was seldom employed. In the event, no GR.3 pilot ever saw an Argentinian fixed-wing aircraft in the air.

Once the GR.3s had been reconfigured for the ground attack role they were in serious business. On 20 May three aircraft, led by Peter Squire, flew a CBU attack on Fox Bay fuel dump. Without an operational FINRAE at the time, they requested

a Sea Harrier 'lead ship' to navigate them to the target, although most of the sortie was completed with their own standby instruments. Jerry Pook and Mark Hare responded to an SAS report of helicopters parked near Mount Kent and flew a surprise attack early the next day, destroying a Chinook and damaging a Puma and a UH-1H Huey with 30mm fire. Although their fast-and-low run did not give them the chance to spot a further twelve helicopters nearby, the attack underlined the importance of reducing the Argentinian rotary wing and short-range fixed-wing assets ahead of the British landings. Jerry Pook also took the first-ever combat damage to an RAF Harrier—a few small-arms 'dings' that were quickly patched up with Speedtape.

Later in the morning Jeff Glover and Bob Iveson, a No 1(F) Flight Commander who had missed 'Maple Flag' to 'attend the show', were scheduled to fly a photo recce near Port Howard. Iveson had to return with undercarriage problems. Glover made his first run, saw nothing of interest and was asked to repeat it. Although it went against the grain to make a second pass at the target, he agreed, but he waited a while and returned on a different heading—which unfortunately put the sun in his eyes. An unseen Blowpipe missile, or, in Glover's opinion, a shell from a 20mm gun, hit his aircraft close to the wing root. The wing folded up as XZ972 headed for the ground and Glover just managed an ejection at almost 600mph, landing in the sea on a partially deployed parachute. Argentinian troops rowed out to collect him and he became the only RAF prisoner-of-war, receiving very correct and generally friendly treatment until his return on 8 July.

After Jeff Glover's capture GR.3 tactics were modified simply to 'lower and faster'. Target approaches below 50ft with weapons release at 150ft were quite common. A second visit to Port Howard was made on 26 May. Bob Iveson and Tony Harper, this time with CBU, put some very accurate ordnance on enemy positions and Iveson felt that he had managed to avenge Glover, who was thought to have been killed.

Sea Harriers and GR.3s chained down side by side on *Hermes'* deck aft (BAe)

May 21 nearly saw the loss of another GR.3 when Flight Lieutenant John Rochefort returned from an armed recce with a bombed-up aircraft and landed it with the left outrigger just over the deck edge. His left wing, resting on his pylon-mounted CBU and 100gal tank, did not drop far enough for the Harrier to roll into the catwalk and overboard. XZ997 was hauled aboard and flown again hours later.

Airfield attacks had priority on 22–26 May and the Harriers encountered heavy AAA at Goose Green, Pebble Island and Port Stanley. Their initial attack on the last of these by four aircraft used a pair of 800 NAS Sea Harriers as flak-suppressors, dropping 1,000lb VT airburst bombs 20 seconds before No 1 arrived. Despite hits by three bombs the runway remained in use. The lack of a dedicated anti-runway weapon was sorely felt. On 24 May the first Texas Instruments Paveway II modification kits to convert 1,000lb bombs into LGBs were air dropped to *Hermes*. However, there were no FACs in position on

the ground to illuminate targets for them at that stage. The following day a different arrangement with the Sea Harriers was tried. Their Blue Fox radar was used to provide accurate range measurement for loft bombing by GR.3s against Port Stanley airfield.

All six GR.3s were in action on 27 May, keeping up the Port Stanley attacks and seeking two 105mm guns near Goose Green which were threatening the 2 Para advance in that area. CBU was dropped on a large troop concentration there by Bob Iveson and Mark Hare, making their second attack of the day in poor visibility without a FAC. Difficulty in identifying exact targets from the cockpit together with poor communications were frequent problems for pilots, often distracting them from potential threats on the ground. Iveson judged that 2 Para needed all the help they could get and decided to risk a third pass using his guns. Sadly, Goose Green's highly accurate 35mm batteries had him in range.[1] Two hits on XZ988 at 100ft altitude brought warning lights on all over his cockpit panels and smoke in the cockpit. His controls froze, cleared again and then began to lose hydraulic

pressure. Iveson managed to arrest a rapid dive by vectoring the aircraft's nose up with the nozzles. With fire intensifying in the cockpit and virtually no control left, he punched-out and landed dangerously close to the burning wreck. He avoided detection by an Argentinian UH-1 Huey that night, holed up in a deserted farmhouse and was picked up two days later by a Royal Marines Gazelle helicopter (XX380) in response to his SARBE beacon.

Goose Green's AAA, which had proved to be far more accurate than Port Stanley's defences and had claimed two British aircraft, became the target for a concentrated attack on 28 May. As the British Army 2 Para force advanced on Goose Green it came under fire from the Oerlikon guns doubling as artillery weapons. Squadron Leader Peter 'Bomber' Harris, with Flight Lieutenant Tony Harper, put some accurate BL.755 on the gun positions from a 50ft run-in while Squadron Leader Pook

---

[1]Skyguard-directed Oerlikon 35mm batteries are capable of firing nine rounds per second, with tracking shown on a radar display and a video screen. Captured examples were found to be extremely accurate and reliable.

added two 30-shot pods of RN 2in RPs. The guns gave no further trouble and 2 Para took the Argentinian surrender of a force twice their number early the next day. The Harrier's role in this had been crucial. Their devastating attacks against troops on open ground were a serious blow to Argentinian firepower and morale.

OPERATION 'SUTTON'

Sea Harrier CAP activity in the second part of May increased as Operation 'Sutton' gathered force on the 21st. While No 1(F) Squadron pounded known Argentinian positions, the Royal Navy squadrons had to keep up to ten Sea Harriers in the air to meet the expected Argentine response. When it came on 21 May it cost the Argentines another fourteen aircraft. Many others turned back with their bombs rather than run the Sea Harrier gauntlet. The day's opening attack was by one of the MB.339A Aeromacchis from Port Stanley, one of only two operational sorties by the detachment during the entire period. Although the light jet caused only minor damage to the Seacat launcher of HMS *Argonaut* along with injuries to three crewmen, its pilot returned to base with his side's first real impression of the size and layout of the British force in San Carlos Water. An indication of the scale of the subsequent reaction came at 1304Z when six Daggers went for the warships protecting the entrance to San Carlos Bay. As they raced across the sea at 50ft, having evaded the CAP and radar detection, one aircraft was destroyed by a Seacat missile and a second by a Seaslug. The formation damaged HMS *Antrim* and HMS *Broadsword* with gunfire but their bombs (one of which ended up in *Antrim*'s 'heads'!) failed to explode. Despite HMS *Brilliant*'s attempts to vector in the CAP fighters, all the surviving Daggers escaped. On a day which Admiral Woodward considered the Royal Navy's first major action since the Second World War, the *Fuerza Aérea Argentina* demonstrated both the vulnerability of the ships and the holes in the CAP arrangements.

A major difficulty for the Sea Harriers operating over the confined space of Falkland Sound was their radar. While Blue Fox had a useful detection range over calm sea, it was not designed for look-down scanning over land. In Simon Hargreaves' opinion, 'Over land it was useless—in fact it was better to turn it off unless you just wanted to use it to scare the Argentinians away. Any CAPs over land or up Falkland Sound would just be cluttered out.' The majority of successful interceptions in the area were accomplished visually after initial vectoring from the anti-air warfare coordinates on Type 22 frigates and Type 42 destroyers.

For the first time the *Fuerza Aérea Argentina*'s few surviving Pucará light attack aircraft were committed to action on 21 May. Lieutenant-Commander Ward, Steve Thomas and 'new boy' Alisdair Craig, on his first sortie, were vectored by HMS *Brilliant* on to a pair which had successfully attacked a British observation post. The manoeuvrable, slow-moving Pucarás presented difficult, elusive targets and one escaped. It took 'Sharkey' Ward three cannon passes to finish the other one (A-511) whose pilot, *Mayor* Carlos Tomba (a 'very brave bloke' in Ward's estimation) baled out and walked back to base at Goose Green.

A second Dagger thrust by three aircraft also escaped unscathed, leaving HMS *Brilliant* with strafing damage to her operations room. Despite injury the ship's Fighter Director Officer vectored Ward and Thomas towards another pair of *Grupo 6* Daggers. One exploded after being struck by an AIM-9L from Thomas's ZA190; a second was sent into an uncontrollable spin by his second missile as it attempted a cannon attack on Ward. 'Sharkey' saw the third Dagger crossing at right angles below him and caught it with a Sidewinder as it tried to escape. As the two RN pilots re-joined formation Ward realised that three 'seagulls' ahead of him were actually light grey CANA A-4Q Skyhawks, part of a coordinated attack by *Grupos 3*, *4* and *5* which crippled HMS *Ardent* and disabled HMS *Argonaut*. Ward and Thomas, short on fuel and armament, handed the situation over to the next CAP section and returned to HMS *Invincible*, with Thomas's ZA190 suffering 20mm groundfire damage to its avionics

bay—the first combat damage to an 801 NAS Sea Harrier.

The Skyhawk attacks had commenced three hours earlier. Mike Blissett and Neill Thomas (CO of 899 NAS) met four *Grupo 4* A-4Cs and destroyed two almost simultaneously with 'Winders, damaging a third with gunfire. Forty minutes later, at 1715Z, Rod Frederiksen and Sub-Lieutenant Andy George were vectored by *Brilliant* towards another incoming flight of four at low level. Frederiksen, flying XZ455, launched an AIM-9L at one of the left-hand pair and its pilot baled out successfully as his aircraft struck the rocky terrain. Both Sea Harrier pilots fired several 30mm bursts at the fleeing Argentinians without effect before having to turn back. (Frederiksen assured the authors that he shot down an A-4 Skyhawk that day rather than the Dagger with which he is credited in some accounts of the war.) As that engagement took its course Lieutenant Clive 'Spag' Morell and Flight Lieutenant John Leeming of 800 NAS took over the southern CAP in Falkland Sound just as another Skyhawk flight was bombing HMS *Ardent*. They were the A-4Qs (spotted by Lieutenant-Commander Ward) of *3 Escuadrilla* which had transferred to Rio Grande after their carrier *25 de Mayo* had withdrawn from the war. From there they mounted only two attacks on the fleet, but sealed the fate of *Ardent*. As they pulled off target an AIM-9L from Morell's XZ457 broke A-4Q 3-A-307 in half and its pilot ejected. Morell had a rare hang-up with his other missile and attacked a second Skyhawk with 30mm, causing considerable damage to its wings. The pilot, José Arco, attempted a landing at Port Stanley but an inoperative undercarriage leg forced him to eject instead. Leeming, one of the 809

Sea Harrier ZA176 (later named *Hot Lips*) on board HMS *Illustrious* as she prepared to sail from Portsmouth on 2 August 1982. It was 809's only cruise as a complete squadron. This Sea Harrier had previously flown 43 combat sorties from *Hermes*, but it achieved international fame in June 1983 when Lieutenant Ian Watson 'landed' it on the Spanish freighter *Alraigo* when he ran short of fuel. (Via R. L. Ward)

NAS replacement aircrew in XZ500, destroyed the third A-4Q with 30mm fire after experiencing Sidewinder launch difficulties. There were just two 'guns only' kills. To the Argentinians the instant loss of over a third of their only squadron with anti-shipping training and appropriate retarded weapons (four 500lb Snakeye bombs on the centreline) was a serious blow.

HMS *Ardent* and 22 of her crew were lost after hits by nine bombs, only two of which failed to explode. In that sense the all-out effort by the Argentinians to frustrate the British landings succeeded, but their heavy losses showed that the CAP system was able to catch the majority of the raiders. RN pilots destroyed nine aircraft on 21 May and shared another with a ship. If the opposition had chosen to use their Mirage IIIEs to distract the CAP, or the AIM-9B missiles which they could have hung on their Skyhawks, their losses might have been reduced. The psychological effect of the Sea Harriers' obvious superiority was such that neither of these tactics was considered worthwhile. May 21 was the Argentinian High Command's big opportunity to disrupt the British landings before land-based defences could be properly established. Although parts of the Argentinian response were obviously coordinated, there seemed to be no overall strategy to try and swamp the fragile CAP line and target the key troop-carrying and picket ships. When the naval vessels' own defensive missile systems proved fatally unreliable on several occasions their vulnerability was painfully obvious. Fortunately, poor training and inappropriately fused bombs denied the Skyhawk and Dagger pilots much of the chaos which they could have caused.

'Bomb Alley' continued to receive regular visitors over the following week, albeit at a reduced rate. 800 NAS found other targets too. Rod Frederiksen and Martin Hale discovered the patrol vessel *Rio Iguazu* which was loaded with munitions for the Goose Green garrison. Hale (in XZ499) strafed it and it was beached. On 23 May Dave Morgan and John Leeming spotted three Pumas and two A-109A helicopters of *CAB 601 en route* to Port Howard. Three

were put out of action by 30mm fire, the third being finished off by Tim Gedge and Dave Braithwaite on the next CAP. The only attack by Argentine jets on 23 May was by a pair of Daggers which began an attack run from the north before breaking off and turning away on a reciprocal course. After the losses of 21 May *Fuerza Aérea Argentina* pilots were much more circumspect in their timing, using advice from their radar controllers about the presence of CAP activity. Andy Auld and Martin Hale were on the northern CAP and Hale picked up the pair of Daggers visually. Unable to catch the first, he launched a missile at the trailing wingman, whose aircraft crashed near Pebble Island.

800 NAS suffered an unexplained loss on 23 May. Four Sea Harriers were each loaded with three 1,000lb VT airburst bombs for Port Stanley airfield once again after reports that short-field arresting gear had been installed there, possibly to operate the *bête noir* Super Etendards. As a precaution the field was struck, unusually at night, but the fourth Sea Harrier to launch, ZA192 flown by Lieutenant-Commander Gordon Batt, was seen to explode in a huge fireball soon after take-off. Possibly he suffered engine failure or became disorientated while trying to formate with the other aircraft in the dark.

Undeterred, the Squadron resumed CAP the next day and picked up contacts in the early afternoon, having missed attacks on the troopships by both Skyhawk groups that morning. Andy Auld (XZ457) got in behind four *Grupo 6* Daggers over Pebble Island, loosed off two AIM-9s in quick succession and felled a pair of them. His CAP partner Dave Smith (ZA193) splashed a third and a fourth escaped by using afterburner. 'Sharkey' Ward rated 25 May as 'probably the worst day of the war as far as Task Force losses were concerned'. It was Argentina's National Day and a show of force was anticipated. There was little the Sea Harriers could have done to prevent the loss of *Atlantic Conveyor* that day. The Task Force had six minutes' warning of the Exocet launch, which destroyed the ship from over 30 miles away. However, in the case of HMS *Coventry*, guarding the northern approaches with HMS *Broad-*

sword, there would have been a good chance of CAP aircraft intervening to save the ship but for a tragic sequence of misfortunes. Neil Thomas and Dave Smith were successfully vectored towards an incoming *Grupo 5* Skyhawk flight which split into two pairs, one aimed at *Broadsword* and the other at *Coventry*. Captain Hart-Dyke, commanding *Coventry*, had already downed two Skyhawks with Sea Darts earlier in the day and he felt confident in the system. *Coventry*'s AWO decided that he could pick up the two A-4Bs on the ship's Type 909 radar and pick them off with Sea Dart again. The Harrier CAP was therefore called off, just outside their Sidewinder release range, and the Skyhawks were allowed to enter the ship's Missile Engagement Zone (MEZ). Normally Sea Harrier interceptions were supposed to happen at least 20 miles outside the MEZ. Neither *Coventry*'s Sea Darts nor *Broadsword*'s Seawolf radars would lock on to the low-flying A-4s as they approached over the land. *Broadsword* was hit by a 1,000lb bomb. The second pair of Skyhawks put three 1,000lb bombs into *Coventry* when she inadvertently sailed slightly across *Broadsword*'s line of radar vision, blocking off her Seawolf battery from an effective launch. All four Skyhawks escaped intact as the CAP Sea Harrier pilots watched *Coventry* capsize and sink.

PAVEWAY

No 1(F) Squadron pilots attempted their first LGB sortie on 30 May. 'Bomber' Harris (XZ989) and Tony Harper (XZ997) were unsuccessful because there was still no laser designator FAC available. Harper dropped his two bombs towards Port Stanley runway from 30,000ft while Harris attempted to 'mark' the runway for them using his LRMTS. The systems proved incompatible. Leaving *Hermes* at the same time, Jerry Pook and John Rochefort went on another helicopter hunt in the Port Stanley area. Pook's XZ963 attracted a storm of small-arms fire as the pair overflew troop concentrations. With fuel streaming from his Harrier, he cleaned the aircraft up but the 'petrol' ran out 30 miles from HMS *Hermes*. A successful ejection put him in the sea for a

Despite the pressure of operational requirements 'down South', 899 NAS kept up a training programme throughout 1982. By December it began to receive back a few of its aircraft. XZ457/713, XZ494/714 and XZ455/715, seen here, all flew with the Task Force and all three downed Argentinian aircraft. (R. L. Ward)

mere nine minutes before an 826 NAS Sea King hauled him out. Two more LGB drops were attempted on 31 May using the three remaining GR.3s against Stanley airport, but they were frustrated again by the lack of suitable designating equipment within range. Battle damage to XZ997, and XV789's need for a three-day maintenance effort to effect the only Pegasus-change of the war period, reduced the GR.3 force to a single aircraft until 1 June when two spares were delivered direct from Ascension Island by Murdo McLeod and Mike Beech. Their 3,000-mile flight took 8 1/2 hours, eight tankers and some careful navigation for the last 800 miles of open sea which they covered without a Victor 'shepherd', although John Leeming assisted them through the final leg in his Sea Harrier. There is no doubt that a broken refuelling probe or an aborted refuelling would have meant the loss of an aircraft and, probably, its pilot.

An important means of extending the range and loiter time of the Task Force's

fighters was completed on 5 June when Royal Engineers built the Port San Carlos FOB, known as 'Sid's Strip' to the RAF and HMS *Sheathbill* to the Navy. Aluminium MEXE planks were laboriously set out to make an 850ft runway, a parking space for four Harriers and a VTOL pad. Originally there was to have been space for ten aircraft but a large number of the 10ft by 2ft planks sank with *Atlantic Conveyor*. Jet fuel was stored in floating bladder tanks just offshore. The honour of making the first landing on the metal mini-airbase went to Simon Hargreaves and Andy Auld on 5 June. After several days with only photo-runs on the agenda, partly as a result of persistent fog, CAPs resumed but the two pilots were caught by fog once again and put down on the 'strip'. They flew four CAP sorties from the planks before returning to *Hermes*.

The FOB quickly became a vital asset. Simon Hargreaves' logbook records seven more visits in the period 7–14 June, one of which did not quite run to plan. As he approached the base after a CAP with Neil Thomas on the 13th the only operational RAF Chinook on the islands (ZA718/BN) caught some of the MEXE planks in its rotor down-blast and lifted them out of position. Contingency plans had already been laid to use the helicopter flight decks on certain RN ships for emergency land-

ings. Hargreaves put ZA177 down on HMS *Intrepid* while Thomas diverted to *Fearless*.[2] They took aboard a light fuel load to enable them to VTO back to 'Sid's Strip' when it was repaired. *Intrepid's* wardroom presented Hargreaves with a case of wine as a gesture of thanks for the Sea Harrier CAP defence: 'Just as they were busily trying to shove it up the back of the aeroplane's equipment bay we got scrambled to meet another raid. We VTO'd off, went on CAP for about two minutes and then had to go into San Carlos again. The wine stayed behind!'

Although that 'raid' was a false alarm, there was Argentinian activity at Port Stanley. The regular C-130E early morning supply aircraft had made it to the airstrip yet again, as it did right up to the end of hostilities. A plan known as Operation 'Canbelow' was aimed at catching stray Canberra B.62 recce flights and the seven C-130E/H low-flying resupply aircraft of *Grupo 1 de Transporte Aéreo*. The 'Sancha' (mother sow) Hercules were the main lifeline for the Argentine troops, making 31 successful flights into Port Stanley in May and June and two large supply drops in the Darwin area. Another 39 flights turned back when warned of the presence of RN fighters. 'Canbelow' was a determined ef-

---

[2]Almost exactly seven years previously G-VTOL had landed on the same spot.

fort to catch these brave airmen in the act. Dawn patrols were set up using the San Carlos FOB but luck was on the side of the *Sanchas*. None of the deliberate attempts to trap them succeeded. 'Sharkey' Ward's detection of C-130E TC-63 was the result of a chance radar return while on CAP. Ward and Steve Thomas were just completing a patrol under the control of HMS *Minerva* when they were alerted to a plot north-west of them. Low on fuel, they turned towards the contact and Ward picked it up on his screen at almost 40 miles—obviously a large target. At that point the C-130 received warnings from Argentinian radar and swung away on a reciprocal heading. Ward and Thomas gave chase, having first ensured that emergency decks could be made available to take the fuel-starved Sea Harriers afterwards. Lieutenant-Commander Ward fired his first AIM-9L as soon as he felt it had a chance of being within range, but it fell a little short. Closing further, he fired again, hitting the fleeing transport in the right wing at just over a mile. 'Sharkey' Ward then emptied XZ451's 30mm magazines into the burning aircraft, which cartwheeled into the sea taking its seven-man crew with it. With around 2,000lb of fuel remaining in each Sea Harrier, Ward and Thomas decided to make for *Invincible* after all, landing with 400lb still in their tanks. No further Hercules or Canberras were caught by Sea Harriers; the only other loss was Canberra B-108, brought down by a Sea Dart on the last day of the war. Lieutenant Andy McHarg closed to within four miles of a Canberra on 1 June but it popped flares and chaff, escaping the fuel-critical 'Sea Jet'. It was one of those occasions on which Sea Harrier pilots wished for just a little more speed and endurance.

There were three more losses to the Harrier force in the last weeks of the war, and one near-miss. Mike Broadwater ejected from ZA174 as he taxied for take-off on a 29 May mission to Port Stanley. *Invincible* swung into the wind and a 40kt airstream blasted across her heaving, wet and slippery deck from the side as she turned. Broadwater's aircraft suddenly lurched 90 degrees to the left, pivoting on

its main undercarriage, and slipped over the side. Its nosewheel steering, designed to give way under excessive side forces, had castored round with the wind and the brakes would not hold the bomb-laden aeroplane. On the same day 'Sharkey' Ward suffered an embarrassing mishap which fortunately turned out to be less serious. As he and Steve Thomas dropped 'thousand pounders' on the 'suspected Super Etendards' at Stanley airfield once again, Ward failed to set his armament mode selector to 'bombs' rather than 'missiles' and loosed off an unguided Sidewinder. Luckily his partner Steve Thomas was some distance behind him at the time. The real 'near miss' was by Lieutenant Charlie Cantan, who managed to bring his Sea Harrier aboard in fog so thick that it was impossible to see across *Invincible*'s flight deck. At 200ft he was able to find the ship only because it shone a searchlight vertically through the fogbank. With this diffused glow as his guide, Cantan settled into the murk and was relieved to make contact with steel rather than the South Atlantic. He had two minutes' fuel remaining when he turned off his engine.

Not so fortunate was 'Morts' Mortimer, 801 NAS's AWI. On an armed recce to Port Stanley he thought he saw an aircraft moving on the runway. He also picked up the flash of a Roland missile launch but at 10,000ft and seven miles' distance he felt relatively safe. Nevertheless, he accelerated away, only to be hit in the rear fuselage—the Roland's only strike during the campaign. Mortimer ejected from XZ456/008, escaped detection by a prowling Pucará and settled down to nine hours in his dinghy off Port Stanley. Eventually Lieutenant-Commander Dudley saw 'Morts'' strobe from his Sea King HAS.5 and pulled him aboard.

The last Harrier GR.3 loss was equally unfortunate, although the pilot again escaped injury. Peter Squire's XZ989/07 was on final approach to 'Sid's Strip' after a frustrating sortie on 8 June when no suitable targets could be found. His aircraft suffered loss of power and made a heavy landing on the grass. It slide across the MEXE runway, inhaling pieces of alu-

minium *en route*, and ended up across a slit trench. The Harrier was later 'Chinooked' to Port Stanley, where it was declared Cat-5 and used for spares. Eventually it was shipped back to Britain, and it ended its days at RAF Gütersloh's Rescue Section as 8849M.

Two more replacement GR.3s arrived on 8 June (XW919 and XZ992) direct from Ascension Island. Both had ALE-40 and 'Blue Eric' jammers fitted. Their countermeasures were first used during strafing attacks on troops near Mount Longden. GR.3s sustained considerable damage from small-arms fire as they flew low-level sorties against targets in the heavily defended hills around Port Stanley. Murdo McLeod's Harrier had several hydraulic lines severed by bullets and he had to use emergency landing gear extension. The following day a bullet passed through his windshield (later repaired with a metal patch) and cut some cockpit wiring. Peter Squire's XZ992 also took a bullet through the cockpit which, even in that cramped space, missed the pilot, while Mick Hare and 'Bomber' Harris survived Blowpipe missiles exploding 100ft above their cockpits. McLeod took his third hit on 12 June but the damage did not become apparent until he returned to *Hermes*. A bullet had punctured XW919's rear RCS duct so that as the aircraft entered a hover hot air began to leak into the tail area, starting a fire which began to melt control cables. He managed to recover safely and the blaze was extinguished, but XW919 was out of the war.

No 1(F) Squadron persisted with the LGBs, whose potential pinpoint accuracy became more desirable as targets within the populated area of Port Stanley presented themselves. A four-ship was launched on 10 June, taking advantage of the fact that a designator FAC was at last in position. However, the aircraft's take-off time was rearranged at short notice and they missed their chance as the FAC was not ready for them. All four returned with their ordnance as they were unable to provide their own target designation. Tony Harper and Nick Gilchrist tried again the following day, aiming to take out an Argentinian command HQ at Stanley

Police house. Once again they were unable to 'lase' successfully with the SAS target marker on the ground and 'dumb bombed' another, less valuable target instead. Their first successful drop took place on 13 June. Several FACs with Ferranti laser designators were placed on high ground around Port Stanley as British troops closed in on the final Argentinian positions. Peter Squire launched two Paveways against a Company HQ on Tumbledown. His first bomb was 400yd short but the second was a direct hit. The 1,000lb bomb, released at 55ft in a 3g, 45-degree climb, reached 1,500ft before being guided into the laser 'basket'. On the afternoon mission Jerry Pook got another

Harrier GR.3 XZ133/V in the markings of the HarDet at RAF Stanley in August 1983. With XZ997, this aircraft flew No 1 Squadron's last sortie of the war, an LGB attack which was called off when the surrender flags were seen. It suffered Cat-4 damage at Stanley when a portable hangar collapsed on it during a storm in July 1982, but the aircraft survived to give another ten years of RAF service. (Via R. L. Ward)

'Delta Hotel' with his LGB on a 105mm gun emplacement. The final LGB attack, and the last of No 1's 126 sorties, was scheduled for 1530Z on the 14th. 'Bomber' Harris had made contact with his FAC and the target was marked when it was reported that white flags had been sighted in Port Stanley. The Harriers were sent back to *Hermes*. There is little doubt that the accuracy of the successful LGB attacks contributed to the collapse of Argentinian morale and the surrender a few hours later. No Harrier unit had any previous experience of LGBs and it was very much a case of 'learning on the job'. Once the initial designation problems had been solved the 'LGB Harriers' could have done considerable further damage to key Argentinian installations if the latter had chosen to continue resistance.

For the Sea Harrier squadrons their final week on CAP included the last big air battle of the war on 8 June. Argentinian observers watched the Royal Fleet Auxiliaries *Sir Tristram* and *Sir Galahad* offloading ammunition at Port Pleasant and the improved weather permitted a counter strike

to be arranged. A joint strike by five Daggers from *Grupo 6* and eight of *Grupo 5*'s A-4B Skyhawks was planned. The Daggers entered from the north, strafing and damaging HMS *Plymouth*, but they then drew the CAP aircraft into a hot pursuit as they escaped unscathed to the northwest. At the same time five A-4Bs (the other three having dropped out with mechanical problems) approached at low level from the south of the islands and bombed the two troopships unopposed. For once the Skyhawks could attack from an altitude which allowed their bombs to fuse correctly and they exploded in both ships, causing the worst British casualties of the war. Although the two phases of the assault demonstrated only very basic coordination strategy, they did succeed in drawing the defences away from an area of crucial need at a time when the CAP was regrettably thin. Part of the problem was that, unbeknown to the Argentinians, 'Sid's Strip' was out of action because of Peter Squire's landing accident, preventing intervention by an 'on-site' Sea Harrier element.

Encouraged by the palpable success of this venture, the *Fuerza Aérea Argentina* decided to make further attacks on the Fitzroy area that afternoon. *Teniente* Vasquez of *Grupo 5* sank one of the landing craft from HMS *Fearless* with a single bomb but his flight of four Skyhawks was immediately pounced upon by Dave Morgan and Dave Smith. Vasquez' A-4B had its tail blown off by Morgan's second AIM-9L, the first 'Lima' having exploded the Skyhawk of *Teniente* Arraras. His Sea Harrier narrowly missed Vasquez's parachute as he baled out. Morgan attempted a gun kill on a third Skyhawk but lost his HUD and could only fire in the general direction of the A-4. His shell splashes alerted Dave Smith to the position of the fleeing Skyhawk and he nailed it with a 'Lima' from three miles, seconds before it crashed on a sandbank. It was 800 NAS's last missile firing of the war. The fourth Skyhawk dropped its external tanks and warload, heading for home, and escaped despite being spotted by an 801 NAS CAP. Lieutenant-Commander Ward and Steve Thomas had a good chance of catching it but were vectored to meet a new incursion from the north. Four Mirage IIIEs of *Grupo 8*, making a rare appearance, turned away from the approaching Sea Harriers and escaped.

The last determined attack by the A-4 force could have been the most damaging. During the events of 8 June the *Fuerza Aérea Argentina* showed most clearly the CAP's inability to tackle a carefully planned series of raids without adequate radar warning. A further demonstration was provided on 13 June when two flights of *Grupo 5* A-4Bs were despatched against advancing British troops in the Mount Kent area. The formation was led by *Capitán* Varela in his A-4B named *El Tordillo*. Approaching over the East Falklands, the aircraft completed a mission without interruption or loss which put bombs very close to the 3rd Commando Brigade HQ where the British Commander, General Moore, was directing the British advance. They passed close to four RN Sea Kings but only fired at and damaged one. But for a misunderstanding between aircrew, they could easily have

placed the rest of their bombs among another large British troop concentration. Luck was on the side of the British that day.

Despite the valiant efforts of the Sea Harrier pilots, *Grupo 5*'s ancient Douglas Skyhawks had destroyed five British warships and seriously damaged another by the end of the war. In all those cases it is now clear that adequate early warning and a greater number of Sea Harriers would have destroyed or deterred virtually all those attackers before they came within sight of their targets. As it was, between 23 May and 14 June *Grupo 4* and *5* Skyhawks, with the Daggers of *Grupo 6*, flew a total of sixteen successful attacks on British land and sea forces, each attack comprising between three and seven bombers. Although aircraft were lost to the ships' missile defences on several of these missions, only three were successfully intercepted by Sea Harriers.

Sea Harrier bombing sorties continued throughout the last stages of the war. Twelve 1,000lb bombs were aimed at Port Stanley yet again on 11 June to try and curtail Pucará flights—without success. 800 NAS's war finished with a couple more ingenious but unsuccessful attempts to catch the elusive C-130Es, as did 801 NAS's. The last of the 599 combat missions was a 'Canbelow' sortie. It drove a pair of Canberras within range of the Sea Dart launchers of HMS *Exeter*, which shot one of the bombers down. In 786 flying hours Lieutenant-Commander Ward's pilots had expended 56,000lb of bombs, 3,061 30mm shells and a dozen Sidewinders. Each pilot averaged 57 sorties. 800 NAS's larger number of aircraft flew 1,126 sorties in all.

One Argentinian target which survived the war was the chain of early-warning radar sets used throughout hostilities to vector attacking aircraft around or away from Sea Harrier patrols.[3] Paradoxically, the tendency to send attacking formations back to the mainland if there was a hint of Sea Harriers in the area was an advantage in that it reduced the number of actual strikes on the British forces. In other ways, the removal of those elements of the radar system which were outside residen-

tial areas would have presented clear advantages, and it is puzzling that this does not appear to have been a priority for air attacks or SAS covert operations.

AFTERMATH

When the surrender came on 14 June the Harrier GR.3s were quickly reconfigured for air defence in case there were Argentinians on the mainland with different ideas. Stanley airfield became a base for Harrier and Sea Harrier defensive operations following a plan which had been organized on HMS *Fearless* before the surrender by a team including Tim Gedge. *Hermes* remained in the TEZ while *Invincible* withdrew for two weeks' recuperation and repairs and then returned to Britain on 4 July when *Invincible* resumed her role. *Hermes'* twelve Sea Harriers returned to Yeovilton between 19 and 21 June. *Invincible* remained in the South Atlantic with ten aircraft and on 14 July it was announced that she would not be sold to Australia after all. Her aircraft were rotated to and from San Carlos, Port Stanley and the carrier itself until she in turn was relieved on 28 August by HMS *Illustrious*. She returned to Portsmouth and her eight aircraft (two had switched to *Illustrious*) were back at Yeovilton on 17 September.

809 NAS, which was aboard *Illustrious* on her arrival in the South Atlantic, had lived up to its Phoenix tail logo and regrouped as a separate squadron during June, the month in which the new ship was commissioned. If the war had continued for much longer it is likely that *Illustrious* would have taken aboard Sidewinder-armed RAF Harrier GR.3s as her fixed-wing component because of the shortage of Sea Harriers.[4] The cessation of hostilities made more aircraft available to 809 NAS.

Port Stanley airfield required considerable rework and extension before it could operate an RAF Phantom FGR.2 detach-

---

[3] Three captured Skyguard units were brought back to the UK and used by the RAF as radar traps to police low-flying routes. They can track aircraft from a range of ten miles up to 25,000ft.
[4] No IV Squadron RAF provided a detachment of six GR.3s led by Squadron Leader Dave Fisher for her work-up.

ment to defend the newly recaptured territory, so Harriers were required to provide interim air defence. 809 NAS went
south to relieve 801 NAS and *Invincible* of
that task. Tim Gedge resumed control of
his squadron and it absorbed some bat-
tle-hardened pilots and aircraft from 800
NAS on their return from the Falklands.
Rod Frederiksen, Martin Hale and Dave
Austin were signed up after some leave and
they were joined later by some other veterans—'Soapy' Watson, Andy George,
Dave Smith, John Leeming (later relieved
by Simon Hargreaves), Dave Morgan,
Dave Braithwaite (one of the original
700A Squadron pilots) and Clive Morell
all served with 809 NAS at various times
between July and December 1982.

Eight Sea Harriers were put through
post-war cycles of maintenance and were
ready by 31 July, Yeovilton's 'Falklands
Celebration' Air Day. One unexpected
maintenance problem manifested itself
during the rehearsal for that occasion. At
one point Yeovilton's Runway 22 was
embarrassingly blocked by a Sea Harrier
at each end, both of which had suffered
nosewheel failure while taxiing. The cause
was wheel-bearing corrosion from months

**In May 1992 Sea Harrier FRS.1s were
still serving on HMS *Invincible* with
800 NAS: conversion to F/A.2 standard
was still two years away. ZD579 was
from the second production batch,
ordered a month after the Falklands
campaign. (Via R. L. Ward)**

on deck in the Falklands arena. Undercarriage inspections were usually done on a
tyre-replacement basis, but constant deck
(rather than runway) operation caused little tyre wear so the problem had gone
unnoticed.

809 NAS aircraft were also given the
twin-Sidewinder rails, which had been
designed originally as a USMC study and
had been trialled by BAe, and new 190gal
drop tanks. These were basically 230gal
Hunter tanks with a section removed. Initially the larger tanks caused slight pitch-
up problems on deck-launch. With 809
NAS were Rod Frederiksen and Taylor
Scott (returning once again to his role as
RN Reservist); the latter had been a crucial member of the nucleus 809 training

**ZA176, which transferred from 809 to
801 NAS, seen in 1983 just before its
unscheduled descent on to the freighter
Alraigo. After repair it was issued to 899
NAS, converted to an F/A .2 and moved to
801 NAS in 1994. (Via R. L. Ward)**

effort during the war and had sailed with
809 as AWI. Both men had wide experience of testing Sea Harriers at A&AEE.
They were able to re-set the aircraft's tailplane trim limits *en voyage* and the new wing
tanks were cleared for use from late September. As an interim measure, four aircraft flew back to Yeovilton from the carrier in the Bay of Biscay when the problem was discovered and came back with
some 100gal versions as a stop-gap. They
were actually suspended on GR.3 pylons

because there was a shortage of Sea Harrier pylons too!

Both the missile and tank improvements could have made a real difference to the punch and endurance of the CAP Sea Harriers if they could have been available a couple of months earlier, but BAe and other manufacturers made an extraordinary effort to provide the Task Force with whatever it needed. Spare parts were always available. During the war period BAe's Kingston-Brough Division produced 4,100 separate items for the Task Force, four times the usual production rate. They included over 300 modification kits for the various armament and wiring changes. The Navy itself produced large numbers of extra items including 56 sets of redesigned Aden gun link chutes, produced at RNAY Fleetlands.

On 17 October Tim Gedge and his wingman Pete Collins escorted the first No 29 Squadron Phantoms into Port Stanley's newly refurbished airfield and the newcomers took over air defence duties on 22 October, freeing *Illustrious* to transfer to the Caribbean. On the ship's return to Britain 809 NAS was disbanded once again, on 17 December 1982.

As the Sea Harrier and Harrier GR.3 aircraft returned to routine squadron work there was plenty of maintenance and rectification to catch up. Their 90 per cent serviceability had been an impressive trib-

ute to a tough, simple aeroplane without very many temperamental systems. A large section of the force spent the war period mainly on *Hermes*' deck in all weathers. The maintainers' ingenuity was tested to the maximum in the attempt to keep the salt moisture out of the airframe and avionics by using various sprays and sealants, rubber compounds and clear plastic film. Availability was sustained partly by compressing maintenance schedules, in consultation with BAe. Fortunately, most inspection and rectification could be done at night or on bad-weather days when the opposition stayed at home. Other peacetime rules, such as keeping armed aircraft out of hangars and not refuelling and re-arming at the same time had to be overlooked. Operating from *Hermes*' crowded deck was also more difficult than usual. Aircraft had to be parked facing the stern and taxied to the stern in order to queue up for take-off.

Of all the returning aircrew the GR.3 pilots were probably the most pleased to be back. Having existed in the cramped conditions of HMS *Hermes*, they were put ashore at Port Stanley in tented accommodation during the Falklands winter. Although their deployment to the South Atlantic had been an outstanding success militarily, one pilot described it to the authors as 'not a particularly happy time. They didn't have much say in their tasking,

ZA194 had a Mirage to its credit while with 800 NAS. On its return to Yeovilton the aircraft was speedily turned around and re-embarked on board HMS *Illustrious*. (Authors)

which consisted mainly of dangerous, mud-moving CAS missions where they took a lot of damage.' Moreover, they were working without their usual nav-attack procedures and against targets for which there was little intelligence information. Their aircraft remained at Port Stanley and were joined by four more replacements to become the Harrier Detachment (HarDet), RAF Stanley, with ten GR.3s, on 4 July. Over the following year aircraft as well as crew were rotated back to the United Kingdom, particularly aircraft which had received battle damage. The HarDet remained in place until November 1982 and thereafter its task was performed by a rota of crews from all RAF Harrier units, including Bob Iveson and other Falklands veterans. On 20 August the following year No 1453 Flight was established and it was responsible for Harrier operations alongside No 29 Squadron (later No 23 Squadron) Phantoms until the opening of the new Mount Pleasant airport in May 1985. Shortly afterwards the Flight was disbanded and its aircraft returned to Wittering.

An order for fourteen new Sea Harrier FRS.1 aircraft (ZD578–582 and ZD607–

615) was announced soon after the cessation of hostilities, which more than compensated for the eight lost to all causes up to that point. Nine more (ZE690–698) were ordered in 1984 so as to raise the standard shipborne complement from five to eight. Four Harrier GR.3 attrition replacements (ZD667–670) were also ordered in July 1983. HMS *Hermes*, which had been in RN service since 1959 but was actually laid down in 1944, was retained by the Royal Navy until November 1983. In May 1987 she was recommissioned by the Indian Navy as INS *Viraat* (Mighty) and was scheduled to operate Sea Harriers for a further ten years alongside INS *Vikrant*.

GR.3 FINALE

When 1453 Flight, defenders of the Falklands, returned to Wittering the end was already in sight for the Harrier GR.3. The first GR.5 had flown in April 1985 and plans were being laid to re-equip at least two of the front-line units with this new, AV-8B-derived variant.[5] Initially it was

Lieutenant-Commander Simon Hargreaves (centre) meets pilots from Eastern European air forces at Yeovilton's D-Day flypast rehearsals, including Czech MiG-23 pilot Josef Sarina. (Via Simon Hargreaves)

planned to update as many as forty GR.3s in order to keep them in service for at least another ten years. The update proposals took several forms, most involving a revised wing. Inadequate stores carriage provision on the GR.3 ruled out the continuing post-Falklands Phase 6 update programme as an answer to the lack of pylon space as this involved rewiring the outer pair for AIM-9 Sidewinders. In 1985 aircraft were still receiving the Phase 6 inputs at St Athan, which took over deep maintenance of GR.3s from Gütersloh and Wittering in 1983. Unlike Sea Harriers, the GR.3s visited the Welsh maintenance base on a flight-hours basis and equipment updates were done at the 2,000hr major inspection stage.

Phase 7 updates would have involved a major redesign of the airframe and once these were ruled out in favour of a completely new Harrier II design it was inevitable that the remaining GR.3s would gradually be sidelined.[6] In fact, the process took longer than expected as a result of lengthy delays in the introduction of the new-generation Harrier. The GR.3 force flew on for another decade after 'Corporate', albeit in ever-diminishing numbers.

Immediately after the Falklands period the force returned to big-league training,

with exercises such as 'Lionheart' (September 1984) in which the Gütersloh squadrons flew 120 sorties from five FOBs in a mere four hours. Exercise 'Coldfire' the following autumn tested the RAFG squadrons' ability to operate from stretches of German autobahn near Paderborn, to the delight of large crowds of spectators. No 1 Squadron periodically practised its 'naval' commitment too. In November 1987 a pair of their GR.3s operated alongside 800 NAS Sea Harriers on HMS *Ark Royal* for Exercise 'Purple Warrior'.

However, the run-down of GR.3 operations began in 1988, the year in which Wittering began to train pilots on the Harrier GR.5. St Athan received its last GR.3 for major servicing the same year. By February 1991 Wittering's GR.3 establishment was reduced to a mere six aircraft to supply the Belize Flight with Harriers and 'current' pilots. On 20 May 1994 Wittering celebrated the 25th Anniversary of the Harrier's service entry with No 1 Squadron. Their intended flypast of 25 aircraft was reduced to ten when appalling weather descended on the base. A lone GR.3 displayed in the murk and XV279, the fourth DB Harrier, was pulled out for ground display. The last flights by GR.3s took place on 29 June 1994 when ZD670/3A and ZD668/3E, the last two Harriers with 20(R) Squadron, flew a round trip from Wittering.

Although most of the surviving GR.3s at the time still had a fair number of hours left on their airframes, the ample supply of GR.5 and follow-on GR.7 Harriers left them no place in the RAF. For a time the Royal Navy thought that a few airframes might be converted to air-to-air 'buddy' tanker configuration to feed their sea-going stablemates, but funding was not made available. Instead, a number of GR.3 Pegasus engines were converted to Mk 106 standard to provide the power for a new generation of Sea Harrier, the F/A.2. Several other GR.3s were supplied to RN bases as aircraft handling trainers or instructional airframes.

---

[5] Described fully in 'Improving the Breed', especially Mount of the Gods.
[6] See 'Improving the Breed', below.

6. Harrier Plus

The Harrier's enthusiastic welcome by the RAF and USMC more than compensated for its awkward birth. For the aircraft's supporters, two years of proven service success vindicated their desire to see the concept developed into a more capable strike fighter. They could not have foreseen just how difficult that process was to be.

The most obvious need was the shed the Harrier's 'short range–low payload' image. Sir Sidney Camm always argued that the aircraft would never attract a wide market until it could equal the performance of 'world standard' fighters like the F-4 Phantom—and offer V/STOL too. Ralph Hooper was among a minority at HSA who maintained that a V/STOL attacker without supersonic performance, or the F-4's large warload, could still be successful. His philosophy was shared by his successor, John Fozard, who felt that the P.1154 had been too ambitious as an initial V/STOL design, even though it might have been workable. Other 'world standard' fighters such as the F-16 were under the microscope as the RAF began to assemble ideas for a follow-on Harrier. AST.403 was their far-reaching Air Staff Target for a replacement for both the Harrier and the Jaguar. Having requested, and then rejected, the supersonic P.1154, the RAF once again saw sonic performance as an attractive feature for a new V/STOL design. As that debate progressed, design initiatives were under way in the United States which would give more tangible shape to the project.

In 1969 HSA had reached a 15-year agreement with McDonnell-Douglas to cover the licence manufacture of the AV-8A. Although that option was not exercised, it also provided for an exchange of V/STOL research data and led to joint

A late production NATC AV-8A (BuNo 159255) keeps station with the first FSD AV-8B (BuNo 161396) over Eastern Missouri. This AV-8B had double-row blow-in doors and no LERX (which were added to meet RAF turning performance requirements). (BAe)

John Fawcett with the second FSD AV-8B, BuNo 161397, which was used for engine, fuel system and intake tests. In addition to its smart black, red and gold on white paint job, it had LERX and the revised single-row blow-in doors. The enlarged LIDs are clearly visible. (Via John Fawcett)

studies for potential successors to the first-generation Harrier. A first nine-month phase of studies was completed in December 1973 and presented to the British and United States governments. Any design outcome was conceived on an equal-partner basis, with airframe work to be shared between the two companies, and Pratt & Whitney were written-in as partners on engine design. In drafting their proposals HSA drew on design experience with the HS.1184 (a big-wing Harrier concept) while McDonnell-Douglas (McAir) used their study of an advanced Harrier, tagged AV-8C (but quite different from the variant which eventually bore that designation), a response to a US Navy Air Sys-

tems Command requirement for an attack type to operate from their planned Sea Control Ships. It was hoped that the USN would become a customer for a new joint project, thereby vastly increasing the world market for the type. The Advanced Harrier would also replace the RAF's GR.3 force and the Marines' AV-8As and A-4M Skyhawks and provide the Royal Navy with something to defend their forthcoming 'through-deck cruisers'.

The Joint Managing Board in charge of the proposals rapidly coordinated its ideas and in 1974 set out its Phase I specification for the AV-16A (originally referred to as the AV-8X), so-called because it sought to double the AV-8A's payload/radius. The Harrier has always been an aircraft designed around an engine and it appeared that a serious redesign of the Pegasus was the key to performance upgrades of that magnitude. Rolls-Royce offered the Pegasus 15, which had been bench-run at 24,500lb thrust, the extra power coming partly from a $2^3/4$in (7cm)

increase in front-fan diameter. For the airframe designers this meant starting with a fuselage redesign, bigger intakes and re-inforced nozzles. To these would be added new avionics, a strengthened undercarriage and, crucially, a new wing to give the additional range and load-lifting factors.

Separate wing designs were undertaken on both sides of the Atlantic as part of Phase II of the process and both were tested in the NASA-Ames wind tunnel. Anticipated performance figures for the AV-16A seem modest in the light of the subsequent AV-8B—a VTO gross weight of 21,500lb, or 25,000lb with a 320ft deck run, and a VTO payload of 2,000lb over a 300nm radius (4,000lb over the same distance with STO). Although the basic AV-16A was to be subsonic, the Board drafted a supersonic variant to satisfy potential customers who still felt that a subsonic attack fighter could not be taken seriously. This was called AV-16S-6 (or HS.1185 at Kingston) and it used a proposed Pegasus 15 with PCB which owed something to Rolls-Royce's BS.100 engine trials for the P.1154 in 1961.

Sadly, 1974 was an unpropitious time to be floating a project the cost estimates for which started at $31 billion, including $500m for engine development, and would probably have risen considerably. Governments were badly shaken by the world oil crisis and subsequent inflation. In Britain the Labour Government was scared off by the likely cost and saw the Advanced Harrier as a tempting target for cancellation. Using the pretext of 'lack of common ground' between the partners, the March 1975 White Paper on Defence took the United Kingdom out of the project. The AV-16A faded out by the year's end, but much had been learned, particularly in the vital area of wing design, and McAir quickly pressed ahead with its own development proposals.

Inevitably, talk of 'selling our V/STOL birthright to the USA' followed the British Defence Minister Roy Mason's decision—

The expression 'big-wing Harrier' makes visual sense in Frank Mormillo's portrait of a 3rd MAW AV-8B. (Frank Mormillo)

and has continued ever since. While separate Harrier studies continued in Britain it was clear that no funding could be found there, or indeed in the United States, for a radical revision of the Pegasus engine, which still seemed basic to a major performance increase. McAir therefore resolved to make do with the F402-RR-404 version and seek performance gains in other ways within the 'minimum change' brief that they were given. Their main impetus was a clearly stated USMC requirement for an improved Harrier. In May 1973 the Marines' Commandant, General R. E. Cushman, issued an SOR (Specific Operating Requirement) for an advanced attack aircraft. Nine months later, in a far-reaching statement, he told the Senate Armed Forces Committee, 'The operational success of the AV-8A has confirmed our belief that a follow-on aircraft will meet our needs for future light attack requirements and permit us to achieve our goal of an all-V/STOL light attack force.' What the Marines wanted was a much simpler aircraft than the AV-16A and they were on their own in the fight to get it. After the demise of the AV-

16 the USN turned to NA Rockwell's XFV-12A, a complex canard V/STOL proposal which never progressed beyond the prototype stage. The RAF was still thinking in terms of an all-British 'Super Harrier' which would probably have been faster and more biased towards air-to-air fighting, and attack sorties in the demanding Northern European scenario.

Without the extra 15 per cent thrust of the Pegasus 15 to deliver the required performance bonus, McAir designers looked instead to aerodynamics and new lightweight materials. A design team led by T. R. Lacey began work on a new wing which would be the key to doubling Harrier's payload/radius. It used NASA's supercritical research data, giving the first military service application to several years of work on the subject. The wing had increased aspect ratio to enhance cruise performance and a 4-degree reduction in sweepback (to 36 degrees) for better longitudinal stability, and the span grew to 30.3ft to allow for an extra pair of pylons. With an increase in thickness/chord ratio from 8.5 per cent to 10 per cent and greater area (230 sq ft), the new wing could accommodate 4,950lb of internal fuel, 2,000lb more than the AV-8A and worth 30 minutes 'on-station' time in combat. This is turn freed the inboard pylons for weapons rather than fuel. Designing a bigger wing was an obvious way of giving more lift capability, but to do so without significantly increasing weight was a major achievement. On the early Harriers the wing had to be kept as small as possible to preserve any real V/STOL uplift ability with marginal engine power. Lacey's team, in collaboration with NAVAIR's Aero-Hydraulic Facility, achieved the required lift and actually saved 330lb weight compared with an equivalent metal structure. To do this they used advanced composite materials for 63 per cent (by weight) of the structure. Conventional metals were used only for the wingtips, leading edges, pylon and outrigger attachment points and centreline rib. Like all Harrier wings, it had to be a one-piece structure, removable for engine changes. It was the world's largest single airframe component to be manufactured in epoxy-resin composite

VMAT-203 were tasked with training Harrier II pilots, initially under the supervision of their CO, Colonel M. D. Ryan. BuNo 162951 is seen here in 1994 with 'KD' codes. (Via Steve Dunkin)

material. The continuous lower skin was fixed; the upper was made detachable for servicing.

COMPOSITES

Although McAir take credit for investing in the manufacturing capacity for composite parts (and used them for the F/A-18 too), much of the research on graphite epoxy and carbon fibre composites was done at RAE Farnborough in the mid-1960s and shared under the 1969 exchange-of-data agreement. The new lamination fabricating buildings were erected at St Louis, one of them a lay-up room where huge 'mats' of carbon fibre material could be cut to shape by laser or NC knife cutter. The laminated sheets were impregnated with epoxy resin and then

placed in a giant autoclave under 200psi pressure and heated to 500°F. Spars and ribs were vacuum-formed. The resulting structure was corrosion-proof, practically fatigue-proof and up to 400 per cent stronger than a similar aluminium fabrication. Resin technology advanced rapidly and by 1983 gave designers the use of composites far stronger than titanium and sufficiently heat resistant to be used near the 'hot end' of jet engines. Bismaleimide (BMI) resins retain their strength up to 450°F.

Kingston's design team used metal as the basis of their proposed wing structure, lacking the access to British composite manufacturing. Partly also this was a result of RAF planning at the time. Unlike the USMC, the RAF placed a high premium on air-to-air survivability for their 'follow-on' Harrier. The existing GR.3 force was tasked with turning back Eastern bloc tank forces in a high-threat environment where self-defence was a better bet than relying on fighter cover. As all five

GR.3 pylons were needed for weapons like CBU or fuel, or a recce pod, there was nowhere to hang a couple of AIM-9 missiles. Overwing pylons *à la* Jaguar were flight-tested but imposed a weight penalty; wing-tip attachments were considered but rejected (as frequently happens in Harrier design circles!). Lacking Government support for an all-new jet with composites, Kingston envisaged designing a replacement 'tin wing' for the GR.3 fleet. This would have been similar to the McAir wing (which would not fit the GR.3) but faster and less draggy. The 'St Louis' wing's only real disadvantage was its 85kt speed penalty on the GR.3/AV-8A's maximum (sea-level) 635kt. Refitting the GR.3 fleet of about 74 aircraft with a larger metal wing and a new digital INS seemed a cheap solution and a means of preserving British design initiative as it still left the way open for later, more radical developments. In practice, it was realised that taking so many GR.3s off the ramps for re-work would cause too serious a reduction in the force's credibility.

As an alternative, the RAF was offered a more expensive 'new' Harrier with Sea Harrier-type forward fuselage and raised cockpit, Pegasus 11-35 engine, leading edge extensions (LEX or LERX) and lift improvement devices (LIDs) which were strakes fitted to the gun pods to increase lift in VTOL mode. A third, and obviously less attractive, possibility was the offer of low-time ex-USMC AV-8A/Cs as attrition replacements on the understanding that they might be converted to GR.3 standard and possibly re-winged too.

While the two major companies appeared to be following very different paths there was still a considerable sharing of ideas. Two HSA concepts were integral to the success of McAir's next design phase: enlarged flaps and LIDs. Both had been considered and rejected at Kingston as they seemed to offer marginal lift increases at a time when a more powerful Pegasus looked to be a simpler and more certain solution to increased V/STOL payloads. McAir subjected them to more extensive research and adopted them for the 'full-size wind-tunnel model' which was used to test the supercritical wing. This

The AV-8B introduced true 'bubble canopy' visibility, helped by an elevated seat position. VMA-331's 'Bombing Bumblebee' insignia appears below the cockpit of 03 VL. (Frank Mormillo)

was actually a crashed and rebuilt AV-8A with a metal replica of the new wing. Strakes were attached to the gun pods and a hinged, retractable 'dam' was attached behind the nosewheel bay. Together, these LIDs formed a three-sided 'fence' which helped to trap hot gases from the nozzles in the VTO position. Normally these gases would escape at high velocity from under the fuselage, creating low-pressure under the wings when the fuselage is close to the ground and sucking the aircraft against the ground—thereby effectively increasing take-off weight. Additionally, some of the hot gases would tend to enter the engine intakes, increasing inlet temperature and causing flow distortion. Both would cause reduced thrust and surge margins. In early tests this simple combination of extended strakes and dam was surprisingly effective, adding over 1,200lb of extra VTO lift.

The enlarged 'positive circulation' flaps interacted with the rear nozzles to produce powerful airflow in a similar way to blown flaps. In STO mode they lowered to 61 degrees and added over 7,600lb to STO lift. A final external change was to the front nozzles. After trials with a number of different shapes in an attempt to direct the

downwards efflux more precisely, McAir devised zero-scarf nozzles with extended square-cut ends. These were tested at Rolls-Royce Patchway (flight-tested in GR.3 XV277) and in the wind tunnel and they added up to 200lb of extra lift by channelling their efflux more efficiently into the area between the inboard pylons, LIDs and 'dam' on each side of the fuselage.

McAir were fortunate in having access to the NASA-Ames wind tunnel to prove these aerodynamic changes. The modified AV-8A, complete with fully instrumented Pegasus, was ready in August 1975 and was mounted on three movable pylons in the huge 40 by 80ft 'open working' section of the tunnel. Tests continued until 18 September 1976 and Phase I of the programme, initiated in May 1975 with the prospect of a USMC order, was wound up in October of that year. The results were good enough to enable Phase II, the Flight Demonstration stage to begin.

TESTING TIMES

To prove the revised airframe, two more AV-8As were modified to YAV-8B standard and flight-tested between November 1978 and February 1981, following the go-ahead from the Department of Defense on 27 July 1976. The two aircraft, BuNos 158394 and 158395, were the final pair

from the first AV-8A production Block. They were given the supercritical wing, with its flattened upper surface and bulged underside, optimised for high subsonic cruise and made of composite materials. The outriggers were relocated inboard, reducing the track from 22ft 2in to 16ft 7in and thereby easing deck handling. The outrigger legs retracted into trailing-edge fairings reminiscent of the AV-16A and P.1154. Revisions to the intakes consisted of an elliptical cowl rim and a double row of blow-in doors in place of the AV-8A's eight per side. This was intended to give extra throat area to the inlet and the revision appeared for a time on the early production aircraft too. In total, 185 flights were made by McAir's Charlie Plummer and his team, with a variety of underwing stores including 300gal tanks on each side of the four 'wet' pylons and, on one occasion, a massive 12,500lb bomb load. Handling, particularly in the hover, was found to be easier and more predictable than in previous models. The No 2 aircraft was lost near the Lake of Ozarks in November 1979 following a flame-out at 37,000ft en route to Whiteman AFB for UK MoD evaluation. After several attempts at a relight the pilot took to his 'chute at 5,000ft. Trials continued without serious delay although surge problems with the engine, which may have caused the accident, were not fully resolved until the F402-RR-406 engine became available in 1984. YAV-8B No 1 performed shipboard tests on *Saipan* (LHA-2) and began ski-jump trials in March 1979 using a ramp built by Fairey Engineering in the UK and erected at Patuxent River. Eventually it joined the NASA Test Fleet as N704NA, and it was still there in 1992.

With such dramatic performance improvements, a minimum-risk interim conversion of the existing AV-8A fleet was briefly considered, following the RAF's investigation of re-lifing their GR.3s. One outcome of this was the AV-8C CILOP programme. Most important among the decisions prompted by YAV-8B experience was the clearance to proceed with construction of four Full-Scale Development (FSD) AV-8Bs, given on 11 November 1981. In the intervening period of delays

Captain Buckley of VMA-513 'on your tail' over the Colorado River, crossing the border between California and Arizona. (Frank Mormillo)

caused by political opposition, McAir had pushed ahead with many other changes to the aircraft. The first of these consisted of further revision of the intake profile and an enlarged wing/fuselage fairing to minimise the severe profile drag noted in the two prototype YAV-8Bs. As no major additional engine funding had been sanctioned, the FSD machines used the good old Pegasus, more or less as it had been for the previous decade. In the F402-RR-404 version, which they used, Patchway's engineers managed to squeeze out a little more thrust—21,180lb against 20,930 for the -402 in the AV-8A. In fact, there had been many improvements to the engine but these mainly affected reliability and ease of maintenance. Cheaper operating costs were more good news to the Defense Systems Acquisition Review Council (DSARC) when, in March 1976, they approved a programme which not only included the two YAV-8Bs and four FSD aircraft but envisaged these as the precursors of 336 production aircraft to replace both AV-8A and A-4M in USMC service. This was to be the realization of General Cushman's vision of an 'all V/STOL light attack force'.

There were still many obstacles ahead, most of them political. In the background were the two major 'image' problems which had always afflicted the Harrier in the USA. One was that it was an 'alien foreign device' which was bought instead of an American product for that most American of institutions, the Marine Corps. A second (in seeming justification of the first) was that it 'couldn't carry a pack of cigarettes the length of a football field'. Ill-informed critics harped upon the fact that the AV-8A was British-built and that its VTOL tactical radius with a couple of Mk 83 bombs was nowhere near that of its stablemate, the all-American Skyhawk. This view, of course, ignored the USMC's preferred STOL operating methods. The AV-8A could carry a respectable 3,000lb of ordnance over a 380nm radius, given a 1,200ft take-off run. In practice, distances-to-target would be much shorter, but this still compared favourably with the A-4M's 4,000lb over a 450nm radius, considering that the Skyhawk was limited to established airfields or complex SATS forward sites.

With the AV-8B the Harrier's comparative performance was elevated to the 'no contest' level. Charlie Plummer demonstrated this on an early FSD sortie. Flying from NATC Patuxent River in an AV-8B with the handicap of 800lb of test gear, he took off from a 700ft ground run, car-

ried seven 500lb bombs for 422 miles, dropped them exactly on target and returned to Pax River with 1,800lb of fuel. He then flew a CAS sortie with twelve 500lb bombs, from a 1,200ft ground run. His 'target' this time was 185 miles away and he returned to make a vertical landing with a 600lb fuel reserve. This was precisely what the Marines wanted. Colonel Stan Lewis, AV-8B Project Manager, explained to a Congressional subcommittee: 'The ability of the AV-8B to operate from short, austere sites is its most valuable feature in the Marines' eyes. It will be able to begin isolation of the battle area of the Marines' landing zones while operating from the decks of amphibious helicopter ships, long before the task force reaches the amphibious objective area. Once ashore the AV-8B will carry its doubled payloads (compared with the AV-8A) from the road segments, captured bombed-out runways, without the need for construction or repair of massive jet bases.'

Elsewhere in the US government less friendly voices were in evidence. Through President Carter's Administration (1976–80) there were many attempts to block the development of the AV-8B by withholding funds. In June 1987 the Armed Forces Committee of the House of Representatives, under Congressman Les Aspin, recommended a plan to 'zero-out' AV-8B production at the end of 1989. This would have stopped production at 180 aircraft, preventing replacement of the A-4M units. The motive in this case was probably to secure Navy funds for the A-6F Intruder (later cancelled) and to push for an all-Hornet Marine Air Component. While FSD testing was under way, Carter's Defense Secretary, Harold Brown, managed to block funds for the project, causing a two-year delay in full procurement plans. In June 1979 he opposed a full Congressional vote, refused to request AV-8 funding, and caused the project to be omitted from the Government's five-year procurement plan. Eventually Congress forced the AV-8B back into the budget, but funding was delayed until 1982. Such delaying tactics obviously increased programme costs, playing into the hands of the cancellation lobby. Eventually, in April 1980, the General Accounting Office recommended that Brown should either proceed with production or cancel the entire programme. Six months later Ronald Reagan was elected into office, heralding a more sympathetic approach to defence issues.

With the entire AV-8B project in financial jeopardy throughout the second half of the 1970s, McAir turned once again to the prospect of shared production and purchase with the United Kingdom. Although the partner companies had been concerned with different design issues since the AV-16A, they began to converge in the late 1970s. Kingston's project (which acquired the inevitable label 'GR.5' at this time), retained the 'tin wing' (aimed at a 50kt speed increase over the YAV-8B version), smaller flaps and a British nav-attack system. However, it took aboard the YAV-8B's revised intake, zero-scarf nozzles and LIDs (or CADs to the RAF). HSA (absorbed into British Aerospace after 1977) also proposed LERX at the wing roots to add 0.5/1.0g to turning performance and permit higher 'alpha' (AOA) in the air-to-air regime. They also added a little wing area, and tests on GR.3 XV277 showed that they delayed separation of airflow at the onset of buffet. In due course these appeared on AV-8B, as did the raised cockpit, which first emerged on the Sea Harrier, improved further with a bubble canopy.

THE RAF REQUIREMENT

The RAF was still keen to have a GR.5 built to its own specifications and BAe understandably preferred the idea of retaining a strong design input to V/STOL development. But in St Louis the prospect of an RAF order for up to 100 AV-8Bs with slight changes to suit the customer was seen as a decisive factor in the political battle to ensure full production of the type. Under the 15-year agreement this would have to be on a shared basis, but at least the Marines order could be eased through the conflicts over funding. Although voices were raised in the United States over the issue of work-sharing, there was reassurance in the name 'McDonnell Douglas AV-8B'. In Britain there was proportionately more outcry over the thought of BAe becoming a mere subcontractor to McAir on the project and losing its V/STOL lead. In fact, the work-share offer was generous enough to leave the RAF

Harrier II '07 VL' low and fast over the Nevada Desert on a live weapons sortie from NAS Fallon with 500lb retard bombs in October 1985. (Via Andy Evans)

Departing the aircraft 'Harrier-style', a pilot saves his groundcrew the trouble of erecting the crew ladder. (Frank Mormillo)

with little option. Conservative Defence Minister John Nott's budget for 1981–82 mentioned a 'complete re-assessment of RAF plans for an advanced VTOL fighter'. Four months later an initial order for 60 GR.5s, based on AV-8B, was shaping up. In August 1981 a Memorandum of Understanding (MoU) was signed, confirming the RAF order as part of an agreement giving McAir 60 per cent of airframe manufacture (in man-hours), with 40 per cent to BAe. The larger USMC order entitled McAir to 75 per cent of final assembly and 100 per cent for any export examples. Rolls-Royce took three-quarters of the Pegasus work, giving 25 per cent to Pratt & Whitney/United Technologies.

British manufacturing participation had, in fact, already begun. By August 1981 BAe had delivered rear fuselage assemblies to St Louis for the four FSD aircraft (BuNos 161396–399). Substantially similar to the structures already provided with the AV-8A batches, the new units had a taller Sea Harrier-type fin. In the McAir complex they were attached to a revised, extended centre fuselage and a completely new front fuselage. Constructed of composite materials and 25 per cent lighter than an equivalent metal fabrication, the front fuselage provided far more equipment space as the pilot's position was raised 10.5in and given a new canopy with a wrap-around single-piece windshield. To counterbalance extra weight in the nose, the fuselage aft of the wing had an 18in extension, stressed for increased aerodynamic loads. A new tailplane of composites, with an aluminium leading edge and a detachable honeycomb trailing edge, replaced the original. This also dispensed with the distinctive leading-edge kink of earlier Harriers, originally introduced as a 'quick fix' on P.1127 XP984 to improve longitudinal stability. Internal fuel capacity in the larger wing increased by 50 per cent. Four of the seven pylons were 'plumbed' for fuel (double the AV-8A's pylon load), allowing the carriage of four 300gal ferry tanks for a ferry range of

2,500nm. Alternatively, full internal fuel plus 9,200lb of stores could be carried—the same as the A-4M. To satisfy the RAF requirement, FSD No 2 and subsequent aircraft also had LERX fitted.

The AV-8B therefore looked very different from its predecessor, but many of the changes were internal. The Harrier was conceived at a time when 'faster and higher' were fighter designers' main targets. By the late 1970s, when absolute performance maxima had begun to level off, more thought was given to the pilot and his ever-increasing workload. The AV-8A operated extensively on old-fashioned, heads-down switch management in a cockpit which seemed an ergonomic slum to 'teen fighter' pilots. McAir made use of their experience with the F-15 Eagle and F/A-18 to redesign the Harrier cockpit and many of its pilot's tasks from scratch.

The starting-point was a set of basic requests from the Marines. For example, they wanted to be able to set up an attack profile with ordnance and be able to use their guns to keep the AAA down. On the AV-8A control panels, that meant an 'either bombs or guns' situation, and some complex switch-shifting to make the change. They also wanted a Harrier with better rearward visibility. A new canopy and less glove-like cockpit meant that the pilot could swivel his head back to see his tailplane and pylons and have a far better view downwards from the canopy sides and over the nose. All of this is vital in a low-level CAS scenario where SAMs and AAA give a pilot split-second warning of

their threats. Also on the request list was OBOGS, an on-board oxygen generating system. Replacing the AV-8A's 5-litre liquid oxygen supply with a 'make your own' system freed the aircraft from frequent LOX replenishments which were not always readily available on Navy vessels or forward bases.

The USMC also wanted an aircraft which was easier to fly. Although some experienced AV-8A pilots came to prefer their aircraft's more 'sporty' handling compared to the more solid AV-8B, the former had suffered major attrition in the mid-1970s when 'nugget' pilots began to go through the training programme. In fact, one of the reasons that the AV-8B was so urgently needed was that attrition had reduced front-line strength by almost 25 per cent by 1982: only 68 of the original 110 USMC Harriers remained in service. In the words of Colonel Harry W. Blot, USMC Programme Manager for the AV-8B, 'It took a superior pilot to be effective in the AV-8A. The AV-8B is a simpler airplane to fly.'

Huge advances in avionics and flight systems technology were available for the AV-8B. One was Sperry's stability augmentation and attitude hold system (SAAHS). This three-axis system was also linked to a departure resistant system (DRS), a combination which minimised pilot workload in VTOL and the transition phase—a frequent source of accidents with the AV-8A. DRS also allowed manoeuvres at extreme AOA, for example in VIFF escape tactics, which would have

The Sierra Nevada mountains provide a stark backdrop for a trio of bombed-up Cherry Point AV-8Bs. Camouflage colours are Dark Green (FS.34064) and Dark Grey (FS.36099). (Via Andy Evans)

caused a loss of control in an AV-8A. SAAHS even enabled hands-off vertical landing. This was demonstrated by McAir test pilot Bill Lowe in February 1983 when he kept his hands off the stick throughout the last 50ft of the vertical descent. Flight refuelling was also made less stressful by the Sperry system.[1]

The second major cockpit improvement was HOTAS (hands-on-throttle-and-stick). By rearranging all the most-used switches and controls on locations on the control stick and throttle lever the pilot's 'head down' time was drastically cut. Armament selection, target acquisition, manoeuvring flap, SAAHS, HUD selection, nosewheel steering, air brake control and air-start are all grouped as touch-recognisable buttons within the pilot's hand-span. HOTAS derived from the F-15 and F/A-18, as did the development of the HUD-based technology which was applied to AV-8B. The Smiths Instruments HUD was retained but upgraded to the SU-128/A model. Whereas the AV-8A

HUD combined data from the baseline system, gun/muzzle aiming symbols and basic flight instrument data, the SU-128/A became the focus (literally) of a wider-ranging system including the Litton ASN-130 INS, AYK-14 mission computer and Hughes angle rate bombing system (ARBS).

ARBS is a distant cousin of the TV camera used in the Walleye guided bomb, combined with a laser spot tracker to give a dual weapon-aiming system. It is virtually unjammable and it enables pilots to reduce the AV-8A's typical 50ft CEP to 20–25ft. Described as a 'smart system for dumb bombs' (AV-8Bs generally do not carry LGBs), ARBS's laser tracker is locked on to a target. Accurate line-of-sight and angle-rate data are then fed into the AYK-14(V) computer and Lear Siegler AN/AYQ-13 stores management system. The 'information highway' for all the data is a Type 1553A multiplex databus of the type installed in a number of current attack aircraft. Attack information is relayed to the HUD, or to a head-down display on the multi-purpose display (MPD). Weapon release is then possible manually, or by using auto mode, which involves following steering commands in the HUD and holding down the bomb release but-

ton until the computer automatically triggers ordnance release. The TV system, which is safer to use than a laser in peacetime training, can also be used to acquire a target purely passively. The pilot selects a small computer-generated window symbol on his HUD, locking the camera on to the target with the target designator control (TDC). Mounted with the laser in the tip of the aircraft's nose, the camera can be slewed to cover the target more exactly or switched to 6x magnification to improve target identification from higher altitudes. ARBS was originally designed for the A-4M and many Skyhawks were to receive it from 1983 onwards. In its ASB-19(V)-2 version for the AV-8B it gave a high degree of accuracy in the dive-attack profiles normally used in CAS sorties.[2]

Below the HUD is an 'up front control panel' which carries the essentials for CNI (communications, navigation and IFF interrogation) control. For more comprehensive information on practically every other aspect of his aircraft's welfare and capability the pilot can rely on his digital data

A reassuring signal from pilot Captain John Scott Walsh indicates that '20 WH' is ready to launch from USS *Guam*. (Via Andy Evans)

indicator (DDI). Tacan information, BIT tests, engine data, time and distance to target, even information from the HUD, can be called up on an MPD on the left of the instrument panel. Other more conventional dials and switches are there as back-up and placed in less immediately obvious locations.

The Marines had always wanted radar in their AV-8As and eventually came to value the moving map display which they deleted from those aircraft. Both of these

objectives were still a decade away but pilots were offered a satisfying package of other goodies in their new bird. To add to its ground-attack punch a new gun, the GAU-12/U Equalizer, was developed, although it was not ready for the AV-8B's service entry. The 25mm weapon replaced the twin 30mm Aden pods of the AV-8A. The twin pod installation was retained to preserve the LIDs effect, larger LID strakes being bolted on when the pods are removed. The gun is the left pod, driven at

Right: With toned-down 'tiger-tail', BuNo 162743 releases a pair of Mk 82 Snakeyes during an April 1987 sortie from Fallon. (Via Andy Evans)

9,000rpm by engine bleed air and firing 3,600 rounds per minute. In the other pod 300 rounds are layered in a magazine which is fed to the gun pod across a 'bridge' which doubles as a lift enhancer. The combination gives about ten seconds' continuous firing.

A number of other upgrades are minor, but important in the AV-8B's forward operating role. The aircraft can be 'hot refuelled' with power on to cut down turnaround times (although AV-8As were rou-

[1]At the time of writing, NASA's Ames Research Center had developed a flight control system and HUD display which permits pilots to make 'blind' landings on a 40 by 70ft pad, using a YAV-8B modified for Vertical Systems Research Aircraft (VSRA) work. New devices were added to the HOTAS controls which effectively allow control to be achieved through fine movements of thumbwheel and trim buttons during such critical 'blind' approaches and landings. The conclusion would be a completely 'hands off' system, with the pilot merely monitoring the HUD cursors, for automatic landings in all-weathers even at sea.
[2]The employment of ARBS, and some of its limitations, is revisited in the ensuing chapters 'An Engine With a Saddle On It' and 'Mount of the Gods'.

125

The GAU-12/U gun system's twin pods are bulky objects, but they add considerably to the AV-8B's VTO performance. Exhaust gases which are ejected into the central space between the four columns of air from the downward-facing nozzles have nowhere to go but up. (Frank Mormillo)

tinely hot refuelled using the flight refuelling probe). Undercarriage wheel brakes are more powerful and the undercarriage members are strengthened and fitted with aluminium wheels to reduce corrosion. An effective all-weather landing system (AWLS) reduces the anxiety of recovery on ship or ashore in poor visibility. Used in conjunction with the INS, it can return the aircraft to its designated landing area at night or in bad weather, taking it to the point where transition to vertical landing

should occur. A superior ECM suite was devised, including AN/ALR-67 RWR and an advanced jamming system known as the Airborne Self-Protection Jammer (ASPJ) which can be carried on a centreline pod. One crucial piece of kit is the AN/ALE-39 chaff/flare dispenser. Many of these items were common to the F/A-18 too. Various state-of-the-art GFE (government-furnished equipment) items were specified, including ARN-118 tacan, two ARC-182 wide-band UHF/VHF radios and the crucial AYK-14 mission computer.

THE FSD PROGRAMME

Flight testing of the four FSD aircraft was begun following the roll-out of BuNo 161396 on 16 October 1981 and its initial hovering tests on 5 November. All four

had the F402-RR-404 engine. FSD 1 tested the AV-8B's general flying characteristics. FSD 2 (161397) was used for engine tests and intake evaluation. It also tackled fuel system proving, flight-refuelling from the KC-130F. This was the first test of the AV-8B's retractable bolt-on refuelling probe, replacing the detachable 'jousting lance' arrangement on AV-8A. The third aircraft (161398) was tasked with avionics and weapons trials, and later with spin testing. When the fourth aircraft flew on 4 June 1983 it closely resembled the definitive production standard. Its initial test programme concentrated on the GAU-12/U gun system.

The AV-8B attained Naval Preliminary Evaluation (NPE) in June 1982 and Initial Operational Test & Evaluation (IOT&E) by VX-5 at Patuxent River. It

Left: VMA-331 Harriers taxy out for a mission from the Combat Center's Expeditionary airfield. 05 VL has LIDs attached in place of gun pods. (Frank Mormillo)

Right, upper: Colonel John 'Hunter' Bioty commented to the authors, 'I'm still amazed when I see a Harrier hovering in mid-air. That's quite a statement after flying the aircraft for over twenty years and 2,700 hours.' Bioty commanded VMA-331, the owners of this AV-8B, from 1988 to 1990. (Frank Mormillo)

Right, lower: The AV-8B's VTOL lift-enhancing combination of LIDs, zero-scarf nozzles and enlarged flaps are all displayed by this hovering Harrier. (Frank Mormillo)

was here that a further revision of the intakes was advocated to improve airflow and add a little more thrust. With characteristic thoroughness McAir set a team of 500 specialists to sort out the problem. Further refinement of the inlet contours was undertaken and the second row of blow-in doors which had been added to the YAV-8B and FSD aircraft was deleted. After much deliberation a single row of seven doors was agreed upon—one less door than featured on the AV-8A. This late redesign took almost six months, by which time early production aircraft were appearing with the double-row doors. All

had to be modified and the production jigs altered.

Weapons and payload trials yielded spectacular results. One aircraft took off with an all-up weight of 29,664lb, including 9,120lb of Mk 82 bombs—some 5,000lb more than the AV-8A's maximum gross weight with little more than 1,000lb extra engine thrust. The Pegasus showed ever-improving reliability and extended service intervals. Whereas the F402-RR-402 of AV-8A days required 'hot end' inspections at 300hr, this extended to 400hr in the -404 version and 500hr in the -406 of later production aircraft.

As the programme matured, many of the Harrier's design goals were exceeded and a serviceable, reliable workhorse rapidly emerged. The evaluators were impressed by other vital if unspectacular virtues which the advanced technology conferred, including a 60 per cent reduction in mmh/fh, a 60 per cent lower requirement for ground equipment and easier access to the airframe and engine. British involvement in the NPE underlined the joint nature of the venture: BAe Chief Test Pilot John Farley joined the flight test programme, and an RAF officer (Falklands veteran Bob Iveson) joined two USMC pilots in making the first batch of 21 test flights.

The next AV-8Bs (BuNos 161573–584) were twelve 'pilot production' jets to get the line established. The first of these flew on 19 August 1983. They were followed by a 'limited production' batch of 21 aircraft, funded in FY83 (BuNos 162068–085). As production built up, McAir invested in specialised tooling, including a $4.5 million Ingersoll drilling machine to reduce production times and costs. This apparatus is installed in a pit 108ft long and it automatically drills 6,500 fastener holes in each wing. It can be programmed to move in six directions, following the contours of the wing's upper surfaces.

The British production line also geared up for its 40 per cent of airframe work on the AV-8B, making centre and rear fuselages, fin and rudder, centreline pylon and RCS—that is, most of the 'metal' structure. The F402-RR-406 (Pegasus 105) began flight tests in December 1984 with a new turbine section which ran 10–20° cooler, reducing overhaul times and prolonging component life. It was installed in AV-8Bs from 1985 onwards. An interim -404A engine was used in the first production batch of 21. By the end of 1983 three production aircraft had flown. On 12 January 1984, at a ceremony at Cherry Point, the USMC training squadron VMAT-203 took charge of the Corps' first AV-8B, BuNo 161573. Coded 'KD/21' it was the first of the 'pilot' batch of a dozen for the unit and it was to have a busy though relatively short lifespan. Transferred to front-line unit VMA-542 it was

USMC TRANSITION DATES

Unit	Name	Code	Pre Harrier	AV-8A	AV-8C	AV-8B Harrier II	Night Attack	AV-8B Plus	Notes
VMA-331	Bumblebees	VL	A-4M until 01/83	–	–	Recomm. 30/01/85	–	–	1
VMA-231	Ace of Spades	CG	Reactivated for Harrier	15/03/73; operational 01/07/73	–	09/85	–	–	2
VMA-223	Bulldogs	WP	A-4M until 07/86	–	–	Late 1987	1992	06/94	
VMA-542	Flying Tigers	WH	F-4B until 06/70	01/11/72	1984–85 alongside AV-8A	04/86	–	07/93	3
VMAT-203	Hawks	KD	TA-4J and A-4M	AV-8A 04/75–03/85; TAV-8A 10/75–11/87	–	AV-8B 12/12/83; TAV-8B 03/87	–	–	4
VMA-311	Tomcats	WL	A-4M until 07/86	–	–	08/86	05/92	–	
VMA-211	Wake Island Avengers	CF	A-4M until 27/02/90	–	–	–	Spring 1990	05/90	
VMA-214	Blacksheep	WE	A-4M until mid-89	–	–	–	Late 1989	–	5
VMA-513	Flying Nightmares	WF	F-4B until 06/70	01/71; operational 04/71	1983–02/87	01/87; operational 20/03/88	09/92	–	6

Notes
1. Recommissioned in 1985 under Lt-Col. J. R. Cranford. Deactivated 30/09/92. Disestblished 01/10/92.
2. Carquals 01/74. Took part in the last cruise of USS *Franklin D. Roosevelt* 09/76; only ever full mixed CV deployment with AV-8s included (10/76–04/77).
3. First Iwakuni Det (with AV-8B) 12/89–06/90.
4. TAV-8B replaced TAV-8A 1987. Squadron formed after operational units.
5. Received first production Night Attack AV-8B 01/09/89. Did first overseas deployment with it 10/91, to Iwakuni.
6. First AV-8B unit in 3rd MAW. Had first USMC AV-8A also (BuNo 158384).

General note
VMA-331, -231, -223 and -542 and VMAT-203 assigned to 2nd MAW at MCAS Cherry Point (until 04/93); VMA-311, -211, 2-14 and -513 assigned to 3rd MAW at MCAS Yuma, Arizona.

shot down on 23 February 1991 during Operation 'Desert Storm', the conflict in which the AV-8B was to prove itself.

A 'RUGGED, DEPENDABLE WORKHORSE'

As AV-8B production gathered momentum it was clear that the combination of delays and consequent cost increases would put the Marines' target of 336 copies in doubt. Their original figure allowed for 160 AV-8Bs to re-equip the three AV-8A units and five A-4M Skyhawk light-attack squadrons, plus 25 for VMAT-203, 27 to be under modification and 124 at-

trition replacements. The last assumed a 4.5 per cent annual wastage rate, compared to 6 per cent for the Skyhawk. Production batches were relatively small and spread over a long timescale, increasing unit costs further. Production of the basic AV-8B could have been completed by 1989, including the RAF's GR.5 order and the eighteen TAV-8Bs for the USMC.

Whereas the RAF chose to continue using its T.4/T.4A trainers, the Marines wanted a two-seater which would replicate the behaviour and control layout of the radically different AV-8B. The TAV-8B had been built into the order from the

outset, rather than after the completion of the single-seat production batches as had happened with the AV-8A/TAV-8A. Nevertheless, the first TAV-8B (BuNo 162574) was the 65th Harrier II off the line and Lieutenant-Colonel Ben Mayer's VMAT-203 did not receive their first example (BuNo 162963, the second to roll off the lines) until 24 July 1987, three years after receipt of their earliest single-place jets. At that juncture there were still seven hard-worked TAV-8As on the Cherry Point ramp, and these much put-upon machines initiated newcomers to V/STOL. Pilots then had to make the mind-shifting translation from ancient to modern cockpit via the simulator before strapping into their first AV-8B. Although this obviously wasted some time, it was felt that the carefully nurtured TAV-8A survivors were still a useful introduction to the new model. Their more demanding V/STOL handling characteristics were valuable in teaching pilots a certain degree of caution before they switched to the more docile 'Bravo'. However, they required early starts for new trainees. With their marginal VTOL thrust, particularly in the hot summer air at Cherry Point, 7 a.m. was the time for TAV-8As to be rolled out for students to have some useful 'push-up' practice. They were retained in this capacity until November 1987, when the new 'twin-sticks' were able to take over. In the spring of 1988 the first TAV-8B-trained class went on to join their operational squadrons.

Despite its curious appearance, the TAV-8B shared most of the single-seater's handling characteristics, although it had no combat capability. Proposals for the design had been submitted to the US Navy early in 1983. In addition to the familiar extended forward fuselage, its vertical tail area was increased and an internal birdstrike-proof windshield was placed in front of the instructor's (rear) cockpit. The two-seat 'family models' were welcomed by the *Hawks* and quickly reinforced the wisdom of their early purchase, even though doing so meant losing eight AV-8Bs from the basic order. McAir test pilot Bill Lowe flew the prototype (BuNo 162747) on 21 October 1986, spending an hour on STO and stall manoeuvres and taking the elongated bird up to 40,000ft and 400kt. He pronounced it trouble-free and also commented favourably on a new Pegasus modification. It was the first to be

equipped with the digital engine control system (DECS) developed by Dowty-Smiths Industries Controls in the United Kingdom and incorporated in production engines from 1987. The system basically removed the pilot's monitoring and adjustment role in engine management throughout the flight regime.

The new jet's service entry made severe demands upon the *Hawks'* resources. Towards the end of the AV-8A era the annual throughput of trainees was about fifteen. This rapidly increased to over fifty annually from 1985 as the 'B' model entered the arena. In twelve years of training AV-8A crew, VMAT-203 had produced some 300 qualified pilots. This had to increase to almost ninety a year to man eight Harrier line squadrons, each with a planned force level of 20 jets and 30 pi-

lots. The *Hawks* had to expand, taking on 45 instructors and 30-plus aircraft. By the end of 1987 the specially marked '100th AV-8B' had left the St Louis complex but there were almost twice that number of pilots qualified to fly it. In many ways the training process was easier than it had been in the 1970s. Students could receive more realistic simulator training in the Cherry Point 'sim', using Evans & Sutherland CT-5A visual systems and McAir-produced software which reproduced the AV-8B's behaviour patterns very faithfully. The aircraft itself posed fewer problems for novices with its SAAHS, less frisky response to small control inputs and simpler cockpit procedures. When DECS engines became available pilots had the option of an instant thrust-dumping mode to shed VTO lift in the event of a hard bounce on

Right, upper: Tanking off a KC-10, this VMA-311 AV-8B(NA) is on TRANSPAC from Japan after a period of detachment to Iwakuni. (Steve Dunkin)

Right, lower: VMA-311 was the first squadron to introduce dispersed-field night operations, flying from roadways and forward sites. 12 WL has the AV-8B(NA) FLIR update. (Steve Dunkin)

landing, which might otherwise have destabilised the aircraft.

Selection for AV-8B training required pilots with above-average ability and after 1980 they could transfer straight from advanced flying training courses. Prior to this, selection was confined to aircrew with high hours on other fast jets. The rotary-wing component of the course was also dropped in the mid-1980s. Replacement crew for the AV-8B units had 62 Harrier flights plus fifteen in the TAV-8A before soloing in the 'B'. The 22-week course included 60hr in the aircraft, taking the pilot to 'combat capable' level before he went on to achieve 'combat ready' status in an operational 'gun' squadron. For ex Skyhawk or Phantom drivers there were ten fewer AV-8B sorties (cutting out some of the ground attack syllabus), while converts from the AV-8A/C needed only fourteen AV-8B flights before re-joining a front-line squadron. VMAT-203 closed down their last AV-8A/C course in April 1985 and the Yuma squadrons put their 'old' Harriers into AMARC throughout 1987.

VMAT-203's first dozen AV-8Bs were necessarily worked hard, each often flying three sorties daily in order to handle the conversion task. By late August 1986 110 crew had qualified since courses began in the spring of 1985. Cherry Point, the world's biggest USMC air base, has four 8,500ft runways and two 'dispersal' sites. Bogue Field, twenty miles away, has a dummy LHA deck for shipboard qualification as well as a full-size 'carrier deck' (complete with arresting gear) where Harrier pilots can practice alongside their Hornet-driving equivalents. Although trials with a Royal Navy-style ski jump were conducted at Patuxent River, the technique was not adopted by the Marines. For their purposes ships are seen mainly as vehicles to transport helicopters and Harriers to the battle zone. After the first few ship-based sorties to prepare the landing ground for the 'grunts', the emphasis is on getting aircraft ashore to operate from a forward site. Pilots therefore concentrate on rehearsing STO/VL sorties, learning to make full use of their aircraft's ability to clear a 50ft obstacle with a 1,200ft

ground run while carrying seven CBU canisters, two Sidewinders and a GAU-12/U gun. Exercises often include surge sorties, when aircraft fly up to eight times a day with only 25 minutes' turnaround each time. The Harriers' self-starting engine and OBOGS all help to make this intense level of usage possible. Training of this kind is carried over into the operational squadrons and it proved to be ideal preparation for their participation in the Gulf conflict.

The first unit to achieve IOC on the AV-8B was VMA-331 *Bumblebees* who had flown their 'racing car' A-4Ms until January 1983. They recommissioned on 30 January 1985 under Lieutenant-Colonel J. R. Cranford and began an eight-year acquaintance with the Harrier which ended with their disestablishment on 1 October 1992 as part of the 'peace dividend'. Their short work-up period included 400hr of weapons qualification at Yuma in the summer of 1984 and a shakedown cruise on board the LPH *Guadalcanal*. One of the first jobs for the squadron's 21 pilots and fifteen Harriers

Left: Marine Harriers in the late 1980s were part of a CAS force which included the OV-10A FAC aircraft, the AH-1J gunship and CH-53E assault helicopters, all seen here at the Combat Center's Expeditionary airfield. (Frank Mormillo)

Right: The Harrier II Plus cockpit, based around two multipurpose colour displays giving digital moving map, ARBS imagery, steering data and radar, weapons and BIT data. At the top right is the digital engine data display. Up front controls (centre panel) concentrate the essential communications, navigation, IFF and weapons controls under a single digital read-out. Above that is the wide-angle HUD. A comparison with early P.1127 cockpit views reveals a leap of several generations in technology. (Via Steve Dunkin)

was to show that their new charges could give their fighter contemporaries a hard time in the air, just as their predecessors had done. In so doing, the pilots pushed their aircraft slightly past the brochure's suggested parameters and found that they departed from controlled flight quite severely under certain DACT circumstances. Some adjustments to the SAAHS were necessary. These were introduced from BuNo 162081 onwards and the *Bumblebees* resumed their very successful contests against F-15s, F-4s and any other comers.

They also had good initial results with ARBS. Lieutenant-Colonel Cranford told the Press: 'This sucker can loft in a 20ft bomb from three miles out. My accurate INS puts me on the IP. I pull up and zoom, say for an attack on a SAM site. I drop on the SAMs before I get in AAA range, then beat feet out of there.' The Harrier also developed a good reputation for reliability. The original USMC requirement for maintenance was a maximum of 15.9mmh/fh and a 1.9hr mean repair time, with a 75 per cent mission-ready rate. Apart from a new lingering problem with their ARC-182 radios, and fuel leaks, VMA-331 were soon beating these targets regularly.

They were followed in the conversion process by the first of the ex-AV-8A units, VMA-231, in September 1985. The *Ace of Spades* squadron reached IOC in July

1986 and made the type's first deployment abroad two months later to participate in the NATO Exercise 'Northern Wedding'. VMA-331 made a similar visit in March–April 1992, taking part in Exercise 'Mallet Blow' when they transferred from USS *Nassau* to RAF Wittering while the ship visited Portsmouth. The six aircraft (appropriately call-signed 'Stinger 1–6') re-embarked via Alconbury on 4 April, having worked alongside RAF Harriers. A third unit, VMA-542 *Flying Tigers*, traded their AV-8A/C models for new Harriers in April 1986, achieving IOC at the year's end. The last of the three AV-8A/C operators, VMA-513, sent its 'Det A' to make the type's final deployment, on board USS *Tarawa*, and then stood down in February

1987, having begun and ended the AV-8A's sixteen-year career. By March 1988 it was in business again with the AV-8B. In the meantime, A-4M unit VMA-311 *Tomcats* at Yuma converted in August 1986, continuing a long tradition of ground-attack experience. The *Tomcats* operated F4U Corsairs for much of the Second World War, flew the first jet sorties in Korea with the Grumman F9F and completed 50,000 combat sorties in South-East Asia. The other three Skyhawk squadrons, VMA-223, -214 and -211, completed transition by 1990 to achieve the current 'Hornet 'n' Harrier' Marine Air Strike component. That other long-serving attacker, the A-6E Intruder, left the USMC by April 1993, taking with it the

VMA-231's Ace of Spades is distinctive even in the drab Harrier Tactical Paint Scheme (HTPS). The Squadron converted to AV-8Bs in September 1985 and were still flying them a decade later. (Via Andy Evans)

Marines' long-range all-weather heavy punch, a task which the Navy resumed unto itself. However, the convenience of having two McDonnell-Douglas products, with many similarities in equipment fit, made for greater efficiency. Hornet and Harrier were to be brought closer together (and the Intruder's all-weather/night capability partly recouped) in the next stage of the development cycle; the AV-8B Harrier II+, equipped with the F/A-18C's AN/APG-65 radar. Prior to the launch of this private-venture Harrier variant in September 1990 there was an interim 'Super Harrier', the AV-8B(NA).

NIGHT ATTACK

Conceived as the result of a $2.1 million design definition contract awarded to McAir late in 1985 and originally called AV-8D, the 'Night Attack' (NA) version had three important updates. First was the GEC forward-looking infra-red sensor attached above the nose in an elongated fairing. GEC Sensors subsequently received an initial £10 million contract for its Electro-Optical Surveillance Division in the summer of 1989 for FLIRs to convert AV-8Bs over two years. USMC interest in FLIRs arose from an NWC China Lake trials programme in which a TA-7C Corsair II did 150hr of tests with a GEC

Marconi night vision system. A pod-mounted FLIR fed images to a HUD and was linked to Catseye NVG for the pilot. Night attack sorties were flown with considerable success, a point which was not lost upon the Harrier squadrons down the road at Yuma.

Having deleted moving-map displays from their AV-8As to simplify them, the Marines were impressed by the digital colour map display developed for the RAF's Harrier GR.5 and Tornado. A Smiths/Honeywell colour MPD was developed, including a moving-map video of maps and charts for each mission. This appeared on the right side of the AV-8B(NA)'s instrument panel, replacing fuel flow and nozzle temperature read-outs. Data for the map screen were stored on laser CD and the entire system, controlled via HOTAS switches, was linked to the third trick in the suite—night vision goggles. FLIR gives 22-degree coverage ahead of the aircraft and the rest of the pilot's field of view can be covered by the helmet-mounted Catseye goggles. Ed Harper, General Manager of the AV-8B programme, was enthusiastic about the new fittings: 'What we've done is expand the hours of the day that we'll be able to employ the weapons system.'

The first NA Harrier (BuNo 162966) flew on 26 June 1987 and immediately began a three-month evaluation at China Lake. At that stage 86 AV-8Bs had been manufactured. VMA-214 received the first production Night Attack Harrier (BuNo 163583) at Yuma on 1 September 1989

and the system was installed in all aircraft from No 167 onwards. VMA-214 *Blacksheep* also had the honour of making the first overseas deployment of the NA model, to Iwakuni in October 1991. Their Yuma base-mates, VMA-211, went direct from the A-4M to the AV-8B(NA) in 1990, and by September 1992 all four MAG-13 units had the nocturnal Harrier.

At Cherry Point VMA-223 *Bulldogs* were first in the night attack business, while VMA-211 *Wake Island Avengers* cruised on board USS *Tarawa* in the summer of 1992 as the build-up for Operation 'Restore Hope' began off Somalia. By the time things had hotted-up there they had been relieved by USS *Tripoli* so they were unable to give the AV-8B(NA) its first exposure to action.

The Marine Corps' plans include an intention to upgrade all surviving AV-8Bs to 'NA' standard eventually. Originally, this was part of a major re-think of Marine air power under the FY87 budget which would have included the acquisition of the re-winged A-6F Intruder (at the expense of at least 100 new-build Harriers) and an eventual total of 602 MV-22A Osprey tilt-rotor assault aircraft. The non-appearance of these two types has been a significant factor in the continued slow-release funding of additional Harriers—and Harrier upgrades. Before the most recent of these, Harrier II+, could be flight-tested, the Marine V/STOL flyers suddenly found themselves faced with a task which would engage a large part of their Harrier assets in a very hot war indeed.

7. 'An Engine With a Saddle On It'

The intricately planned 'Desert Shield'/ 'Desert Storm' air campaign of 1990–91 was remarkable partly for the number of aircrew who had to undertake missions for which their training strategies had not really prepared them. OA/A-10A Warthog pilots often found themselves flying at night, searching out targets by using the IR seeker heads of their AGM-65D/G Maverick missiles, set to 3x or 6x magnification. At the same time, F-111F Aard-

AV-8B BuNo 163289 with temporary camouflage applied for 'Desert Shield'. In the case of this squadron, VMA-223 *Bulldogs*, the warpaint was not required: the unit supplied a contingency Det to Rota which was not called into battle. The *Bulldogs*' 'rudder art' dates back to May 1942 when, as the 'Rainbow Squadron', VMF-223 was the first step in reconstructing USMC air power after Pearl Harbor. They became the *Bulldogs* the following year. (Via Andy Evans)

vark flyers were destroying Iraqi tanks at a rate per sortie seven times higher than the A-10 tankbusters, who were supposed to be doing that job by day only. The F-111F was conceived as a long-range nuclear interdiction aircraft. Meanwhile, F-15E 'Mud Hen' pilots, expecting similar long-range, first-pass strike sorties too, found themselves roaming the skies of southern Iraq trying to spot mobile 'Scud' launchers on a search-and-destroy basis. War creates its own priorities, and often they do not accord with the predictions of air staff procurement planners! For the USMC Harrier II squadrons, trained to provide short-range CAS for their advancing ground troops, there were many surprises but not much textbook CAS. According to MAG-13(FWD)'s commanding officer, Major John Bioty, 'CAS was the priority mission for all Harriers. However, most sorties (about 85–90 per cent) were

flown against interdiction-type targets in southern and central Kuwait.'

Few would have predicted, either, that, of the 44,145 US combat sorties flown during the 43 days of the war, 19 per cent would be by USMC aircraft compared with 14 per cent for the USN, who had about fifty more aircraft in the area. Of this Marine total a large proportion were by the 170-plus helicopters and 78 F/A-18Cs in the theatre, but no fewer than 3,380 sorties were logged by the 66 shore-based Harriers and twenty on board USS *Nassau* (LHA-4). In total, some 7.7 per cent of all US combat sorties were by AV-8Bs in a war which involved a total of around 4,000 aircraft from all US operational units.

However, post-conflict bean-counting of this sort was far into the future for the folk at MCAS Cherry Point in August 1990. To many of them, the pressing con-

cerns included finding out where Kuwait was, or adjusting to the prospect of another long absence from home only weeks after returning from a six-month Unit Deployment Program (UDP) stint at Iwakuni, Japan. Saddam Hussein's invasion of Kuwait on Thursday 2 August 1990 triggered a flurry of diplomatic activity in Washington. By 7 August Saudi Arabian leaders had been persuaded of the urgency of the Iraqi threat and America's willingness to counter it. President Bush ordered the deployment of US forces to 'effect the withdrawal of all Iraqi forces from Kuwait'. The same day several AV-8B squadron commanders were asked how soon they could deploy to Bahrain. Only a week later the clear skies over MCAS Yuma were full of Harriers heading east to Cherry Point. Between 18 and 21 August two squadrons set out on the $17\frac{1}{2}$hr flight to Bahrain, with a half-way stopover at Rota, Spain.

When the call to action came, six Marine squadrons, plus the training unit, had converted to the AV-8B, while VMA-211 and VMA-214 were still working up on the AV-8B(NA) at Yuma. Only about fifteen night-attack Harriers had reached these two squadrons, so there was no possibility of its very useful extra capability being available for the deployment. VMA-542 had recently returned from Iwakuni, where a set of fairly new pilots had gained valuable flying experience, including some live ordnance range work in South Korea and Okinawa. Their replacements at Iwakuni were VMA-231, who took up station on 4 June. The *Bumblebees* (VMA-331) were scheduled to deploy to USS *Nassau* as part of the 4th Marine Expeditionary Brigade (MEB), which embarked for the Persian Gulf in August. Meanwhile VMA-513 were scheduled to relieve VMA-231 at Iwakuni in November 1990 (little realising that their six-month slot there would extend to eleven), but they had a six-aircraft Det available for deployment at sea too. MAG-13's VMA-311 *Tomcats* were the first to fly out to the Gulf, in company with VMA-542. That left one 'gun' squadron, VMA-223 *Bulldogs* from Cherry Point's 2nd MAW, and VMAT-203 *Hawks*.[1] In fact, VMA-223 did deploy too

after a fashion, sending six aircraft to NAS Rota in January 1991 as a contingency force. These were returned to the USA on 23 February and the *Bulldogs* prepared for a Mediterranean cruise in USS *Wasp* in June. Of the six front-line AV-8B squadrons, five therefore took a direct part in the war and the sixth was half-way there.

Lieutenant-Colonel Dick White, commander of VMA-311 *Tomcats*, was one of the squadron bosses who received that 7 August call. His twenty jets traversed the United States to Cherry Point on 15 August. There they had their standard green camouflage stripes overpainted by NADEP in light grey to give a two-tone grey effect (like all Gulf-deployed Harriers) which retained the distinctive 'posing Tomcat' tail motif. On the 18th the aircraft were armed with 300 rounds of 25mm ammunition and a pair of AIM-9Ms, plus tanks, and took off for Rota. There they enjoyed a final night with a free choice of beverages before moving on to the alcohol-free Arab zone. Flight refuelling at night had not been a compulsory part of the training syllabus and most pilots had to take up to eleven 'plugs' from a KC-10A before landfall at Sheikh Isa AB, Bahrain. Several were conducted during severe thunderstorms over the Atlantic. Captain Craig Berryman described the experience: 'None of us had ever tanked behind a KC-10 before. Just out of Nova Scotia one of our jets hit a refuelling basket too hard and ripped it off. Because it was dark all we saw was a huge fireball behind the tanker when the hose ripped free. We thought we'd lost a jet before even getting to the combat zone. After the big flash our eyes re-focused and we could see a Harrier backing away from our now-useless tanker. The KC-10 and AV-8B diverted to Nova Scotia and the spare tanker took over. A repair team was immediately flown out of Cherry Point and both caught up with us in two days. Quite impressive repair work!'

Eventually they were to move once again to the newly prepared forward operating base near King Abdul Aziz Naval Base at Jubail in Saudi Arabia, about 100 miles from the Kuwait border. Although there was a 7,000ft runway in existence it

had a disintegrating surface which was a perpetual FOD hazard to the Harriers. However, it was the kind of base where a Marine could feel at home: the training camp back home at Twenty-Nine Palms in the Mojave Desert was good preparation for life without water and under canvas. When the *Tomcats* left Yuma the temperature there was 125°F and they thought it could not be any hotter in Bahrain. When they landed there it was 130°F and there was 80 per cent humidity. Fuel was in tactical bladders, placed to enable aircraft to 'hot-refuel'. Accommodation was in tents at the car park of the local football stadium, which also offered showers and foot lockers for the maintainers to store Harrier spares. There was also a tented 'club' with a non-alcoholic bar: desalinated warm water was the normal drink. In due course the hardstanding area was extended with a 3,500ft AM-2 metal taxy track which would accommodate the eventual total of 66 AV-8Bs plus the twenty OV-10A/D Broncos of VMO-1 and VMO-2 which provided forward air control–airborne (FAC-A) for the Marine attackers.

Following closely on the *Tomcats*' heels was VMA-542. Before leaving Cherry Point they had done a little jet-swapping with other units, including VMAT-203, so that they could deploy with the latest DECS-equipped engines in all twenty Harriers. This was in order to minimise engine 'tuning' and fuel-system difficulties in the varying temperatures of the desert environment. Rolls-Royce Rep Mr Russ Hammond was on site to cosset the Pegasus engines. The squadron 'fixers' worked overtime updating their service records on the new aircraft and replacing any high-time components. This effort was to be well rewarded: their aircraft turned in an exemplary availability rate during the eight months they were destined to spend in Saudi Arabia. In fact, the aircraft gave even less minor trouble than they did in normal daily hot-weather operations at

---

[1]Unlike its British counterparts, 899 NAS and No 20(R) Squadron RAF, VMAT-203 does not have a reserve combat status, although it became a source of aircraft and experienced crews for the deployable units.

Yuma. The *Tomcats* had similarly good results, with nineteen out of twenty aircraft ready for action each day.

During their three months at Sheikh Isa VMA-542 had time to practise long-range navigation using INS, and to adjust their internal EW equipment to likely threats in the area. Their Sanders AN/ALQ-164 pods did not arrive until the Squadron moved to Abdul Aziz. Further training was then needed as the crews were unfamiliar with this device. ALQ-164 was mainly a deception pod, designed to fool enemy radar into 'seeing' the AV-8B some distance away from its actual position in the air. The supply of these pods was speeded up and there was an adequate number for all aircraft by the start of the war. VMA-311 survived on only five pods. Early in the conflict only one pod per division of four Harriers was used, and their importance diminished as Allied air supremacy advanced. Craig Berryman observed that 'the Iraqis in Kuwait tended to use their early warning radars to get a quick look at where the aircraft were coming from and then launched barrages of AAA and SAMs in that general direction. I never saw any indication of CW homing radar being used, as for SA-6 or Hawk missiles.' Colonel John 'Hunter' Bioty added: 'The Coalition SEAD effort virtually shut down the Iraqi radar guided missile threat. The primary threat was optically directed AAA barrage fire and IT "pocket-rocket"

Left, top: VMA-231 from MAG-32 at Cherry Point was the third Harrier unit to join MAG-13 at King Abdul Aziz. The' bomb' under the cockpit of BuNo 162962 records 40 missions. Above it is the Arabic 'Free Kuwait' slogan. (Andy Evans)

Left, centre: With six Mk 7 CBU dispensers hung on its pylons, a MAG-13 AV-8B prepares for a BAI sortie from King Abdul Aziz base. The Mk 7 could be adapted for a variety of submunitions, most commonly the Mk 20 Rockeye II anti-armour bomblets. (Via Andy Evans)

Left, bottom: An AV-8B on jacks for servicing in an 'instant' hangar. Its canopy is sealed in an attempt to keep out the sand, although pilots reported sand ingress even with the canopy closed. (Via Andy Evans)

SAMs. The main jamming effort of the ALQ-164 pod was against detection/tracking radars. No other pods were in use.' In addition, aircraft were equipped with ALR-67 receivers which had been updated twice with geo-tailored Persian Gulf 'libraries'.

Most of VMA-542's time at the Bahrain base was spent maintaining a four-ship twenty-four-hour alert in case of an extension of Saddam's invasion. High-altitude navigation and low-level ground attack was practised at unrestricted altitudes until the USAF lost an F-15E, an RF-4C and an F-111F in rapid succession. Pilot disorientation at very low altitude over hazy, featureless terrain was thought to be the cause. All aircraft were given a strict 1,000ft minimum ceiling AGL, rather than the 50–100ft which many crews felt was a more realistic preparation for the likely scenario ahead. Suitable 'targets' in the desert were hard to find and more than one innocent camel (and its owner) doubtless appeared in the TV 'window' of an AV-8B pilot's ARBS display.

Sheikh Isa rapidly became overcrowded as the US force build-up continued. Eventually it housed ten USMC F/A-18 Hornet and A-6/EA-6 Intruder units plus two USAF ones with F-4G/RF-4C Phantoms. Pilots began to resent having to walk over

a mile to find their aircraft on the newly-built base area in temperatures over 53°C. Worst of all for quick-reaction, CAS-dedicated crews was the 30–35 minutes' flying time to any likely targets in Kuwait. They needed much shorter reaction times and the move to join the *Tomcats* at Abdul Aziz in November 1990 was welcome—except, perhaps, to the groundcrews who mostly had a sweltering nine-hour bus journey to the new location.

A third squadron, VMA-231, joined the expanding MAG-13 component at Abdul Aziz on 22 December 1990, following President Bush's announcement of increased force levels. Their flight from Iwakuni, where they were relieved by fourteen VMA-513 aircraft, took all of two weeks. They staged through Wake Island, Hawaii, Yuma, Cherry Point and Rota—an 18,000-mile trip. All their Harriers, which were the first to receive the full Harrier Tactical Paint Scheme, were declared mission-ready the day after arrival. The Harrier establishment under MAG-13 (Forward Deployed) of the 3rd MAW at Jubail was completed in the same month by VMA-513 Det B. Their six non-Iwakuni-bound Harriers were shipped in aboard USS *Tarawa* with the 5th MEB and flown in to Abdul Aziz base. Before the 'land war' stage of the conflict began, USS

Nassau arrived off the Saudi coast with the 4th MEB (MAG-40) units, including VMA-331, led by Lieutenant-Colonel C. Fitzgerald.

To reduce reaction times further still a very basic forward operating site was established north-west of King Abdul Aziz at Tanajib, an oil company airfield a mere 45 miles from the Kuwait border with a short, single taxiway and a small concrete area. It was given the basic facilities to operate twelve aircraft, refuelling and rearming them, refilling water tanks and performing basic repairs, all within five minutes of the border.

THE HARRIERS' ROLE

As the political situation deteriorated through January and action seemed imminent, MAG-13 were told that they would be held in reserve during the opening phases of 'Desert Storm'. Once the air offensive was complete the Harriers would then provide CAS ahead of their own advancing troops during the liberation of Kuwait. In fact, having the USMC 'independent air force', dedicated to sup-

VMA-542's '02 WH' prepares for an 'oil-trench torching' mission with four Mk 77 Mod 5 napalm bombs in late February 1991. (Via Andy Evans)

porting its own troops, in the war zone was rather awkward for the planners of the campaign. General 'Buster' Glossom, chief targeter and commander of all USAF units in theatre, was aware that he had to allow for MAG-13's *raison d'être* which was to react *ad hoc* to the Marines' battlefield needs rather than to fit neatly into a decisive master plan. Iraqi airfields, air defences and communications had to be neutralised in the opening attacks. Following that phase, the biggest threat to a Coalition advance into Kuwait was Iraqi armour and artillery; much of this outranged US/Coalition guns and could have delayed an advance considerably. USCENTCOM commander General Norman Schwarzkopf and Chief of Staff General Colin Powell were advised that they might face 3,700 artillery pieces, an unknown number of rocket launchers, 5,700 main battle tanks and 5,000 AFVs. They elected to reduce this total by half through the use of air power before committing ground troops to action. The Harrier squadrons' role in that process actually began much sooner than they expected.

Initially, Lieutenant-General Walter Boomer, overall commander of the Marines in the area, told AV-8B units that they would eventually take part in the process of battlefield preparation (Phase 3 in Schwarzkopf's plan) and then in the ground war (Phase 4). This would follow the destruction of strategic targets such as airfields within Iraq (Phase 1) and of air defences in Kuwait and the Iraqi border (Phase 2). However, as the opening day of hostilities approached Major-General Moore, 3rd MAW commander, met all his squadron commanders to tell them that they would after all take part in the massive opening round of air strikes on 17 January. VMA-311's CO, Lieutenant-Colonel Dick White, was 'fragged' to take a twelve-aircraft strike on positions in Kuwait, with a follow-up attack later the same day. In the end, the lack of EA-6B ECM aircraft due to the demands of the bigger strikes in Iraq caused these sorties to be cancelled.

At 6.45 a.m. on 17 January four MAG-13 Harriers were on the usual alert status when a VMO-2 FAC detected Iraqi artillery which was shelling parts of the coastal town of Khafji. Marines in the vicinity were thought to be at risk, so the quartet was called up. Two were from VMA-311, led by their XO, the other two were flown by Captain Scott Walsh of VMA-542 and the *Tigers'* CO, Lieutenant-Colonel Ted Herman—with the Squadron flag in his cockpit. Loaded on the *Tigers'* pylons were four Mk 83 1,000lb LDGP bombs per Harrier, while the *Tomcats* toted Rockeyes; all four carried a single AIM-9M, an AN/ALQ-164 pod and a full load of 25mm cartridges. The Harriers took off on the AV-8B's first combat mission. Their FAC marked the target with a Zuni rocket as they came in from the sea under low cloud and sighted the gun emplacements in their ARBS cameras. There was little AAA so the aircraft returned for three gun passes to finish off the two 122mm artillery pieces which still survived from the six attacked with bombs. The *Equalizer's* mixture of 25mm armour-piercing, incendiary and HE shells was very effective against thick-skinned targets as well as vehicles. As they departed the area their FAC reported all the Iraqi weapons totally destroyed. Some understandable euphoria back at King Abdul Aziz was dampened the next day by the loss of the FAC who had guided the Harriers so effectively. Chief Warrant Officer Guy 'Gunner' Hunter and his pilot Colonel Cliff Acree were hit in OV-10A (BuNo 155435) and made POWs.

Flying FAC in Vietnam-vintage Broncos was a dangerous business in such heavily defended airspace.[2] VMO pilots tried to remain above 5,000ft to stay above the worst of the AAA, but poor visibility often forced them lower to identify targets. It was a tribute to their skill in performing this vital component in the MAG-13 effort that only two OV-10s were lost. The second (BuNo 155424), from VMO-1, fell to a SAM on 25 February and its pilot, Major Joseph Small, became a POW; Captain David Spellacy, the FAC, was killed. Relief came in the second week of battle in the form of VMFA(AW)-121 with a squadron of brand-new F/A-18D 'Fast FAC' Hornets. Flying from Sheikh Isa with the call-sign 'Combat', these two-seaters carried a formidable load of equipment: two LAU-10 Zuni pods were employed for target-marking, a Hughes AAR-50 or Ford AAS-38 FLIR pod could be carried on one of the fuselage missile stations and a McDonnell-Douglas ASQ-173 LST/SCAM (laser designator/strike camera pod) could be carried on the other. A combination of fuel tanks, four Mk 83 bombs and AIM-9 self-defence missiles completed the punch, while NVG cockpits and a full communications suite, including data-link, made the job of controlling AV-8B strikes, by day or night, much easier.

Although there were early difficulties, the FAC-A team learned fast. 'Initially', Craig Berryman remembered, 'the F/A-18D "Delta" pilots' marks were poor—often the WP rocket would be 1,000m or more from the intended target. I'm told that by the end of the war the F/A-18D and AV-8B made a lethal team. The biggest problem at first was fuel management. Every mission I was on, the FAC-A was at the tanker when we got to the target area. The OV-10s didn't get much work after Lieutenant-Colonel Acree and CWO 4 Hunter were shot down. For most of the time they weren't allowed to fly north of the Kuwait border. Assets were being saved for when the ground war started, anticipating a huge requirement for CAS and FAC-A. During "Desert Shield" we worked a lot with the OV-10s, especially the OV-10D with its laser designator.'

Berryman's opening mission was at 1600 on 'Day One'. 'As we were cleared for take-off, the air traffic controller said "Good luck and good hunting!" That was my first real thought that I was going to kill someone. As we crossed the border we started getting AWACS calls that an "unknown" was rapidly closing in our direction. Things got tense as the distance closed to "merge plot" just as we got to the target area. I wondered if we would have to jettison our ordnance for an air-to-air engagement, but it turned out to be one of our aircraft returning from a mission further north.

---

[2] During 'Desert Shield' MAG-13(FWD) also practised CAS with Army units in western Saudi Arabia using AH-1 Cobras as FAC helicopters.

had to talk Harriers to their targets using a basic INS designation. INS tended to drift a little during hard manoeuvring and pilots would have welcomed GPS and the laser ring gyro. A typical 40–45-degree dive attack was initiated at about 15,000ft and 525kt. Chaff would be popped on the way down to fool AAA radars and missiles. Bombs would be released at around 6–7,000ft, minimizing exposure inside the 10,000ft lethal zone for AAA.[4] Flares were usually used on the pull-out to counter IR missiles. Some pilots preferred to use flares on the dive too, but there was the risk that this could get the gunners' attention. The lack of flares in the AV-8B was always a sore point. Craig Berryman remarks: 'The A-10As had 480; we had 60. We had to save ours until we thought we really needed them. The AV-8B(NA) had 180 but they were "down" for the duration of the war with problems with the -408 engine.' The light grey Harriers were hard to see otherwise. Even that inevitable 20–

'As we each took turn diving on the artillery positions we could see AAA bursting around the other man's jet. But during your delivery you became so focused on keeping the "pipper" on target that this was about all you saw until the bombs left the jet and you started your climb back to safety. All of us were shot at in our dives but none of us had seen it in our own dives. After the bombs we switched to the 25mm gun and came back in to strafe—probably not the smartest thing, but this was combat! I also remember the flight home, being afraid our own fighters or air defence would shoot us down.

'Attack profiles were typically a high altitude ingress (15,000–20,000ft) to a 45-degree dive with a high release to stay above small-arms fire and light AAA.[3] Airspeeds tended to be 500kt plus. Speed was life. That was the lesson I forgot when I was shot down.'

Pilots on that first Khafji mission were impressed by the accuracy of ARBS under combat conditions and it continued to perform well throughout the war. It was of limited use at night. For the TV to work, flares had to be used to illuminate the enemy positions, but therefore also the Marines' own. This technique was little used, but the laser spot-tracker (LST) was a very effective and much-used night designation method. Its performance could be degraded by smoke, in which case FAC-As

[3]In fact no Harriers were hit by AAA during the war. One returned with a small hole in the tailplane but this was determined to be the result of a 'strike' by a piece of 25mm debris from the Harrier's own gun.
[4]Colonel John Bioty added: 'Prior to entering Kuwait, airspace contact was made with the Direct Air Support Center (DASC) and the pilot was given a mission. Ingress to the target was flown at 500 KTAS and all combat checks were completed. The flight would then ramp down [descend] to roll-in altitude (20K for low drag weapons and 15K for cluster munitions). If CAS was required any time during the mission, Harriers were diverted immediately. On CAS sorties weapon release was left up to the pilot and was based on the situation of the ground troops. During the battle for Khafji, for instance, pilots descended to lower altitudes and some weapon releases or strafing attacks were done at 2,500ft or lower.'

30 seconds inside the ground defence's envelope gave the enemy a chance to shoulder-launch a small IR SAM towards the Harriers' vulnerable jet nozzles. Although nowhere near as powerful a missile-magnet as an afterburning jet, the Harrier's hot nozzles, positioned below the wing, produced an IR signature somewhere in between those of the A-4 Skyhawk and A-6 Intruder. From above, the wing shielded the nozzles against fighter-launched IR seekers. From below, where the SA-7 and SA-14 launchers waited in their hundreds, there was a tempting heat source to latch on to.

A missile hit on the single-engine AV-8B would invariably disable the aircraft, whereas a twin-engine type with larger tailpipes might survive. Colonel Bioty was frank: 'IR missiles exploded in the area of the hot nozzle and in most cases blew the nozzle off, rendering the aircraft uncontrollable. Marine F/A-18s were also hit by IR missiles. These aircraft were able to land safely because the missile exploded in the tailpipe area rather than in the mid section of the jet. In future wars, however, IR missiles will probably have "lead angle bias" and impact in a jet's mid section.'

Effective mutual support from a sharp-eyed wingman was the best defence. At 6,000ft there were only seconds between a missile launch and disaster; a marginally late missile call to a pilot concentrating on his ARBS was usually too late. Because of the difficulty in seeing small IR missiles with their minimal smoke trails and high closing speed, Harrier crews were keen to have a missile approach warning system (MAWS) to detect missile plumes and give them a better chance of evasion. RAF Harrier GR.7s have a Plessey MAWS in their tailcone, and after 'Desert Storm' plans were made to fit the AV-8B fleet with an AN/AAR-44(V) system to provide similar coverage. From pilot Craig Berryman's viewpoint, 'a MAWS would have been extremely beneficial. It would probably have saved four out of the five AV-8B losses and maybe both pilots who were killed.'

Two tactical decisions helped to keep losses down. Second-pass attacks were avoided as a rule and slightly different attack profiles were used on each sortie. Many pilots opted in any case for the 'one pass, haul ass' approach. FACs as a rule preferred pilots to drop bombs one at a time so that results could be assessed and re-attacks ordered if necessary. Pilots had to rely on the FAC's advice about potential threats from the ground. Changes were also made in the tactical formations used for strike sorties. In the first few days of 'Desert Storm' the MAG-13 units flew four- to six-ship strikes, sometimes with EA-6B ECM and fighter cover. Over most of Kuwait the AN/ALQ-164 was not considered adequate protection, particularly on some of the limited SEAD sorties flown at this time by Harriers. This approach was replaced by the 'pairs' principle. Attacks were made by AV-8Bs in twos, offering better mutual support and hitting the target from different headings about 10 seconds apart. In VMA-542 the pairs often flew together for the rest of the war. VMA-311 also decided that the standard four-ship division was, according to Craig Berryman, 'too hard to manoeuvre around the battlefield and get everyone across the target in an expeditious manner. The extra eyes were certainly missed for self-defence, but with the air-to-air threat minimal and a sporadic AAA/SAM threat it was worth the trade-off.'

On the run-in to an attack ARBS would have exact speed and height data from the aircraft's other systems. The pilot locked up the target using the TV camera, which used background contrast to identify its objective. ARBS then used computer inputs to measure the closing rate between the aircraft and the target by assessing the alteration in slant angle of the target as it passed under the aircraft's nose. Generally, this method delivered very accurate bombing solutions at the Marines' usual 40–45-degree dive angle, but operating the camera to achieve a lock-on in low-level, shallow-angle attacks was more difficult as background contrast was usually less defined. There was also less time to operate the camera's slew control to acquire the target. Smoke and haze, increasingly serious problems as the war developed, could also degrade TV imagery. The RAF have found the system slightly less effective for the low-level mission profiles which they use. In the Gulf, Harrier pilots found the ARBS's 6x magnification TV facility particularly useful for inspecting targets after rolling in to the attack. Many Iraqi tanks had already been hit, or were decoys, and this could be used at night, too, as long as a designator aircraft or ground-based illuminator could be set up for the mission.

Using the GAU-12 gun could be a good way of suppressing identifiable flak sources but it could have the disadvantage of dis-

Before deploying to King Abdul Aziz, VMA-542 spent three months in 'Tent City' at Sheikh Isa airfield, Bahrain. (Via Andy Evans)

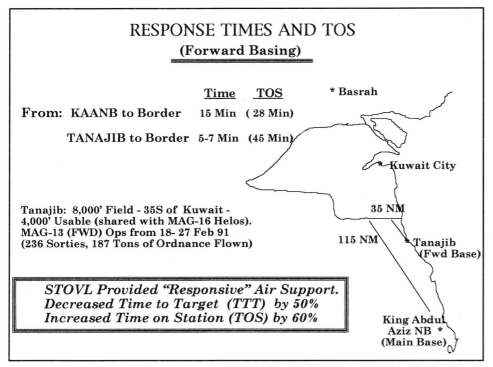

RESPONSE TIMES AND TOS
(Forward Basing)

	Time	TOS
From: KAANB to Border	15 Min	(28 Min)
TANAJIB to Border	5-7 Min	(45 Min)

*Basrah

Kuwait City

35 NM

115 NM

*Tanajib
(Fwd Base)

Tanajib: 8,000' Field - 35S of Kuwait -
4,000' Usable (shared with MAG-16 Helos).
MAG-13 (FWD) Ops from 18- 27 Feb 91
(236 Sorties, 187 Tons of Ordnance Flown)

King Abdul
Aziz NB *
(Main Base)

STOVL Provided "Responsive" Air Support.
Decreased Time to Target (TTT) by 50%
Increased Time on Station (TOS) by 60%

tracting a pilot from keeping his aircraft correctly lined up for an accurate drop. As a back-up to ARBS, CCIP mode could be used where it was impossible to obtain an effective camera lock-on. The pilot had to watch a cursor and bomb-line in his HUD, keeping the CCIP cross exactly on target. When the cursor and bomb line met it was time to press the red bomb release button on top of the control column.

After their successful Khafji operation the MAG-13 squadrons' missions just kept on coming. Their daily Air Tasking Order (ATO) usually listed three kinds of targets. First were priority targets chosen by Marine Expeditionary Force planners, each with a primary and secondary target. These tended to be armour, artillery or communications centres. In the second category were targets of opportunity, requested by a FAC and coordinated by the Direct Air Support Centre (DASC), to be issued to the Harrier units as a Joint Tactical Air Request (JTAR). A FAC would then work the target with a flight of AV-8Bs. For the third category each squadron was allotted a 15 by 15min 'kill box' in which they could seek targets of opportunity. This pattern was established early in the war and MAG-13 had fairly exclusive 'hunting rights' over their sections of

the battlefield, operating independently of other air operations for most of the time. They became the USMC's own long-range artillery, available at short notice on a 'cab rank' basis. Air refuelling was seldom necessary because of the short mission duration. On average this was about an hour, with much shorter flight times in cases where Tanajib was used as the jumping-off point. Unlike most combat aircraft in the area, the Harriers were independent of the overworked tanker force. This in itself was liberating for the squadron mission schedulers and helped to sustain their high sortie rates. An AV-8B's internal fuel was usually sufficient for pilots to reach the home strip well before their headsets broadcast the Harrier's 'low fuel' warning via an automated female voice, known universally as 'Bitchin' Betty'.

Harrier activity at King Abdul Aziz developed into a pattern which prevailed until the beginning of the land war in February. In many ways the base environment resembled FOB training sites like Twenty-Nine Palms in the USA except that regular deployments to those bases would usually include a balanced force of eight aircraft detachments from AV-8B, OV-10A, AH-1J/T and CH-46 squadrons. Base defence for an Expeditionary Unit usually

included a light anti-aircraft missile battalion (LAAMBN) battery, a forward anti-aircraft defence (FAAD) unit and Hawk SAM batteries. Tented accommodation and canvas 'hides' for the Harriers were standard, as were the bladder-type fuel stores, topped-up periodically by visiting KC-130F/T tankers from a VMGR unit.

HARRIER SORTIES

Although the MAG-13 base facilities were sufficient to generate up to three sorties per Harrier per day, things seldom reached that level until the last few days of 'Desert Storm'. Pilots usually flew 'day on, day off' until then, while armourers and fixers worked 'twelve hours on, twelve hours off'. Their training had prepared them for frequent high-intensity missions. One technique used in Stateside training was the 'daisy chain', which involved one AV-8B landing vertically on a FOB pad while another taxied from the pad to refuel and rearm and a third aircraft made a STOL take-off with another load of 'pig iron'. With 66 Harriers on site at King Abdul Aziz, this process would rapidly have saturated the Saudi airspace beyond the limits of safe deconfliction by controllers.

For the day's sorties the ordnancemen would hang their wares, usually six Rockeye CBU or six 500lb bombs (1,000lb Mk 83 bombs, the standard USN 'serious metal', were in rather short supply), and then fill in the time with cards and coffee until the next flight was due out. Frequent 'Scud' attack warnings were helpful in alleviating tedium. Food was often consumed on the flight line in the form of foil-wrapped MREs (meals, ready to eat). Pre-flighting the aircraft included a sand-check to ensure that the insidious fine Saudi grains had all been brushed or vacuumed out of intakes, cockpits and even HUDs (a scenario not envisaged by Scrimgeour's pioneering TES outfit, which had covered most other contingencies, although these were part of the routine at Yuma for obvious reasons). After strapping into the capacious cockpit (by AV-8A standards) a pilot would switch on power from the internal battery to fire up his APU. When this was running, BIT checks were accomplished and the INS

Sorties Flown/Ordnance Expended

UNIT	SORTIES/HOURS	ORDNANCE	TIME-FRAME
MAG-13 AV-8s	3138 / 3769 Hrs	2937 Tons	17 Jan - 28 Feb 91
MAG-40 AV-8s	242 / 279 Hrs*		20 Feb - 28 Feb 91*
TOTALS	3380 / 4048 Hrs	6 Million Pounds in Desert Storm	

*VMA-331 entered the War on 20 Feb 91 from the USS Nassau in the Gulf. On the 3rd day of the Ground War, they flew 56 Sorties (19 A/C) for a rate of nearly 3 sorties per A/C.

STOVL Allowed Flexible Basing. Sorties Were Flown Without Tankers, thus Reducing the CinC's Logistics Requirements.

initialised, the engine start switch went from 'Off' to 'Start', the throttle to 'Idle' rpm and flaps to the STOL position. If all was well and the INS was running accurately (vital for navigation in poor visibility and featureless landscapes), the aircraft could taxy out. The Pegasus was then run up to 27 per cent and to 55 per cent rpm to check acceleration times on the DDI and ensure that they were between 3.6 and 4.6 seconds. With power set at 50 per cent, the water injection switch was engaged, increasing mass flow through the engine and allowing higher jet-pipe temperatures (JPT) by cooling engine components. Jet nozzles were set to 10 degrees down and the STO nozzle stop at 60 degrees. After a final check of engine intake pressures the throttle was pushed to maximum power and brakes released. At 90kt the nozzle lever was slammed to the 60-degree detent, lifting the Harrier into the air after a ground-run of less than 1,000ft. With 12 degrees AOA displayed the nozzles could be rotated fully aft, the gear raised and the aircraft levelled off at 2–3,000ft at a cruise speed of 425–430kt.

Following the steering indications in his HUD provided by the INS for the 20–30 minute flight, a pilot soon had to call up the 'weapons select' command on his DDI

once the FAC had cleared his flight into the target area. Weapons stations could be selected for single bomb release, or combinations. Triple ejection racks (TERs) were carried early in the war but pilots preferred the simpler and less draggy arrangement of one bomb per pylon. On the DDI bomb-dropping intervals (in milliseconds, as such equating to tens of feet at 500kt) and fusing commands could also be set. Fuses were usually fitted to the noses and tails of bombs so that the pilot had the option of selecting either over the target area. If Mk 82 SE (Snakeye) bombs were aboard, nose fusing was set to release the 'safe' wires which deploy the bomb's four tail cruciform air brakes. Choosing the tail fuse on a Snakeye converted it back to a normal 'slick' bomb because the wires would remain in place.

Having completed his attack, a pilot awaited instant BDA (bombs damage assessment) from his eagle-eyed FAC-A or, if he was bombing close to the Coalition lines, from an ANGLICO, the USMC Air Naval Gunfire Liaison Company FAC. AV-8Bs did not carry strike cameras. It was possible, but risky, for a wingman to use his ARBS camera to assess the results of his leader's drop. BDA was a perpetual problem. General Schwarzkopf later de-

scribed it as 'abysmal', due largely to the lack of sufficient tactical reconnaissance aircraft, the worst weather in the area for fourteen years and the lack of high-definition video recorders in the strike aircraft. (Colonel Bioty checked his day-to-day sortie figures for the authors and noted that AV-8 operations were severely affected by weather on only five of the 42 days of war. Ceilings of 7,000ft or less were present on 27–28 February.) Regrettably, the Marines had retired their own RF-4B Phantom battlefield recce jets the previous August and relied partly on UAVs (unmanned air vehicles) for BDA reports.[5]

On his return from the sortie, with arming wires trailing loose from his empty pylons, or possibly a set of undelivered ordnance if the target was unavailable due to a weather abort, the pilot began his initial approach to the crowded base at 1,500ft. Flaps were lowered, water switched on and transition begun half a mile from touchdown for a vertical descent. Usually, short landings on 1,500–2,000ft of runway were possible, but on a crowded base a vertical descent could be made by selecting the 40-degree nozzle position and allowing speed to decay to 140kt. Gradually the nozzle control was moved to the 81-degree 'hover-stop' position and speed reduced further by adjusting nozzles between 'hover stop' and 'braking stop' angles, taking the jet to a point 100ft above the landing site and maintaining heading with the RCS. Gradual power reduction allowed the Harrier to settle on the ground, whereupon power and water injection were cut, the nozzles swung aft and the nosewheel steering engaged to taxy in. The whole process was easier in the Harrier II whose wing still generated useful lift at speeds below 50kt with nozzles in the 60-degree position. In that configuration, AV-8As would be heading for the deck at forward speeds below 90kt. At King Abdul Aziz it

[5]John Bioty: 'The lack of the RF-4B recce unit was sorely felt in the quest for tactical photo-reconnaissance of the battlefield. Some target photos were available but they were old and in short supply. RPVs [UAVs] helped during the later stages of war but their video had to be "developed" and took time to get to the attacking aircrews.'

AV-8 Sortie Generation
Desert Storm

	Planned	Flown
Sustained: (2.0 sorties/day)	102	101*
Surge: (3.6 Sorties/day)	184	160*

*MAG-13 (Fwd) Flew near sustained rate for 37 days, near surge rate for 5 days * Note: 12 A/C remained on continual "strip alert" - throughout the war.*

was quite usual to launch two or three Harriers at once from different sections of the runway. To the Marines, 800ft of concrete is the bottom line in establishing an FOB from which to operate Harriers over a 300-mile tactical radius.

Each squadron launched up to twenty sorties a day in the first week of war but night flying became established as the conflict intensified. The AV-8B's attack systems were designed for identifying and designating targets from below 15,000ft, with ARBS laser as an option for day attacks. Colonel John Bioty reckoned that 'In daytime, smoke and fire on the battlefield allowed the ARBS lock to drift. Many pilots delivered their ordnance in the ARBS/CCIP mode. In this fashion, ARBS provided target height information but the pilot manually released the weapons. ARBS did provide target situational awareness because of its magnification. Pilots would lock on to a suspected target then glance in the cockpit to the ARBS display in an attempt to identify it. Better results could have been obtained at night with the AV-8B(NA) FLIR addition—and its extra Tracor ALE-39 dispensers would have been welcome too by day. For night operations it would have eliminated the optical/IR SAM threat because these sys-

tems were not a factor at night.' Iraqi troop movements and armour redeployments were usually done in darkness and an effective night attack system would have enabled more damage to be done. AV-8Bs were cleared to fire the AGM-65E Maverick with semi-active laser (SAL) guidance. The Marines were the only users of this variant which required a ground FAC to designate targets for its seeker. A lack of these facilities at the right times meant that actual firings were restricted to five in the whole war, although MAG-13 had 210 missiles 'on hand'. Two did not guide and 'went stupid' owing to loss or interruption of laser energy from the lasing aircraft (usually an OV-10). Three laser Mavericks were direct hits. Colonel John Bioty described one of them: 'Early in February 1991 MAG-13(FWD) received word from the Kuwaiti "underground" that senior officers of the Iraqi 5th Mechanised Division were planning a coordinating meeting at 9 p.m. at a gas station three miles south of Kuwait City. Target coordinates were passed to the aircrews. An OV-10 was airborne that evening and in position to lase the target. A section of AV-8s armed with AGM-65Es launched at 8.30 p.m. and checked in with the OV-10. The Bronco reported seeing armoured

cars pull up to the building and military personnel get out. After the final armoured vehicle arrived at 9.05 p.m. and people entered the building, it was lased by the OV-10 crew and a Maverick launched by a Harrier. It scored a direct hit on the building. Later, during the debrief, the OV-10 crew described the event in more graphic detail: "It was beautiful", they said; just as the last Iraqi soldier closed the door the Maverick went right through the same door. The explosion was awesome.' No 'TV Mavericks' (the AGM-65B electro-optical guided version) were used, but some pilots felt that this weapon would have given them a useful and accurate stand-off capability against heavily defended priority targets. Paveway II LGBs such as GBU-12D/B and GBU-16B/B were hardly used because the medium/low altitude attack profiles using ARBS were judged sufficiently accurate to make LGBs unnecessary. Contrary to 'Gulf mythology', only 9 per cent of the bomb tonnage dropped during the war was precision guided, and less than one-tenth of that 9 per cent was dropped by USN or USMC aircraft—mostly F/A-18s.

Of the other weapons used, Mk 20 Rockeye II was the most common. In a typical 40–45-degree dive attack its bomblets were effective in a 300 by 200ft area. A version of the ISC Technologies Mk 7, the Mk 20 was developed by the Naval Weapons Center and it had been in use since the middle of the Vietnam War. The weapon contained 247 Mk 118 dart-shaped bomblets which were capable of penetrating armour. Turrets were seen to fly off a number of older Iraqi tanks after Mk 20 CBU hits. Another variant, the CBU-59 anti-personnel/anti-*matériel* (APAM) was also used. CBU-55A fuel–air explosives (FAE) were occasionally carried in the days immediately before the ground war began in an attempt to explode minefields with a large detonation immediately above them, but the results were disappointing. Also at that stage the Harriers made their much-publicised napalm drops on the oil-filled trenches which the Iraqis had set up on the Kuwaiti border, as a wall of fire to hold back the advancing Coalition armies. Perhaps the Iraqis would have had more success in this than the AV-8Bs, but the Mk 77 Mod 5 fire bombs, each containing 63gal of fuel and 'imbiber beads', failed to ignite anything. Pilots put this down partly to the age of the ordnance, and they hated the mission because the strict 1,000ft straight-and-level delivery put them within easy reach of enemy ground fire. Other than these weapons, the majority of ordnance carried by AV-8Bs came from the vast stocks of Mk 82 and Mk 83 bombs. Although AIM-9M Sidewinders were hung on one pylon for the first few days, the Iraqi fighter threat was quickly neutralised elsewhere and the missiles were put back in store; none were fired from Harriers.

On the ground the enemy defences were omni-present. VMA-542 commander Ted 'Mongoose' Herman said that, around many targets, 'we knew that every square inch of land was covered by triple-A and missiles'. On his first mission he was aware of 'incredible amounts of small-calibre triple-A'. Inevitably there were losses. VMA-331 were the first to lose a pilot and his aircraft, although it was an operational loss on approach to USS *Nassau*. Captain Michael Craig Berryman's was the first combat shoot-down:

'On August 2nd 1990 my unit got the call. We would be the first Marine fixed-wing squadron going into the Persian Gulf area to hold off Saddam Hussein. When my division headed out for our first combat mission my heart gotta pumpin'! I wondered if all this training I had done for the last five years was going to be enough. I found out the first time I put my Harrier into a dive and put her nose on a real target—my training took over. [On 28 January Berryman was scheduled to lead a two-ship attack with Captain Joe Hines on an Iraqi "Frog" missile site which had been firing on Marines near the town of Khafji. As the pilots walked to their AV-8Bs their Intelligence Officer ran up to warn them of a SAM site in the target

area. They failed to locate the "Frog" site but then did notice a large convoy heading south towards Khafji, the spearhead of Saddam's ill-fated incursion into the town.]

'I went into a 45-degree dive, gaining airspeed from 450 to 550kt. Suddenly, without warning, the inflight refuelling probe just popped out. It got sucked out by the aerodynamic pressure. The airplane turned sideways in a dangerous braking action due to the probe. [Berryman pulled away, allowing Joe Hines to hit the target.] I broke one of the cardinal rules of CAS. You never go back for a second run on a target unless Marines are dying on the ground. [Having recycled his probe, he made a second attack with Hines covering him.] As I went for the second pass the probe got sucked out again. I had to fight to recover the aircraft. As I started pulling up and away I reached down to recycle the probe, got some airspeed back and got away from the small-arms fire. [As Berryman hauled the skidding Harrier away Hines noticed a flash on the ground and a missile streaked towards his companion's Harrier, coded '02 WL', before he could radio a warning.] I didn't see the missile because I was looking down to recycle the probe. The first thing I felt was the airplane get hit from the port side and

get pushed a few feet through the air. Then [there was] a huge explosion and the airplane went end over end, and sideways at the same time. Quite a ride! I was thinking, "If I can just get to the water I can punch out". Our intelligence people had shown us photos of what the Iraqis were doing to the captured Kuwaiti Resistance fighters, and it was ugly. I didn't want to go through that so I thought about staying in the plane and accepting death on impact. And then I thought that idea was stupid. [With his Harrier in an inverted flat spin he reached for the exit handle and 1.2 seconds later the MDC shattered the canopy as advertised.] I watched the maps get sucked out of the cockpit, then the ejection seat fired. I saw nothing but grey as the g-forces drained the blood from my head.

Berryman became a target for Iraqi AK.47 fire as he drifted down, unseen by his wingman, to be listed MIA. Landing safely, he ran towards a sand dune, still pursued by Iraqi bullets, and found himself face to face with an Iraqi APC crew. Surrounded and captured, he received the first of many severe beatings and was dragged off to prison in Baghdad for interrogation. He continues: 'One guard grabbed my hand and held it out on the table. The interrogator took out a knife

Captain John Scott Walsh (right) models the ubiquitous desert hat at Sheikh Isa while his VMA-542 colleague opts for more conventional gear. (Via Andy Evans)

AV-8B LOSSES, 'DESERT SHIELD'/'STORM'

Date	BuNo	Code	Unit	Pilot	Remarks
22/01/91	162954	11 VL	VMA-331	1Lt Manuel Rivera Jr	Killed; operational loss; USS *Nassau*
28/01/91	163518	02 WL	VMA-311	Capt Michael C. Berryman	POW
09/02/91	162081	09 CG	VMA-231	Capt Russell A. C. Sanbourn	Jump 57; POW
23/02/91	161573	21 WH	VMA-542	Capt James N. Wilbourne	KIA
25/02/91	163190	12 WH	VMA-542	Capt Scott Walsh	Rescued
27/02/91	163740	14 VL	VMA-331	Capt Reginald C. Underwood	KIA; USS *Nassau*

and drove it into the table beside my hand and said, "I'm going to ask you five questions and if I don't like the answers I'm going to cut off a finger for each wrong answer.'

Shocked into complete silence, the pilot survived that experience and was returned to his cell to complete 37 days as a POW. The only relief was the partial destruction of the prison building by USAF F-117As with 2,000lb LGBs: 'The bombs were so close before impact you could hear their fins making corrections to target. No POWs were seriously injured. The Iraqis were forced to move us to another camp where there were eleven Americans in one cell. We drew so much strength from each other by being together, and being able to talk for the first time, that no matter what the Iraqis tried they wouldn't break our spirit.'

While air operations continued into February, the stress on pilots flying up to three missions daily began to tell. There was little respite apart from occasional visits by selected personnel to the Cunard liner *Princess* for 'R&R'. Moored well off Bahrain, the ship was known as 'The Love Boat' because it offered some home comforts that the aircrew were unable to find in their host country, such as a few beers and some young ladies to talk to.

The routine was broken on 29 January by Saddam's sudden decision to mount a heavy armoured assault on the border town of Kahfji, just as General Schwarzkopf declared total air supremacy over Kuwait and Iraq. Post-war reports by Iraqi defectors suggest that the attack was meant to be the prelude to a major hostage-taking raid, ahead of Saddam's planned invasion of Saudi Arabia. It was repelled by USMC AH-1W SeaCobras, AV-8Bs and USAF aircraft in four separate actions which cost the Iraqis over 100 tanks and vehicles and huge numbers of prisoners. On one strike AV-8Bs destroyed 22 tanks. Several USMC recce teams in the town were able to escape as the air strikes took their toll and Coalition troops recaptured the town.

VMA-331, at sea on board USS *Nassau*, were almost involved in CAS for a classic USMC amphibious landing. The presence of a large seaborne expeditionary force off the Kuwait coast, and the assumption by the Iraqis that it would natu-

John Walsh in flying gear, with personalised Mk 20 Rockeye. (Via Andy Evans)

rally make such a landing, was used to distract large sections of Saddam's army from the actual US/Coalition advances in the western part of the theatre. At one stage General Schwarzkopf did contemplate a real landing at the coastal town of Ash Shuaybah, code-named 'Desert Saber'. He was persuaded that the inevitable USMC casualties would be unacceptable to the American people. However, the USMC Harriers were involved in several feint attacks which were supposed to suggest an imminent coastal assault, including Operation 'Slash'. This was a limited attack, on 20 February, on Faylaka Island. After heavy shelling by USS *Wisconsin* and USS *Missouri*, USAF MC-130E 'Combat Talon' Hercules dropped three colossal BLU-82/B 15,000lb blast bombs (in what became known as the 'Blues Brothers' attack). VMA-331 were tasked with supporting strikes on AAA sites. A second mock invasion by the 4th MEB was made at R'as as Sabiyah with sixty helicopters supported by AV-8Bs. This drew even more Iraqi troops to defend the area.

After the night of 23–24 February, when the ground war began with a series of armoured thrusts into Kuwait, the AV-8Bs' sortie rate increased markedly. At last their primary CAS function could be employed as the Marines pushed north, preventing an orderly Iraqi escape from Kuwait. February 23 also brought VMA-542's first loss. At 1930 Captain James 'Trey' Wilbourne was involved in an attack on Ali al Salem airfield with Mk 83 bombs. He dropped them successfully but the next thing his wingman saw was a flash just beyond the target where Wilbourne's AV-8B, the first one handed over to the USMC, had hit the ground, killing its pilot.[6] The squadron suffered its second Harrier loss two days later as MAG-13 aircraft destroyed Iraqi armour ahead of the advancing 2nd Marine Division. Captain Scott 'Vapor' Walsh was on his 39th combat mission and his second of the day. Flying from Tanajib FOB, he was attacking an armoured column in bad visibility below a 9,000ft cloud base. He became separated from his leader, losing mutual support, and took an IR missile in the right rear nozzle. With flames streaming from

AV-8B BuNo 163424 of VMA-542, loaded with Rockeyes, heads for the battle front. (Via Andy Evans)

the aircraft's wing, he found a Fast-FAC to escort him out of the area and attempted a landing at a tiny desert airstrip. His undercarriage had partly extended and he had persuaded the faltering Harrier to within 1,000ft of touchdown when the hydraulics gave out and control became impossible. Walsh tugged the ejection handle as his aircraft turned on its back and he hit the ground seconds after his chute opened. He was collected, uninjured, by a USMC vehicle and returned to duty.

The only VMA-231 loss was on 9 February. Captain Russell 'Bart' (after Bart Simpson) Sanborn also fell to an IR SAM, probably an SA-7, and was captured before he could dig himself an overnight 'hide'. One of VMA-331's seaborne Harriers was the final loss of the war. Captain Reginald Underwood was killed in uncertain circumstances while attacking in restricted visibility on the last day of fighting.[7] Inevitably the five combat losses provoked comment about the AV-8B's survivability and resulted in plans to protect its hydraulic lines and install MAWS. In fact, five losses in 3,380 low-altitude missions over some of the most heavily defended battlefield territory in history was an extremely impressive survival rate. In the 1973 Arab-Israeli war the IDF/AF lost 109 aircraft (including approximately four dozen Skyhawks), 48 of them to SAMs in nineteen days of combat. The AV-8B, of a similar size to and with an IR/radar sig-

nature comparable to that of the Skyhawk, faced later-generation SAMs and the same deadly ZSU-23 AAA. In the first three days of their war the IDF/AF sustained a 4.1 per cent loss rate (i.e. one for approximately every 25 sorties); the rate for the AV-8B units in the Gulf was 0.15 per cent, nearly 30 times lower. Obviously direct comparisons are not possible, but in the Gulf context AV-8B losses were certainly not out of line with those for other USAF/USN types, except perhaps the A-10 which sustained the same number of losses with more than twice the number of aircraft (144) over 8,100 sorties. However, the AV-8B did not have yards of armour plate and disposable engines and flying surfaces!

During the last five days of the war the AV-8B squadrons flew around the clock, recording astonishing sortie rates. Of the 242 flown by VMA-331—the first ever

[6] James Wilbourne III (call-sign 'LZ') was flying a night mission, ruling out an IR SAM hit—the only loss which could not be confirmed as an IR missile 'hit'. Pilot disorientation could have been a factor due to reported heavy smoke and haze. In Colonel John Bioty's opinion, Wilbourne 'became disorientated or released his ordnance below a safe recovery altitude. He was carrying four 1,000lb bombs and his aircraft impacted in a near nose-level attitude, just beyond the target. The Air Group considered this a combat loss because it could not be proven otherwise.'
[7] This loss is described more fully below.

VMAQ-2's EA-6B Prowlers provided EW cover for as many Harrier strikes as possible. BuNo 158035/00 CY was one of twelve Prowlers deployed to Sheikh Isa in August 1990. (Via Andy Evans)

from an LHA ship—most were during this period. Lieutenant-Colonel Dick White's *Tomcats* flew 1,017 combat missions, dropping 850 tons of ordnance in all, with pilots completing three sorties a day during the final week. On several days the Squadron generated 60 sorties with its 18–19 aircraft. Colonel John 'Hunter' Bioty, who commanded MAG-13 (FWD) with its four AV-8B units at Jubail, told the authors, 'The Harrier was a "prime" sortie generator during "Desert Storm" and kept constant pressure on Iraqi troops in the central and southern Kuwait areas. As a result, both Marine divisions faced little resistance in their quest to retake Kuwait City. On a personal note, I can relate having led a section of AV-8Bs against Iraqi troops on the "Highway of Death" on 26 February 1991. Reporting in at 6 a.m. to our F/A-18D Fast-FAC, I was told to interdict armoured vehicles and troops north of the city. Having landed back at King Abdul Aziz Base, I drove over to General "Royal" Moore's HQ at 10 a.m. and personally reported on the situation. He asked me how my sortie went. I told him all three

were successful. Because of our forward basing at Tanajib, just 35 miles south of the Kuwaiti border, I was able to land, refuel, rearm and get airborne two more times that morning!'

On board USS *Nassau*, VMA-331 completed 56 deck-launched missions in one day, far more than a conventional Navy fighter unit could have achieved, given the slower cycle of launch and recovery required by catapults/arresting gear methods on larger ships. *Tarawa* class LHAs were built with the AV-8B in the design equations. They have a full-length 834 by 131ft flight deck and large areas of hangar accommodation. Normally they carry a Special Operations Capable Marine Expeditionary Unit (SOCME) with a six-aircraft Harrier detachment, but a full squadron of twenty VMA-331 aircraft could be taken instead.

VMA-331's war had been difficult from the outset. Deployed to USS *Nassau* off North Carolina on 18 August 1990, the Squadron had tried to stay proficient during the voyage to the Gulf but, as one officer put it, 'Our biggest enemy for much of the time was the ship itself.' They were frustrated by all manner of limitations: lack of fresh water for Pegasus anti-corrosion wash-downs, complaints about the use of their 'minimag' night lights to inspect engines at night when deck-lifts were

prohibited, even the high-fat ship's diet. They arrived late in the war, having already lost a pilot in training—Captain Manny 'Buick' Rivera, whose Harrier went into a rapid descent on a night approach to *Nassau* while it was just offshore and crashed on the beach. The squadron had unexpectedly been put on a night CAS tasking, but none of its pilots had flown a night sortie for over four months.

Their first mission was the 20 February diversionary attack against Faylaka Island's AAA defences. An 0540 attack was launched in rain, darkness and 800ft overcast, with the aircraft loaded with Mk 82 bombs fitted with Mk 376 tail fuses and Mk 43 TDD (target detector devices) to give an airburst function. One of the aircraft, flown by Captain 'Woody' Underwood, also carried an AN/ALQ-164 DECM pod. The primary Faylaka target was 'socked in' so the four Harriers went north to Bubiyan, the 'secondary', and bombed from 37,000ft on INS 'like Air Force B-52s'. Dodging an unguided SA-2 which exploded in the middle of the formation, they about-turned for *Nassau*. VMA-331's real share of combat came with the initiation of the ground war into Kuwait. They were soon flying 60 sorties a day in support of the rapidly advancing Marine ground forces.

On the last 'shooting' day of the war, 27 February, Major Ben Hancock led a division of four VMA-331 Harriers against a target near Safwan, southern Iraq. Their F/A-18D FAC-A, 'Combat 05', reported weather at 10,000ft ceiling, overcast with seven miles' visibility, degraded by smoke from burning oil wells. Captain Kevin 'Peewee' Herrmann,

Right, upper: Craig Berryman with one of VMA-311's Harriers after his first mission, 16 January 1991. (USMC via Craig Berryman)

Right, lower: The wreck of Craig Berryman's Harrier (BuNo 163518/02 WL) on 4 March 1991, the day before his release from prison in Baghdad. His squadron sent a search party to examine and photograph the crash site, thinking that they might discover his remains in the wreckage. (USMC via Craig Berryman)

Colonel John Bioty, CO of MAG-13 FWD, took this photograph of the Al Burgan oilfields west of Kuwait City, set alight by Saddam Hussein's retreating troops. (John Bioty)

'Woody' Underwood and the Squadron CO, Lieutenant-Colonel John 'Mystic' Fitzgerald, followed Hancock towards the target at 450kt in loose 'fighter wing' (abeam of each other with a mile's separation). 'Combat 05' called them on to the target, not realising that they had actually flown too far north to some incorrect co-ordinates. As they prepared to roll-in 'Mystic' Fitzgerald called 'Break, break! Flares!' as multiple SAMs headed for the division. Two made for 'Woody''s aircraft and it took a hit in the left hot nozzle. 'Mystic' almost caught a third but he managed to enter the cloud base and lost it. Underwood was heard to transmit 'I can't control it' seconds before his AV-8B struck the ground in an orange fireball. At 'bingo' fuel the other three pilots had to dump their bombs and return to the ship. Analysis of the sortie showed that the mistaken coordinates had taken them over the well-defended centre of the Iraqi Republican Guard's Hummurabi Division. Despite reports that Reg Underwood had ejected and survived (probably deception trans-

missions by the Iraqis to lure in the rescuers), it became clear after the war that he had not. His remains were returned to his native state of Kentucky in March 1991.

The AV-8B—the 'engine with a saddle on it', as one pilot thought of it—had demonstrated with outstanding success its ability to operate from all the platforms for which it was designed. Above all, it turned in remarkable figures for availability. Helped by excellent spares supply-lines, all squadrons reported steady '95 per cent plus' ready rates throughout the war. In a letter to the Persian Gulf War Commission, General Norman Schwarzkopf named the seven weapons systems which he felt had significantly contributed to the Coalition's quick success in 'Desert Storm'. Only three of them were aircraft: the F-117A 'Stealth', the AH-64 Apache—and the AV-8B Harrier.

At the beginning of March 1991 58 AV-8Bs, marked with their prodigious bomb scores, were still at King Abdul Aziz, but the return to the USA was in progress. VMA-231 and VMA-542 sent the major-

ity of their Harriers to Rota on 16 March and they returned to the United States aboard USS *Saratoga* and USS *John F. Kennedy*. The remaining seven ran out of tankers on the Rota leg when two out of three KC-10As provided went unserviceable. They had to retrace their paths to King Abdul Aziz and wait two weeks for the next tanker slot on the crowded transatlantic return routes. They finally arrived at Cherry Point on 1 April. VMA-311's nineteen survivors were the 'first in—last out', flying the Atlantic to Cherry Point on 13 April en route to Yuma. Of the two MEB units, VMA-331 sailed out of the Gulf on 10 March and VMA-513 Det B rejoined USS *Tarawa* the same day. No-one had any doubt that, if the need arose, they could be back and in action very quickly indeed.

8. Super Harrier Plus

The experience of the Gulf War greatly reinforced confidence in the AV-8B and the USMC's V/STOL philosophy. Actually, the number of US Navy ships with Harrier support capability increased steadily from 1988 onwards. Seven assault ships in the 18,300-ton *Iwo Jima* class (LPH), five *Tarawa* class (LHA), each of 39,300 tons and a planned total of eleven *Wasp* class (LHD) carriers of 40,532 tons are Harrier-capable. The big *Wasp*s, five of which are intended as *Iwo Jima* replacements, can take full Harrier squadrons of 20 aircraft and six SH-60B helicopters. They strongly resemble the USN's planned Sea Control Ships of the 1970s, and will probably replace some supercarrier commitments in the near future, especially as the ageing F-14 Tomcat fleet is gradually phased out and a reducing Navy becomes increasingly stretched. In addition, deck landing vessels of the *Whidbey Island* class (LSD) can take small Harrier detachments. With such flexibility to deploy Harriers quickly to areas of need, the case for continued improvement to the aircraft, and for an eventual replacement, steadily gathered force.

In drafting proposals for the Harrier 3, as it was originally dubbed, Rolls-Royce's Pegasus 11-61 engine was central to a further series of improvements. Originally rig-tested at Patchway, Bristol, in 1987, it was based on a demonstrator engine called XG-15, funded by Rolls-Royce and the MoD in 1984.[1] Alan Baxter, one of Rolls-Royce's Senior Engineers, provided some background on the 11-61: 'It is surprising, on looking back, to realise that between the Pegasus 6 (Mk 101) of 1965 and the 11-21 (Mk 105) of 1980 the thrust had grown by only 3,000lb, although it is true to say that much effort had gone into improving the efficiency and reliability of the engine to the point where, in 1980, there were over twenty engines that had exceeded 2,000hr lives. With the continuing introduction of more aircraft equipment and payload, the engine was clearly overdue for a significant growth in thrust.' The company's XG-15 demonstrator delivered its anticipated extra 15 per cent power, which equated to another 3,000lb of thrust (under tropical day conditions).

Derived from the Mk 105, the 11-61 had a number of internal improvements—a new front fan with increased pressure ratio (the model 64B), a better combustor, an extra low-pressure bearing, reduced pressure loss in the diffuser and single-crystal blades in both LP and HP turbines. Advances in steel manufacture enabled the cooling process to be controlled in such a way that the electromagnetic/crystalline domain in the metal aligned themselves in one direction rather than randomly, forming a single-crystal structure. Any additional crystals were 'picked off' during the cooling cycle. The process gives up to 40°C improvement in heat resistance and lower 'creep', but it makes the blade more fragile during manufacture. To manage

The first R-R Pegasus 11-61 being installed in ZD402 in April 1989. The aircraft's first ground-run at full power was made on 13 April and Heinz Frick flew it four days later. (Via Alan Baxter)

[1] The 'X' stood for 'extra' and '15' for the extra 15 per cent thrust which the demonstrator engine provided.

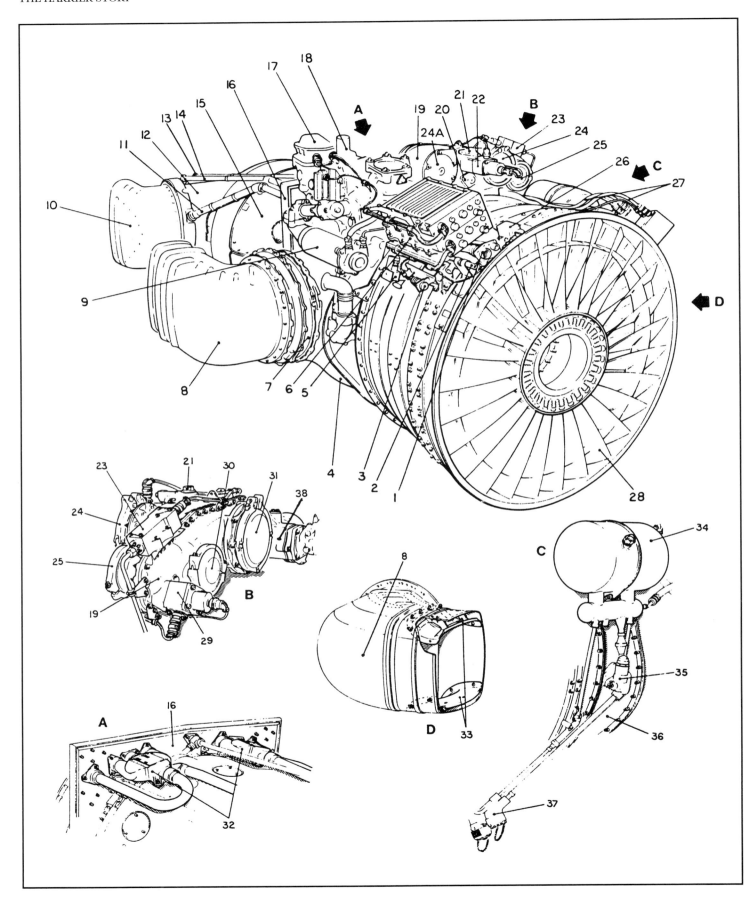

Left: Pegasus 11-61 assembly. 1. Electrical general services and manual fuel control connections. 2. T1 air sensor (VIGV control). 3. Engine monitoring system (EMS) connector. 4. LP compressor delivery duct. 5. OBOGS shut-off valve connector. 6. Digital engine control unit (DECU) No 1 (upper); digital engine control unit (DECU) No 2 (lower). 7. Intermediate delivery duct. 8. Front (LP exhaust) nozzle. 9. Fuel cooled oil cooler. 10. Rear (exhaust duct) nozzle. 11. Rear nozzle bearing cooling air tube. 12. Bifurcated exhaust duct. 13. Water injection supply tube. 14. Rear environmental control system (ECS) air supply tube. 15. Combustion chamber/turbine casing heat insulation shield. 16. Fireproof bulkhead. 17. Fuel metering unit. 18. Manual fuel control system. 18. Accessory gearbox. 20. Oil low pressure warning switch. 21. HP compressor hand turning shaft cover. 22. LP compressor speed probe. 23. EMS HP compressor delivery (P3) transducer. 24. Generator drive pad, left hand side (mounts integrated drive generator, including constant speed drive and AC generator of 30kVa capacity). 24A. Generator drive pad, right-hand side (currently blanked). 25. No 1 hydraulic pump drive pad. 26. EMS vibration signal charge amplifier. 27. High energy ignition leads. 28. LP compressor. 29. HP compressor speed probe. 30. No 2 hydraulic pump drive pad. 31. Gas turbine starter/auxiliary power unit (GTS/APU) mounting pad. 32. Bleed air heat exchangers (precoolers). 33. Front nozzle trimmers. 34. Oil tank. 35. Oil pressure relief valve. 36. Intermediate case. 37. Oil tank drain and pressure filling coupling. 38. VIGV control unit.

Right, upper: Pegasus 11-61 design features.

Right, lower: Thrust vectoring

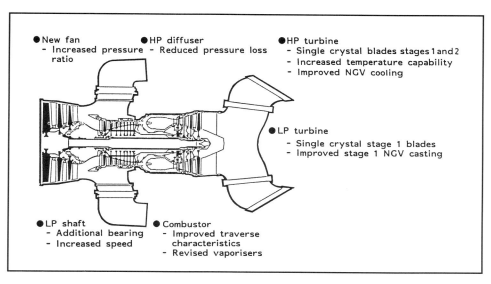

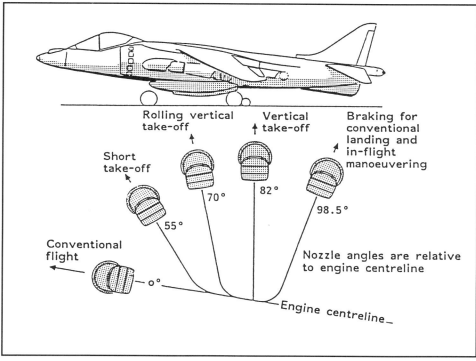

the engine's fuel system, full authority, twin-channel digital engine control (FADEC) was incorporated from the outset.

Flight testing of the new Pegasus took place in Harrier GR.5 ZD402 which was delivered to Patchway by road on 28 March 1989. The aircraft was fitted with a MODAS flight data recorder and MARS strain gauge and it received a smart blue-black/white paint job. A delegation from McAir and NATC arrived at Patchway on 15 May to see the installation of the first engine (Pegasus No 967).

Ground runs were done at the 'Palm Beach' Harrier site at Filton (so called because it had once been decorated with potted palms as a film set for the thriller *Cone of Silence*) with the aircraft tethered, causing considerable surface damage to the 'Beach' when the aircraft's nozzles were deflected downwards beyond 30 degrees. Heinz Frick made the first flight on 9 June, and fifty-seven others followed, shared among Frick, Andy Sephton and Chris Roberts. NATC pilot G. Hoppe flew an evaluation for the USMC on Flight 56 and McDonnell-Douglas Chief Test Pi-

lot Jack Jackson flew another. The only problem that arose was a popping, thumping noise, noticed by all pilots, mainly in VTOL mode. It was solved by fitting the second 11-61 engine (No 968).

The results of the 11-61 tests were so encouraging that it seemed a good opportunity to try and beat the existing Harrier time-to-height records. In the International Record regulations, Class H (for vertical take-off aircraft) specifies that the aircraft should start from rest, but a short rolling VTO is allowed. There were four records to beat—the 3,000m, 6,000m,

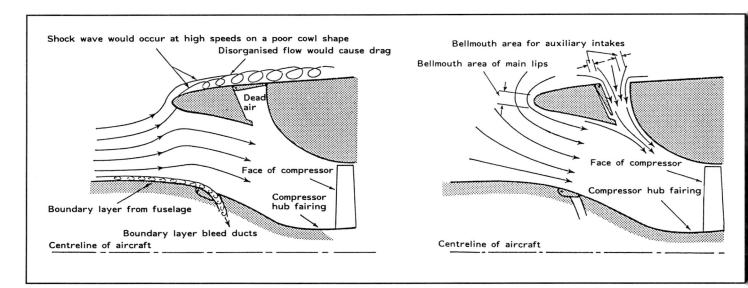

Shock wave would occur at high speeds on a poor cowl shape
Disorganised flow would cause drag
Dead air
Face of compressor
Compressor hub fairing
Boundary layer from fuselage
Boundary layer bleed ducts
Centreline of aircraft

Bellmouth area for auxiliary intakes
Bellmouth area of main lips
Face of compressor
Compressor hub fairing
Centreline of aircraft

Left, upper: Plan views of Pegasus 11-61 intake flow pattern in conventional flight (far left) and in V/STOL flight (near left).

Left, lower: The Pegasus 11-61 engine for the Harrier II Plus was test-flown in Harrier GR.5 ZD402 in June 1989. The unusual colour scheme was a mix of Roundel Blue (75 per cent) and black (25 per cent), prepared by BAe at Dunsfold; wing and tail-tips were white. (Via Andy Sephton)

Below right: US Marine Corps interest in the Pegasus 11-61 engine was represented in the flight-testing by Glenn 'Gremlin' Hoppe from the Naval Air Test Center, seen here with Andy Sephton, Dave MacKay (A&AEE) and the 11-61 test-bed. (Via Andy Sephton)

9,000m and 12,000m altitudes. Alan Baxter described the preparations: 'Four separate flights were allocated. In this way the absolute minimum fuel could be carried for each attempt. The wing pylons were removed. Additionally, the wiring was modified to allow the use of lift-off engine ratings with the nozzles aft and water injection to be available at airspeeds above 250kt. Short rolling take-offs were made at the Short Lift Wet (SLW) rating with nozzles at 70 degrees. Different profiles were flown for each of the flights by Andy Sephton and Heinz Frick: for example, the 3,000-metre attempt involved a level acceleration to 220kt, then a 3g pull-up to the vertical.' Monitoring of the flights at Filton was provided by a representative of the Royal Aero Club and awards were made to the two pilots for new records as shown in the accompanying table. Shortly afterwards the two prototype 11-61 engines were flown to St Louis for continuation flight tests and then to Edwards AFB for a further 43 flights from October 1989, leading to service clearance as the Pegasus F402-RR-408. Harrier XV402 was handed back to the MoD(PE) and subsequently reallocated to No 1 Squadron.

While Pegasus 11-61 engine development proceeded the Marines were experiencing difficulty with some of their earlier engines. There were several cases of engine failure due to contaminated lubri-

Left, top: VMA-542, under Lieutenant-Colonel Kevin Leffler, received the first batch of Harrier II Plus aircraft in 1993 at Cherry Point. Here '06 WH' releases a pair of blue (training) Snakeyes. (Via Andy Evans)

Left, centre: A radome which is slightly reminiscent of an earlier St Louis product, the F-4 Phantom, gives the 'Plus' a sleeker look than the Sea Harrier F/A.2. VMA-542's 'lo-viz' tiger insignia is all but invisible below the windshield. (Andy Evans)

Left, bottom: VMA-223 *Bulldogs* began to receive radar-equipped Harrier II Plus variants in June 1994 at Cherry Point, including BuNo 164558 (MAP)

cation channels for the inlet guide vanes (IGVs), causing them to jam in the closed position. This reduced the airflow to the engine, inappropriately causing overheating and compressor failure. There were also teething problems with some F402-RR-404 and -406 engines which had been retrofitted with DECS (adding an 'A' suffix to the engine designation), In two cases AV-8Bs were thought to have crashed because fuel had been cut off due to a mismatch between DECS and several engines which were said by the USMC to have received inadequate testing prior to installation. The cause is more likely to have been the method of switching DECS on and off in the AV-8B. A control lever was employed which was lowered (rather like a car hand-brake) to engage DECS at the bottom of its travel. If vibration or incomplete lowering caused the lever to move slightly the system would disengage. Unless the pilot realised the error and selected manual reversion the fuel supply would be cut off. The Marines assured Rolls-Royce that their pilots would be trained to avoid this problem, but a second on/off switch was installed—which probably made the situation even more complex. Improved software helped. For their DECS-equipped GR.5 the RAF specified a more straightforward arrangement.

Having resolved these problems, Rolls-Royce and the USMC were faced with some more unexpected snags with the -408 (11-61) Pegasus soon after it entered Marine Corps service. Several of the early

HARRIER TIME-TO-HEIGHT RECORDS				
Flt no	Altitude (m)	Pilot	Time (sec)	Previous record (sec)
49	6,000	H. Frick	55.38	60.65
50	9,000	A. Sephton	81.00	86.66
51	12,000	H. Frick	126.63	142.70
52	3,000	A. Sephton	36.38	39.48

Right, upper: Strapping into the cockpit of a 'Plus'. The HOTAS stick, up-front controller, HUD and multifunction displays have replaced almost all the old 'steam gauges'. (Andy Evans)

Right, lower: These Harrier II Plus aircraft have the three-tone Tactical Paint Scheme, using shades FS.361189 Dark Sea Gray on upper surfaces, FS.36231 Dark Gull Gray on the sides of the aircraft and FS.36230 (Dark Ghost Gray) on the undersides. (Andy Evans)

production engines were installed in new-build AV-8B(NA)s, and two failures, one leading to a crash, occurred to the Yuma-based VMA-211 and VMA-214 in February 1991. Rolls-Royce Senior Engineer Martin Rogers was one of the team sent to investigate: 'The first case occurred in a high-g pull-out. The guy ran in at high power and high altitude, which heats up the engine core and casing. He then dived in an attack profile, throttling back to maintain the correct speed. This cooled the engine casing slightly and it started to shrink. As he pulled out of the dive he slammed the throttle open, heating the core rapidly and causing centrifugal expansion. At the same time the severe g-forces caused downward bending of the front fan and its blade tips touched the abrasive coating inside the engine casing. His Pegasus went into surge but he managed to recover the AV-8B. While this was being investigated a second aircraft [BuNo 163873] had the same problem, but the engine caught fire and the aircraft was lost.'

At that point the Night Attackers were grounded and a modification programme was initiated to enable Marine pilots to resume their macho tactics. 'Fan blades were changed from titanium to steel, the abradable coating was altered, compressor blade-tips had their clearance fractionally increased and the compressor casing was strengthened. All the 11-61 engines which had been delivered were returned to Filton for these modifications and the Marines are now very happy with them.' AV-8B(NA) operations continued in the meantime with the F402-RR-406A engine as a retrofit.

In USMC service the 11-61 engine was rated at 23,400lb thrust against 21,450lb for the -406A, although it had been run at 23,800lb on test. The de-rating was a means of prolonging servicing intervals. Once the new engine had been established as the basis of the powerplant for the AV-8B(NA) and its successor, the Harrier II-Plus (as it became known), McAir designed a radar into the project too.

LIGHTWEIGHT RADAR

Pilots had long requested a lightweight radar to increase their air-to-air, attack and navigation options. Installation of the comparatively basic Blue Fox in the Sea Harrier ten years previously had shown how radar could convert the basic Harrier I into an effective sea defence fighter. Hughes Electronics of El Segundo, California, had performed minor miracles in producing an amazingly versatile multimode, pulse-doppler set small enough to fit the F/A-18A Hornet. Their AN/APG-65 set, with a planar antenna squeezed into a 34in diameter radome, offered nine air-to-air modes, furnishing target location and guidance for SARH (semi-active radar-homing) Raytheon AIM-7F/M Sparrow and Hughes (second source Raytheon) midcourse-guided/terminal autonomously radar-guiding AIM-120 air-

to-air missiles (AMRAAM). It could also provide range and bearing for Harpoon and Sea Eagle anti-ship missiles, with an effective search range of up to 80nm, plus navigation and 'blind bombing'. For the AV-8B's even smaller nose—to which a new radome had to fit flush—the radar's antenna had to be reduced by about 2in in diameter. This caused a reduction in tracking capability of only 10 per cent.

The need to preserve the aircraft's CG meant that the APG-65's power supply and target data processor were installed in the rear fuselage equipment bay, though the nose contains essential transmitter and receiver/exciter 'black boxes' as part of the overall Harrier II+ nasal modifications.

The AN/APG-65(V) works in a number of air-to-air modes, all synthesised into

'clean' presentations on the radar display, though the primary cues used are those which lace the HUD. For air-to-air it boasts range-while-search (RWS), track-while-scan (TWS) and simultaneous velocity search. These are all used to help acquire and keep tabs on contacts at BVR ranges, and to help establish the ideal attack geometry to launch an AMRAAM or two; or, in surveying snapshots, to close

A division of *Tigers* AV-8B Plus aircraft, showing the relocated 'wind vane' on the nose, pushed to one side by the FLIR's boxy fairing. Behind the intakes are the curved LERX and ahead of the fin are extra 'scabbed-on' ALE-40 units. (Via Andy Evans)

multiple-shoot, enabling the 'system' to hold 'track files' on various targets assigned AMRAAMs while also keeping a look-out for more potential 'bandits'. Missile launch parameters are all furnished on the HUD, to help the pilot steer his aircraft on course for the target and decide when to unleash the missile cargo at optimum firing range.

Like their Royal Navy counterparts the F/A.2s (described in the next chapter), select AV-8B+ aircraft at sea would be required to perform a dedicated CAP mission for an amphibious assault force over the beach-head, and early warning for the ship too, engaging targets at BVR distances with the AMRAAM. With the missile launched, mid-course guidance updates are periodically despatched to each AMRAAM to correct for changes in target position, until the weapon locks-on autonomously to its intended victim during the final phase of intercept, leaving the Harrier to 'knock off'. (This can be accomplished earlier, but it entrusts the missile with greater responsibilities). One hundred and ninety-eight 'candy bar'-shaped projectiles in each missile's warhead then erupt on impact or in close proximity to the target, blowing off a tail or wing, or (more commonly) rupturing fuel, electrical and hydraulic lines. Maximum 'kill' distances at medium altitude vary between 20 and 40 miles, depending on whether an attack is made head-on or in a tail-chase and whether or not the missile has to climb in a 'look-up, shoot-up' mode, where the rocket fuel gets burnt up more quickly for every yard of reach. But it is equally effective at medium ranges and even right down to where Sidewinders would be more far more expedient. In these instances the missiles could be locked on target prior to launch, pretty much guaranteeing a 'kill' every time.

At closer quarters in a great slice or chase, the radar can be switched to auto-acquisition mode, wherein it will lock on automatically when the target enters its narrow scan; the pilot manoeuvres his aircraft physically to place the quarry within it on the HUD, probably using the radar-derived target cursor displayed there to pre-empt squinting about, and sighting whenever possible so as to make doubly sure the target is indeed hostile. AIM-9M Sidewinders may be cued for pre-launch lock-on (signified by a 'chirp') or gun muzzles brought to bear. The choice would be dependent on closing speeds and target aspect angle, and on whether or not the target was 'squarely in the sights' within mark one eyeball range as opposed to being a nondescript speck of a silhouette against the sky.

For air-to-ground work, the radar offers moving target indicator (MTI) capability, as well as an air-to-ground ranging mode which assists the ballistics number-cruncher continually compute optimum 'bombs away' during a traditional, high-speed strike against fixed targets. These can be made 'blind' using stored coordinates, but the best option is to set up a radar attack for a preassigned 'box' and then revert to a hybrid visual-radar bomb pass against a specific target of opportunity sighted through the (updated) SU-158 HUD. With the aid of the FLIR image projected on to it, night is pretty much as good as day under all conditions save severe precipitation or smoke.

For long range target acquisition and general overland navigation, where heads-down work does not prove to be problematic, the system offers doppler-sharpened and synthetic aperture radar ground-mapping modes, making relatively light work of discriminating reasonably radar-significant targets and terrain features, reducing the chances of getting lost in a heavy navigation-aid-jammed environment, while also providing some additional systems redundancy. Moreover, the radar provides a sea search mode, useful not only for acquiring enemy shipping in choppy seas at long range for an AGM-84 Harpoon volley but also to assist a combat-weary aviator locate his own floating aerodrome when the ship is operating in 'quiet' electromagnetic noise conditions in order to elude the enemy. Splicing a big radome

in as surreptitiously as possible for a vis-ident (visual identification). RWS provides the greatest surveillance volume in terms of target range, range rate, azimuth and elevation, and is typically used first to help acquire a 'bogey' for preliminary interrogation, and lock-on at arm's length if no friendly IFF returns are generated, for hand-off to an AMRAAM. TWS mode is customarily used for a multiple-target/

on to the Harrier and cramming it with the AN/APG-65(V) placed the aircraft in a new league—and none of the competition, bar the latest models of Sea Harrier, boasts V/STOL capability to boot!

In other respects the Harrier II Plus retained all the modifications introduced in the AV-8B(NA) (BuNo 163853 and up), including an extra four Tracor AN/ALE-39 countermeasures dispensers 'scabbed' on to the upper rear fuselage. Added to these were wiring bundles for GPS Navstar, and an automatic target hand-off (ATHS) system for exchange of target data with fellow fighters and FACs through modems. Updated communications systems are also being incorporated into the aircraft, using the overwing UHF antenna which became standard after BuNo 162077 (and which was retrofitted to earlier builds under AV8AFC-223). This also serves as the aerial for the AN/APX-100 IFF system. Provisions were also added for a recce pod, though it is likely that twin-seat Harriers may become increasingly engaged in the FOB fast-FAC and armed recce roles, using portable high-resolution video cameras linked to a real-time re-ceiver, at around the juncture that a useful sensor suite can be packaged in a light-weight centreline pod for day-to-day work.

OTHER CHANGES

Structural changes embrace the LERX, which were enlarged to the '100 per cent' version used on RAF GR.7 models, while the wing was given the eight-pylon configuration of the RAF versions by installing two extra missile pylons ahead of the outrigger fairings.[2] All the additions increased gross take-off weight to 31,000lb, including 7,759lb of internal fuel and 13,200lb of stores. A less apparent but vital improvement, resulting from the steady evolution of structures and materials used in the Harrier, was the 6,000hr fatigue life inherent in the airframe. Composite materials and 'economy-minded' design has resulted in a Harrier which lasts longer. Most of the preliminary structural work was both designed and tested 'in house' by McDonnell-Douglas at St Louis. The company now boasts its own Phantom Works and an allied V/STOL R&D Center. Current projects include new composite wing extensions, allowing greater cruise economy plus wingtip Sidewinder carriage (freeing wing pylons from the task), redesigned LIDs to boost VTOL payload (a feature which would be particularly welcomed in the light of the weight increases associated with the new radar fits), a ceramic-matrix composite exhaust blast shield (replacing the existing nickel-alloy version), and independent fore and aft nozzle control—though the last is aimed squarely at evaluating completely new V/STOL technologies.[3]

In the same way that AV-8B production had been ensured partly by a guarantee of export customers, the AV-8B+ was the subject of a Memorandum of Understanding (MoU), signed on 28 September 1990 by Spain, Italy and the USA. It involved the core manufacturers, McDonnell-Douglas, BAe, Rolls-Royce, Hughes and Smiths Industries and 'offset' contractors Construcciones Aeronauticas SA (CASA) of Spain and Alenia in Italy.[4] Implicit in the MoU was a joint minimum order of 100 aircraft which was seen as a means of attracting further USMC 'business'—and the prospect of additional exports. At the time of writing a potential Japanese order could begin that process.

On receipt of a $20 million contract from Naval Air Systems Command in December 1990, McAir modified AV-8B No 205 (BuNo 164129) as an FSD airframe. Test pilot Jackie Jackson flew it, a month ahead of schedule, on 22 September 1992. On its nose were the flags of the three customers. The aircraft was tested initially at NAWC-AD through Feb-

An AV-8B Plus with LIDs in place of gun pods in the markings of *Esc 009* of the Spanish Navy, ahead of delivery in 1996. (Via Steve Dunkin)

ruary 1993 for airframe and systems trials before being transferred to NAWC-Wpns at China Lake (where it was later joined by the first production aircraft, following the latter's delivery on 23 April) for radar evaluations. The second brand new production example went to VX-5 for OT&E, while the third—part of a 27 aircraft order, all adapted to the new task on the St Louis lines on the tail-end of the AV-8B order books—was test flown for carrier suitability prior to being delivered to VMA-542 at MCAS Cherry Point on 25 June 1993. By July 1994 there were seven sharp-nosed grey shapes on the *Tigers'* flightline, and deliveries to the USMC continued through November, when new production shifted to the exports.

Of greater significance was the agreement for the Marines to fund the remanufacture of a substantial number of AV-8Bs to B+ standard too. In 1990 the Corps had hoped that their entire fleet (at least 114 aircraft) could be re-lifed as Harrier II-Plus models, but the total was reduced to 73 in the eventual May 1994 contract. IOC for the rebuilds was set for 1997 and contract completion for 2002 at a global figure of $1.7 billion. Each rebuild involves reconstructing the aircraft around an entirely new fuselage, a cheaper option than extending and modifying the existing one. In all, the process takes twelve months per airframe. The II-Plus aircraft will be concentrated in the 32nd MAG, which includes VMA-223, VMA-231 and VMA-542.

A work-sharing arrangement was devised between McDonnell-Douglas and the Naval Aviation Depot (NADEP) at Cherry Point, where the AV-8Bs are disassembled and inspected. The majority of structural modifications, apart from those associated with the new fuselage, are performed and tested at NADEP while the St Louis line carries out final assembly of the new and re-used components involved in the programme.

On 18 September 1995 Jackie Jackson flew the first remanufactured 'II-Plus' from St Louis, only 42 minutes after fellow test pilot Fred Madenwald took the company's prototype F/A-18E Super Hornet aloft for the first time. By the middle of the year 'II-Plus' aircraft were flying alongside the standard B model in several AV-8 units. VMA-223 at Cherry Point operated twelve Harrier II+s and eleven AV-8Bs under Lieutenant-Colonel Douglas Lovejoy. Earlier in the year his squadron decamped *en masse* to Indian Springs Auxiliary Field near Nellis AFB for training lasting a whole month. Their standard syllabus called for each pilot to do one week per month 'night cycle' (NVG) training in the new variant. Occasionally II+ aircraft were supplied on loan to other units to enable them to fulfil their night training commitment. During 1995 they were in high demand!

---

[2] Earlier AV-8Bs feature provisions for these extra pylon stations, known as 1A and 7A, but they were not certified for Sidewinder use until very recently.

[3] Primarily for the JAST (Joint-Service Advanced Strike Technology) demonstrator programme, which is in competitive development in the USA. Refer to the final chapter, 'The Next Leap Forward'.

[4] CASA and Alenia each have a 15 per cent stake in the programme. Meeting the Spanish *Armada* order for sixteen aircraft, CASA is performing final assembly of aircraft nos 4–16, the first three having been supplied 'off the shelf' from St Louis. The first CASA-assembled AV-8B+ (BuNo 165029) flew on 11 December 1995. Four more will be delivered in 1996 and three in 1997. Alenia was behind schedule at the time of writing. Refer to the chapter 'Export Variants' for further details.

9. From War to War

Operation 'Corporate' had put Sea Harrier to the test early in its career and the experience inevitably yielded lessons for the future. There were deeper consequences for the Sea Harrier itself than there were for the training programme. 899 (HQ) NAS's training philosophy had been proven in the Falklands and there were no major changes to be made. Plenty of other air arms were anxious to study that success at first hand: the squadron hosted many 'study delegations' from as far away as Japan in the second half of 1982. The Sea Harrier FRS.1 had clearly been an outstanding success in the roles for which it had been intended, but long term redesign initiatives were begun in 1983 to equip it with a more effective lookdown/shoot-down radar and a BVR missile system. The outcome of those modifications was to be a very much more capable fighter, using technology which was not available when Sea Harrier was first conceived.

In the six years between 'Corporate' and the placing of contracts for a major Sea Harrier upgrade there were other additions to the aircraft's repertoire. The 34th and last aircraft of the original 'build', ZA195, replaced the unfortunate XZ450 and, with XZ440, it continued development trials of the BAe Dynamics Sea Eagle anti-shipping missile until March 1986. Entering service the following year, Sea Eagle's fully active radar and 'fire-and-forget' design enabled it to be used by single-seat aircraft like the Sea Harrier. In July 1984 XZ440 of the Joint Services Trials Unit flew a live-firing sortie which caused major damage to the target, the redundant missile destroyer HMS *Devonshire*. Based on BAe's Martel tactical/SEAD missile, the 13$\frac{1}{2}$ft-long (4.14m)

Sea Eagle has a Microturbojet engine which drives it and its 500lb (226.8kg) warhead at almost 700mph over a 70nm range. Guidance is inertial, with a Marconi active radar for the terminal phase. Sea Eagle offered similar performance to the AM.39 Exocet used in the Falklands, but with more effective guidance and a far larger warhead. Training for Sea Eagle is almost entirely simulated, with very few live rounds. Firing it is 'largely a non-event' according to one 800 NAS pilot. 'You just fire it and go home. Live firing is largely a means of quality-testing the weapons's reliability.'

The Sea Harrier's post-Falklands Phase I Update (completed by 1987) included Sea Eagle capability and introduced the twin-Sidewinder launch rails which 809 NAS had trialled earlier. In peacetime they are seldom used, however, because of the weight penalty. MADGE, 'nozzle-inching' and 190gal wing tanks were also standardised under Phase I and they all helped the aircraft to remain viable as it entered its second decade of service. An increase in front-line squadron strength to eight aircraft was another result of South Atlantic experience. The original five-aircraft allocation was parsimonious and a reflection of the limited space aboard *Invincible* class ships with their original Air Wing composition.

An equally significant change to the standard RN Air Wing was the introduction of the AEW component which was so much missed during 'Corporate'. Placing ships on forward radar picket duty as a substitute for airborne radar warning had proved far too risky and inadequate. British carriers were incapable of operating any off-the-shelf fixed-wing AEW types (such as the Grumman E-2C

Hawkeye), and the only practicable alternative was to use a helicopter to carry a sufficiently powerful search radar. Two Sea King HAS.2As were modified by Thorne-EMI and Westland, using an existing AEW conversion study by the Yeovil-based helicopter manufacturer, all in an extraordinarily short nine-week period.[1] Such were the exigencies of combat. Although they were not ready in time for the Falklands affair, acceptance trials were completed by 30 July 1982, so that HMS *Illustrious* was able to include the two development aircraft ('Cyclops' 1 and 2) in her Air Wing for her August–December 1982 cruise to the South Atlantic. Thorn-EMI's Searchwater radar, developed for use in the cancelled Nimrod AEW.3, was mounted in a radome 6ft in diameter, suspended from a hydraulic arm which swings backwards through 90 degrees to raise the structure when the aircraft is on the ground. The radar is protected by a flexible Kevlar radome which is inflated by two small fans (hence the helicopter's nickname, 'Bag'). When lowered, it gives 360-degree coverage over a radius exceeding 100 miles from 10,000ft altitude. Modifications also include Racal's MIR 2 'Orange Crop' ECM (capable of jamming AM.39 Exocet) and the Cossor Jubilee Guardsman IFF unit.

The ungainly but extremely effective 'Bag' can patrol for up to 3$\frac{1}{4}$hr, but VERTREP refuelling in the hover can extend this. Appropriately, the first operational unit for the ten conversions was 824 NAS, formerly a Gannet AEW.3 operator. Their first commander, Lieutenant-Commander Peter Flutter, was an ex-Gan-

---

[1] Sea Kings XV650 and XV704. Ten aircraft were eventually converted, drawn from the HAS.2A serial batch XV649–714.

net Observer. Control of the Sea King AEW.2As passed to 849 NAS who usually operate 'A' and 'B' Flights, one per Air Wing, with three 'Bags' each. In mid-1995 'A' Flight (*Aardvarks*) operated their trio from HMS *Invincible*, providing fighter control for the Sea Harriers involved in Operation 'Sharp Guard' off Bosnia. Current Sea Harrier pilots are in no doubt that the ingenious 'Bag' is essential to their way of life, although its radar is shortly to receive a major upgrade. At present, its radar picture is 'inferior to the Sea Harrier F/A.2's', according to one of Yeovilton's Fighter Directors.

From 1985, when HMS *Ark Royal* became available, the Royal Navy began to operate its carriers on a rota which maintained two in service while the third was held in reserve or was undergoing refit. Sea Harrier ZA195 was the first to land on the deck of *Ark Royal*, in July 1985. There were 38 of the aircraft in RN service at that time. By 1992 only eleven of the original 'Falklands' Sea Harriers were still on charge, seventeen having been lost during the conflict and in subsequent accidents, but deliveries of 23 new aircraft enabled the Air Groups to make long deployments, while a comparatively well-stocked 899 NAS could still run a comprehensive training programme. A number of Falklands veterans remained with the squadrons: Lieutenant-Commander Mike 'Soapy' Watson commanded 800 NAS in 1987–89 and then took over 801 in March, 1990. 'Fred' Frederiksen ran 800 NAS in the mid-1980s before joining BAe as Chief

Sea Harrier FRS.2 Project Pilot in 1988. Squadrons tended to declare to the same carriers during the 1980s: 801 has been associated with HMS *Ark Royal* since 1985, while 800 was part of HMS *Illustrious*' Air Wing until 1989, joining *Invincible* thereafter. 801 returned to *Invincible* when 'The Ark' was laid up in January 1995.

All three carriers made extended cruises throughout the 1980s and early 1990s, visiting the Far East, Australia and the United States. There were frequent exercises with NATO partners too. In June 1983 one of these demonstrated the Sea

Sea Harrier ZD615 of 899 NAS/OEU, the third conversion off the F/A.2 line. (Via HMS *Heron*)

Harrier's ability to put down in unscheduled confined spaces. Sub-Lieutenant Ian Watson, flying ZA176/001 on a sea-search for the French carrier *Foch*, lost contact with HMS *Illustrious* and then became generally lost when his when his NAVHARS gave him an incorrect heading. Low on fuel and without a radio, he dead-reckoned into a shipping lane and picked up the freighter *Alraigo* on his Blue Fox. Rather than abandoning his jet alongside, Watson quickly calculated that he had enough fuel to attempt an impromptu vertical landing on a flat area of containers occupying the small vessel's main deck. The Sea Harrier's main landing gear rolled back slightly, off the edge of the containers and the jet settled back on to its tail at an angle, resting on its empty gun

pods and a damaged AIM-9 acquisition round. ZA176 was eventually transferred to a larger BP tanker and finally returned to Yeovilton on a low-loader where it was repaired and handed over to 899 NAS. Any sense of personal risk which the crew of *Alraigo* may have felt at this unorthodox visitation was tempered by a Lloyd's Insurance award of £29,000 to the Captain and £209,000 among the rest of the crew. In all, £412,000 was paid to the owners, but the Navy retained an aircraft which was still in service twelve years later. Ian Watson remained with 801 NAS, although his Squadron has not pursued this early form of SCADS deck-landing since then.[2]

Another unconventional landing was pulled off by 800 NAS when HMS *Illustrious* sent two 'SHARS' to visit NAS Pensacola, Florida, during Exercise 'Global 86' for the US Navy's 75th Anniversary show that May. The CO, Lieutenant-Commander A, Siebert, flew ZA191 with

Lieutenant Ellis in ZD609. During their display Ellis put his aircraft down on its gun pods and wing tanks after an under-carriage malfunction. ZD609 had its fin and tailplane removed to be shipped back to Britain. Lieutenant-Commander Siebert, meanwhile, flew his aircraft 4,750 miles back to Yeovilton via Cherry Point, Brunswick, Goose Bay, Sondestrom and Keflavik. It was the longest-ever unsupported flight by a Sea Harrier. Siebert did all his own basic 'first level' maintenance *en route* using tools and spares carried in the empty gun pods. In a small aircraft like the Sea Harrier, storage space is at a premium and baggage pods are not carried. Gun pods are usually fitted even if the Aden cannon are not installed, because they improve VTOL lift characteristics.

Joint operations with other navies were also regularly practised. In June 1989, 801

[2]For details of SCADS see below, 'The Next Leap Forward'.

NAS and the Spanish AV-8 squadrons trained jointly at both Rota and Yeovilton. Cross-decking with the Spanish carrier *Príncipe de Asturias* took place when a quartet of Sea Harriers spent two days aboard. *Ark Royal* returned the compliment between 4 and 6 July in the North Sea, when four EAV-8Bs were aboard for air defence. The Spanish contingent, led by *Capitán de Corbetta* J. Arcusa, did a week of ACM practice at Yeovilton before the deployment. A repeat exercise code-named 'Dragon Hammer' took place in May 1990 when HMS *Invincible* operated aircraft from *Príncipe de Asturias* and the Italian carrier *Giuseppe Garibaldi*.

The RAF also kept their Harrier Force current on 'deck ops' with exercises like 'Hardy Crab' in May 1985, when HMS *Invincible* was used as a 'base' for practice low-level attacks over south-west England. One of the last long-distance deployments involving Sea Harrier FRS.1s took 800 NAS in HMS *Invincible* to the South China Sea for Exercise 'Starfish' in September 1992. In a curious reversal of the situation ten years earlier, A-4 Skyhawks were able to score a number of missile 'kills' against Sea Harriers. The difference was that the Skyhawks were RNZAF A-4Ks updated with HOTAS cockpits, an APG-66 radar similar to the F-16's and AIM-9L Sidewinders. It was a reminder that cockpit technology had advanced considerably since the FRS.1 took to the sky.

Sea Harrier training was refined by 899 NAS throughout the 1980s as the Squadron took over the CONVEX stage from No 233 OCU. (899 NAS's AWI at the time of writing was the last RN pilot to fly the Harrier GR.3 during his training.) Students used Wittering only for practice in FOB and confined-site operations. Having completed basic training, novice pilots usually had a Sea King flight to experience hovering, followed by three T.4N flights with one of the three squadron QFIs. Conventional landings were made at this stage and then repeated by the student in a single-seater. Students then commenced VTOL 'push-ups' with a QFI on a radio link in the time-honoured fashion. This stage concluded with mastery of the transition from winged flight to the hover.

A second phase concentrated on Air Warfare, with radar interceptions of increasingly elusive targets, usually FRADU Hunters. Ground attack began with visits to the nearest range, Pembrey, although ranges in the north-east of England were used at a later stage of training. As always, the emphasis was on air-to-air tactics, including two-versus-one and VIFF later in the course, and climaxing in visits to Decimomannu's electronic range to take on other NATO 'players'. The training programme aimed to keep about forty pilots 'current' on the Sea Harrier.

One of the ways in which continuation training was provided was 899 NAS's participation in NATO Tactical Leadership Programme (TLP) 'meets'. In 1993–94, for example, two FRS.1s (ZD614 and ZD607) were detached to Florennes in Belgium, flying 'hostile CAP' in a series of exercises. Radar and air-to-air sorties dominated the training syllabus in terms

The F/A.2 cockpit (seat removed) shows marked differences from the FRS.1, principally the two multifunction display screens, up front controller and HOTAS stick. (BAe)

of hours too. In 1985 a typical Sea Harrier course included 34 radar sorties totalling 36hr plus a further fifteen 1hr-long sorties for night radar qualification. With nine additional air-to-air flights, the total 'fighter' time occupied 61 of the course's 97 flying hours.

In the same year 899 NAS put a T.4N aboard a carrier and launched from a ski-jump at sea, both 'first time' events. Although two-seaters can deck-operate perfectly well, they are very rarely flown from carriers. Problems do arise in that the T.4N NAVHARS cannot be plugged into the ship's INAS and can only be kept 'current' with the Harrier's APU running, updating itself from the ship's inertial sys-

October 1962 and XP984 to Thorney Island, with a fire in its engine bay, in March 1965. Barrie Tonkinson also landed a T.2 at Boscombe in this configuration in July 1970, although the Harrier subsequently burned out. In later Harriers the Pegasus rarely seized up if there was a failure, so a degree of hydraulic power was provided by the 'windmilling' engine. In the Sea Harrier's case the 'de-RATting' was perhaps more logical because dead-stick carrier landings were obviously not an option. Sea Harriers tended to fly higher than their RAF counterparts too, allowing pilots a little longer to deal with the situation.

BLUE VIXEN

However, far more than minor airframe modifications was needed to produce a credible Sea Harrier for the 1990s. In the autumn of 1987 a BAe Advanced Projects team visited HMS *Ark Royal* to observe operations as background to their studies of advanced variants. These deliberations extended back to 1983 when it became clear that a new radar would be available to cure the Sea Harrier FRS.1's lack of look-down/shoot-down capability. This facility was made even more necessary by the advent of Soviet sea-skimming missiles and shipborne fighters such as the Yak-36. When the FRS.1 was designed such electronics were not available 'off the shelf', but the mid-1990s saw the introduction of lightweight pulse-doppler radars which offered multi-mode operation, track-while-scan, multi-target engagement, tighter surface target acquisi-

tems. T.4Ns are also a tight fit on the deck lift and their large sideways-opening canopies present handling problems in high winds. The Royal Navy never felt the need of a two-seater just to teach VTOL/ STOVL on carriers—another tribute to the Harrier's basic ease of handling.

Although its avionics were beginning to date the FRS.1, the airframe and the Pegasus 104 were a reliable and versatile combination throughout the 1980s. A few engines in 1986–87 suffered a reduction in surge margins and occasional flame-out/fireball problems at high AOA. It was discovered that manufacturing tolerances for some of the engine components had

been slightly altered, and the solution was simply to reintroduce the original specifications.

In common with other first-generation Harriers, the FRS.1 fleet had their RAT removed during the 1980s as an economy measure. In earlier, lighter P.1127s the RAT did allow the pilot to use his flying controls a little longer if the engine failed. He could use the extra seconds to gain height for an ejection with the aircraft under straight-and-level control. Several aircraft with failed engines were actually recovered using RAT-power. Test pilot Hugh Merewether brought two P.1127s back safely, XP972 to Tangmere on 30

from a series of at least three consecutive 'hits' on the target by its pulses it can give an exact calculation of range and velocity.

As a multi-mode radar, Blue Vixen can be switched to LPRF for ground mapping, which it does better than Blue Fox. In all it can cover eleven modes, including look-up, look-down, velocity search, air combat, single-target track and track-while-scan in air-to-air configuration. For air-to-ground it can do sea-surface search, beacon interrogation, ranging and freezing data in addition to mapping. Blue Vixen originated in company-funded studies in the 1970s which gave rise to the Red Fox export proposal and, in due course, the ECR-90 which developed into a radar for the EFA/Eurofighter 2000. It drew on Ferranti's Blue Falcon research programme and its design was well advanced by 1987.

While radar development proceeded British Aerospace considered other improvements. An early study included wing-tip AIM-9/ASRAAM rails to free the outboard pylons for other loads. This proposal was deleted to save weight, but it was revived on McAir's AV-8B Technology Demonstrator in 1994. In the same BAe redesign the outboard pylons were used for a pair of AIM-120 AMRAAM missiles on Frazer-Nash Common Rail Launchers which could also take Sidewinders. Two more AIM-120s were hung on underfuselage LAU-106 mounts, replacing gun pods or LIDs at some cost to VTOL performance. AIM-120 is the successor to the AIM-7 Sparrow III. Its incorporation in Sea Harrier's weapon system provides a BVR capability which vastly increases its potential as a fighter. It removed the advantage enjoyed by the 'big boys' who could lob a BVR missile and retreat before a Sea Harrier pilot could close to AIM-9 range. The choice of Blue Vixen was closely associated with AMRAAM's role as the revised Sea Harrier's primary armament, and it became the first aircraft outside the United States to have an armament system designed around the missile. Blue Vixen transfers target bearing and velocity data to the missile and updates it *en route* to the target

tion and greater resistance to jamming. The FRS.1's Blue Fox was a low-PRF (pulse-repetition frequency) set. It emitted a series of regular radio frequency pulses controlled by an electronic 'clock' and measured the time lag between emissions and subsequent returns bounced off a target, thus determining the Sea Harrier's distance from its target. High-PRF radars send out pulses which are much closer together and determine the target's velocity by calculating the doppler shift in the frequency when the pulses return to the receiver antenna. In simple terms, low PRF is best for measuring range, while high PRF is better for calculating velocity.

LPRF works well when searching for targets in 'look up' mode against a clear sky background, but it is poor at 'look down' detection of targets against ground clutter, as Falklands pilots discovered. HPRF works well in look-down mode because it can more easily recognize moving objects against a relatively static background. Ferranti designed the Blue Vixen, which is a medium PRF (MPRF) radar. It sends out a mixture of low and high PRF pulses and can assess both range and velocity accurately in look-up and look-down modes, including head-on target tracking. MPRF takes more computing power to calculate the grouped radar returns, but through a secure, jam-proof data-link until the missile's own active seeker takes over for the terminal guidance phase.

One of the radar's greatest strengths is its capacity to guide all four AIM-120s to different targets simultaneously, a capability previously enjoyed only by fighters in the F-14 Tomcat league. In tests at the White Sands and Eglin ranges an F-15C launched four AIM-120s against four QF-100D drones. Despite energetic manoeuvres and copious chaff and countermeasures emissions by the target 'Huns', all were reduced to scrap metal. AMRAAM is lighter than AIM-7 Sparrow but the placement of missile pylons and launch rails on Sea Harrier had to be calculated to avoid CG problems. The Mach 4 missile is much faster than its predecessor and far less visible in flight because of a much reduced smoke plume.

Blue Vixen and AMRAAM were the centrepieces of an extensive revision of Sea Harrier's avionics, weaponry and cockpit which constituted the Phase 2 upgrade package. In fact it was a full Mid-Life Update (MLU), sufficient to bring about a redesignation—Sea Harrier FRS.2. In February 1985 BAe and Ferranti received a project definition contract for upgrading thirty FRS.1 aircraft. Cost-cutting reduced some of the wishlist items in the MLU, removing JTIDS (Joint Tactical Information Distribution System), a secure radio system which transmits data on targets and threats from command centres to the aircraft's cockpit displays. It also replaces tacan, provides secure voice communication and is resistant to jamming. JTIDS data exchange would enable Sea Harriers to work more effectively as a team of two, or four, sharing common data on their HUDs which could be transmitted direct from an

AWACS aircraft or passed from one Sea Harrier to another. It could certainly be handled by the spare capacity in the multiple-redundant 1553B databus which connects the aircraft's HUD, NAVHARS, radar and weapon system and allows them to communicate with each other. There is also room for GPS Navstar in future updates, and the Navy hopes that both systems will be funded in the late 1990s.

Also 'chopped' were LERX similar to those on the AV-8B/GR.5 to improve turn performance, detachable extended wingtips and the Zeus RWR/ECM suite designed for the RAF's Harrier II variants. On the latter issue the RN settled for an upgrade to the existing Marconi ARI.18223 RWR, providing warning of hostile radar lock-ons rather than an integrated ECM system.

Aerodynamic changes were minimal. A 15in (0.35m) fuselage plug was added aft of the wing to extend the fuselage, counterbalance the radar and provide more avionics space. Blue Vixen's main processor is located there. The wing gained an extra fence and a slight kink in the leading edge. Much more far-reaching changes affected the cockpit. An F/A-18-style HOTAS control concept was introduced, simplifying the entire flight control, radar and armament switchology and allowing 'heads up' flying. In place of many traditional 'steam gauge' instruments a pair of monochrome video displays occupied a large area of front panel, radar on the right and a multi-function Ferranti MED 2066 raster head-down display on the left. An up-front controller was located below the HUD, offering many of the essential 'ba-

Right, upper: The BAe ACMI range over the North Sea is the favoured air combat training arena for Yeovilton's Sea Harriers. They carry AIM-9 acquisition rounds for ACT. (Authors)

Right, lower: Still decorated with camera-tracking markers, F/A.2 (FRS.2) ZA195, the first conversion, makes a brief visit to RNAS Yeovilton in July 1992. (Authors)

The 'unscarfed' nozzles, seen here on a T.4N, remain relatively unchanged since the early Harrier GR.1 and continue to propel the latest F/A.2. (Authors)

sic flying' inputs such as navigation functions which previously appeared on a keyboard unit on the right side of the FRS.1 cockpit. It was repositioned at chin height to be more visible and accessible. The threat-warning display remained in the same position as the FRS.1's, rather inconveniently tucked away on the lower left of the cockpit.

Although the highly desirable Pegasus 11-61 was a possibility for the FRS.2, it had to make do with the same Mk 104 variant as the FRS.1. Zero-scarf nozzles were proposed to give marginal thrust improvement, but these too fell victim to the budget-trimmers.

Blue Vixen was flight-tested in two BAe 125 test-beds, beginning with the RAE's XW930 on 26 August 1988.[3] Its complex air-to-air modes were worked out in this aircraft, including multiple target engagements. BAe 125 Series 600B ZF130 then joined the programme, fitted out with a 'virtual FRS.2' cockpit in place of the co-pilot's position, and most of the FRS.2 avionics. A missile simulator was installed to feed AMRAAM characteristics to the Blue Vixen so that it could replicate launch and guidance procedures. An underwing AIM-9 acquisition round was also carried, giving the 'executive jet' an unusually bullish aura. Tests with the BAe 125s enabled all parts of the FRS.2 avionics system to

be integrated smoothly via some extensive computer software redesign and de-bugging. In the absence of a Hunter T.8M equivalent to train pilots on the new radar, the RN would have plenty of use for the BAe 125s too, but funding was only provided for a simulator update.

REBUILDING PROGRAMME

BAe received a £170 million contract in December 1988 for FRS.2 rebuilds over a time-scale which was five years later than originally envisaged. A further contract in March 1990 allowed for ten new-build FRS.2s. This was increased to fifteen in 1992 and then eighteen in January 1994 (ZH796–813). The intended number of FRS.1 conversions has fluctuated slightly but currently stands at 31, including the two Development Batch airframes ZA195 and XZ439. Heinz Frick took the first of these aloft on 19 September 1988 and reported a 'faultless' maiden flight. It flew initially without radar. The first trial Blue Vixen was screwed into XZ429 and both aircraft undertook a ten-day sea trial on HMS *Ark Royal* in November 1990. Rod Frederiksen was by then Chief Project Pilot for the FRS.2 and Simon Hargreaves was Senior Royal Navy pilot at the A&AEE. They made the first FRS.2 carrier landings together on 6 November and completed forty sorties from the ship, test-

ing all the possible launch configurations. Together with BAe's Graham Tomlinson and Flight Lieutenant Dave Mackay, they checked for CG problems with four AMRAAMs aboard and handling with the flight-refuelling probe in place. Night flights enabled them to evaluate the new cockpit displays and lighting for nocturnal interceptions. Flight characteristics were predictably similar to those of the FRS.1, despite slight weight increases. MoD(PE)'s FRS.2 fleet was joined by XZ497, the first 'production' conversion, which did the 'cold hangar' environmental control tests. AMRAAM flight-testing took place in the United States using XZ439 complete with leering sharkmouth. It made the journey to Eglin AFB on the new *Atlantic Conveyor* in January 1993. Successful firings were made against MQM-107 drones and two QF-106As were also sent spinning in some rather expensive but successful trials. A camera mounted in a modified ML practice bomb container recorded the events. Sidewinder and 30mm gun tests were done in Britain in January 1994 and the Navy took delivery of its first service aircraft, ZE695, on 2 April. Alan Millican, BAe's Quality Director, 'handed the keys' to Rear Admiral Ian Garnett, FONAC, while CTP Graham Tomlinson wrung out XZ497 in a spirited flight demonstration.

Despite rumours that 809 NAS might rise again as the FRS.2 IFTU, it was decided to establish a Sea Harrier Operational Evaluation Unit (SHOEU), co-located at Boscombe Down and Yeovilton.

[3] Lieutenant-Commander Andy Sinclair and his associates of the Directorate of Test & Evaluation, Boscombe Down, were key players throughout the development. Prior to BAe 125 testing, a BAC One-Eleven was used to integrate many of the various avionics (Blue Vixen, 1553 databus, bus controller and missiles), and test a breadboard 'A' version of the radar, collecting data on signal characteristics at various PRFs. This was aimed at software development and optimisation of the various radar operating modes. From this work the 'B' version radar possessing production features was built and fitted to the BAe 125s.

It set up shop at A&AEE on 1 June 1993 with four RN pilots. ZE695 was actually the first aircraft to reach the unit, with ZD615 following on 3 September 1993. Both jets joined in 899 NAS's annual APC at Akrotiri that month and six FRS.2s were used by the OEU during that year. Of these, XZ495 was lost during armament trials on the Lundy range after engine failure, caused in all probability by a FOD-damaged compressor blade. Co-location enabled Yeovilton's handlers to get used to the new systems, and it was decided to keep the OEU in being throughout the Sea Harrier's operational life, providing continuing support for new developments and tactics. At the time of writing three OEU FRS.2s spend most of their time at Boscombe Down.

The conversion programme gathered pace through 1993, with each rebuild taking up to twelve months, depending on the maintenance state of the airframe on arrival at St Athan for a pre-modification Works Programme. After an initial strip-down at Dunsfold, aircraft were trans-ferred to BAe's Brough plant or structural re-work, then returned to Dunsfold for completion. By March 1994 sufficient re-builds had been completed for 899 NAS to begin FRS.2 conversion training for its first four squadron pilots.

The advent of the new Sea Harrier has had an enormous impact upon training and upon the muscle-power of the front-line squadrons. Aircrew at Yeovilton were unanimous in emphasizing the difference between the two variants. Lieutenant Hugh Rathbone said that FRS.2 'revolu-tionized our approach to Sea Harrier tac-tics, putting us up there with the best and enabling us to hold our own well into the twenty-first century. With FRS.2 we always win, even against Tornado F.3. The RAF are a bit sad because with FRS.1 they al-ways won, forcing us within BVR range to attempt an AIM-9 shot, by which time the Tornado would have done a "Fox One" radar-missile kill. They have a bet-ter overall picture of the fight, but JTIDS would remove that advantage too.' While pilots acknowledge that the FRS.2 had to

Above: One of 800 NAS's first batch of F/A.2s, ZD611, back on the flight-line after a training sortie in April 1995. (Authors)

Right: Sea Harrier ZD582/122 of 800 NAS returns to the ramp after an ACM sortie. The markings of its former owners, 899 NAS, remain on the fin. (Authors)

be a 'minimum change' project, with none of the airframe improvements seen in the RAF's second-generation Harrier, they welcome the retention of the original small wing which confers a speed advantage of around 100mph over the attack-orientated GR.7. The slightly improved manoeuvra-bility of the big-wing Harrier is not missed either. 'Sea Harrier isn't an agile F-16-type fighter anyway,' explained Hugh Rath-bone. 'The idea is to take advantage of the radar and AMRAAM and knock out the enemy at 20 or 30 miles. In order to maximise AMRAAM's range advantage you need to sea-launch as fast as possible to meet the threat, and Sea Harrier's go-faster wing is an advantage. We can fire four AMRAAMs, zap four intruders at high or low level and go back for more.' With the new armament Sea Harrier pilots could finally demonstrate that a 'real fighter' does not have to have flames blasting out of its tail-end and Mach 2 performance to be a dominant player.

While 899 NAS pilots still made regular deployments to 'Deci', the Mediterranean ranges were regarded in the mid-1990s as being most useful for air-to-ground training. BVR missile technique became the priority in training, with the AIM-9 occupying more of a back-up role, and the serious missile-slugging work moved to the BAe ACMI air combat range over the North Sea. Based around six oil rig-like towers, the system can track up to 36 aircraft simultaneously in combat scenarios reminiscent of 'Red Flag' at Nellis AFB. At a mere £8,000 per half-hour session, the range slots have to be booked well in advance and carefully planned, but it is still the cheapest way of providing Sea Harrier pilots with experience of the multi-target ACM which they require. 899 NAS usually deploys four aircraft to Waddington (the prime control site) for up

to two weeks, and pilots can debrief there after their sorties, or at Coningsby, Lakenheath or even Leeuwarden in Holland, which has the same three-scan debrief facility and is linked to the range system.

Visitors can often raise enough opposition from other forces to arrange anything up to twelve-versus-twelve ACM scraps. The popularity of the ACMI range means that there is seldom any shortage of NATO F-16s or USAFE F-15s to play against. Sea Harriers are fitted with ACMI data-relay pods underwing for their range sorties. 899 NAS's aircraft, usually operating with 'Fist' or 'Winder' call-signs, as opposed to 800 NAS's 'Satan' and 801 NAS's 'Vixen' or 'Seafire' labels, usually occupy three half-hour slots on a range day. Typically these would run from 0800 to 0900, landing back at Waddington at 0930. After a 90min turnaround the second 'match' would take place at 1130 and the third at 1500. Under pressure, two parallel sorties could be flown at once on the two halves of the range. ACMI visits usually include one or two CONVEX stu-

dents for whom it is their first encounter with the 'big picture'. They face 'one-versus-four' or 'one-versus-unknown' opponents, and the two-week course has to provide a steady build-up of complexity in the ACM situations they face. An 800 NAS pilot put the situation very concisely to the authors: 'You learn to fly the Sea Harrier FRS.2 from the debrief afterwards.'

Sea Harrier pilots felt that they were being slightly disadvantaged in the range-scoring process at ACMI because Sparrow parameters were still in use, whereas 'AMRAAM should easily outrange all other users' missiles'. Training for AMRAAM cannot simulate all its advantages—the smokeless motor for example. 899's AWI felt that being unable to use a smoke trail to check the missile's flight-path was no loss, 'except for the personal enjoyment of seeing it go towards the target. It's best that the guy doesn't see it coming'. AMRAAM is an all-aspect missile, although the lateral 'beam shot' against a crossing target is still the most difficult. Head-on launches are easier and they can be made from greater range than any likely

Conversion to Sea Harrier F/A.2 standard involved the addition of a small leading-edge kink to the wing, inboard of the main pylons. Otherwise the wing resembles that of the basic GR.1 model and confers a 100mph speed advantage over the GR.5/7 variants. (Via HMS Heron)

opposer's shots. Simon Hargreaves' enthusiasm for the radar/missile combination was unstinted: 'We've skipped at least two generations of aeroplanes in one go. The F/A-18 is roughly equivalent but in terms of weapons performance the Sea Harrier's radar is superior to the APG-65. They really got it right. In air-to-air modes it interleaves PRFs cleverly and the pilot just sits there and points the scanner in the right direction. The 1's and 0's look after themselves. And yet, to all intents and purposes, it's still the same aircraft as the FRS.1. The new radome doesn't alter the flight characteristics, apart from some early problems with surge margins. The only problem with AMRAAM is the lack of a UK range big enough to fire it. Live firings have to be done in the USA, at great expense, using Point Mugu, Roosevelt Roads or Eglin.' 899 NAS were due to begin live firings in 1996.

Although the injection of FRS.2 technology affected Sea Harrier operations more than anything else since the type's introduction, the basic training syllabus still operates around the 'same old Wittering CONVEX syllabus of the 1970s,' according to 899 NAS's CO. Currently running at 110hr, it occupies two 'terms' (e.g. December to June, or April to December etc.): 'Training for a multi-role aeroplane needs the longest OCU course in the UK. Students have to learn bits of Tornado F.3 syllabus, bits of Tornado GR.1, bits of Jaguar, bits of Harrier GR.7. They concentrate on the air-to-air environment (about 60 per cent of the operational phase). Their Full Mission Simulator (FMS) is very good and they get an awful lot of time in it.' A major 18-month upgrade was needed to modify the 'sim' to FRS.2 standard.[4] Training for the FRS.1 stopped in November 1993 and the first FRS.2 converts did not appear until Easter 1994, so there was an interim pe-

riod when neither group had the use of a simulator.

Teaching pilots to avoid the Harrier's idiosyncrasies is by now firmly entrenched in the syllabus, particularly the dangers of intake stall, unstable VTO or transition. Simon Hargreaves saw it as a 'slow pedantic, building-block approach, making sure you reinforce the lessons that need to be rammed home. It uses the experience of the RAF in the late 1960s and the USMC. You change the syllabus at your peril. So far we haven't lost a single pilot to the sort of accidents which occurred in the early

days, due to better understanding of stability and control.' Weapons training includes an annual allowance of two live Sidewinder firings per squadron. 'Academic' range work for ground attack is done at Pembrey but students soon become familiar with the range, so for their OPEX (operational phase) they are sent to a range they have not visited before,

[4] Ground crews also have their own VEGA Group/Ogle Design Cockpit Orientation Trainer for the FRS.2 as part of 27 computer workstations to help trainees learn the techniques of avionics fault-diagnosis.

such as Spadeadam or Cowdenbeath. Their sortie will often include tanking and a live 1,000lb bomb drop. One such sortie by a student in April 1995 involved a 4hr 20min mission with two tanking 'bounces' over the North Sea, two attacks at Spadeadam with a ground FAC, a medium range recce through Yorkshire and some 45-degree attack work at Donna Nook followed by a tanker prod on the way home. This type of sortie was representative of an end-of-course exercise with an emphasis on the Bosnia-type operations which dominated training in 1994–95.

DEPLOYMENT

Conversion of the two front-line Sea Harrier squadrons began in October 1994, following the receipt by 801 NAS of XZ455 and ZA716 on the 5th of the month. The Squadron made an ACMI visit to Waddington in November and reached full strength in January 1995, ready for a deployment to the Adriatic for six months. By that time the pilots were getting used to calling their aircraft the Sea Harrier F/A.2 rather than FRS.2. The redesignation was announced in July 1994 as a result of the aircraft's ability to deliver the Paveway

II laser-guided bomb. At the same time the Royal Navy's deletion of the WE.177 nuclear weapon from its inventory meant dropping the 'S' for (nuclear) Strike and the substitution of an 'A' as in 'F/A-18'.[5] Although the F95 camera remains aboard and is often used to provide recce ('R') intelligence, it is no longer credited in the title.

Sea Harrier activity in the vicinity of the embattled former Yugoslavia began when HMS *Ark Royal* took 800 NAS's eight FRS.1s on station in the Adriatic from 27 January 1993. Operation 'Deny Flight', enforcing UN Security Council Resolution 816, began in April before the ship was relieved by HMS *Invincible* with 800 NAS in July. 800 NAS also had to fly in support of Operation 'Sharp Guard' (initiated on 15 June), which required NATO naval vessels to monitor and enforce sanctions against ships entering the territorial waters of the former Yugoslavia. With over 100 NATO jets available to support the UN Protection Force's show of strength, the Sea Harrier squadrons were tasked with CAS or CAP by the controlling 5 ATAF HQ at Vicenza. Soon after taking up station 800 NAS were flying twelve 'intimidation' sorties daily in an attempt to encourage the Bosnian Serbs to move from high ground around Sarajevo. By the time HMS *Invincible* handed over to *Ark Royal* again in February 1994 there were nearly 350 aircraft from twelve nations committed to UNPROFOR's needs. On 9 February the Serbs were ordered (for the first time) to move heavy weapons outside a twelve-mile exclusion zone around Sarajevo. General Rose called 800 NAS to action on 22 February when a Swedish convoy of soldiers was fired upon from Bosnian Serb positions. However, the Sea Harriers and a flight of 52nd FW A-10As were called off by the UN Commander, *Général* Jean Cot because there were no obvious targets.

[5]Mk/B.57 warhead-based bombs and depth charges were withdrawn from USN service following President Bush's directive of 27 September 1991, removed from ships and placed into storage pending dismantling as and when the ships docked for resupply. The Royal Navy 'traded in' its B.57 weapons at about the same time.

801 NAS were asked to fly top cover for a British aid convoy which managed to reach the besieged Muslim town of Maglai on 16 March. Once again the RN jets were only permitted to scare the Serb gunners, who were shelling the town, with ALE-40 flares. At the end of March the town of Gorazde came under attack and 801 NAS were given a CAS tasking, but the dreadful weather and mountainous terrain meant that the Sea Harrier pair had great difficulty in finding their target. The pilots could hear on their radios the sound of shells falling close to the troops calling for assistance. On his sixth pass, still trying to get a target solution, the pilot of FRS.1 XZ498 ejected after an SA-7 missile exploded on one of the aircraft's hot nozzles.[6] He landed to the west of the town with slight injuries and received cover from USN F-14 Tomcats as he made his way to the protection of an SAS unit operating in the Muslim area. Under the control of an EC-130E, a pair of French Puma helicopters stood ready to attempt a pick-up but were grounded by a severe fire-fight in the area. A-10A Warthogs were whistled up for more top-cover but bad visibil-

ity kept them from the target area. Eventually the SAS, who were awaiting the Pumas in any case to lift out one of their own casualties, walked through Serb lines and made their way to a pick-up point where the helicopters extracted them and the 'SHAR' pilot.

Ark Royal returned to Britain and a state of 'reduced readiness' (i.e. storage) while HMS *Illustrious* was returned to service. HMS *Invincible*'s second Adriatic cruise was the last with Sea Harrier FRS.1 aboard. Following a four-month 'assisted maintenance' period at Portsmouth and a two-week 'shake-down' cruise in June with two SHOEU F/A.2s aboard, the carrier headed for the Adriatic on 28 August. Two more OEU F/A.2s joined ship as she headed south with six FRS.1s com-

Above: ZD615/712 of the OEU pulls a tight turn over the sea, where its Medium Sea Grey camouflage works well. Some 899/OEU F/A.2s were delivered in Dark Sea Grey with black codes. (BAe)

Below: As Harrier T.4Ns were upgraded to T.8 standard they received the glossy black trainer scheme: ZD603 was the first, in May 1995. The T.8 has a similar front cockpit to that of the Sea Harrier F/A.2, with HUD, up-front controller and multifunction displays. Although it lacks radar, it can carry AIM-9 acquisition rounds and the ACMI pod. The Royal Navy expects to receive up to five T.8 updates eventually. (Authors' collection)

Right: Sea Harrier ZD612/724 of the OEU formates with ZD615/723. Although it is still the West's smallest combat aircraft, the Sea Harrier F/A.2 can match any other fighter in service in the air combat arena. (Via HMS *Heron*)

[6]At the time of writing, names of aircrew flying operations in the Bosnia-Hercegovina area remain classified.

prising 800 NAS's complement. The F/A.2s were on ship to prove satisfactory integration with the Air Wing and to take a first look at the jet 'in theatre'. F/A.2s flew CAP and OCA (offensive counter-air) missions alongside their 800 NAS partners. There was nearly a second loss on 22 November. A pair of F/A.2s were on a recce near Bihac the day after NATO aircraft struck Udbina airfield to prevent its use, when two SA-2 'Guideline' SAMs were fired at them from a site near Okota. One of the Vietnam-vintage weapons exploded within two miles of one Sea Harrier and the other passed close by. An 800 NAS pilot told the authors that the F/A.2 pilot was 'able to take evasive action due to an excellent "spot" by his wingman. It could have been very embarrassing otherwise!'

In fact the embarrassment was reserved for the Bosnian Serb air defences, which were subjected to a massive 5 ATAF photo recce sweep the following day and the destruction of four SAM sites by 48th FW F-15Es and HARM missiles. For their Adriatic tours the FRS.1 Sea Harrier received updated IFF (Mk XII Mode 4) and a strap-on GPS system attached to the instrument panel coaming. They also carried Vinten recce pods in addition to their F95 cameras. AIM-9M Sidewinders replaced the long-serving 'Lima' models.

The Sea Harrier F/A.2's first full carrier deployment began on 26 January 1995, when HMS *Illustrious* set sail with six 801 NAS aircraft aboard. With improvements to her four Olympus engines, a 12-degree ski-jump and larger crewroom and hangar space, *Illustrious* took on the first Adriatic deployment of the year. Her aircraft included Falklands veteran XZ455, used by Bertie Penfold and 'Fred' Frederiksen to destroy two Argentine aircraft. In its second 'life' and second conflict it joined the other Sea Harriers in demonstrating great success at radar-tracking low-flying Bosnian Serb helicopters against heavy ground clutter. CAP sorties usually lasted up to four hours with two TriStar tanker join-ups. Maintaining the Bosnia 'No Fly Zone' (NFZ) continued, together with the commitment to provide protective air cover for UNPROFOR and the UN 'safe areas' in Serb-held territory. The 'Sea Jet' demonstrated its 'swing-role' character well, moving from air superiority to CAS to recce without reconfiguration. In the latter role, F95 camera shots revealed unexpected Serb artillery positions. As 'Deny Flight' sorties continued late into 1995, HMS *Invincible*'s F/A.2 aircraft received Texas Instruments GEN-X active expendable radar decoys, which are ejected from the standard AN/ALE-40(V)4 chaff/flare dispenser.

Left, top: Falklands veteran XZ455 joined 801 NAS aboard HMS *Illustrious* in January 1995 to help enforce the Bosnia 'No-Fly Zone'. (Via R. L. Ward)

Left, centre: This jet, XZ457, scored four confirmed kills in the Falklands, earning its name *The Sharp End*. In fact, the nickname was applied for RN photographer Neil 'Joe' Mercer's photo collection to raise money for the Fleet Air Arm Memorial Church at Yeovilton. (Via R. L. Ward)

Left, bottom: Two OEU Sea Harrier F/A.2s accompanied 800 NAS's FRS.1 squadron aboard HMS *Invincible* for her Adriatic cruise in the summer of 1994. (Via R. L. Ward)

Right: Flying over HMS *Ark Royal*, Sea Harrier XZ495 keeps station on ZD615/712. The former was used by 'Sharkey' Ward in the opening skirmishes of the Falklands conflict on 1 May 1982 when he damaged a Mentor of *4 Esc* with 30mm fire. Almost twelve years later it was lost in the Bristol Channel—the first F/A.2 casualty. (BAe)

During Operation 'Determined Force', which began on 30 August 1995 in response to continued Bosnian Serb shelling of Sarajevo, Sea Harrier F/A.2s attacked several command and control sites with 1,000lb bombs. By that time the Adriatic watch had passed back to 800 NAS. 801 NAS returned to Yeovilton on 27 July from HMS *Illustrious*, 800's six aircraft (including two other South Atlantic campaigners, XZ459 and XZ492) having flown out to join *Invincible* a week previously. The need to maintain a constant carrier presence in the Adriatic dominated the activities of the small Sea Harrier force from 1993 onwards. It came at a time when the squadrons were already under pressure because of the requirement to convert pilots to F/A.2 and 'lose' aircraft for long periods to the BAe conversion line. 801 NAS made its transition in October 1994 and Yeovilton received ten F/A.2 conversions during that year. 800 NAS began conversion in March 1995, re-declaring to an operational Air Group in July after Area Capability Training for the Bosnia scenario. The squadron took AMRAAM on its first operational deployment and carried LGBs in action for the

first time. Cross-decking took place with Spanish and Italian AV-8Bs, including DACT sessions.

An immediate consequence of the re-build programme was the reduction of front-line squadron size to six rather than eight aircraft. Without about six Sea Harriers on the conversion lines at Brough and Dunsfold and others in pre-conversion maintenance at St Athan, the small size of the Sea Harrier force was once again painfully apparent. However, the process advanced rapidly. In early April 1995 ZD581/124 sat in a corner of Yeovilton's Aircraft Maintenance Group (AMGO) hangar, the last FRS.1 to await the con-version line.

The first four aircraft from the 'new build' batch of Sea Harrier F/A.2s neared completion in September 1995, with eight additional aircraft in prospect. Engines for the new 'SHARS' are refurbished Pegasus Mk 103s stripped out of the RAF's redun-dant Harrier GR.3 force. Bringing the engines up to Mk 106 standard for the Navy requires a rebuilding programme at Rolls-Royce Patchway and this has re-sulted in a disparity of several months between the delivery of the airframe and that of the engine, with consequent de-lays to the flow of new aircraft. Pilots and maintainers at Yeovilton were unanimous in advocating the Pegasus 11-61. 899 NAS's senior maintainer described it as

'the answer to all our problems, but we need someone to buy it for us'. An addi-tional blow to Sea Harrier availability in 1994–95 was the discovery of a corrosion problem in the tail area of several F/A.2s. Corrosion control is one of the biggest worries for maintainers on ship and shore and it is usually picked up by Survey Ops (SOPs) periodically. In Sea Harriers it has been most apparent in the nosewheel and main undercarriage leg. As a long-term aid to their efforts, dehumidification systems are to be installed in Yeovilton's hangars and aboard the carriers. On return from a flight a Sea Harrier will be connected up to the system and blown through with dry air.

MAINTENANCE

During the F/A.2 conversion programme aircraft were sent to St Athan for a maintenance Work Programme in which they were 'standardized' by having all their individual faults remedied. They were then sent to BAe for the F/A.2 treatment and returned to Yeovilton's AMG (NASU until 1988) for acceptance checks. At a time of great pressure on aircraft availability the AMG were alarmed to discover serious corrosion around rear fuselage Frame 46, a metal diaphragm where the bullet fairing on the tail connects to the rear of the aircraft. This fault escaped attention at St Athan and Brough simply because an inspection of that area was not required by those organisations. As a result, six gleaming 'new' F/A.2s had to be grounded for up to three months while the relevant structural box-section in the tail area was replaced or rebuilt. 800 NAS suffered delays in converting to the F/A.2 and had to 'borrow' aircraft from 899 NAS. RAF teams from Wittering were sent to assist, but had only one jig for the repair process. The corrosion affected mainly the older airframes: XZ459 was the first to be discovered.

In mid-1995 several Sea Harriers were approaching 3,500 airframe hours. The youngest had 1,800hr 'on the clock'. Extra weight resulting from the F/A.2 conversion does little to help the fatigue index. The basic age of the thirty-year old airframe design shows in other ways too. Yeovilton's Air Engineering Department (AED) has found the F/A.2 a harder air-

Left, upper: Sea Harrier ZD613 of 801 NAS, firmly chained to HMS *Illustrious* in the winter of 1995. (Via R. L. Ward)

Left, centre: Repairs to the corroded tail section of an F/A.2 being undertaken by Yeovilton's AMG. (Authors)

Left, bottom: An F/A.2 has its radar inspected at Yeovilton's AED hangar. (Authors)

Right: In April 1995 800 NAS Sea Harriers appeared in Dark Sea Grey (foreground) with black codes and standard Type B roundels or in Medium Sea Grey with 'lo-viz' roundels. (Authors)

craft to work on than the FRS.1. Apart from early headaches over the new avionics there is 'lots more gear in it. Things that were hard to get to before are now virtually impossible. We end up having to remove quite a lot of gear just to get to things. When we go on detachment people who fly more modern aircraft can't quite believe how difficult our aircraft are to work on.' Thus spoke a senior 'fixer' who had spent fourteen years dealing with the problem.

The AED aims to inspect Sea Harriers every 30 weeks, with a three-week turnaround cycle . Every 18–24 months they go across to the AMG for second-line Scheduled Unit Maintenance (SUM). There they are stripped, de-panelled and deprived of engines, seats and wings. A Quality Assurance Team does a two-day 'main strip' survey of the aeroplane and a SUM Work Package is devised to include remedial work and updates. This process was accelerated from September 1995 by the installation of new computer diagnostic equipment to plan the SUM to the best effect. Usually it takes a ten-man team about fourteen weeks (5,000 man-hours) to recover the aircraft to operational life. If major defects are discovered, RAF teams are called in from the St Athan MU.

Several accidents involved main undercarriage collapses due to fatigue failures (ZD610 on 17 July 1990, XZ499 on 2 February 1992 and ZD579 on 25 January 1993, for example). St Athan's workshops were able to manufacture and fit new drag beams for the main undercarriage mountings after one such incident, and they frequently manufacture parts which are not easily available as 'spares' from BAe.

Perhaps inevitably, the pressure of operations generates some bizarre maintenance problems. XZ440 was with 800 NAS in HMS *Illustrious*'s hangars in October 1989. While it was being refuelled a surge in the ship's systems caused the wing-tank over-pressure relief valve to fail. Air was unable to escape from the wing tanks as fuel was forced in and they were massively over-pressurised, causing huge ruptures and a cascade of fuel on to the hangar floor. The wing was removed and written off while the rest of the aircraft was rated as Cat-4 damaged and has not yet reappeared as an F/A.2 conversion, although Brough intended to convert it for re-issue in 1996. Another 800 NAS FRS.1 (XZ492) suffered wing damage while landing at Leuchars. Its jet efflux caused the runway barrier to lift and wrap itself around the starboard outrigger, which was ripped off. The aircraft was pulled to the ground and came to rest on its right pylon and damaged wing. A replacement wing was trucked up from Yeovilton's AMG but it got jammed under a bridge en route and damaged. In the end, XZ492 had to bor-

row another wing from XZ451, which arrived by a different road route. On at least three occasions the detachable wing concept has enabled bird-stricken Sea Harriers to be returned by road to the AMG from as far away as West Freugh.

Most of the maintainers' jobs are rather more routine. Resprays are done at St Athan using polyurethane finish rather than the less durable acrylics which were tried in the 1980s. Acrylics tended to peel off even when a special clear coat was applied to the leading edges of intakes and flying surfaces to try and hold it down. So far, nothing has beaten 800 NAS's Falklands-period 'distemper brush' approach to aircraft painting for sheer durability! One of the most regular tasks is FOD damage inspection of engine compressor blades, particularly since the loss of the OEU's XZ495 to this cause. Mostly this is done by running fingertips along the edges of the blades of the first-stage com-

pressors. Any FOD 'nick' of more than 5thou decrees the engine to be unserviceable until the damage has been 'feathered out'. Damage deeper into the engine is less likely as the majority of FOD is usually 'centrifuged' out of the cold nozzles, but if it is detected by a 'scope' inspection the engine has to be removed for repair. Landings on grass are 'avoided like the plague' if the AED maintainers have their way! Maintenance man-hours for the F/A.2 had not been established at the time of writing, partly because the usual cycle of Works Programme scheduling had been suspended during the main period of F/A.2 conversions. When the FRS.1 entered service the figure was about 10–15:1mmh/fh, rising to 20:1 as aircraft aged. The AMG's Deputy Director, DEPAMGO Appleby, reckoned that the F/A.2 would probably average 20–25:1 because of its increased complexity and intensive utilization.

October 20 1995, a day short of the 35th anniversary of Bill Bedford's first two-minute hover in prototype P.1127 XP831, was the day chosen by BAe to hand over their first new-build Sea Harrier F/A.2. Rear-Admiral Terry Loughran received ZH796 (NB01) on behalf of the Royal Navy at a ceremony attended by Bill Bedford. It was the first new fixed-wing aircraft to be delivered to the Royal Navy since 1988, when their last Sea Harrier FRS.1, ZE698, was handed over. Looking to the future, Rear-Admiral Loughran anticipated further joint deck operations involving Sea Harriers and RAF GR.7s.

Below left: Small FOD nicks are carefully feathered out on slightly damaged fan blades like those at the top of the picture. (Authors)

Below right: A much more seriously 'FODded' fan on a Rolls-Royce test-bed Harrier GR.5. (Via Andy Sephton)

10. Mount of the Gods

Great Britain's commitment to the AV-8B as the basis for its Second Generation Harrier was settled by the Memorandum of Understanding of 25 June 1981, which confirmed an order for sixty GR.5 aircraft (plus two Development Batch examples) based on the USMC variant. Although the RAF had initially stated that AV-8B was not a suitable replacement for the Harrier GR.3 (their ASR.409 requirement), by March 1981 the only quibbles were over the AV-8B's turn rate.

Externally similar to the AV-8B, the aircraft in fact introduced numerous changes to adapt it to the RAF's needs. In the cockpit, Martin-Baker's Mk 12 seat replaced the Stencel model, and the Ferranti moving-map display (similar to the front-seat 'repeater' unit in Tornado GR.1), which draws upon a film library of detailed maps installed in the aircraft, was updated and reinstated. A Ferranti FIN.1075 INAS replaced the Litton AN/ASN-130 of the AV-8B. Designed by Ferranti Defence Sys-

tems' Edinburgh-based Navigation Systems Department, FIN.1075 employs a floated, rate-integrating gyro platform and

The first GR.5(DB), ZD318 was painted in two-tone grey, a scheme which was tested on RAFG Harrier GR.3 XV738 in the 'Match Coat' trials of 1984. A two-tone green scheme (also tested on a GR.3 XV 804 and intended originally for the whole GR.3 fleet) was eventually sprayed on GR.5s instead. Both GR.5(DB)s were initially given the grey scheme. (BAe)

comes from the same line of development as the FIN.1070 for EFA/Eurofighter 2000.

Externally, a pair of AIM-9 launcher pylons were cleverly incorporated ahead of the undercarriage outrigger fairings, with protective silicon tiles on the wing surface behind them to provide insulation from the Sidewinder's fiery exhaust. The outboard and intermediate pylons were also strengthened to enable them to carry the bulky 600lb BL.755 CBU. Reinforcement of the local wing structure had to be in the form of a metal component to avoid changes to the basic composite wing on the St Louis production line. Further strengthening of the wing leading edges, nose cone, windshield and intake lips gave

added bird-strike resistance for the NATO low-level scenario. Much of the bird-proofing originally built into the Harrier GR.1/AV-8A had been designed out of the AV-8B as the Marines did not see it as a priority for the kind of flying they were used to. The RAF wanted it back in again.

In place of the AV-8B's GAU-12/U Equalizer gun the MoD chose a twin Aden 25mm installation, saving 200lb and offering less drag. The GR.5's gun pods were lighter and narrower than the AV-8B's, giving slightly more effective 'LID' characteristics. In reducing the gun's calibre from 30mm to 25mm the Royal Ordnance Establishment increased its cyclic rate of fire from 1,300 to 1,750rpm. Aden 25 uses ammunition which is similar to the

For seven years No 233 OCU flew Harrier GR.5s (and later, GR.7s) alongside a diminishing number of GR.3s. In this photograph, the unit's first operational GR.5 (ZD324) takes priority as a bomb-laden GR.3 pulls aside gracefully for the newcomer. (BAe)

Oerlikon KBA (25 by 137mm) rounds employed in the GAU-12/U. The muzzle velocity of the chosen STANAG 4173 shell is 1,050m/sec (3,450fs) against 790m/sec (2,590fs) for the KBA, making it more accurate at short range. It has percussive rather than electrical ignition, which many consider safer in an HERO environment. The Aden 25 was designed as an 'all-round' gun, equally capable in air-to-ground and air combat, whereas the

Equalizer is optimised for strafing. Despite its advantages and rapid initial development, the Aden gun suffered from prolonged teething problems and at the time of writing is still not fully cleared for service use. Persistent difficulties occurred with gun-barrel life and with interfacing the gun with its pod and ammunition.

Other equipment changes included an accident recorder and MIRLS (miniature infra-red linescan), also based on the system in the Tornado GR.1A. More significantly perhaps, Marconi's ARI 23333 Zeus EW system was fitted in place of the Litton AN/ALR-67 and 'strap-on' Lockheed-Sanders AN/ALQ-164(V); it works along very similar principles, but without the drag penalties associated with

the American pod, the Zeus jammer having been packaged into an Aden 25 gun pod. Flight Lieutenant Chris Huckstep, on his third RAF Harrier tour and with over 1,700hr on the two generations in early 1992, described the Marconi Zeus radar warning receiver and automatic jammer as 'an extremely important piece of equipment. It works like this. A computer has fed into it all the different frequencies of various kinds of threats; each radar, each missile, has its own features that can be identified. The data base [working in C–J bands] also knows things like the lethal range of a given missile. When the receiver picks up a frequency, it displays the direction and type with a symbol on the RWR scope. The greater the threat, the more it

The standard GR5/7 colour scheme of NATO Dark Green uppersides and Lichen Green undersides on GR.5 ZD346, here testing a load of seven Improved BL.755 CBUs and a pair of AIM-9G Sidewinders. (BAe)

moves towards the outer edge of the display. So, the pilot knows what is looking at him, what has locked on to him, what has been launched at him and whether it is in range or not, and he can determine which of several threats is the most important. He can programme the computer to display a threat as a certain number, and tailor it to various environments. The Zeus, knowing the frequency of the threat, automatically selects the appropriate jamming response and this is reflected on the

Left: Rolls-Royce GR.5 test-bed ZD466 in the hover. This Harrier was in use at Filton from January 1990 to July 1991 on engine trials. (Via Andy Sephton)

Right, upper: RAF Wittering's No 1 Squadron began to deploy its GR.5s to NATO exercises in Norway soon after they achieved operational status. Traditional 'snow' camouflage was daubed on. (Andy Evans)

Right, lower: Blotches of temporary Arctic camouflage here incorporate No 1 Squadron's insignia. (Andy Evans)

in trials designated Operation 'Horsefly'. Zeus's £100 million contract price indicates the perceived importance of anti-missile protection. For less than 300lb total weight Zeus and MAWS are intended to give 360-degree protection against a wide range of IR and radar-homing missiles, and hostile radars. It was certainly the kind of protection which AV-8B pilots would have appreciated in the SAM-lacerated skies of Iraq and Kuwait. However, MAWS's lengthy gestation meant that it could not have been available to them (nor was their own, home-grown version at that stage). In fact, clearance trials were still proceeding in 1994, but it seems to work well with the new chaff/flare fit.

In all, seven AV-8B systems were changed in the design of the GR.5, including the all-weather landing system, which was deleted. Additional costs resulting

scope. The system also tells the pilot how many chaff and flare rounds remain in his dispenser.'[1] This includes a 'library' of over 1,000 known types of emitter, and the reaction time is claimed to be less than one second. Zeus includes sensors located in wingtip bulges, in the nose 'prong' antennae and in the tail, to help detect and analyse enemy radar activity. Plessey's MAWS, a lightweight radar in the tail-boom, is coupled to Zeus to issue warning data on missiles in flight, and it can be coupled to the chaff/flare dispensers automatically.[2] Expendables comprise TACDS V-10 flare dispensers and a French Phimat chaff pod, but the latter has more recently been supplanted by CelsiusTech BOL dispensers fitted to each outrigger, packaged like a 'small loaf of bread' measuring about $2^{1}/_{2}$ by 3in (6 by 8cm) in cross-section and packing in 160

0.3in (8mm) thick chaff 'slices'. These are dispensed electromechanically, released one at a time in any number of patterns. Mounting them on the two outriggers offers both rapid dispensing and the advantage that the wingtip vortices help spread the chaff, providing rapid blooming—essential at countering radars with short pulse lengths and range gates, such as those used by enemy fighters and forward ground defences used to track targets for missile attack—so that it is able quickly to build up a series of distracting clouds in bursts, each offering a realistic Harrier-sized radar cross-section. The system also frees the pylon previously used for the Phimat chaff-dispensing pod. The GR.5/ 7 was the first aircraft to receive this compact and effective new Swedish system.

MAWS was extensively tested at NWC China Lake in 1989 using a Harrier GR.5

[1] Based on an interview with John Roberts, kindly provided by the interviewer. Marconi Space & Defence Systems received their Zeus contract in November 1983 and the Northrop Corporation provided the jamming transmitters. Extensive trials took place at China Lake and Zeus was released for service trials in mid-1990.
[2] The Plessey MAWS weighs only 25lb but cost £10 million to develop! Like Zeus itself, development of the MAWS continued after the Harrier II's entry into service and it was not ready for use in 1989. It differs from the American Harrier II MAWS system, which relies on detecting launch 'flashes' and missile plumes in the ultra-violet part of the spectrum (hence the curious-looking sensor fitted underneath the nose of American II-Plusses) as opposed to doppler techniques. None of these are fail-safe, but they go a long way towards improving survivability in an era of increasing electro-optically guided weapons which are relatively 'stealthy' in the CAS/BAI arena, where supplies of shoulder-launched weapons are often abundant.

by the company as a private venture. It has a solid-state transmitter and full cryptographic capability, making it compatible with the US Mk XII system. Radio equipment in the GR.5 was the GEC Avionics AD.3500, which gave line-of-sight tactical communications, clear and secure speech and two emergency channels.

In every other respect a 'minimum change' policy applied to the GR.5. Whenever possible, components from the GR.1/AV-8A had been already carried over into the AV-8B design, or modified, to save cost. The Dowty-designed undercarriage, for example, was simply beefed-up to cope with increased weights. Other components which had proved unreliable in the original design (such as the AV-8A's water tank gauge) were replaced. A new gauge was designed by Simmonds Precision in the United States and produced by Flight Refuelling in the UK, as was the retractable refuelling probe.

One surprise was the retention of ARBS. In 1980 it was widely supposed that the RAF would want to install an improved version of LRMTS, which had proved popular in service, or a more advanced laser. The AV-8B's databus could have allowed such a system to be fitted using a suitable interface module and appropriate software. Once again, cost limits obtained and the Hughes angle-rate system was retained despite misgivings in the RAF. It was seen as an ideal system for the Marines' predominantly clear-visibility, 45-degree dive-attack profile, but less good for the RAF's favoured level-pass attack at low altitude. Flight Lieutenant Chris Huckstep reckoned that 'In bad weather or under threat, there is little time to find the target and get set up properly'.[3]

Although the basic testing of AV-8B and GR.5 obviously ran parallel as far as airframe 'read-across' was concerned, the equipment fit which distinguished the RAF version was not tested until four years after the AV-B's operational fit was established. However, the benefits of having a Harrier with twice the GR.3's 3,000hr fatigue life were welcomed. So was the AV-

from these alterations ran to £40 million and there were inevitable delays in the programme. FIN.1075 underwent a four-year refinement process after Ferranti received the initial order in April 1985. Poor reliability in the early stages meant reversion to the Litton unit for the RAF's first batch of aircraft, and even after service entry thirty-two more Litton AN/ASN-130 had to be ordered as interim equipment for the first batch of RAFG Harrier GR.5s while persistent problems with water ingress were sorted out. FIN.1075 was finally declared healthy in mid-1989.

Less favoured was the BAe Dynamics MIRLS project. Designed to provide an inbuilt, all-weather reconnaissance capability, the system was delayed, rose far beyond cost estimates and was eventually cancelled, leaving the Harrier without its traditional 'tac recce' function. At the same

time, the progressive withdrawal of the GR.3 variant meant that all the RAF's Vinten four-camera recce pods were mothballed. It was assumed that MIRLS would quickly supersede them. In fact, the wedge-shaped bulge beneath the GR.5's nose which would have contained the linescan unit was loaded with ballast instead. (It was deleted from the later GR.7 variant and removed from remanufactured GR.5s.) Because MIRLS was intended to record its IR imagery on to videotape, the Harrier's wet-film processing and interpretation facility was also phased out towards the end of the GR.3 era in 1989 and had to be resuscitated later.

Finally, the Harrier GR.5's IFF transponder was different from the AV-8B's Bendix AN/APX-100. In the spring of 1987 Cossor were awarded a contract for 72 units, known as IFF.4760, developed

[3]See Note 2.

8B's more solid 'feel' in flight, due to the very effective Sperry SAAHS. Pilots appreciated the slightly more roomy HOTAS cockpit with its more logical layout. Above all, they appreciated having 50 per cent more internal fuel (and four times as much externally) than the GR.3, and a 70 per cent increase in ordnance. For the manufacturers involved, the greater proportion of British equipment shifted the balance of production to a 50/50 share between McAir and BAe rather than the 60/40 AV-8B deal. Rolls-Royce kept 75 per cent of the engine workload. The Pegasus Mk 105 chosen for the GR.5 was rated at 21,750lb thrust (only 250lb greater than the GR.3's powerplant and 300lb more than the AV-8B's F402-RR-406A which was de-rated to increase time between overhauls, or TBO).

DECS

An important innovation for the Pegasus in 1982 was DECS (Digital Engine Control System) developed at Rolls-Royce Patchway with the assistance of Dowty at Cheltenham and Smith Industries at Basingstoke. Until then all marks of Pegasus had used mechanical fuel control systems. John Fawcett, who did most of the test-flying of DECS, explained to the authors what the system achieved. 'First, it enabled an engine or a fuel system to be changed without the need to carry out engine runs and flight tests to set up the system, as was the case with the old hydro-mechanical system. This was a great advantage as the Harrier needs to be tied down to run at high power, which in a dispersed "hide" site is virtually impossible.' Rolls-Royce Senior Flight Test Engineer Alan Baxter provided further background: 'The Pegasus control requirements were severe, as early engines had virtually no surge margin at all. Consequently the hydro-mechanical system had to be tailored to suit the characteristics of the engine, a time-consuming affair which nevertheless was achieved satisfactorily. The control system was always difficult to set up as it had a number of adjustments, all of which appeared to interact with the rest, and it was not until the advent of full-authority digital fuel control systems that the oppor-

tunity presented itself of developing an electronic control for the Pegasus. This was done under contract [A61A 2331] from the MoD, using Pegasus II No 922. The DECS sat on the fan casing of the engine on top of a much-simplified hydro-mechanical system.' It was supplied with fuel for cooling purposes and backed up by a manual fuel system.

Ground running began on 17 December 1981, using GR.3 XV277 which became the Rolls-Royce test-bed at Filton from October 1979 to October 1987, performing seven major engine test programmes. Its cockpit equipment usually consisted of little more than a radio and stand-by instruments. DECS flight-testing lasted from 11 March 1982 until XV277's last flight in 1987. (It was driven to Yeovilton's AMG by lorry on 29 November 1988 at the end of its flying days.) Initially, John Fawcett made take-offs and landings using the back-up manual system until DECS reliability was established. A second prototype system (No 145) was fitted for a new test flight series beginning on 7 January 1983, during which Fawcett engaged DECS during a hover, STO, VL and transition. From October 1983 to December 1984 development versions of the Mk 105 engine (11-21J) and F402-RR-406 (11-21K) were flown using MODAS (Modular Onboard Data Acquisition System) for computer analysis purposes. Following this, flight testing of the production DECS began in January 1985.

John Fawcett found that the major problems encountered were 'due to slow response. This was most evident during vertical landing and close-formation flying. On landing, the DECS needed to make sure the pilot was on the ground and really intended to slam the throttle to idle. The time taken for the computer to respond to these inputs and pull back engine power was in the order of 0.5 seconds. It should be remembered that the DECS microprocessor shared its vintage with the Sinclair ZX Spectrum home computer! The natural spring in the Harrier undercarriage meant that this delay caused the aircraft to bounce; the height of the bounce depended on the rate of descent. (The "record' was 6ft by an RAF

pilot!) A Harrier landing on a ship descends at around 6ft per second and this would cause a 3ft bounce. I discovered when I flew AV-8B Ship 2 (BuNo 161397) that its more highly damped undercarriage reduced the bounce, but it was still unacceptable to the Marines as an aircraft might slide dangerously if it bounced when landing on a ship. Attempts to solve the problem using software fixes failed and a mechanical fuel-bleed system had to be used, based on a revised PDR solenoid.' This was the basis of the 'thrust-dumping' mode incorporated in production DECS-equipped engines. Slow throttle response was also apparent in air-to-air refuelling. John Fawcett flew XV277 fitted with a refuelling probe and made a number of 'dry prods' at lower engine rpm, where the problem was most apparent. Software amendments eventually cured this difficulty.

One major improvement brought about by DECS was the cure for a tendency in previous Pegasus engines to stagnate at 92 per cent thrust. For the RAF's STO routine this was not a major problem, but the USMC had already lost an AV-8B 'off the bow' because of it. The aircraft and its pilot were 'keel-hauled' by the ship and the Marines were naturally anxious to avoid similar accidents. DECS guaranteed 100 per cent thrust for take-off, although Rolls-Royce had already put other 'mods' into the Pegasus to alleviate the problem.

From the pilot's point of view, DECS also simplified hovering and VTOL. John Fawcett continued: 'When a Harrier was manoeuvred in the hover using the old system, engine bleed air was needed to power the RCS "puffer" ducts. This caused a slight reduction in specific engine fan speed, for which the pilot had to compensate with more throttle. DECS automatically detected the reduction and added more fuel to restore the situation and maintain the thrust level demanded by the chosen throttle lever angle.'

A development Mk 105 Pegasus 11-21 was ready in time for installation in the first Harrier GR.5 (DB 1, ZD318). It was rolled out on 23 April 1985 and flown by Mike Snelling at Dunsfold on the 30th.

GR.5s were assembled at Kingston using wings, pylons and front fuselages from the 'Home of the Phantom' at St Louis, and other parts made by BAe under the work-share agreement which had begun the supply of UK-produced parts to the AV-8B production line in February 1981. Three other DB aircraft followed (ZD319–321) and the lengthy process of flight-testing the UK-specified equipment began. In most respects the GR.5 airframe was already a known quantity and the RAF's 210,000 hours of V/STOL flying, with 75 per cent at low-level, enabled the service induction of the revised Harrier to be prepared with confidence. However, the lengthy delays in avionics which affected

Pylon-power, Harrier-style. On the outboard station of this No 1 Squadron GR.5 hangs a Phimat chaff dispenser. (Andy Evans)

the test programme meant that the first RAF GR.5, ZD323, was not delivered to Wittering for familiarization purposes until 29 May 1987. Armament trials were prolonged too. Several aircraft were involved, including ZD319 which did ordnance trials at West Freugh in August 1986. Apart from the Aden 25 gun's extended problems, the programme had only achieved clearance of AIM-9L and practice bombs for service use by February 1991, nearly two years after the first operational squadron converted to the type. Largely this was a knock-on result of earlier delays with the avionics. However, the RAF's operational introduction of the GR.5 also happened rather later than expected as well.

One of the major factors in the delayed service entry was the loss of ZD325 on one of its final BAe pre-service test sorties on 22 October 1987. Taylor Scott, who had been such a vital figure in the Sea

Harrier programme, was making oxygen checks at 30,000ft over Salisbury Plain when contact with the aircraft was lost and it was tracked on radar heading west, straight and level. It was intercepted by a USAFE F-15C, whose pilot reported that the Harrier's canopy was shattered but that the unoccupied ejector seat was still in place. ZD325 flew on for 90 minutes, eventually plunging into the sea when its fuel ran out, some 250nm south-west of Ireland. The wreck sank into 600ft of water and was never lifted. Taylor Scott's body was found near the village of Winterbourne Stoke, Wiltshire, and it was clear that the Martin-Baker Mk 12H seat's manual separating system had been activated, firing the parachute-deployed rocket (PDR) through the canopy. This in turn deployed the pilot's drogue chute, dragging him through the canopy. His seat remained aboard, all straps and connec-

tions with the pilot having been released as part of the manual separation process. A popular theory in the Harrier community suggests that Scott's cockpit 'wander' lamp (a small light on a flexible stalk) may have become lodged under the manual override firing rod. If the seat had then been lowered in flight it could have caused the obstruction to distort the firing rod, triggering the PDR. Although Martin-Baker subsequently modified the seat with a shield over the rod, the investigation of the accident remained inconclusive, causing a delay of nine months in the commencement of pilot training and hampering the GR.5's service début. By May 1988 Undersecretary of State for Defence William Reeves announced that 'cumulative delays had increased the delay in service entry to eleven months'.

GR.5 INTO SERVICE

Wittering received its first operational GR.5 (ZD324) on 1 July 1987, but it did not make its first operational flight until 30 March the following year. Deliveries recommenced in May 1988, and No 1 Squadron had eight aircraft under its wing by the year's end. The Squadron reached full operational establishment by February 1989, albeit with Litton INAS units replacing the delayed FIN.1075. Ferranti equipment began to be retrofitted from July 1989.

Originally it had been planned to convert two RAFG Harrier units only, transferring low-time GR.3s to No 1 Squadron. The lack of suitable aircraft at the time frustrated that plan and No 1 became the first with the Harrier II some twenty years after introducing the 'Harrier I' to RAF service. No 233 OCU under Wing Commander Peter Day was well prepared for the conversion programme, having re-established the Harrier Conversion Team (HCT) in February 1987 with Squadron Leader Jonathan Baynton and two other pilots, all of whom had trained with the Marines at Cherry Point on the AV-8B simulator. They were not able to make their first GR.5 flights until 30 March 1988 (using ZD324), because of the 'cumulative delays'. No 233 OCU's first course (HCT 1) began on 18 July 1988,

using the EAV-8B simulator at Rota, Spain, which McAir had provided for the last stages of the seven-week course. All No 1 Squadron's pilots were GR.5-capable by the end of April 1989, together with most of No 233 OCU's aircrew. HCT 1 gave eight days of ground school and sixteen sorties, five of which were ARBS range sorties. Many of the earliest converts were GR.3 men who needed only six hours of 'handling' training, four hours of formation and air combat plus five range sorties and simulated attack profiles (SAPs). No 1 was fully operational by autumn 1989 under Wing Commander Iain Harvey and declared to SACEUR Strategic Reserve (Air) on 2 October. The OCU aircraft were worked hard to catch up on the conversion process, logging 1,200hr flying time in their first year. One GR.5 amassed 330hr 'on the clock'. The task then shifted to the RAFG No 2 Group Harrier units, with deliveries of ZD376 to Gütersloh for familiarisation in December 1988 and ZD401 to No 3 Squadron the following May to begin the transition. In advance of its conversion No 3(F) Squadron had gradually accumulated most of the older GR.3s to 'use up', completing operations on this model by 29 November 1989, when a nine-ship GR.5 formation was put up to celebrate the event. The influx of new GR.5 airframes was very rapid, a backlog having developed during the hiatus following Scott's tragic accident. For a time, No 233 OCU had more aircraft than its pilot conversion courses could handle and several went into MU storage at Shawbury. At the start of 1989 it had four different types of Harrier: ten GR.5s, seven GR.3s, eight T.4s and a pair of T.4As.

No IV(AC) Squadron, originally planned as the first GR.5 unit when it was thought that the sixty GR.5s originally ordered would only be sufficient to equip the RAFG units plus training and attrition, had wound-down its 'recce' speciality by 31 May 1989 in anticipation of losing its GR.3s with their photo-pods. (No 1 Squadron's photo-recce operation ceased at the same time.) In fact, No IV was the last to receive the new model, resulting in an eighteen-month period with-

out recce capability for its GR.3s. Wing Commander Malcolm White presided over the end of the Squadron's GR.3 era on 7 December 1990, and a week later received ZG473 from the SAOEU, an aircraft which leap-frogged the GR.5 stage and took the squadron straight to the definitive Night Attack Harrier for the RAF, the GR.7.

NIGHTBIRD

At about £20 million a copy, the Harrier GR.7 represented the fruits of the United Kingdom's investment in the joint BAe/McAir effort which produced the Marines' AV-8B(NA). It was preceded at Kingston by an interim model, the GR.5A, nineteen of which were manufactured. They had much of the GR.7's cockpit layout, wiring for some of the forthcoming night attack equipment and a little of the revised

avionics. ZD320 was the 'prototype' GR.5A and it was stored with the majority of the batch at 27 MU Shawbury at the end of 1989 to await conversion to definitive GR.7 standard. In due course all surviving GR.5 models went through the GR.7 'update line' following the delivery of the last *ab initio* GR.7, ZG862, on 2 June 1992. The GR.5A batch were the last to be processed. A £16 million contract was announced on 11 November 1990 for the upgrade of 58 GR.5/5A Harriers with digital moving maps, FLIR and NVG cockpits. The first new-build GR.7s (ZG471–473) were sent to 'A' Squadron of the A&AEE from May to August 1990 to continue trials, following the type's first flight on 29 November 1989. Three others flew with SAOEU in 1990 alongside T.4As XW267/SA and XW269/BD.

The emphasis on night attack for the RAF's Harrier Force was a corollary of reduced East–West tensions as the 'Cold War' ended, causing a re-think of the Harrier's tasking. Its primary role shifted from CAS to BAI (or, to be more precise, FOFA—follow-on force attack—which meant interdicting enemy armour reinforcements behind the forward battle area) and longer-range interdiction. As hostile troop and armour movements tend to be made under cover of darkness, it was logical to apply FLIR and night-vision technology to the Harrier concept to enable it to deal with those targets. In a relatively small airframe it was not possible to consider equipping the Harrier as an all-weather/night striker in the Tornado category, but advances in lightweight FLIR and night vision goggles promised a considerable clear-weather, night-attack capa-

bility. The choice of GEC-Marconi's FLIR sensor for the AV-8B(NA) in the summer of 1989 was the outcome of extensive tests at China Lake which included evaluation of Catseye NVG. Parallel tests were run in Britain under the 'Nightbird' project, a joint RAE/DRA programme which had begun in 1986 using the rather heavy, clumsy goggles available at that time aboard Andover, Hunter T.7 and Harrier T.4A test aircraft. A new lightweight, balanced NVG helmet/goggle set was developed in 1988 alongside a programme called Penetrate, which included work on

Left: Making an interesting comparison with the Harrier II Plus cockpit, the GR.7 office offers similar multifunction screens, but with FLIR imagery appearing on the right-hand screen and a moving map on the left. (BAe)

Right, upper: Comparison of Harrier GR.5 and GR.5A/7 profiles.

Right, lower: Squadron Leader Gerry Humphries of No 1 Squadron models the GEC Nightbird NVG set. (Andy Evans)

HUD display gives an intense image by shining a dot on to the HUD screen, which is good for daylight use. A raster version gives a TV-type picture on the HUD, which is much better for night or low light, using the picture from the FLIR.' Ferranti's new model combined both possibilities in one unit.

On the Harrier GR.7 the FLIR unit was mounted in a box fairing similar to the AV-8B(NA)'s ahead of the windshield, as close to the pilot's sight-line as possible, avoiding parallax on the HUD. With FLIR imagery projected, the pilot also had standard navigation and instrumentation data before him in the HUD, and target data from FLIR replacing the daylight-only ARBS. FLIR imagery could also be switched to a multi-function display screen on the instrument panel instead by using a HOTAS control button. Contrast could be switched by using another button which changed the imagery from 'hot = black' to 'hot = white', rather like positive and negative photography. The GEC-Marconi FLIR installation covers a field of view about 20 degrees ahead of the aircraft, co-inciding with the pilot's line of vision through the windshield, straight ahead. To obtain night vision beyond that rather narrow swathe, GEC's Nightbird NVG set is used. Goggles are mounted on a swivel attached to the pilot's helmet and swung upwards when not required. NVGs are mounted far enough ahead of the pilot's eyes for him to look under them at FLIR imagery in his display screen or at his digital colour map display—the first of its kind to be installed in a British aircraft. Goggles are used in a number of RAF aircraft, including the Wessex HC.2. A pilot of one these No 234 Squadron res-

perspective cockpit displays with FLIR imagery projected on to a raster HUD display. This was backed up by inputs from a new GEC-Marconi digital map display and terrain referenced navigation system (TRNS). GEC Avionics Guidance Systems Division at Rochester received the order for their Digital Colour Map Unit (DCMU) towards the end of 1987. It was the first solid-state mapping unit, replacing film-based mechanical systems. The computer which stored its terrain imagery could retain data on a geographical area the size of Europe. Information could be presented in several scale sizes with orientation varying from 'north at the top of the display' to 'direction of flight-track at

top'. Targets, waypoints, defences and ground obstacles could be overlaid on the display for clarity.

An A&AEE Buccaneer S.2 (complete with 'Nightbird' nose art), a Tornado GR.1 and a Jaguar T.2A were added to this important programme in due course. One of the three Harrier T.4As (XW269) used for Nightbird had an experimental FLIR fitted into its LRMTS nose cone and a development version of the Ferranti Type 4510 cursive/raster HUD, with an FD5000 video camera. Andy Sephton, who flew many of the Nightbird Harrier trials from RAF Lyneham in 'T-Bird' XW269 explained the advantages of this type of HUD: 'The standard (cursive

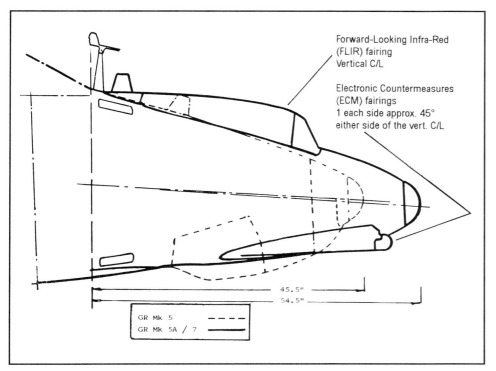

Forward-Looking Infra-Red
(FLIR) fairing
Vertical C/L

Electronic Countermeasures
(ECM) fairings
1 each side approx. 45°
either side of the vert. C/L

45.5"
54.5"

GR Mk 5
GR Mk 5A / 7

cue helicopters told the authors that looking through them is 'rather like peering through a pair of bog-roll tubes. They give a field of view extending about 40 degrees and they are extremely effective in the lowest light conditions. They work by amplifying the available light in the wavelength between visible light and infra-red. Their effectiveness obviously varies according to the ambient light level. A full moon gives conditions similar to daylight in terms of clarity, but without colour—except green.' Nightbird pilots found that flying towards a full moon created genuine dazzle and sorties had to be planned to keep a full moon behind or to the side of the aircraft. Artificial lighting in built-up areas can also overload the goggles.

All NVG-equipped aircraft have to receive extensive cockpit lighting changes. Even small amounts of red light in the cockpit block out the goggles completely and a low, even, blue glow is required. Normal map-reading navigation is possible too, although certain colours will not be visible on a paper map. Pilots also have to get used to travelling at high speed with no sense of depth-of-field through the goggles. Rain can degrade NVG/FLIR definition badly.

RAE Bedford developed a night-landing light system for Harrier FOBs known as the Bedford Experimental Lighting System (BELS). It consisted simply of a supermarket 240V bathroom light tube with a 12V charge across it. Without NVGs the resultant glow is invisible, but the goggles make the light stand out clearly and several can be used to mark the hover position at a FOB in covert conditions.

NVG flying with the GR.7 began on 11 December 1990 and included a visit to VMA-211 at Yuma by three aircraft in March 1991 for trials alongside AV-8B(NA) exponents of the 'dark art'. Three SAOEU pilots led by Wing Commander Keith Grumbley flew 70hr of night sorties, including low-level attacks. Two of the pilots, Flight Lieutenants Paul Gunnell and Steve Hawkins, completed the trials session later in the United Kingdom with a night SAP from West Freugh to the Garvie Island range in February 1992, dropping live 1,000lb bombs. Their

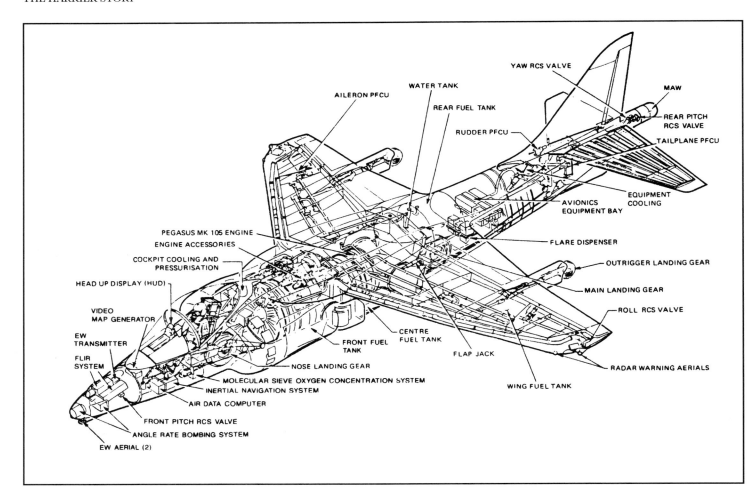

AILERON PFCU
WATER TANK
REAR FUEL TANK
YAW RCS VALVE
MAW
REAR PITCH RCS VALVE
RUDDER PFCU
TAILPLANE PFCU
EQUIPMENT COOLING
AVIONICS EQUIPMENT BAY
PEGASUS MK 105 ENGINE
ENGINE ACCESSORIES
FLARE DISPENSER
COCKPIT COOLING AND PRESSURISATION
OUTRIGGER LANDING GEAR
HEAD UP DISPLAY (HUD)
MAIN LANDING GEAR
VIDEO MAP GENERATOR
ROLL RCS VALVE
EW TRANSMITTER
CENTRE FUEL TANK
FLIR SYSTEM
FRONT FUEL TANK
FLAP JACK
RADAR WARNING AERIALS
NOSE LANDING GEAR
MOLECULAR SIEVE OXYGEN CONCENTRATION SYSTEM
WING FUEL TANK
INERTIAL NAVIGATION SYSTEM
AIR DATA COMPUTER
FRONT PITCH RCS VALVE
ANGLE RATE BOMBING SYSTEM
EW AERIAL (2)

Left, upper: Interior layout, GR.7.

Left, lower: The SAOEU operated four GR.7s for MoD(PE) trials programmes in 1992 at Boscombe Down and BAe Dunsfold. Armament testing with TIALD and LGBs was included. (Via Andy Evans)

Right, top: SAOEU's insignia was replaced by that of the AWC in 1995, as seen on GR.7 ZG501. (Authors)

Right, centre: FLIR imagery of Wittering's main runway, projected on to a GR.7's HUD. (Gerry Humphries via Andy Evans)

Right, bottom: A detachment of No IV Squadron GR.7s visited Belize in September 1993 to demonstrate the speed with which such a deployment could be made in an emergency. ZG532/CC still has the Squadron's high-visibility tail markings. (Andy Suddards)

FIN.1075G INAS units were modified to receive data from a GPS unit mounted on the fuselage spine. This installation was apparently capable of ensuring a positional accuracy to within 100ft over the 30nm sortie.

Apart from its FLIR fairing, the GR.7 is visually distinguishable from the GR.5 by its 9in nose extension, with the twin 'tusks' of the definitive Zeus system projecting beneath it. As part of the development programme, Rod Frederiksen delivered factory-fresh GR.5A ZD466 to Filton on 24 January 1990 for Rolls-Royce to test the effect of both GR.5 and GR.7 nose profiles on engine surge margins. The GR.7 nose structure arrived late, in September 1990, and could not be fitted straight away because plastic filler used in its manufacture kept flaking off, posing a FOD hazard. When CTP Andy Sephton was finally able to conduct comparative flight trials in the summer of 1990 it was concluded, after 37 flights, that there was little difference in the effect of the two nasal variants upon surge margins or stress levels in the fan blades. When ZD466 returned to BAe on 25 July 1991 it marked the end of fixed-wing flying from the Patchway Flight Test Facility after more than 70 years.

While GR.7 trials continued, the GR.5 rapidly gained popularity with its pilots.

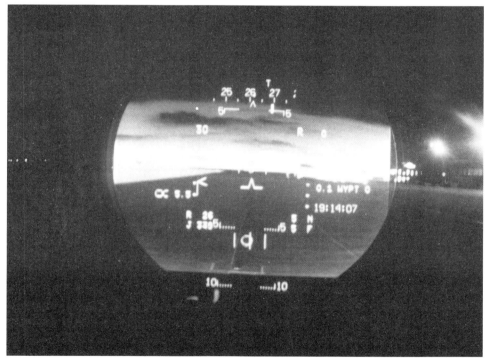

Having made its first AIM-9L firings at a Valley APC in July 1989, No 1 Squadron donned white splodges of arctic camouflage for its deployment to Bardufoss, Norway. The visit was repeated in March and April 1990 for Exercise 'Cold Winter'. On that occasion Phimat chaff pods were taken along, pending clearance of the Zeus system. By September 1990, when the Battle of Britain 50th Anniversary flypast was staged, all three box formations of Harriers contained the GR.5 variant. Changes of plan concerning the allocation of the new Harriers had resulted in an additional order (of 16 July 1986) for another eighteen GR.5s. This was further increased to thirty-four (on 19 April 1988), bringing the total order to 96. In fact, the last 27 were built from the ground up as GR.7s. The 1986 order reversed the MoD's original plans to equip the RAFG units with new Harriers while the UK-based No 1 Squadron would have kept re-lifed GR.3s. These upgrades would have been low-time airframes fitted with a variant of the BAe metal 'big wing' originally conceived for the 'all-British GR.5' project. In fact, the cancellation of the GR.3 re-life programme (and the lack of sufficiently sprightly GR.3 airframes) made extra GR.5s a more attractive option.

OCU COURSES

No 233 OCU had its GR.5 courses in full swing by the end of 1989. The OCU organised itself into two sections: 'A' Squadron, which concentrated on weapons training at the 'advanced' end of the course under the tuition of six Fighter/Reconnaissance Instructors; and 'B' Squadron, which provided Basic Conversion Training. When Wittering's GR.5 simulator was installed in 1991, twenty-four additional personnel were required to man it. They offered a much cheaper service than the previous visits to Rota or Cherry Point 'sims' for AV-8B experience. No 233 OCU also ran an Aircraft Rectification Flight with 250 men in all. With the GR.5 came a new approach to Harrier maintenance. Instead of returning its aircraft to the St Athan MU for 1,000hr major overhauls, as it had in the GR.3 days, GR.5 airframes were given Minor,

Primary Star and Two-Star maintenance inspections on base. The use of LRUs for many of the avionics cut maintenance times. Quick checks on engines and other systems were made possible by the introduction of HIMS (Harrier Information Management System), produced by Scicon. Ferranti designed their AST.1200 test set to check the operation of their FIN.1075 INAS. In the case of major damage, airframes could be returned to BAe and engines to Rolls-Royce. One of the goals of the AV-8B/GR.5 programme was a 60 per cent reduction in maintenance compared with the earlier models. Access to frequently serviced components was easier and the composite main airframe sections were designed to be substantially fatigue- and maintenance-free. Wittering's Harrier fixers learned from the USMC the technique of metal-patching damaged composite areas. Small wounds, such as a lightning-strike hole in the wing of ZD326 in 1989, simply had aluminium patches riveted over them'; larger areas, such as a crunched wingtip, were sawn out and replaced by a metal section.

Pilots entering the OCU's courses in 1989–90 spent a week on Gazelle helicopters at Shawbury to gain familiarity with vertical and hovering flight, followed by ten days on the GR.3, T.4 and simulator, including twelve hours of flying. Seventeen more solo GR.3 flights were made. At this point RN Sea Harrier trainees moved to Yeovilton's 899 NAS course, and RAF candidates advanced to GR.5 ground school to learn about the aircraft they would actually fly, with its totally different cockpit. A Harrier Avionics Systems Trainer (HAST) assisted in this process, followed by ten days of simulator sessions.

The Wittering 'sim' (later to be matched by one at Laarbruch) was built to replicate flying conditions throughout the world, using satellite data to generate the required scenarios. An extremely detailed, fully simulated display appears immediately ahead of the pilot, while the peripheral areas are blocked in with more basic computer-generated 'landscapes'. As the pilot alters his eye position the 'high detail' area shifts accordingly, providing VTOL virtual reality via a specially modi-

fied helmet equipped with a small camera. Finally, the student entered the CONVEX stage, making sixteen short familiarisation sorties followed by twenty combat preparation flights in which ACM, formation and night-flying and low-level navigation were taught. In-flight refuelling was at first limited to altitudes below 10,000ft because of development difficulties with the GR.5's 'airmix' (rather than the less healthy pure oxygen) breathing system for the pilot.

Having completed all that to his QFI's satisfaction, the student then flew his eight weapons sorties with 'A' Squadron followed by several which culminated in a series of SAPs in which he had to plan the mission and lead a pair of Harriers. Although live weapons drops were included, CBLS 200 practice bomb dispensers were used less than in the GR.3 syllabus because dropping real ordnance would have been merely an exercise for the aircraft's automated nav-attack gear rather than the pilot's skill. QFIs were more interested in seeing that their students were capable of reaching the target and achieving an ARBS lock-on to the target. No 233 OCU had about fourteen pilots at various stages of its courses at any given time.

Pilots quickly learned to appreciate the simplicity of the GR.5's state-of-the-art systems. Although INAS line-up was done in the usual way by entering latitude and longitude digits read from the aircraft's parking spot, most of the other avionics and systems were accessed and checked via the two multipurpose cockpit displays (MPCD). While the INAS aligns, a pilot can do the traditional walk-around checks before climbing back in to strap in and 'pull the pins'. BIT tests of the engine and fuel systems, flying controls and navigation systems are also done on the MPCDs. The Harrier is then taxied out with nozzles at between 60 and 65 degrees and braked at the runway threshold. Nozzles are then swung to the level-flight angle to avoid runway damage. The pilot then dials the required take-off mode in his HUD (VTO, STO etc.) so that he can check nozzle and automatically cycled flap angles, jet-pipe temperature and engine rpm at a glance. Engine acceleration times are then checked with the Pegasus run to 55 per cent and nozzles are quickly tested with a downward 'flick'. With brakes off and full combat thrust applied, the Pegasus delivers its full 21,000lb-plus in a little over two seconds. Flying speed is reached in around 5 seconds with nozzles at 20 degrees, depending on the aircraft's weight. The flaps rise progressively, controlled by a computer programme which receives speed and AOA inputs.

OPERATIONS

When they entered operational squadron service in 1990 pilots would have found the Harrier Force operational routine much as it had been in the GR.3's heyday. Dispersed operations from FOBs were practised by the RAFG units in three an-

nual exercises including 'Hazel Flute' (the initials echo the 'HF' of 'Harrier Force', as with the more recent 'Hill Foil' series of exercises). Each squadron had three predetermined forward sites and the Station Commander relocated to a Forward Wing Operations Centre (FWOC) off-base. Both squadrons divided into three detachments of six aircraft, each 'det' with a series of 'step-up' sites for rapid dispersal if the main site was compromised. On the FOBs the GR.3-style aluminium plank dispersals had to be re-laid to allow for the GR.5's narrower outrigger track. Aircraft departed and returned to the forward site singly to reduce the possibility of detection. Finding the site on return was always a problem, and pilots aimed to sight it from around 150ft approach altitude, helped by improved navaids. Weather limi-

tations were dependent on the 'temperature of the battle'. Normally a 1,500ft cloudbase and 3nm visibility were required for peacetime operations, but in wartime take-offs would be made if the cloudbase crept above tree-top level.

However, there are changes in emphasis. The new Harrier's increased appetite for fuel and weaponry soon put the traditional Logistics Park supply method under severe strain, while the Harrier's shift of role from CAS to BAI, or deeper interdiction against airfield and radar sites, meant that a larger prepared STOL op-

Nightbird nose art on the A&AEE's T.4A XW269 at RAF Lyneham in November 1986. A FLIR unit is incorporated into the LRMTS nose-cone. Andy Sephton is standing to the right of the 'blindfolded crow' artwork. (Andy Sephton)

erating surface gave a better chance of flying those missions. More work was done to explore the use of car parks, short road areas and concreted areas around industrial buildings, all with netting 'hides' attached to the sides of on-site buildings to look like a continuation of the structure itself.[4] Larger buildings could be adapted to become temporary shelters for a flight of Harriers as well. However, as German housewives began to contemplate the prospect of battle-laden Harriers emerging from their local hypermarkets in times of international stress, a more serious inhibition became apparent. In 1990 the German government gradually tightened the regulations controlling low-level flying until a minimum 1,000ft ceiling was imposed. Clearly, this was useless for realistic training of ground-hugging Harrier mud-movers. RAFG squadron commanders began to look back to Britain for suitable training facilities. Ranges in the Netherlands and Belgium were available but none offered the extended low-level, multi-target sorties which could be planned within the United Kingdom's low-flying system. In 1990 the RAF was flying about

150,000 low-level sorties annually in the UK alone, mostly in the 250–600ft altitude range with occasional 'de-limits' in remote areas.

The case for regular FOB exercises in the Laarbruch area was weakened further by increasing German objections to the use of forest sites for such noisy, traffic-intensive activities. Tree-felling or other changes to the terrain were already precluded. In any case, the gradual relaxation of tensions with the former Soviet Union after 1991 placed a large question mark over the need for concealed-site exercises on such a large scale.

With its superior weapons-carrying capacity, the GR.5 was able to exercise the armourers more thoroughly with a wider range of ordnance requirements. Hunting Engineering's Improved BL.755 contained among its 147 bomblets parachute-retarded, armour-piercing missiles for use against the upper surfaces of armoured vehicles. In 1990 replacements were scheduled, including Hunting's stand-off SWAARM (Smart Weapon, Anti-Armour) and Marconi's Brimstone, also an anti-armour guided weapon, to fulfil

The kinked leading edge of the GR.5/7 wing is evident in this view. White intake interiors on most Harriers are a means of reducing the aircraft's visibility head-on. (MoD)

SR(A).1236. Matra 68mm rocket pods were used by No 1 Squadron, which retained its anti-shipping roe. The Harrier GR.5 could take a 1,000lb bomb on its centreline pylon, or 2,000lb of stores on the inboard or centre-wing pylons, or 250gal fuel tanks. BL.755 or other stores up to 630lb could be suspended on the outer pylons with AIM-9s for self-defence on their 'outrigger' launchers. If practice bombs were required, ML Aviation's CBLS 200 container was fitted, with 3kg bombs from Portsmouth Aviation. Throughout the GR.5's career Aden 25 guns were not carried due to clearance delays and the empty pods remained 'plugged' at their business ends.

[4]Some of this netting, held in reserve for wartime use, features radar-absorbing 'stealth' properties too, so as to make location of the FOBs by radar-reconnaissance and/or by radar prior to a strike run a tough proposition. Work in this area remains classified on both sides of the Atlantic.

As new-build GR.7s began to reach the RAF in 1991, the prospects for more advanced weapons systems opened up. In the Gulf War GEC-Marconi's TIALD (Thermal Imaging and Laser Designator) pod had been used successfully on the Tornado. As it included an automatic target-tracking feature, obviating the need constantly to keep its crosshairs manually centred on the target after lock-on (requiring a second set of hands in the cockpit), its use on the Harrier GR.7 was a logical next step, clearing the way for LGBs to be added to the arsenal. In March 1995 BAe received a project definition study for the integration of the Texas Instruments Paveway III Low-Level LGB with the GR.7, with TIALD as the designator. The pod had already been used in SAOEU trials on a GR.7, mounted on an inboard pylon alongside all-up 549 kg (1,210lb) LGBs. In the one-man cockpit target acquisition would mostly be slaved to the HUD; locked, the pilot would then 'pull up' and loft his Paveway III, and belly-over in an arc, while the pod continued to track the target and the bomb flies its smoother, proportionately guided ballistic trajectory to the target. Paveway III does not use range-reducing 'bang-bang' steering to the laser spot. Laser designation would be switched on during the last few seconds of bomb flight, the calculated time-to-impact being furnished in alphanumerics on the HUD. Also on the long-term shopping list for the Harrier in 1995 was CASOM (Conventional Stand-Off Missile) under RAF requirement SR(A).1238 for a missile with a concrete-penetrating warhead and a 250–400km (155–250 mile) range. The candidates included Rafael's Popeye 2, the McDonnell Douglas/Hunting Grand Slam, Aérospatiale's ASURA and a variant of the Tomahawk cruise missile.

Due to enter service during 1998 is the BAe AIM-132 ASRAAM (Advanced Short-Range Air-to-Air Missile). RAF GR.7s are the first aircraft scheduled to use it, and will conduct much of the operational trial work to 'bed the weapon down' for the EFA/Eurofighter 2000. As its name implies, this is ostensibly a short-range 'heat' weapon designed to supersede Sidewinder, although, launched at altitude, it is said to offer an impressive 30-mile reach.[5] At the time of writing ASRAAM is undergoing live-fire trials at the US Eglin and China Lake ranges, aboard USAF F-16s. It offers off-boresight shooting at up to 60 degrees (the RAF requirement, though it is theoretically capable of tracking at angles of up to 90 degrees) by means of a wide-angle, Hughes-developed 128 by 128 pixel element, 'staring' focal plane array seeker which offers clutter rejection in the look-down, shoot-down mode as well as massive resistance to IR jamming. This 'staring' array can image the heat from the entire aircraft rather than just its exhaust plume. At close quarters it can be aimed way off bore-sight—off to the left and right, or up, through the large one-piece windshield, within the current effective 60-degree cone of vision—by means of a helmet-mounted sight. This capability, and a BVR imaging capability optimised for medium-range shooting in the 15–30 mile range regime, are not scheduled for the interim Harrier GR.7 fit with the first batch of weapons, which are intended primarily for self-defence, as they would compromise the current NVG option. However, a helmet sight would become available as the GR.7 expands its bag of tricks to encompass a strike escort role. The missile itself employs relaxed static stability so that it can be taken through extremely high-g, tight changes of heading by its four little tail flippers, and it is said to outperform many of the latest thrust-vectoring weapons like the remarkable Russian R.73 'Archer'. Essentially it offers both long-range, head-on aspect launch possibilities as well as a 'getting out of a tight corner', high-angle, off-boresight, close-in engagement capability. It will give the Harrier GR.7 a terrific punch, and Sea Harrier crews relish the prospect of having some in their inventory, for use in 'policing actions' as a back-up to AMRAAM, where 'vis-ident' becomes crucial and there actually exists limited scope for BVR shoots.[6]

Deliveries of GR.7s were interrupted for almost two months in August–September 1991 as a result of a series of fire-related accidents. The first occurred to ZG743/CA of No IV(AC) Squadron on 29 May 1991, near Gütersloh. Its pilot ejected after the Harrier sustained generator failure followed closely by the loss of all back-up systems. Recovery and examination of the burned-out wreck proved difficult, but it seemed likely that a fire had begun before the jet crashed. Two further incidents happened in July, the first to another IV Squadron GR.7 which managed to recover to Gütersloh with a fire in its rear fuselage and had to be returned to BAe for an extensive rebuild. Two weeks later, on 29 July, ZD353/H of No 233 OCU, a GR.5, just made it back to Wittering's runway with a similar blaze in its back end. It too got trucked to Brough for major surgery. Examination of the July casualties quickly revealed a fault in the wiring of the loom distributing power from the transformer/rectifier unit in the rear equipment bay. Carbon insulation on the Kapton wires had worn away because of friction, causing arcing and fires. The power-switching panel in the rectifier was also found to be working at its maximum capacity, so that it could not absorb any unexpected power surges. All GR.5s and GR.7s were grounded for over seven weeks while larger connector tags were attached to the wiring looms to ensure separation.

---

[5] Born out of the British exploratory project 'Tail Dog', ASRAAM was originally conceived as a multinational effort to develop a Sidewinder replacement concurrent with American AMRAAM development. The project collapsed in the late 1980s but was later revived when the RAF rewrote its requirement, and in 1992 BAe Dynamics received a £570 million contract from the MoD for development and production of the first Lot of missiles. The United States has been treading its own path with competitive development between Hughes and Raytheon for the AIM-9X, though ASRAAM still features as an outsider in that competition. AIM-9X will begin to be deployed on Harrier II-Plus around the turn of the century, although it shares little technology with the current L/M Sidewinder variants, apart from the possibility of reworked missile bodies.
[6] AMRAAM works best at BVR distances, where at least two controlling agencies are required for positive confirmation of 'bandits' (AWACS and GCI both, usually) within current NATO operating rules. A pseudo-imaging 'heat' weapon like ASRAAM offers a built-in target discriminating facility. The abandoned American AIM-9R imaging Sidewinder project offered a similar facility.

Lighter Tefzel wiring was used and the power-switching panel was improved. Half the fleet was back in the air by late September, but pilots were at first ordered to stay within twenty minutes' flying time of an airfield with substantial fire-fighting equipment. The RAF refused to take delivery of the final fourteen GR.7s and threatened to invoke a late-delivery penalty clause which would have cost BAe up to £40,000 per Harrier.

To compound their problems, BAe were then informed that a number of GR.5s and USMC AV-8Bs had been found with acoustic stress cracking in their rear fuselages around the hot nozzle area. A quick-fix consisting of metal patching and other minor structural strengthening

actually took each aircraft out of service for up to three weeks from September 1991. The longer-term solution involved rebuilding the affected centre-fuselage area with additional stringers and thicker titanium skin between Frames 30 and 33. This was done to AV-8Bs when they received Night Attack or II+ rebuilds, and to GR.5s on the GR.7 update line.

By the end of 1991 the GR.7 was well established in the two Gütersloh units. No IV Squadron had only one GR.5 alongside its fifteen GR.7s, while Wing Commander Richard Thomas's No 3(F) Squadron still operated a mix of GR.5, GR.5A and six GR.7s, the first GR.7 (ZG479) having flown in on 30 November 1990. Back at Wittering, No 1 Squad-

ron had a dozen GR.5s while No 233 OCU flew its usual assortment of variants, excluding the GR.7. In September 1992 the OCU followed the fashion of adopting a 'shadow' nameplate. After the run-down of No 20 Squadron's Tornado GR.1 operations at Laarbruch in May 1992, their designation passed to No 233 OCU, who became 20(R) Squadron and altered their markings accordingly. At the time, their commander was Falklands veteran Wing Commander Tony Harper. All GR.5s gradually accumulated at Wittering, the RAFG squadrons operating a wholly GR.7 force. No 1 Squadron eventually received its first GR.7s in June 1992 (ZD461/01 and ZD434/02) while No 233 OCU's Mk 7s began to roll off the GR.5 conversion line in June 1993 to supplement a few new-build aircraft which had already arrived.

At the end of 1992 the RAFG Harrier Force moved into Laarbruch, No 3 Squadron on 16 November and No IV on the 27th, each with a 'diamond nine' formation on arrival. Flypasts were also mounted to mark the closure of the old 'clutch' airfield at Gütersloh. Updates to the GR.7 had continued through the year. In November 1992 five of No 1 Squadron's aircraft had Global Positioning System (GPS) units installed, detectable by a small white disc antenna on the aircraft's back. This navigation enhancement coincided with a widening of the Harrier Force's sphere of action at that time. Four No 1 Squadron GR.7s went to Yuma, Arizona, for low-level training alongside the AV-8B(NA) flyers in April 1993. No 3 Squadron deployed Harriers to Kuantan, Malaysia, in September 1992 as part of a large South-East Asian air defence exercise involving RAF Tornado F.3s, and it also contributed to the United Kingdom's

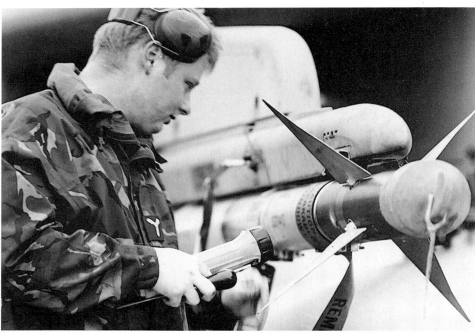

Left, upper: Harrier GR.7 ZG478 returning to Incirlik n autumn 1994 with CBU, AIM-9s and Phimat pod underwing and a camera pod on the centreline. (Via Andy Evans)

Left, lower: Checking the seeker head on an AIM-9L Sidewinder with a torch beam before a 'Warden' sortie. (Via Andy Evans)

major air defence test, 'Elder Forest 92' at RAF Leeming. No 1 Squadron also sent aircraft to a 'Red Flag' at Nellis AFB, while No 233 OCU ventured even further afield, sending ZD378/AL to display at Chile's FIDAE 92 air show. Sadly, its pilot made a short landing which was 'conventional' but for the lack of a lowered undercarriage. His GR.5 sustained only minor squashing of its gun pods. RAFG field deployments continued too. The first GR.7 exercise of this kind was 'Hill Foil' in the first twelve days of June 1992, in the Sennelager training area.

OPERATION 'WARDEN'

The most dramatic indication of the Harrier's increasing importance within the RAF's overall strategy was its decision to deploy GR.7s as part of Britain's commitment to Operation 'Warden', the protective overflights of Kurdish 'safe areas' of northern Iraq, as part of Operation 'Provide Comfort'. RAF aircraft were among those from four air forces committed to the task. By April 1993 nine Laarbruch aircraft had been painted in medium grey ARTF (Alkali Removable Temporary Finish), ready to take over the 'Warden' flights from Coltishall's Jaguars. This constituted a change of policy in that No 1 Squadron was previously the unit charged with fulfilling 'out of theatre' commitments while 2 Group units 'held the line' in West Germany. 'Warden' marked the first deployment of the Harrier Force as a unified organization with participation by all the Harrier squadrons. Early Harrier pilots would also have been pleased to see a developed version of their aircraft confidently placed in the role previously occupied by the traditionally more potent Jaguar—and capable of performing it better too. The first four Harriers (RAFAIR

9621–9625) departed Laarbruch on 2 April 1993, with four more (RAFAIR 9626-9629) on the 8th. They were coded 'WA' (ZD447), 'WB' etc. to indicate membership of the Warden Det, but all other unit insignia were overpainted with the grey temporary finish. Once they were established at Incirlik AB, Turkey, all three front-line Harrier Force squadrons took two-month turns at manning the detachment. In all, fourteen GR.7s received the grey paint job and definitive TACDS V-10 flare dispensers under the rear fuselage by the end of 1993. Wiring modifications were made (taking up to 650 man-hours per Harrier) to enable the aircraft to carry recce pods because their tasking, like the Jaguars before them, was essentially armed

reconnaissance. As the 'Warden' commitment continued into 1994, crews and aircraft were also drawn from No 20(R) Squadron, imposing a difficult burden on Strike Command in managing the movement of personnel, aircraft and equipment.

In their surveillance role the Harriers kept watch on Iraqi activity around the safe havens established in northern Iraq. Radar and air defence sites, troop movements and airfields were kept under observation by recce packages which often included over thirty aircraft. An E-3A Sentry took up position over the area to be surveyed, followed by an F-15C Eagle fighter sweep. A 429 ECS EF-111A then overflew the area to check for hostile elec-

Right, upper: Another armed reconnaissance flight over northern Iraq begins as a pilot rolls his Harrier out to the active runway. (Via Andy Evans)

Right, lower: This heavy burden of fuel, BL.755 CBU, Sidewinders and Phimat gives some idea of the GR.7's lifting capacity compared with first-generation Harriers. (Via Andy Evans)

vided their Vicon 18-603 GP pod which
contains a 91cm LOROP (long-range
oblique photography) camera using
12.7cm wide high-definition film. SAOEU
tested another Vicon pod, the 18-403 with
IR linescan and a panoramic camera, in
1990, and the Vicon 57 multi-sensor/
LOROP pod. The availability of such a
range of lightweight pods gives the Harrier GR.7 a considerable recce capability
which would previously have been fulfilled
by a more complex dedicated reconnaissance type. Most 'Warden' photography
was from medium or low altitude, and the
results were available from the RIC within
a couple of hours. Harriers also took along
a pair of AIM-9Ls, two BL.755 CBUs and
Phimat or BOL chaff. A GR.7 was able
to carry a greater warload than the Jaguar over the same range.

The Incirlik Det suffered an operational
loss on 23 November 1993 when ZD432/
WF (No IV Squadron) had an engine
surge while refuelling from a VC-10 80
miles south of the Iraq–Turkey border. Its
pilot accidentally shut off the HP fuel
cock—a surprisingly common error—and
the engine died. He ejected at 1,500ft near
Dahluk and was well looked after by the
locals, who stood guard over the wrecked
jet until No IV Squadron's CO, Wing
Commander David Haward, arrived to
reward them with some free livestock.

The Harrier GR.7's introduction coincided with a change in the RAF's perception of the aircraft's role. Not only did
CAS begin to take second seat to BAI, but
the advent of new weapons, many of
which were tested by RAF Tornado and
Jaguar units in the Gulf War, enabled the
Harrier Force to add a medium-altitude
attack role to its repertoire. Paveway LGBs,
CRV-7 70mm rockets in 19-shot LAU-
5003 pods and CBU-87 became available
to supplement or replace BL.755 and

tronic emissions, followed by the recce
force of up to six Harriers with F-15C or
F-16C top cover courtesy of USAFE. The
GR.7s usually operated in three pairs,
each one covering up to a dozen photo-
targets.

'Warden' required a revival of the Harrier's reconnaissance capability which had
been phased out in 1989. When MIRLS
was cancelled it was hoped that USMC-
style recce pods with IR linescan sensors
would be made available for RAF use.
Lack of funding dictated that the old GR.3
Vinten pods, with four F95 cameras and

a forward-facing F135, had to be dusted
off and returned to service. Pilots were
given extra training in the 'lost art' of
photo-recce flying. The Recce Intelligence
Centres at Wittering and Gütersloh, which
had been closed at the end of May 1989,
yielded equipment for the re-establishment
of a Recce Interpretation Centre (RIC) at
Incirlik. Later, the Vinten GP.1 pod was
made available, with wet-film imagery on
a 550-frame cassette, a horizon-to-horizon
sweep camera and a movable camera
which the pilot can lock on to a selected
target for multiple shots. Vinten also pro-

Matra 155 rockets. The other major enhancement in capability was the introduction of night attack technology at squadron level, following the successful Nightbird trials.

No 1 Squadron was tasked with a two-year operational study of NVGs in the low-level BAI mission. Operating in a potentially high-threat environment for this type of mission meant that medium-altitude deliveries were too risky and the GR.7 was forced back down to its traditional tree-top altitudes. When NVG training began it was acknowledged that ejection

with the goggles in place would add to the hazards of lo-lo sorties by posing a threat of severe injury. The Mk 12 seat was therefore modified to Mk II standard with a small charge in the line connecting the bulky NVG to the pilot's Mk 4 helmet. This causes the goggles to separate and drop back into the cockpit as the ejector seat fires. AV-8B(NA) pilots still have to remove their NVG manually in these conditions, and they are not usually employed for take-off and landing, whereas the RAF models can be. GR.7s also received a new cockpit HUD video to monitor night train-

ing. GPS Navstar, a great help in night navigation, was fitted to all the aircraft which were prepared for use in Operation 'Warden' and it is hoped that the modification will eventually be applied to the whole fleet.

Initially No 1 Squadron intended to create a specialist Night Flight within its establishment but it was soon decided to convert the whole unit. Their first GR.7 sortie was flown on 2 June 1992 and it became an all-GR.7 unit by November that year. By January 1993 fourteen pilots were NVG-qualified. A conversion course was devised which took pilots 50hr to become night combat ready. Flying began at medium altitude and included formation work (greatly assisted by the electroluminescent strips fitted to Harrier II variants), tanking and range drops. Further low-altitude attack sorties were made, leading to a couple of SAPs with hostile fighter 'interception' included. Pilots then put in six months of practice over a variety of terrains and ambient light conditions before they were officially qualified to 'leap in the dark'. They also learned to plan night sorties, which require great preparation and are best conducted in good weather to give FLIR/NVG imagery of acceptable quality. Small but hazardous obstructions such as pylons and cables are noted with more than usual care as they cannot be picked up on night visual aids.

When their conversion was complete a number of No 1 Squadron personnel were posted to No 3(F) Squadron at Laarbruch to help with NVG training. Most of the pilots' 25 conversion sorties were flown in Britain, some using a special NVG low-level route. Ten of No 3's aircraft detached to RAF Marham in December 1994 to 'get in some night hours' and another batch visited RAF Leeming the following month. Limited by the rule that in the United Kingdom low-flying must cease at midnight, pilots had to fit in their 25 flights whenever they could, and this is obviously less easy in the summer months. No IV Squadron were scheduled to undertake their NVG conversion in the winter of

1995–96. Harrier pilots have taken to night flying without undue difficulty and with an excellent safety record. No 3(F) pilots continued their conversion through the summer of 1995 with a series of two-week detachments to RAF Coltishall, RAF Leeming, RAF Marham and the Test & Evaluation airfield at West Freugh. This seems to be the likely pattern for the next few years as aircrew slot in their NVG time around other commitments. Night capability has enormously enhanced the Harrier's usefulness as the RAF's other night-attacker alongside the all-weather Tornado.

One of No 1 Squadron's longest-standing Harrier traditions has been to provide the RAF's 'carrier-based role'. This was allowed to lapse in the latter stages of the GR.3 era and was not revived until the summer of 1994, although pilots from No 3 Squadron did make practice ski-jumps at Yeovilton at the beginning of that year. Three SAOEU GR.7s (ZG472, ZG475 and ZG501) embarked on HMS *Illustrious* for a widely publicised sea deployment under Wing Commander Nick Slater. All three had the GPS modification. Flight Lieutenant Chris Norden had the distinction of making the first deck-landing in a GR.7. The larger dimensions of the new model made it a tight fit on the ship's deck-lifts. When the trials ended on 8 July the pilots had achieved some success in solving one of the oldest problems with 'Crab Harriers' at sea—getting the INAS to align and remain 'current'. GPS updates helped

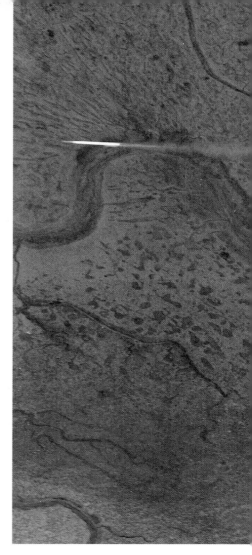

with this, although it was found that FIN.1075G still had some problems under heavy sea conditions. Aircraft launches were made at a variety of weights up to within 1,000lb of the 31,000lb maximum. In all, forty flights were made, including exercises with F-8E(FN) Crusaders from the French carrier *Foch*. To many observers the trials on *Illustrious* showed just how viable a mixed force of Sea Harriers and GR.7s would be. Simon Hargreaves, who flew his Sea Harrier from HMS *Hermes* alongside RAF GR.3s in the Falklands, was in no doubt about the potential: 'A squadron of Sea Harrier F/A.2s and one of Harrier GR.7s would be an excellent

Taxying out for a 'Hazel Flute' sortie from RAF Bentwaters in September 1994, ZG504 has an ARTF grey finish. Codes were applied beginning with 'W' for 'Warden' to Harrier Force aircraft which were made available for duty at Incirlik AB, Turkey. (Via R. L .Ward)

On the range: ZD376 releases a rocket projectile. (Sergeant Rick Brewell/RAF)

combination, particularly if we can get Sea Eagle on GR.7s. Then you've got a long-range punch with a very viable fighter escort and sweep, whilst at the same time retaining Sea Harrier's air-to-ground role. The only problems are political inter-service rivalry. Putting GR.7s on carriers looks like "light blue" endorsing carriers at sea at a time when a replacement for HMS *Invincible* will be demanding large amounts of the defence budget. But it would be the perfect role for the GR.7. It will be happening, I'm sure.' For the limited-war, Adriatic-type situations which British forces are currently training for, such a combination would seem the ideal rapid-reaction package.

TRAINING EXERCISES

In the mid-1990s Harrier units continue to participate in their established training exercises. No 1 Squadron sent a detachment to Bodø between 4 and 20 March 1994 for 'Arctic Express' with RAF Jaguars and Tornados. The previous year's visit to Norway included a demonstration of the GR.7's toughness. Three aircraft were on a familiarisation flight over Kaafjord when ZD469/08 flew into two steel cables suspended from pylons across the water. The Harrier took a fair amount of damage to its various leading edges and a quantity of Norwegian fishing gear was uprooted, but the aircraft landed safely. 'Hazel Flute' took place at the former USAF base, RAF Bentwaters, in September 1994. Twenty-two GR.7s from all three front-line units took part together for the first time in anticipation of the Harrier Force becoming a component in NATO's Quick Reaction Force (Air) from January 1995. A variety of FOB-type locations were set up on the base, including airfield buildings to represent urban sites and traditional 'forest' sites elsewhere. All personnel (over a thousand) made do with tented accommodation and the aircraft did not see the insides of any of the numerous cosy HAS structures around the airfield. For complete authenticity, mobile radar equipment and airfield control facilities were driven to the base and convoys of supplies and munitions were laid on two days before the jets arrived. Bentwaters was chosen mainly because it represented a typical disused airfield such as Harrier Force components might encounter in wartime operations. It also fuelled speculation that the Bentwaters/Woodbridge complex (actually refurbished by the Americans just prior to their withdrawal two years previously) might become the future base for the two RAFG Harrier squadrons. Defence Secretary Malcolm Rifkind announced on 14 July 1994 that Laarbruch would close in 1999

Left: Wing Commander C. R. Loader of No 3 Squadron emerges from his aircraft's hide at Chivenor in May 1995. (R. L. Ward)

Right, upper: 'Urban' hides on the runway at Chivenor for Exercise 'Hill Foil'. Normally these would be erected beside or between existing buildings. (R. L. Ward)

Right, lower: A view of ZG 478 with its 'WY' codes replaced by the 'last two' of the serial (78). This system was in turn was superseded by one using the aircraft's build number (in this case '68'), for use in 'Deny Flight' operations at Gioia de Colle. ARTF grey was replaced by a permanent two-tone grey scheme which is intended for all RAF strike/attack aircraft. Here the aircraft is releasing flares from its TACDS V-10 system. (Via Andy Evans)

as part of the Front Line First review. Both No 2 Group squadrons were therefore scheduled to return to the United Kingdom. In practical terms the cost of restoring Bentwaters to active RAF use and converting its US-style 110V power system to British standards was excessive. Coltishall or Cottesmore seem more likely homes at the time of writing.

'Hazel Flute' for 1995 took place at RAF Chivenor, following an earlier 'Hill Foil' at the base in May using 24 Harriers from all three squadrons. It was effectively a two-week 'Taceval' for No 1(F) and No 3(F) personnel, whereas 'Hill Foil' is regarded as a 'Maxeval', testing all aspects of squadron efficiency. Sixteen pilots and 1,000 support 'troops' descended on the bare base to set up tented quarters once again. This exercise gave pilots the chance

RAF/RN HARRIER/SEA HARRIER ANNUAL ATTRITION

Year	Harrier	Sea Harrier						
1969	2	—	1978	1	—	1988	2	—
1970	2	—	1979	6	—	1989	1	2
1971	2	—	1980	3	1	1990	2*	2
1972	8	—	1981	3	—	1991	3	1
1973	5	—	1982	7	7	1992	1	1
1974	3	—	1983	6	3	1993	2	—
1975	3	—	1984	2	2	1994	1	3
1976	4	—	1985	2	1	1995	1	1
1977	—	—	1986	3	1	1996	2?*	2
			1987	4	1			

* Includes T.4Ns (XZ445 in 1990) in RN use.

Harrier Force exercises tended to involve all front-line units, although there were still single-squadron examples, such as 'Brilliant Invader 95', which included No 3 Squadron as an 'enemy' long-range interdiction element. 'Air Warrior 94' took ten Harriers and twenty aircrew from the whole Harrier Force to make the GR.7's first appearance in the United States. Held at Nellis AFB between 9 and 29 August, the Air Combat Command-sponsored exercise enabled pilots to practise CAS with 52nd FW A-10As and US Army Apaches. Live drops of CBU-87 and 1,000lb bombs were included, with early-morning sorties a speciality. The exercise provided valuable experience, but cost limitations are the main cap on more frequent involvement in this kind of training. Aircrew would certainly welcome more of it, and its value was certainly evident when the Harrier's third combat assignment began in July 1995.

Twelve GR.7s from No IV(AC) Squadron relieved the Jaguars of No 6 Squadron which recorded the 5,000th hour of Jaguar operational flying over the Balkans shortly before returning to Coltishall on 31 July. No IV's Harriers came from a newly established central pool of aircraft drawn from all units. They were given non-squadron tail codes in white relating to their build numbers (e.g. ZD376/24)— a new departure for the RAF. Permanent two-tone grey paint schemes were applied and the Harriers passed through Dunsfold for a series of equipment updates before leaving for Italy. They were called to action when the patience of UN Commanders finally snapped following a Bosnian Serb mortar attack on Sarajevo on 28 August 1995 which killed 37 people. On 30 August NATO aircraft carried out the biggest air attacks in the organisation's history. Operation 'Deliberate Force' involved 80 aircraft in attacks on radar, missile and command centre sites around Sarajevo on the first day and it extended over the following 48 hours to include similar targets around other UN 'safe havens'. Nine Harriers flew some of the 300 sorties against 23 targets during that period, using two 1,000lb CPU-123/B LGBs or 'iron' bombs apiece, plus a pair

to practise NVG/FLIR sorties on the local ranges at night and in poor visibility from 11 to 22 September. The base came under frequent simulated air attack to test the six Rapier sites which were set up around Chivenor. BAI local sorties were flown over the Welsh range routes and out to ranges in the north-east of England. For No 3 Squadron 'Hazel Flute' was a sharpening-up exercise, preparing them to replace No IV Squadron at Gioa del Colle in October 1995 for Operation 'Deny Flight'.

BOSNIA

The increasing role of the Harrier Force within NATO's Rapid Reaction response has tended to unify operations of all the Harrier units because the Force has to be able to supply sixteen aircraft in support of NATO's needs at short notice. Any of the three squadrons must now be ready to meet this requirement, which has also brought an increase in squadron size from twelve to sixteen aircraft. In 1995 twelve additional Harriers were released from attrition storage to enable this to happen.

of AIM-9Ls and 250gal tanks. Their Aden gun pods remained 'plugged'. The first strikes began at 1 a.m. BST on 30 August with attacks on radar installations, followed by a second wave at 2.50 a.m. in which No IV Squadron attacked an ammunition dump at Lukavica and a munitions factory at Vugosca. Further attacks against air defences in the Majavica hills near Tuzla and on missile sites around Gorazde and Mostar took place later that day.

Harriers were limited to reconnaissance flights during the first part of 31 August owing to poor weather, supplying recce data to the mobile RIC at Gioa del Colle. Harriers were put in a 'holding pattern' over the coast in the hope that the weather would clear over their targets, but they returned with their 'thousand pounders' still on their pylons. September 1 brought fresh attacks on a missile site at Sokolac and radar installations near Foca, Mostar and Gorazde, taking the NATO mission

total to 500 sorties by the time a pause was announced to allow the Serbs to remove their heavy weapons from around Sarajevo. Harrier recce sorties continued over the next two days to provide BDA. With the resumption of air strikes against the intransigent Serbs, No IV's pilots again taxied their droop-winged birds on to Gioia's rain-soaked runway, rolling past the base's silver F-84F Thunderstreak gate-guard and lining up for a conventional take-off to maximise warload. Fur-

ther attacks were made on munitions dumps at Lukavica, and the range of targets extended further to include military installations around the Serb capital at Pale. In improving weather conditions, four-ship Harrier formations attacked an ammunition dump near Pale and other military installations up to 14 September, when the air strike option was put on hold.

NEW VARIANTS

As the Harrier GR.7 established itself in service, the RAF was already looking ahead to two new variants. The designation GR.9 was reserved in 1989 for a projected GR.7 with the much-desired Pegasus 11-61 of the AV-8B Plus and the AIM-120 AMRAAM missile system of the Sea Harrier F/A.2, along with terrain-referenced navigation. A radar in the Hughes AN/APG-65 class would also be needed for this very up-market Harrier, which at present remains a 'paper aeroplane'. At the very least the Harrier Force would welcome the 11-61 engine to compensate for the GR.7's weight increase over the GR.5 and the consequent erosion in its hovering performance. One minor performance enhancer for the GR.7 which was allowed was the so-called '100 per cent' LERX modification, borrowed from the AV-8B(NA). GR.7 ZG506 was the first to receive the 0.702m (7¹/2 sq ft) per wing enlarged LERX area which was intended to improve turning performance, and it was retrofitted to many GR.7s in 1995. Minor alterations to the Honeywell AN/ASW-46(V)2 SAAHS were needed to compensate for the destabilising effect of the LERX by slightly increasing tailplane movements.

A more urgent requirement was a two-seat Harrier which could provide appropriate Harrier II training in place of the GR.3-orientated T.4A. After rapidly dismissing the idea of fitting GR.7 avionics to the obsolescent T.4, the MoD issued a requirement for ten new aircraft in Octo-

The advent of the T.10 in 1995 enabled No 20(R) Squadron to provide training on an aircraft whose handling characteristics are very similar to those of the GR7. ZH634 was operated by the Boscombe Down Fixed Wing Test Squadron. (Authors)

ber 1989. (The T.4 rebuild would have been designated T.6, using FLIR and some other GR.7 systems, but basic differences in aircraft handling precluded the option.) After further meetings of the MoD Procurement Committee in January 1990 an order for fourteen (later thirteen) TAV-8B derivatives (ZH653–665) was announced on 28 February. The new trainer, designated the T.10, was to have full GR.7 weapons capability, Martin-Baker Mk 12 seats and the Pegasus 105 engine. Surviving T.4/T.4As with an appreciable number of flying hours left were scheduled for conversion to T.8 standard for re-issue to the Royal Navy. Assembly of all but the first aircraft was completed on a new production line at BAe Warton because of the pressure of GR.7 and F/A.2 work at Dunsfold. The first aircraft, ZH653 (TX01) flew on 7 April 1994 with Jim Ludford and Graham Tomlinson aboard, and it moved from Dunsfold to Boscombe Down for flight testing in July. ZH654 undertook hot-weather trials in Oman from 10 April the following year, which underlined the T.10's rather marginal hover performance and renewed wishes for a more powerful Pegasus. No 20(R) Squadron received ZH657/M for familiarization on 30 January 1995, and flew their first operational sortie in ZH658/N on 1 March. The Squadron was scheduled to receive seven T.10s, with one (ZH661/10) going to No 1 Squad-

ron in April 1995 and at least two to the RAFG units. ZH665 became the first No 20(R) Squadron casualty on 26 July, suffering Cat-4 damage after running short of fuel and crash-landing at Wittering without injury to the crew.

Pilots have predictably found the new trainer easier to handle than the small-wing T.4, partly due to the SAAHS 'auto-stab'. Its introduction has simplified the training syllabus, although pilots once again needed to travel to MCAS Yuma's AV-8B simulator in 1995 while the Wittering unit was upgraded to GR.7 standard. Trainees now get two sorties in the T.10 before their first GR.7 'hop', whereas previously they came from the T.4 and simulator to a solo in the GR.7 with an instructor in attendance in a 'chase' Harrier and two others strategically positioned on the ground. No 20(R) Squadron's 1995 Harrier Long Course under Wing Commander Glenn Edge comprised 98 sorties over 31 weeks. Night attack clearance for the T.10 and the reinstatement of the GR.7 simulator were foreseen as opportunities for considerable future development in training procedures.

11. Harriers For Sale

HSA's Hunter had been a considerable export success, with over a half of the 1,972 production run being sold new, refurbished or as licence-built items to eighteen different countries. The company naturally hoped to fill its order books once again with a type which carried forward the simple practicality of the Hunter and added the revolutionary bonus of V/STOL. Those hopes were not fulfilled for a large number of complex reasons. However, the fact that developed Harriers are still in production and being sold to foreign customers, albeit in small numbers, some thirty-five years after the prototype flight, is surely a confirmation of the basic soundness of the product. At the time of writing there is still a strong export potential in new markets, and a much wider sales horizon for a twenty-first century follow-on design.

The RAF has been a V/STOL exponent for over a third of its existence, with Harriers currently taking an increasing share of its operational commitments. A V/STOL follow-on is an inevitable requirement for the Royal Navy and those navies which are building or planning 'Harrier carrier' ships. In the United States, the Marines remain solidly behind V/STOL and current plans envisage commonality of design which would also embrace USN and some USAF requirements, thereby massively increasing the world-wide interest in V/STOL or Advanced STO/VL warplanes.

Confidence of this sort was not apparent in the 1960s. To some extent the launch of the Harrier as an exportable commodity was inhibited by the political uncertainty surrounding the whole concept. In its original, supersonic P.1154 configuration the image of V/STOL was damaged particularly by the farcical collapse of NATO's NBMR-3 competition and by continued hostility from the United States, where the TFX/F-111 'commonality' idea was being promoted as the way forward for tactical fighters. In retrospect it is clear the P.1154 would not have been a feasible prospect as a dispersed-site warplane. In the opinion of G. W. 'Johnnie' Johnson, a crucial figure in the Harrier sales effort from 1969 onwards, the demise of P.1154 was inevitable and not entirely unwelcome. 'Without the hard-won experience of Harrier it would have been extremely unreliable and, operationally, would have caused so much damage on take-off from unprepared surfaces that the attraction of "dispersed anywhere" would not have applied, and the "mobile" force would have been back to runways, albeit small ones.' Ralph Hooper felt that if the P.1154 had gone ahead at that time it would have killed V/STOL stone dead. If both the RAF and RN had rejected the aircraft for these reasons there would have been virtually no hope of attracting other orders. Throughout its first decade of service potential customers for the Harrier looked to the RAF for a lead.

The RAF had earlier shown an interest in an operational P.1127 via OR.345 (1960–61), but the lure of supersonics persuaded many of its decision-makers to take the P.1154 option. OR.345 lapsed in 1961 and widespread RAF interest in a P.1127 derivative was not revived until the cancellation of the P.1154(RAF) in February 1965. In the meantime the TES Kestrel experience had been a crucial stage in promoting the jet for RAF use, but no further interest was forthcoming from the other TES participants. Germany remained tied to the (dead-end) VAK-191 as a way of reviving its own aviation industry, and to the massive F-104 Starfighter programme. In America any immediate evolution of the Kestrel was squashed by SAC and the 'big carrier' lobby and their prestigious 'megabuck' projects, which did not include small ships with small numbers of aircraft. It was an example which the world's air forces, many of them reliant on US equipment, found difficult to ignore.

John Crampton, the first Technical Sales Manager for the P.1127, joined Hawker's sales team in 1959 and became Kingston's Technical Sales Manager in 1961. He maintained that the P.1127 always had an operational potential: 'It was not "experimental" in the way that the Rolls-Royce "Bedstead" or Short SC.1 were.' However, as his former sales colleague Johnnie Johnson pointed out, it was 'always a concept vehicle. With such a revolutionary idea there was the worst of all aeronautical worlds: a new and very different airframe and a new engine being operated in what could fairly be described as an unusual manner. It is easy to forget just how many unknowns there were.' For the sales team, 'until the aircraft could be demonstrated to and, more importantly, flown by potential operators, there was nothing to do except talk'. While the HSA team continued to encourage customer interest, increasing RAF involvement gradually took the P.1127 format to the production Harrier stage by 1965.

Once that point had been reached and the company had an operational aircraft to market, the sales effort pushed ahead strongly. It naturally concentrated upon the Harrier's dispersed-site capability at a time when the USSR's rapidly expanding arsenal of tactical 'nukes' put every air-

Armada **AV-8S Harriers were delivered in USN colours (Light Gull Grey and white) and received BuAer serials, in this case 161178.** *Esc 8a* **was the first Harrier unit to operate regularly from a ship's deck.** (BAe)

field west of the border in jeopardy. Whereas the P.1127/Kestrel's lack of conspicuous warfighting capability (in some ways emphasised by the TES aircraft with their de-rated engines and 'warload' consisting of one camera) had possibly diminished the type's sales potential, the fully fledged Harrier GR.1 was portrayed as a wholly new tactical concept. Bomb- and rocket-laden aircraft were depicted operating from invincible dispersed sites long after the supersonic 'wonderjets' had been grounded by cratered runways. The late-1960s slogan ran, 'Harrier—it changes everything'. The experience of the Six-Day War in June 1967 in which the air forces of four Middle East nations were demolished in a matter of hours by Israeli pre-emptive air attacks should have convinced more governments of the vulnerability of their air assets. Possibly the 'it changes everything' slogan was in itself

slightly intimidating to the world's air forces, tied as they were to well-established infrastructures (and careers) which depended on airfields, runways and conventional aircraft and tactics. Possibly, too, the Harrier's revolutionary character was somewhat oversold in the early stages. Rather than suggesting that it made all other combat types obsolete it might have been more appropriate to market Harrier as a specialized component in a nation's defences, which would perform functions which other aircraft could not do at all. That was actually the RAF's approach as it developed a role for the jet alongside its Jaguars, Phantoms and Vulcans and evolved the principles of 'survivable tactical air power'.

However, hindsight is, as usual, unhelpful. In the depths of the Cold War the marketing strategy probably seemed right for the military, but procurement decisions are inevitably made by politicians who have many other pressures upon them. Certainly, to nations who did not see themselves as potential Soviet targets in the Central European War scenario the dispersed-field aspect seemed irrelevant.

They could find cheaper conventional aircraft with bigger warloads on Uncle Sam's second-hand sales lists.

FRANCE

Among the countries which seemed possible NATO customers in the earliest days was France. John Crampton saw it as 'a constant sales target largely because of the partly French (Wibault Gyropter) origins of the idea. We tried to cash in on that and tried hardest when the moment seemed ripest. And it seemed likely that Dassault always torpedoed our efforts.' In Johnnie Johnson's estimation, 'The French were always interested, having tried VTOL themselves with Balzac. I should guess that through the years every active aviator in the *Aéronavale* was flown in a Harrier, and in my view this was mostly to keep Dassault on his toes.' HSA's two-seat Harrier G-VTOL was demonstrated on the French carrier *Foch* in November 1973 during a two-week exercise off the Brest peninsula.[1] Its night and bad-weather ca-

[1] A Harrier GR.1 bearing the spurious serial XY125 also flew from the helicopter carrier *Jeanne d'Arc* in October 1973.

pability were shown and the aircraft fitted the ship's deck-lift and hangars. The *Aéronavale* decided to stay with its F-8E(FN) Crusaders and Super Etendards, with the longer-term objective of replacing the Crusaders with Dassault's Rafale by 1998. In January 1989 the French considered leasing Sea Harriers as a temporary replacement for the Crusaders. A delegation visited RNAS Yeovilton and there was talk of a substantial lease agreement pending delivery of the Rafale M. The plan failed to materialise, as did an alternative proposal to lease F/A-18 Hornets. Instead, seventeen Crusaders were re-worked once again, allowing them to complete 34 years of carrier service since their *Aéronavale* début in 1965.

GERMANY

West Germany seemed another obvious user because of the vulnerability of its airfields. An initial interest in the project, expressed through the TES Kestrel involvement, gave way to support for domestic projects and an obligation to buy US-built aircraft to offset the cost of basing American forces in West Germany.

SPAIN

Following HSA's major success in supplying the USMC's need for a V/STOL attack aircraft, the European sales breakthrough came in August 1973 with an initial Spanish contract for six single-seat Harriers and a pair of two-seaters.[2] The main credit for the sale undoubtedly goes

[2]For the USMC background story see above, 'It Changes Everything'.

Current Spanish plans involve updating EAV-8Bs (including 01-912, seen here landing on *Príncipe de Asturias*) to Harrier II Plus configuration. (Via R. L. Ward).

to John Crampton, although he was quick to play down his role in a deal which he described to the authors as 'a salesman's dream . . . The Spanish Navy's DOR, Admiral Suanzes, was determined to get the Harrier into his country's navy. The customer wanted to buy the aeroplane as much as the salesman wanted to sell it. Of course, John Farley's wonderful demonstration helped a lot.' That demonstration took place in October 1972 when Farley flew direct from Dunsfold to the Spanish helicopter carrier *Dédalo* (formerly the US Navy's converted cruiser hull CVL-28 *Cabot*) off Barcelona. His flight had to be direct because, in the rather strained political atmosphere of the Gibraltar debate between Spain and Great Britain, permission to overfly Spain was refused. Several months previously Harold Wilson's government had cancelled an order for frigates which were to be built in British shipyards for the Spanish Navy. *Dédalo* had to be moved from her Mediterranean station south of Portugal to a more northerly location so that the 'demo' Harrier could reach her.

In this rather embarrassing climate the Harrier made a vertical landing on the carrier, failing to ignite her wooden deck as some had feared it would, and two days of flight trials followed. On the return trip from *Dédalo* the Harrier took off with part-filled 330gal ferry tanks, requiring some full-forward stick on lift-off. Shortly afterwards it suffered a virtually complete elec-

trical failure. Farley had to fly visually below a 300ft cloudbase without navaids. Flying slowly, with partial flaps he made landfall and map-read his way to Istres, just west of the Marseilles control zone. As he approached the runway at Istres' Flight Test Centre with the Harrier's transponder squawking 'emergency', a pair of Mirages were being scrambled to investigate. Their leader was about to taxy on to the runway as the Harrier came into view. Mirage brakes were rapidly applied and Farley selected 'braking stop' on his nozzle control while approaching quite fast. He was so pleased to see a runway that he momentarily forgot the ferry tanks underwing and their effect on handling in the braking stop. As the Harrier's nose pitched sharply upwards, full forward stick and plenty of throttle were needed to maintain equilibrium. With its tail scraping the ground the jet came to rest in 200yd. 'The Istres Controller must have been amazed at such an unorthodox arrival,' mused the pilot. 'Maybe he thought that was how Harriers normally stopped.' Apart from unorthodox situations such as this, where slopping fuel could upset the CG, the large ferry tanks had very little effect on handling.

HSA's Harrier sales pitch was aided by a Spanish law forbidding the use of fixed-wing, carrier-borne aircraft by the Navy. Their planners argued persuasively, and eventually successfully, that the Harrier did not take off and land conventionally but

was really a fixed-wing helicopter and did not contravene the law. In Britain the sale was opposed by the Labour Party, who were hostile towards the Franco government in Spain. The order therefore had to be routed through the USN as part of the USMC's FY 1974 AV-8A purchase. On the export paperwork the Harriers were therefore labelled T/AV-8A(SP), or later AV-8S, while Kingston called them Harrier Mk 50, or Mk 55, and the Spanish chose the designation VA-1 Matador, with VAE-1 for the two-seaters! Partly the deal was arranged in this way to make it 'uncancellable' by any future Labour government. The Harriers were officially sold to the United States and put on the AV-8 final assembly line at St Louis before delivery to Spain, with *Armada*-compatible radio sets replacing the RAF kit. When a second batch of five (Mk 55) single-seaters was ordered in 1977 General Franco was dead and King Juan Carlos' democratic government was able to deal direct with Britain. The only visible difference between the two batches was the logo 'Armada' in place of 'Marina' on the rear fuselage. Whereas the first batch had US-style insignia and BuNos applied before being air-freighted from Mildenhall like the other USMC AV-8As, the second five did not carry BuNos (although they were allocated). The first of this quintet, coded 008-9, departed from Dunsfold for Cognac on 27 June 1980, escorted by two AV-8Ss (048-6 and 008-8).

With no experience of fixed-wing naval operations to draw upon and one rather ancient carrier on a five-year lease from the US Navy, the *Arma Aérea de la Armada* relied on the United States for AV-8S training. Ten pilots with at least 500hr of background experience on SH-3D and AB-204B helicopters aboard *Dédalo* were sent on US Navy fixed-wing conversion courses, followed by AV-8A experience courtesy of McDonnell-Douglas and a joint UK/US team led by Squadron Leader Ken Jones. A new squadron, *8a*

Escuadrilla, was commissioned at Mayport, Florida, on 29 September 1976, after an intensive six-month training programme in which one AV-8S (008-5) was lost, though its pilot ejected. *Dédalo*, its wooden deck covered with a protective metal VTOL area, arrived off Florida for a month's carquals, returning to Spain at the end of 1976. Two USMC pilots stayed with the squadron at its Rota base and helped it to achieve IOC in March 1977. A second group of pilots, without rotary-wing backgrounds, followed the full USN basic training syllabus and then transferred to RAF Wittering's Harrier OCU. Thereafter training was gradually shifted to Rota in Spain as first-generation Harrier courses came to an end in Britain and the USA.

In service *Dédalo* usually carried up to six Matadors and its ASW helicopter component. USMC-style dorsal antennas were fitted to allow communications between Matadors and helicopters. The jets' primary role was air defence, with a brace of AIM-9P (later 'Lima' model) Sidewinders and guns. For their seldom-used secondary CAS role for the Spanish Marines, the whole range of USMC ordnance could be delivered using the Baseline nav/attack suite. Until 1986 the squadron detached annually to Manises-Valencia for weapons training on the Caudé range, with the Air

Force providing Mirage IIIEE or F.1CE fighters for DACT at other times.

Escuadrilla 008 was responsible for developing techniques of seaborne V/STOL operation for the *Armada* and its experience was of benefit to subsequent users too. Rapid launches of up to four aircraft in pairs could be made from *Dédalo*'s rather confined deck using a criss-cross pattern of aircraft running diagonally from positions at the left or right after deck. Although the USMC had made several carrier deployments, *Esc 008* was the first Harrier unit to operate regularly at sea. Pilots deployed on *Dédalo* spent long periods on station in the Mediterranean or Eastern Atlantic. NATO cross-decking exercises with other carriers included 'Ocean Safari 81' with the AV-8A Det from USS *Saipan* and USS *Guam*. Matadors also teased the odd F-14A Tomcat in ACM sorties. Once the Royal Navy's Sea Harrier units were operational there were frequent visits to Yeovilton—and an increasing wish by many *Armada* pilots for the radar-equipped 'SHAR' as a follow-on type to fulfil their air-defence role more effectively. On one of those visits a programme was instigated to equip the Spanish jets with Marconi Skyguardian 2000 RHWS sets. In June 1985 four aircraft spent a fortnight at the RN base practising ski-jump techniques for use on *Dédalo*'s

replacement, the carrier *Príncipe de Asturias* (R11).

When Admiral Elmo Zumwalt's Sea Control Ship failed to impress the USN's 'big carrier league' in the 1970s, Spain, which was to have been a subcontractor for the project, decided to proceed with a modified version of the design. With American support, the 16,700-ton *Príncipe de Asturias* was laid down at Spain's Empressa Nacional Bazán shipyard in 1977. The first-ever purpose-built 'Harrier-carrier', it incorporated a 12-degree ski-jump and space for a 20-strong air group including up to ten AV-8s. Launched in 1982 and commissioned seven years later, *Príncipe de Asturias* was designed to operate the surviving AV-8B jets and a batch of twelve EAV-8Bs (VA-2 Matador II, though the 'Matador' title was used even less than in the AV-8S era), ordered in 1983. Spain was the first export

Right: EAV-8B 01-901 (BuNo 163010), the first to be delivered to the *Armada*, was lost in an accident near Rota two years after delivery. (BAe)

Below: *Armada* EAV-8Bs have fleet defence as a priority and regularly train for AIM-9M and GAU-12 gun engagements. This 'clean' pair has only the enlarged AV-8B style LIDs fitted. (R. L. Ward)

customer for the chunky AV-8B, the first three of which were delivered from 6 October 1987 onwards, direct from St Louis. Their nine-hour delivery flight required eight KC-10 'plugs' en route.

As with Spain's purchase of EF/A-18 Hornets, substantial US financial underpinning was provided. A new squadron, *9a Escuadrilla*, commissioned on 29 September 1976 under its commander, Joaquin Arcusa, its ten pilots having passed through MCAS Cherry Point's AV-8B course. Training passed to the Spanish/USN naval base at Rota with the delivery in April 1987 of an EAV-8B simulator built by Ceselsa in Madrid. Rota also had a 'deck' marked out for carrier training as part of a syllabus which included 100hr of EAV-8B conversion training, with 30hr in the 'sim'. Several *Esc 8a* pilots upgraded to the new variant and the mission remained much as before. EAV-8Bs have the full range of USMC countermeasures and weapons, with DECS-equipped engines. Until the withdrawal of the remaining AV-8S aircraft in 1985 *Príncipe de Asturias* normally operated four of each type, with the AV-8B complement being increased to six for the ship's contribution to Operation 'Deny Flight' off Bosnia in February 1994. Spain has contracted to sell its AV-8S Matador Is (see Thailand, below).

The *Armada*'s desire for a radar-equipped fighter to make use of *Príncipe de Asturias*' night-flying facilities, and to improve air defence, was realised in 1990 when Spain responded to McAir's invitation to join with Italy in the AV-8B Harrier II Plus programme. From the American viewpoint the export deal helped to guarantee production of the 'II Plus' for the USMC, but it also provided Spain and Italy with highly capable seaborne fight-

Left, upper: EAV-8B 01-912 makes a smart but ear-splitting lift-off. (Via R. L. Ward)

Left, lower: Italy's first pair of TAV-8s, ordered in 1989, were the forerunners of a Harrier II Plus order which could total 24. Italy is the first country so far to receive the trainer version ahead of the single-seater Harrier. (Authors' collection)

ers. In Spain the Harrier II Plus APG-65 radar and 'glass' cockpit were already familiar from the same company's EF/A-18A with the *Ejercito del Aire*, and *Esc 9a* pilots were posted to *Esc 152* at Zaragoza AB from September 1994 to gain experience with the equipment. An order for eight new-build aircraft was confirmed in March 1993 at a fixed price of $527 million, with delivery to begin in 1996. Final assembly was contracted to CASA in Spain, who already handled AV-8 maintenance for the *Armada*. In addition, the eleven 'stock' AV-8Bs were destined for the 'II Plus' conversion line at St Louis and a single TAV-8B was ordered. Training for the new variant's night systems began at Rota in 1995 using USMC officers on detachment, including Captain Steve 'Shoes' Dunkin.

ITALY

Italy's interest in the Harrier was encouraged by a flight demonstration on their ship *Andrea Doria* in 1967 and rekindled in June 1970, when Wing Commander Ken Hayr called at Ciampino Airport, Rome, with five aircraft *en route* to No 1 Squadron's first APC at Akrotiri. *Generale* G. C. Graziani was given a cockpit briefing and the visit generated considerable excitement. When the HSA Middle East sales tour staged through Naples in 1972 the Italian Air Force particularly requested a sales presentation. However, it was the Navy which had a specific requirement for a V/STOL combat aircraft and in 1983 its preference was for the Sea Harrier. Serious consideration was given to a purchase of twelve aircraft as a trade-off against Royal Navy selection of the Otomat-Teseo SSM. In fact, the United Kingdom opted for the AGM-84 Harpoon instead, but a much more serious obstacle for Italy was a 1929 law, similar to Spain's, prohibiting the Italian Navy from using fixed-wing aircraft and allocating all such activity to the Air Force. Johnnie Johnson commented: 'Even if the Navy got their aircraft they were to be flown by Air Force pilots. Put another way, the Air Force was being asked to invest in its own retirement fund by giving up pilots to allow the Navy to acquire a capa-

bility that the Air Force had spent years fighting against. It was a re-run of the RAF/RN battles of the 1930s.'

The seriousness of naval aspirations was reinforced by the launch of the 13,240-ton *Giuseppe Garibaldi* (C-55) with a 6-degree ski-jump bow at the end of a full-length flight deck, which was clearly intended to handle something hotter than a helicopter. It was announced that the ski-jump was built to 'protect the flight deck from excessive spray'! Sea trials followed, using RN Sea Harriers and the AV-8As from USS *Guam*.

An amendment to the Mussolini-inspired law curtailing naval aviation was proposed in July 1985, and at the same time there was renewed speculation about a Sea Harrier deal, to be offset by British purchase of the A-129 Mangusta anti-tank helicopter. During the four years' delay while the issue was once again argued out, interest swung towards the AV-8B instead. There is little doubt that McAir promoted the AV-8B quite strongly against the Sea Harrier, helping to stall the decision to allow the improved Harrier II Plus to become available as direct competition. On 26 January 1989 Law No 2654 was passed, allowing aircraft over 1,500kg (3,300lb) in weight to fly with the Navy. An order for two TAV-8Bs (MM55032 and -033) and sixteen Harrier II Plusses followed shortly afterwards, with an option on eight more. (BuNos 165007–165027 have been allocated.) Like the Spanish aircraft, they were intended primarily for air defence with a secondary CAS tasking. As part of the tri-national agreement all but the first three single-seaters were to be assembled locally, in this case at the Alenia factory using components from the BAe and McAir production lines.

Deliveries of the radar-equipped Harrier IIs began with MM7199, the first of three diverted from the FY 91 USMC allocation on 20 April 1994, almost a decade after the launch of the *Giuseppe Garibaldi*. The Harriers went straight to MCAS Cherry Point, where Tactical Air Combat Training System (TACTS) began under the supervision of VMAT-203. Contact was made with *Garibaldi*'s deck for

The Italian *Aviazione per la Marina* is in the process of acquiring 27 TA/AV-8B+ Harriers. (McDonnell-Douglas)

the first time in November 1994 for carquals, using the two TAV-8Bs also. By the time operations began with the first St Louis-built aircraft (BuNos 164563–565/ MM7199–201), almost four years had elapsed between the delivery of the two-seaters and their one-man stablemates. Both TAV-8Bs received uprated F402-RR-408 engines in 1994 to improve their hot-weather hover performance. Alenia's assembly line for the rest of the order was due to start delivering hardware at the end of 1995. Italy's work-share agreement with BAe/McAir included Pegasus sub-contracting for Fiat Avio, gun parts (Breda), pylon components (Aerea), hydraulics (Magnaghi) and parts for the radar/missile systems with other companies. Alenia were also contracted to handle the majority of the MMI Harriers' maintenance using components sourced through

a Joint Development Office in the United States.

The Harrier II Plus's first operational assignment with the MMI's *1 Gruppo Aereo* (*Grupaer*) was to provide fire support for the evacuation of UN troops from Somalia, beginning January 1995. Over 100 combat hours were notched up, with 25mm cannon and rocket pods aboard. A 100 per cent availability target was achieved up to the cessation of operations on 22 March 1995. Thereafter *1 Grupaer* moved straight to Exercise 'Tridente 95' in the Mediterranean before returning to base at Grottaglie, near Taranto. Italy intends to build a second, slight larger 'Harrier-carrier', probably to be named either *Giuseppe Mazzini* or *Conte di Cavour*, and hopes for a third, ensuring further aircraft orders. In 1995 talks were held by Italy, Spain, Britain and France to discuss the joint development of a new generation of carriers to replace HMS *Invincible* in 2015. For Spain, the policy marked an extension of its *Alta Mar* (high seas) plan, formulated to

protect its worldwide fishing operations as well as offering increased NATO participation. Although twenty years elapsed between Hugh Merewether's first Harrier DB landing on *Andrea Doria* and the AV-8B deal, the MMI has now become one of the most enthusiastic proponents of seaborne V/STOL.

SWITZERLAND

As an operator of British jet fighters since 1946, and Hunters since 1958, the Swiss Air Force seemed a very likely Harrier customer. In 1970–71 it began to look for a replacement for its DH Venom fleet. A Swiss Harrier order was, in Johnnie Johnson's view, 'the biggest one to get away. If you were to design an aircraft specifically for Switzerland it would come out looking like a Harrier. It's a small country with few airfields and terrain that inhibits the construction of more. I should think that 80 per cent of senior Kingston management visited Switzerland to spread the gospel.' The sales effort was supported by flight demonstrations in 1971, and John Farley's logbook for the period records just how intensive the effort became:

'Harrier GR.1 XV742 [then at Dunsfold as a trials aircraft] with civil registration G-VSTO [because the Swiss would not allow a military aircraft to fly to Switzerland]. Dunsfold–Malpensa–Lugarno 10 June 1971.

'11 June 2 x demos - Lugarno
'12 June Lugarno to Grenchen
'12 June demo at Grenchen in
           pouring rain!
'12 June Grenchen to Lugarno
'13 June 3 x demos at Lugarno,
           including formation with
           VIP HS125
'15 June Lugarno–Malpensa–Zürich
'16 June demo Zürich
'17 June Zürich–Dunsfold
'In Harrier GR.1A XV748 (OCU) for second Swiss push:

'21 June Dunsfold–Zürich–Lugarno
'21 June 1 x demo
'22 June 2 x demo
'23 June 3 x demo
'24 June 3 x demo plus 1 x photo
           flight with HS125
'25 June Lugarno–Zürich–Dunsfold'

The correspondent for *Flight International* watched the demonstrations at Lugarno/Agno and Grenchen, rating them 'the finest Harrier demonstrations ever given'. Bill Bedford and John Farley spent a considerable time planning the flights, knowing that their aircraft was not, in fact, among the six types officially under consideration as a Venom replacement. The Lugarno demo included a rolling take-off from the perimeter track followed by a 60kt climb at 60 degrees, keeping to the steep contours of the hill to the south of the airfield. After a work-out at speeds from 0 to 600mph, XV742 was brought down the same hill-slope profile in a steep decelerating transition to a landing on the narrow valley airstrip.

Swiss interest—and indecision—continued through 1973. HSA borrowed XV276 from Rolls-Royce to allow a Swiss evaluation pilot, H. Stauffer, to fly it. Sadly, his flight from Dunsfold lasted a mere two minutes. Rather than moving the nozzle control aft following take-off he inadvert-ently closed the HP fuel cock, ejecting as the Harrier went ballistic. Possibly the experience tipped the balance. Johnnie Johnson: 'Perhaps the rest of Switzerland figured that if he couldn't do it, nobody could!'

A year later the protracted decision-making process took another turn. Switzerland evaluated the Northrop F-5E, eventually ordering 72 aircraft in 1976. For good measure a further 60 refurbished Hunters were ordered too. Most of the F-5Es were assembled in Switzerland, which actually added $180,000 to the unit cost. Compared with the Harrier, the F-5E Tiger offered limited supersonic speed and a small radar, possibly making it a more obvious 'self-defence' type. Underlying the decision was a recognition of the huge investment which the country had undertaken in constructing its heavily defended airfields, with 'hangars' blasted out of mountainsides and well-hidden runways. A country which considers its airfields to be relatively invulnerable is less likely than most to appreciate the off-site advantages of the Harrier. HSA at least had the compensation of a renewed Hunter deal, but a hundred Harriers in Swiss markings would have been a much better boost to the export drive.

CANADA

In addition to the crucial USMC AV-8 sale there was some hope of Canadian uptake. A sales presentation was made early in the Harrier's history with the possibility that the aircraft could be used as part of Canada's NATO contribution in Europe.

ARGENTINA

Representatives of the Argentine forces were regular attenders at early Harrier presentations and at sea trials from 1971 onwards. Having acquired the aircraft carrier *Veinticinco de Mayo*, they were encouraged to follow the Royal Navy example and opt for Sea Harrier, but budget restrictions dictated ex-USN Skyhawks instead. As John Crampton remarked, 'Just how close we came to a sale is hard to determine. Just as well we did not succeed, perhaps?' John Farley flew Harrier GR.1 XV757 to *Veinticinco de Mayo* from Dunsfold on 9 September 1969, returning to Dunsfold after an hour aboard. The ship was en route to Argentina on its delivery trip from Holland.

BRAZIL

The Brazilians saw a need for a seaborne Harrier to fulfil patrol tasks which the US Navy had asked them to take on, but the Brazilian government was unable to fund a refurbishment for its only carrier, *Minas Gerais*. The ship, like *Veinticinco de Mayo* a former RN *Colossus* class vessel, was withdrawn in 1987. It would have been unable to handle modern conventional jets and the Brazilians had viewed the Harrier as a clear answer to their problems. As part of the sales pitch HSA's demonstrator G-VTOL appeared at Brazil's first aeronautical exposition, the São Paulo International Aerospace Show, in 1973. Don Riches and John Farley flew it in challenging 'hot and high' conditions at the show, 2,100ft above sea level in temperatures of 30°C. Farley also did six landings and take-offs from *Minas Gerais* in G-VTOL off Santa Cruz in Brazil in 28 September 1973.

CHILE

Early in 1990 the country was seen as a possible market for refurbished RAF Harrier GR.3s after the withdrawal of an arms embargo. Two Harrier GR.3s from No 1417 Flight, Belize, performed at FIDAE '90 in Santiago but no order was forthcoming.

AFRICA

There was some discussion of a possible sale of refurbished Harrier GR.3s to Zimbabwe in 1989 during a visit by the British Prime Minister but inadequate funding ruled this out. Johnnie Johnson recalled a potential sale to Uganda also: 'We were driven by the Heath Government to spend time in Uganda at the time of General Idi Amin, on the grounds that he was the last bastion of freedom in Africa and should be supported. We demonstrated the Harrier to him while he was on a Scottish holiday and the whole thing was supposed to be taken very seriously at the time.'

THE MIDDLE EAST

In Johnnie Johnson's opinion the turning point in the sales campaign was the appearance of G-VTOL, HSA's two-seat demonstrator. In 1970 the management decided to fund a single T. Mk 52 Harrier, based on the T.2 and equipped by the usual 'parts' suppliers on an 'embodiment loan' basis. Initially fitted with the Pegasus Mk 102 (the first two-seater to receive it), and later the Mk 103 'big motor', 'Gee-Veetol' had an enlarged communications fit for world-wide demonstration work and a series of striking one-off colour schemes. It also received the 'reserve' military serial ZA250 in addition to its highly appropriate DTI registration. First flown on 16 September 1971, G-VTOL was crucial to the export drive. 'It allowed other pilots to experience V/STOL and to discover for themselves that only quite average flying skills were required. Until then there was an understandable reluctance on the part of MoD to allow one of their single-seat Harriers to be flown by some unknown person at the request of HSA. All the (sales) efforts before 1972 were handi-capped by our inability to allow people to fly, or to demonstrate in their home countries. Many from the Middle East, for example, saw the aircraft being demonstrated at Farnborough or Le Bourget on a cool autumn or spring afternoon and asked, reasonably enough, how it would perform at a '35°C in swirling dust'.

Four Harrier sales tours were organised (three by Johnson), all using G-VTOL. In planning the Middle East tour HSA intended to go strongly for a series of 'genuine prospects in Abu Dhabi, Iran, Kuwait, Saudi Arabia—and India'.

IRAN

G-VTOL and its attendant HS.748 support aircraft arrived at Teheran on 24 June 1972 on the first leg of the tour, which had staged through Naples and Akrotiri. Johnnie Johnson organised the logistics for the whole tour. His report on Iran read: 'Our programme for Teheran was confused since, whilst we were there, the Shah was at Boscombe Down watching a Harrier demonstration.' The team was advised to do nothing until the Shah reported his views on the aircraft back to his Air Force. Although the tour had stopped at Teheran at the Iranians' request, the Shah's movements were surrounded by such deep secrecy that HSA's Iranian agent did not know that his leader was actually at Boscombe Down. Twenty-three years on Johnnie Johnson is convinced that Iranian interest was sincere, despite these bizarre circumstances. Their intention at that time seems to have been to base Harriers at Bandar Abbas to be on hand in possible conflicts with Gulf states. Iranian attention shifted towards the Sea Harrier in 1976 when it was reported than an order for thirty aircraft was imminent together with at least two British-built *Invincible* class ships. Shortly before his overthrow at the

G-VTOL/ZA250 in its original colour scheme. For modellers, it comprised overall Middle Blue (BS381C:109) with nose flash, tail cone and upperwing panels in Bright Red-BEA (ICI Spec. F407/711). The fin and upper fuselage were white. 'G-VTOL' appeared underwing in Light Aircraft Grey (BS381C:627) and in Middle Blue on the fin. (BAe)

end of 1978 the Shah sent an aide and
military team to London for a briefing on
Harrier ship operations.

KUWAIT

During their four unproductive days in
Teheran the sales team carried out some
repairs to persistent minor faults in G-
VTOL and attempted to fix a troublesome
drop tank before moving on to Kuwait.
On the day appointed for the demonstration there the Prime Minister, Sheikh
Saad, was called away to address a parlia-
mentary session on the Sterling crisis, while
the Head of the Armed Forces, General
Mubarrak, had to go to Beirut for medical treatment. HSA's demo went ahead in
the absence of these two key decision-
makers and the commanders of the local
Lightning and Hunter squadrons were
given G-VTOL trips in temperatures of
44°C. Once again the faulty drop-tank
played up and on one landing both
mainwheel tyres burst. The exhausted
maintenance team sorted out all the technical glitches in the 'cool' of the evening
of 29 June and prepared G-VTOL for its
next venue: Bombay.

INDIA

'The weather at Bombay defies description,' wrote Johnnie Johnson. 'The clos-
est analogy I can find is standing under a
tepid shower for twelve hours fully clothed.
When we arrived (in the HS.748) the Harrier had been parked in the open for
twenty-four hours without even covers
over the canopies and it was saturated.'
His first task was to locate some liquid
oxygen (LOX) for the aircraft and this was
found at the local steel plant—which
turned out to be the only source of correctly pressurized LOX in the whole of
India. G-VTOL departed for the Indian
naval base at Cochin on 2 July, returning
after a few minutes with a whole menu of
electrical faults including total HUD and
INAS failure. 'A second attempt at take-
off was aborted when innumerable electrical snags appeared during the take-off
run. Meanwhile, the monsoon continued
and every time a panel was removed to
trace a fault, more water entered the un-
protected systems bays.' Eventually Indian
Airlines were persuaded to lend the team
a hangar and the jet was allowed to dry
out overnight.

The next morning it was pushed out
and started and everything was 'on line'.
G-VTOL arrived in Cochin on 3 July,
where John Farley gave his first Indian
Navy passenger, Captain Tahiliani, a familiarisation flight. Cochin was the shore
base for a series of demo flights from India's aircraft carrier, INS *Vikrant* (R-11; laid
down as the RN light fleet carrier HMS

The first Sea Harrier FRS.51 (IN 601) for the Indian Navy, still carrying its Class B serial G-9-478. (BAe)

Hercules). Farley had studied photographs of *Vikrant*'s flight deck, used normally for Sea Hawks and Alizés, before the tour and had requested lines to be painted for G-VTOL's deck operations.[3] He flew the aircraft aboard *Vikrant* on 5 July with Tahiliani aboard, making eleven more solo sorties at various weights, up to 'max fuel' including full 100gal combat tanks, over a 585ft take-off run. His return to Cochin, with a fully serviceable Harrier, was a great moment for the HSA team: 'This tremendous success lifted the spirits of the whole team because it was so apparent that the Indian Navy had seen the light,' Johnson reported. Ten more sorties were flown from *Vikrant* on 6 July, meeting all the targets, and opportunities to fly more Navy personnel from Cochin were curtailed only by a lack of LOX. Having been let down over the LOX supply at Bangalore, the weary HS.748 crew embarked on yet another round trip to Bombay to charge up their LOX containers. Even so, three very senior INS personnel had flown in G-VTOL and all had taken the controls for portions of their sorties, including sample take-offs, hovers and transitions. At the farewell party at Cochin, Johnson remembers that 'we were all left with the feeling that they had been convinced that the Harrier was the right aircraft for their requirements'.

G-VTOL's demonstrations won the aircraft many supporters in the Indian military establishment at a time when the candidates for their Navy's Hawker Sea Hawk replacement seemed limited to the low-cost A-4 Skyhawk (later embargoed by the USA) or the Dassault Etendard. The Yak-36MP Forger was also briefly considered. Discussions rumbled on for a further five years and in October 1977 Defence Minister Jagjivan Ram announced that 'a V/STOL fighter' would be ordered as part of an upgrade for *Vikrant*. A Sea Harrier order was confirmed a year later, but it took a further fourteen months before this specified publicly six Sea Harrier FRS.1s and two two-seaters.

India despatched a group of technical personnel to Kingston in September 1980 as the core of the Sea Harrier Project Team. INS pilots began to train in Britain in 1982, going initially to RAF Brawdy where the INS Sea Hawk squadron, No 300 *White Tigers*, had originally commissioned in 1960. After training there with No 2 TWU, the pilots joined the Harrier CONVEX at Wittering and then moved to RNAS Yeovilton for a year on the Sea Harrier. Their first aircraft (IN602) was handed over at Dunsfold on 27 January 1983 to the Indian High Commissioner, and a Muhurtham ceremony was performed involving garlands of marigolds on the Sea Harrier's nose and a mixture of coconut milk, lemon and incense on its nosewheel. This ancient Vedic ritual was a form of blessing on a new venture and it was also meant to appease the elements. Immediately afterwards the weather lightened up, allowing CTP Farley to perform a 'rocket climb' demo.[4]

By February 1983, 899 NAS at Yeovilton was hosting nearly 200 INS personnel. Already pushed by the demands, and aftermath, of the Falklands campaign, the Squadron borrowed an extra RAF T.4 to help with conversion, and G-VTOL on occasion too. The INTU (Indian Navy Training Unit) was established within the Squadron using three INS Sea Harriers and both INS two-seaters. The Sea Harriers were standard FRS.1s (known as Mk 51s) with their LOX systems replaced by an on-board oxygen generating system (OBOGS), providing gaseous oxygen in place of hard-to-get LOX.[5] A US embargo on the AIM-9 Sidewinder required this 'standard' missile to be replaced by the French Matra R550 Magic, already in use by the Indian Air Force. Changes to the IFF and radar were also necessary. Both Harrier T Mk 60 trainers were essentially Pegasus 103-equipped T.4Ns with a revised cockpit layout to include some of the Mk 51 systems. In order to give longer hovering times in high climatic temperatures, the Pegasus water-injection system was modified to give a half-rate flow.

All aircraft from the first batch were delivered by March 1984. The first three

were flown direct to the INS base at Goa-Dabolim in December 1983, a 4,800-mile trip staging via Malta, Egypt and Dubai. 300 Squadron recommissioned on the new type under Commander Arun Prakash, becoming operational in July 1984. Flying from *Vikrant* began early in 1985 following a spectacular public display by the six Sea Harriers over New Delhi. The arrival of a Singer-Link-Miles simulator in March 1984 signalled the commencement of a domestically run training programme which since 1990 has centred on the Sea Harrier Operational Flying Training Unit (SHOFTU, actually 'B' Flight of 551 Squadron). Operational flying has included large-scale exercises with IAF units, anti-shipping and night-intercept practice, with sea-search, accompanying the Navy's huge Tu-142M and Ilyushin Il-38 reconnaissance aircraft.

When the first order for eight aircraft was placed it was anticipated that India's long-term plans would require up to 48 Sea Harriers in total. In fact, fluctuations in policy have so far allowed the total to reach only 23 and four trainers. Additional orders have been for ten (IN607–616 and T.60 IN653) in 1985 and seven (IN617–623 plus T.60 IN654) in October 1986. The extra aircraft were required to equip India's second carrier. When INTU pilots practised deck landings on Falklands veteran HMS *Hermes* in 1982 they could hardly have imagined that it would become one of their own bases five years later. After refurbishment the ship became INS *Viraat* and it was delivered to India in August 1987, operating a familiar mixture of Sea Harriers and Sea Kings like the now refurbished, ski-jump-equipped *Vikrant*. In the same month, negotiations began for a third carrier to be built at an unspecified foreign yard for delivery by 1999, though consideration was also given to the possibility of acquiring one of the three RN *Invincible* class ships, should one have become available. In mid-1985 the

[3]See above, 'Sea Jet'.
[4]See Appendix by John Farley discussing his display routines.
[5]OBOGS uses a ceramic filter to strain out non-oxygen elements from engine bleed-air. It has since become a standard item on the later generation Harrier IIs as well.

Indian government was looking at the Russian carrier *Admiral Gorshkov* and the French ship *Clémenceau* as possible replacements for INS *Vikrant*. Further Sea Harrier orders would probably result from additional 'blue water' expansion of this kind, but in 1995 upgrades of the existing Sea Harrier fleet were also under review. BAe and Israel Aircraft Industries collaborated to devise a radar and armament update which would be cheaper than the full F/A.2 rebuilt (already rejected by India on cost grounds). Based on the Israeli ELTA EL/M 2032 pulse-doppler fire-control radar and BAe ASRAAM missile, the modifications could include new avionics and the ELTA 8240 EW suite plus engine refurbishment and structural modifications to take the aircraft to the year 2010. A decision was expected early in 1996 to replace the two hard-pressed T.60 trainers with new T.8s (or reworked T.4s). The RAF's last two T.4s (ZB600 and ZB602) were delivered to Dunsfold at the end of 1995 for refurbishment and probable sale to the INS.

ABU DHABI

In July 1972 the HSA sales tour entered its last leg. The final Indian presentation in Delhi, for the Indian Air Force, took place on 10 July and was 'so well attended by senior officers that only Air Commanders and above qualified for chairs'. Delays occurred because the Indian authorities decided to remove all HSA's promotional slide and movie projection equipment so that a carpet could be put down just before the presentation began. Afterwards, G-VTOL demonstrated at the airport, though the pilot (who had been promised a clear circuit) had to dodge constant air traffic and the flight was curtailed. The team left India with the feeling that the Air Force was 'less firm than the Navy in stating their need for the Harrier' and headed for Abu Dhabi.

For the final demonstration of the tour HSA test pilot Tony Hawkes was required to fly for the Ruler and the Crown Prince (who also happened to be Defence Minister) of Abu Dhabi from a desert air strip 1,000ft above sea level. Familiarisation flights were also planned for various military personnel. Sadly, G-VTOL was hovered backwards into its own dust-cloud during the first demonstration. The pilot lost sight of his horizon and made a heavy landing, snapping off the starboard outrigger and seriously bending the nose. As it hit the sand Johnnie Johnson 'heard the sound of a £5 million sale disappearing'. He is convinced that both Abu Dhabi and Kuwait would have been customers, with the possibility of others in the area following their lead.

JAPAN

In July 1995 the JMSDF (Japanese Maritime Self-Defence Force) expressed an interest in the purchase of up to five Harrier T.10s as 'Navy and support trainers'. If a contract results it will consolidate an interest in the Harrier which has extended over thirty-three years. John Crampton: 'The Japanese interest goes back to 1962 when I was despatched to Japan to join a Bristol Engine team in giving a presentation to the JSDF on the potential of the P.1127. It must be remembered that at that time Japan was making under licence the Bristol Orpheus, which formed the gas generator element of the engine which became known as the Pegasus. Japan was therefore "halfway to making a Pegasus".' Johnnie Johnson: 'Anything the Japanese buy needs to be capable of local manufacture. Their non-aggressor role means that they have to fight hard for a budget and cannot countenance a strike aircraft. Harrier met many of the defensive roles that they have, especially for the disputed islands.'

The Harrier was demonstrated at Japan's Nagoya Air Show in October 1971. G-VTOL was to have appeared but it was damaged in a landing accident when its pilot 'ran out of runway' at Dunsfold. An RAF GR.1A was substituted, flown out to Japan in a Belfast. By March 1990 speculation about a Harrier purchase arose once again. The Harrier II Plus was thought to be the likely subject of a twelve-aircraft deal, based on light carriers for sea-lane defence. An alternative which the Japanese are also known to favour is the

SkyHook concept.[6] At the time of writing it seems likely that at least one of these options may be close to realization.

CHINA

A Chinese delegation visited Dunsfold in December 1978 where they viewed and approved a demonstration by Harrier GR.3 XV762, on loan from No 233 OCU. They subsequently requested a Harrier flight. John Farley was asked to let the Number Two man in the Fighter Command of the People's Liberation Army 'have a little fly in G-VTOL and do the main manoeuvres'. It was then revealed that the pilot in question spoke no English. With characteristic thoroughness, Farley insisted on three interpreters to avoid any possibility of misunderstanding. He then wrote down every word he intended to say to the Chinaman (known as Mr Mah), covering flight and emergency procedures in exactly the way they would be conveyed to him, and had them translated into simple instructions in Chinese, each with a signal in Morse code written alongside it. A signalling system was devised. When Mr Mah heard his name in his headset he had to look up and meet Farley's eyes in the 'front pilot''s cockpit

rear-view mirror to reassure his mentor that he was listening. A Morse instruction was then given orally (with 'dit' meaning a wing-borne manoeuvre, 'dah' a jet-borne one, etc.) and Mr Mah then had to consult his notepad to find the instruction corresponding to the Morse signal. He then nodded at the mirror and took the controls. If in doubt, Mr Mah just had to oscillate the stick to pass over control again. It was a highly original method of conducting a basic Harrier conversion course, but it worked well and G-VTOL returned intact.

A year later a BAe presentation was given in Peking; in April 1979, the year in which Prime Minister Thatcher welcomed Chairman Hua Kuo-feng, the first Communist Chinese leader to visit Britain, she spoke of China's 'crucial role in world affairs' and supported diplomatic efforts to divorce China from the Soviet Union. Military trade deals with Britain and France were seen as an expedient move in this attempt. BAe was convinced that Chinese interest in the Harrier was sincere and possibly convertible into an order for a hundred, with a further 200 to be built locally by Shenyang. There were reservations about exporting British technology to China, although civil airliner deals had already been negotiated.

At the presentation it became clear that the Chinese operational requirement actually involved using Harriers, based on the Sea Harrier format, to patrol a huge area bordering Russia. They would have been moved around a number of forward sites to counter possible Russian incursions. Most of those sites were apparently going to be in 'hot and high' locations with ambient temperatures of 30–40°C and a consequent degradation in the Harrier's hover performance. The BAe team, and John Farley in particular, had genuine doubts about whether they would be fulfilling the Kingston philosophy of providing for the customer's real needs if they pressed ahead with the deal. He provided the Chinese with realistic performance figures, given the likely operational scenario (such as could be deduced from the secretive Chinese). The fact that they did not pursue the deal had more to do with a severe shrinkage in Chinese defence expenditure, improved Sino-Soviet relations and a failure on their part to understand the Western concept of inflation in setting the price for the aircraft. They regarded the last as 'cheating'. Their faith in the Harrier was re-stated, ironically, when the Chinese heard of the Sea Harrier's spectacular success in the Falklands. Mr Mah contacted Kingston again and indicated that if they had realized that the aircraft was that good the Chinese would have found a means of affording it anyway!

THAILAND

The first deal involving 'pre-owned' Harriers enabled Spain to supply seven AV-8S and two TAV-8S Matadors to Thailand, allowing the *Arma Aérea de la Armada* to concentrate on enlarging its Harrier II Plus fleet. Thai pilots began training in the United States at the end of 1995, passing through the US Navy's basic courses at Meridian, Mississippi, and Kingsville, Texas. At the time of writing they were due to begin AV-8S conversion at Rota, Spain, in June 1996, remaining there until March 1998. The new Thai squadron, with fifteen pilots, is due to be based at U-Tapao and their mission will be to patrol the Thai coast and detect 'pirate' vessels.

IN 601 on the flight-line at RNAS Yeovilton, where India's first batch of Sea Harrier pilots was trained in 1983. (Via R. L. Ward)

Captain Steve Dunkin, involved in training Spain's Harrier II Plus pilots at Rota, commented that 'the real problem is language—the Thais will be taught by the Spanish in English!' Spain's Bazán shipyard began constructing a 'helicopter/Harrier-carrier' HMTS *Chakkrinareubet*, in 1992. Designated OPHC 911 (Offshore Patrol Helicopter Carrier), the ship is similar to Spain's *Príncipe de Asturias*, but it is about 15m (49ft) shorter and has a 12-degree ski-jump. It is due to be handed to the Royal Thai Navy in December 1996. A second ship was ordered from Germany in 1991, though the modifications to the vessel, including a ski-jump to permit AV-8 operations, will have to be carried out elsewhere because Germany is not allowed to export offensive military equipment. Several AMARC-resident AV-8A/C airframes have also been purchased from the USA for spares, but it would seem feasible to refurbish a number of these ex-USMC airframes with low hours for use on Thailand's second carrier.

REVIEW

There is no disguising the fact that, despite energetic and effective sales efforts on the part of the HSA/BAe management and McDonnell-Douglas, the export sales of the Harrier 'family' have so far been disappointing. Compared with a 1967 target sale of 2,000 aircraft, the 'score' nearly thirty years on has barely crept above 800. Of those, 322 have gone to the British forces and 396 to the USMC (not counting remanufactured airframes). A mere 86 new-build 'foreign export' sales have been recorded for all Harrier variants in that time. It is of little comfort to the manufacturers' accountants to know that the worldwide impact and significance of that small force is out of all proportion to its numerical size. In very many cases sales were close to being agreed and there were unique political reasons in the majority of cases where agreement could not be reached.

The Harrier has been a 'slow burner', a revolutionary concept which has taken over three decades to become accepted as a part of military aviation in many parts of the world. In Johnnie Johnson's words, 'You have to do a lot of preaching to win a convert.' In places where the Harrier was unknown, incomprehension and amazement abounded. One senior BAe sales executive told the authors how he was approached by an Iraqi delegate at a sales briefing and asked whether the Harrier's hovering capability was really designed to make weapon-aiming easier! At the large USN facility at Naples the sight of a Harrier decelerating to transition to a vertical landing was enough to cause all the base's emergency vehicles to start heading for the runway in anticipation of what they took to be an impending crash. That was eighteen months after the type entered service with the US Marines.

A quarter of a century on, many more 'Harrier-carriers' are being constructed or planned, to capitalise on the naval potential of the design and to give countries which could not afford big aircraft carriers a real naval aviation combat capability. SkyHook still holds real possibilities, and the long debate over the Harrier's successor will ensure that there is still plenty of development potential in an idea which may have seemed little more than a novelty in 1960.

No 300 Squadron's white tiger insignia first appeared on the unit's Hawker Sea Hawks. (Via R. L. Ward)

12. The Next Leap Forward

SCADS

The use of Harriers aboard naval vessels has become well established in the last two decades, but there have been many other projected extensions of the 'Harriers-at-sea' concept. For the Falklands campaign the container ships *Atlantic Conveyor* and *Contender Bezant* became temporary Harrier transport/support vessels, with limited flying facilities. These wartime emergency methods were the outcome of studies, on both sides of the Atlantic, of the possibilities of exploiting the large deck area of container vessels. They were seen as a readily available, quickly convertible, cheap augmentation of an existing carrier force. After the Falklands, British Aerospace continued to develop ideas which evolved into the Shipborne Containerised Air Defence System (SCADS). Any vessel capable of providing a 120m (395ft) deck-run for take-off could be equipped with the SCADS installation in about two days. Containerized support 'kits' for up to six installations would be loaded aboard, plus Seawolf anti-missile systems, air defence radar, missile countermeasures, command and control equipment, accommodation and logistical support. About 230 standard ISO 20ft containers would be required, and a runway with a ski-jump, built from sections of British Army Medium Girder Bridge. A SCADS-equipped container ship would be used primarily for area air defence, and its Harrier complement could be augmented by ASW helicopters.

McDonnell-Douglas have extended the concept in the 1990s and projected the multi-mission Harrier II Plus operating from towed or anchored barges, converted oil tankers (with an 'over-lay' flight deck installed) and even oil rigs. The aircraft's internal starting system, OBOGS and minimal maintenance reduce ground support requirements to the point where such rudimentary 'bases' become feasible.

SKYHOOK

An even more radical proposal to establish the need for a dedicated flight deck was proposed by BAe/Dowty Boulton-Paul in the late 1980s. SkyHook's origins apparently lay in a conversation between two BAe test pilots and a designer. John Farley had just returned to Dunsfold from an unpleasant deck landing on the French carrier *Foch*. The rolling motion of her slippery deck had almost caused his Harrier to slip overboard after the landing was completed. Farley expressed rather strongly to designer John Fozard his feeling that there should be some means of 'grabbing' a V/STOL aircraft once it had made deck contact and securing it immediately in heavy seas and bad-weather landings. Test pilot Heinz Frick said, 'Why not grab it while it's still in the hover?'. He worked on the notion and formulated a shipborne crane device which could swing out over a ship's side. Its 'hook' end was stabilized over the sea bed and a Harrier simply had to be hovered in its usual pre-deck landing position, but immediately beneath the end of the gantry. Frick designed a simple visual aid, giving the same visual cues that all pilots use in close-formation flying, for the pilot to position his aircraft within a couple of feet of the 'hook-on' location. The crane then lowered and locked on to the Harrier using similar space-stabilizing principles to the Boeing 'Flying Boom' aerial refuelling system.

Having securely 'caught' the Harrier, using sensors which extended a jack-rod to lock into a fixed pick-up probe built into the aircraft's spine, the crane then swung it inboard and placed it, either on its undercarriage or 'wheels up', on a trestle which could be pre-loaded with weapons or fuel tanks ready for immediate attachment to its pylons. Once the aircraft had been swung over the deck the SkyHook's robotics switched from 'space stabilisation' (over the sea bed) to stabilisation relative to the ship. Mobile trestles with aircraft aboard could be moved easily to hangar spaces, on or below decks, and 'parked' more tightly than conventionally stowed aircraft.

'Take-off' from the SkyHook was accomplished by swinging the aircraft over the side, starting up and running cockpit checks. With nozzles pointing down, the pilot then signalled for the central jack-rod of the supporting gantry, connected to his aircraft's pylon, to extend the suspended Harrier downwards and away from the four sway-brace pads which steadied it on the gantry. At full power, the Harrier was gently 'pushed up' a little. The crane, sensing an up-load, unlocked and withdrew its extending jack-rod upwards, leaving the aircraft in the hover and free to move away. Two SkyHook assemblies could be installed on larger ships to increase the sortie rate. The technology used to stabilize and operate SkyHook was well established—essentially a flight simulator motion base (upside down), and a velocity sensor. Land-based trials with G-VTOL and other Harriers, conducted by Heinz Frick and two other pilots, with the hover 'visual aid' device mounted on a fire service hydraulic turntable, showed that it was quite easy to position a Harrier in the correct 'grab' situation, even in gusty conditions.

G-VTOL in yet another colour scheme. On the light grey fin is Heinz Frick's 'SkyHook' cartoon. The Harrier is demonstrating a hook-up the crane unit. Ahead of its nose is the system of lights used to position the aircraft for a 'grab' by the central shaft of the hooking device and its four locating pads. (BAe)

So far SkyHook has not advanced beyond basic feasibility studies and there is no immediate commercial prospect. However, several nations have expressed interest, especially Japan, which has a requirement to operate aircraft at sea but is not allowed ships large enough for deck-borne operations.

VAAC HARRIER

The second prototype Harrier T.2, XW175, spent its entire life after its delivery in July 1969 on development trials. In January 1983 the Cranfield Institute of Technology was contracted to modify the aircraft for testing control systems which could be used in V/STOL designs to follow on from the Harrier family. It was first upgraded to T.4A standard and then its rear cockpit was rebuilt for VAAC (Vectored thrust Aircraft Active Control) technology, making it the first fly-by-wire V/STOL aircraft. The system evolved around a re-programmable digital flight-control computer and programmable HUD, using software 'control laws'. The standard Harrier control system and performance was digitally copied, flying control inputs, RCS, throttle, flaps and nozzle angle all being reduced via software to a system whereby the pilot flew the aircraft with two control sticks, one controlling speed and the other direction. Eventually all control functions were combined into a single stick, which included a throttle control built into a single trim-switch, freeing the pilot's left hand to operate radios, radar or an armament panel. This reduction in workload was so massive that in February 1993 a civil PPL holder was strapped into XW175's back seat and he was able to transition to the hover and land the Harrier at his first attempt. The aircraft still had the 'two-lever' cockpit at that stage, first flown with computer control in May 1990.

The VAAC project pilot at RAE (later DRA) Bedford was Flight Lieutenant Dan Griffith, and his pioneering work paved the way for VTOL aircraft which would be simpler to handle, more efficient and capable of exploring vectored thrust in 'unstable' airframe configurations to expand the manoeuvring envelope.

AV-8B PLUS, PLUS

In the United States, McDonnell-Douglas modified AV-8B BuNo 161397 as a Harrier Technology Demonstrator with the eventual aim of testing an equally radical control system. Initially the project was conceived to show how the modification, design and building of aircraft could be rationalised to make the process quicker and cheaper. In 1995 the AV-8B appeared with wingtip AIM-9 rails (an oft-proposed Harrier 'mod') but McAir later installed zero-scarf rear nozzles to reduce IR signature and designed improved LIDs. Long-term intentions for the Demonstrator included a 30cm (11.8in) centre fuselage stretch and fly-by-light (fibre optic) controls.

Other AV-8B initiatives from St Louis in 1995 included a proposal to install three-man 'people pods' in place of underwing fuel tanks for the rapid transit of Special Forces personnel to forward sites. The 21ft long pods would be pressurized and soundproofed, with small portholes to take the edge off the claustrophobia. They could also be used for the rapid evacuation of wounded troops in situations where the Harrier's speed advantage over a helicopter might save a life.

ASTOVL, JAST, CALF

The firm basis of operational success achieved by the Harrier family has promoted a continuous research effort on both sides of the Atlantic with the aim of establishing basic design principles for a 'third-generation Harrier'. In most respects the eventual outcome will probably be a very different aircraft indeed from 'Harrier II' and the finer points of its likely configuration are beyond the scope of this book. However, many of the proposals so far put forward for the next century's V/STOL fighters have their roots in 1950s research, and one can be traced right back to Michel Wibault's original Gyropter.

Just as the P.1127/'Harrier I' was an aircraft built around (and because of) a radically new powerplant concept, the next 'leap' for V/STOL will also depend on advances in engine technology. Recent evolution of the existing Pegasus has concentrated on reliability and reduced servicing costs rather than on trying to extract yet more thrust. After test-bed runs with the BS.100 and PCB Pegasus 2 in 1962–65 and 1980–81, Bristol Engines/Rolls-Royce continued fairly low-key research into PCB as a means of converting Pegasus into a more powerful, supersonic 'driver'. Harrier GR.1 (DB) XV280 was used for the first series of ground tests with a Pegasus 2A (PCB) between 1985 and 1990 and was subsequently dumped at the Foulness test site (though its cockpit ended up at RNAS Yeovilton for instruction purposes). A second PCB test-bed, made up from sections of P.1127 XP976 and GR.1 XV798 (written-off in a No 20 Squadron accident at Wildenrath), used a PCB Pegasus 2 with variable-area nozzles. The aircraft was suspended in a huge gantry at Shoeburyness and the engine's extended, drooped nozzles were designed to explore the problems of hot gas re-ingestion and digital fuel control. Ground erosion by columns of superheated air at over 2,000°F (1095°C) remained the biggest handicap with PCB engines of this type. No PCB-capable Pegasus was actually flown, and the 'lash-up' XV798, with its four-foot centre fuselage extension, completed its trials in 1994 and was donated to the Rolls-Royce Heritage Trust.

Supersonic performance remains as a prerequisite for most follow-on Harrier proposals and the quest for an appropriate power source has taken a number of directions. In January 1986 a five-year joint UK/US study began, comparing four powerplant concepts jointly funded by NASA and the British Ministry of Defence. They included augmented ejector lift (tested and rejected in a simpler from with the Lockheed XV-4B in 1964); a remote augmented lift system (a single deflected nozzle behind the cockpit); and a tandem fan (in which air from a first-stage shaft-driven fan could be diverted downwards for VTOL while the core turbine—taking its air from auxiliary inlets—exhausted its efflux via a deflected rear nozzle). All the above systems were essentially two-nozzle layouts, with RCS for stability. BAe/Rolls-Royce also experimented with advanced vectored engines which revived the original BE.48-style three-nozzle system, but with PCB in the front pair.

All four proposals had been dropped by 1990 and the Defense Advanced Research Projects Agency (DARPA, later ARPA) in the USA began new studies with an emphasis on 'stealth' characteristics. Two years later a new initiative called 'Thundercat' requested Advanced STO/VL (ASTOVL) proposals for submission by 24 November 1992. RFPs were to be based on remotely driven lift-fans, either shaft driven via a clutch (shades of Gyropter) or by engine gases (as in the 1960s Ryan XV-5A). This competition was to have led to the selection of two designs for prototype construction after a final decision in mid-1995.

The original 'Thundercat'/ASTOVL designs were a Lockheed/Pratt & Whitney proposal resembling the F-22, with a shaft-driven fan exhausting downwards behind the cockpit and a 'stealthy' jet efflux 'slot' at the rear. McDonnell-Douglas/General Electric proposed a similar arrangement with Pegasus-type vectoring nozzles at the rear and a gas-driven, downward-directed fan behind the cockpit. (In August 1995 McAir announced that the gas-driven fan was being abandoned and replaced by a vertically mounted lift engine). Exhaust gases from its YF120 engine could be diverted rearwards for forward flight, or into the vectored nozzles. In March 1993 BAe/Rolls-Royce signed up with McDonnell-Douglas as partners on this project. Two other designs emerged from Northrop/Grumman with similarities to the McDonnell-Douglas/BAe entry, and another from Boeing based on a single F119 engine in a delta airframe.

In essence, ASTOVL is a USMC requirement for an AV-8B replacement but its vast development cost could only be met if it would also satisfy the USAF need for an F-16 replacement. The latter aspect led to a concept known as CALF (Common Affordable Lightweight Fighter) in mid-1995, with the object of producing two prototypes, designated X-32, by mid-1996. In the latter part of 1994 the project was also merged with the USAF/USN technology demonstration programme known as JAST (Joint Advanced Strike Technology), the aim of which is to harness technologies to produce a stealthy Joint Strike Fighter (JSF) to replace most of the existing US tactical fighter inventory and AV-8Bs with a single type from 2007 onwards.

This left the British Government with the prospect of a go-it-alone project (which would be too expensive) or accepting the US-driven JAST/ASTOVL/CALF design as a Harrier/Sea Harrier replacement, if it ever reaches production as a 'jump-jet' JSF. Despite opposition from US Defense Secretary John Deutsch, who ruled out British participation in the design stages, agreements were signed in 1995 to involve BAe, and possibly other European manufacturers and Japan, in the basic design decisions. With a potential US requirement for over 3,000 aircraft, and only 100 for British needs, it is inevitable that the bulk of design and manufacturing work will finally have shifted to the United States for the next 'Harrier' generation. Finding a single design to fulfil all the conflicting mission requirements of its potential customers makes the 'commonality' arguments over P.1154 in the 1960s seem trivial, but at the same time it is a reminder of the destructive effects of trying to compromise too far. This time it may well be that economic pressures will force that compromise on air arms which require an aircraft in the ASTOVL class, because there will be no other alternative available to them.

Appendices

APPENDIX A: PEGASUS MAIN VARIANTS

Pegasus 1 (BE.53/2) 9,000lb. August 1957. Two-stage overhung fan (from Olympus). 7-stage HP compressor (from Orpheus). Cannular combustor and single-stage HP turbine (Orpheus). 2-stage LP turbine. Four nozzles (2 hot, 2 cold). First ran September 1959.

Pegasus 2 (BE.53/3) 11,000lb. February 1960. Orpheus 6 HP spool (higher pressure) extra power needed to feed RCS. Later rated at 12,000lb. P.1127.

Pegasus 3 13,500lb. April 1961. 8-stage HP spool and HP turbine with 2 stages, using improved compressor blades. Cleared for 30hr 'life'. Offered 14,000lb thrust short-term for take-off.

Pegasus 5 15,000 lb. June 1962. New 3-stage fan as part of major redesign which included annular combustor, air-cooled HP turbine, variable inlet guide vanes on compressor. Cleared for 50hr 'life'. For Kestrel. Flew April 1964. 15,500lb thrust available for take-off. Designed for 18,000lb but de-rated.

Pegasus 6/Mk 101 19,000lb. March 1965. New titanium fan, new combustor including water-injection, improved fuel system. 2-vane nozzles. Air-cooled 2nd stage HP turbine. Cleared for 300hr 'life'. For Harrier GR.1. In service April 1969.

Pegasus 10/Mk 102 20,500lb. 1969. 20°C increase in TET. 32% increase in water flow. 400hr 'life'. Mk 802 (export). USMC designation F402-RR-400. In service 1971 with Harrier GR.1A and early AV-8A.

Pegasus 11/Mk 103 21,500lb.1969. Increased airflow. Improvements to fuel and water-injection systems. Emergency manual fuel control fitted. 800hr 'life'; hot-end inspection at 300hr. Mk 803 (export). F402-RR-401 and -402 (USMC production), rated at 20,930lb in AV-8A. This marked the end of major thrust increases from Pegasus. It offered 40% more thrust than Pegasus 5.

Pegasus 104 21,500lb. 1976. Fan casing aluminium rather than magnesium/zirconium. Corrosion protection. Increased capacity gearbox. For Sea Harrier. First flight August 1978.

Pegasus 105 21,750lb. 1984. Uprated gearbox. F402-RR-404/404A for YAV-8B, early AV-8B, where de-rated to 21,150lb. Also for Harrier GR.5/7. DECS in -404A version. 400hr 'hot end' inspection TBO.

Pegasus 106 21,450lb. 1985. -406A has DECS. More powerful HP turbine with single-crystal blades. F402-RR-406/406A in later AV-8B; Mk 152-42 in EAV-8B.

Pegasus 11-61E 23,800lb. 1987. Turbine as in Pegasus 106. New front fan (Type 64B). New combustor. First flight June 1989. F402-RR-408 in AV-8B, Harrier II+.

Derivative
BS.100 30,000lb. 1964. New Pegasus variant with PCB in cold nozzles, aimed originally at P.1154 project.

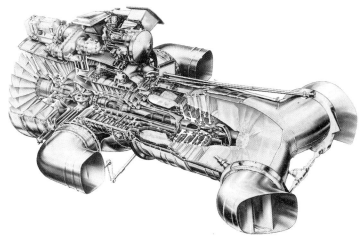

Rolls-Royce Pegasus Mk 104

Rolls-Royce Pegasus 11-21

APPENDIX B: HARRIER FAMILY TREE

One of the Hawker Siddeley Kestrels, at Farnborough in 1966.

An AV-8B Harrier II Plus, with APG-65 radar.

Big Wing Harrier

BAe design for new wing (8.7% bigger than AV-8B wing) Retrofittable to GR Mk 3 and basis for improved a/c Dropped in favour of concurrent AV-8B design

GR Mk 3

50 converted GR Mk 1/1As and 40 new builds
Same as GR Mk 1 except:
– LRMTS in extended nose (some GR Mk 1/1As had LRMTS)
– FF: 9 Jan 76
– GW: 25,200lb
– Engine: Pegasus 11 Mk 103 of 21,500lb thrust

AV-8S

Spanish Navy designation: VA.1 Matador
UK export designation: (first 6) Mk 50, (next 5) Mk 55
Same as AV-8A except:
– Engine: Pegasus 11 Mk 150 of 21,500lb thrust

GR Mk 1A

41 converted GR Mk 1s
Same as GR Mk 1 except:
– Engine: Pegasus 10 Mk 102 of 20,500lb thrust

AV-8A

UK export designation: Mk 50
102 CAS a/c for USMC procured 1969–74
Fitted to US specification, including Sidewinder capability
FF: 20 Nov 70
GW: 25,200lb
Engine: Pegasus 11 F402-RR-402 of 21,500lb thrust

P.1127

1957: Private venture by Hawker Siddeley; 6 aircraft built for UK Ministry of Aviation
FF (tethered) 21 Oct 60; (untethered) 19 Nov 60
Engine: Pegasus 3 of 13,500lb thrust

Kestrel F(GA) Mk 1

1962: 9 ordered for Tripartite (US/UK/Germany) Sqn
1966: 6 equipped US Tri-Service Team (USN/USAF/USA); designated XV-6A (formerly VZ-12)
FF: Mar 64
Engine: Pegasus 5 of 15,500lb thrust

GR Mk 1

World's first V/STOL combat aircraft
78 built for RAF
Max weapon load of 5,000lb
FF: 28 Dec 67
GW: 23,000lb
Engine: Pegasus 6 Mk 101 of 19,000lb thrust

T Mk 2

Trainer version of GR Mk 1
Longer forward fuselage and counterbalance in tail
FF: 3 Oct 69
GW: 24,000lb
Engine: Pegasus 6 Mk 101 of 20,500lb thrust

T Mk 4A

New aircraft built to T Mk 4 standard
None equipped with LRMTS
GW: 26,200lb
Engine: Pegasus 11 Mk 103 of 21,500lb thrust

T Mk 2A

Converted T Mk 2
Same as T Mk 2 except:
– Engine: Pegasus 10 Mk 102 of 20,500lb thrust

T Mk 4

Converted T Mk 2/2A
Same as T Mk 2 except:
– Some equipped with LRMTS
– GW: 26,300lb
– Engine: Pegasus 11 Mk 103 of 21,500lb thrust

T Mk 6

Same as T Mk 2 except:
– Night vision equipment for training GR Mk 7 pilots
None built: superseded by T Mk 10

T Mk 52

2-seat demonstrator built using Company funds (BAe)
First civilian jet V/STOL aircraft in UK
UK civil registration G-VTOL
FF: 16 Sep 71
Engine: Pegasus 11 Mk 103 of 21,500lb thrust

FRS Mk 51

23 FRS Mk 1 Sea Harriers for Indian Navy
Same as FRS Mk 1 except:
– FF: 6 Aug 82
– Engine: Pegasus 11 Mk 151-32 of 21,500lb thrust

Mk 80

Export version of FRS Mk 1
Same as FRS Mk 1 except:
– Blue Fox radar replaced by LRMTS
None built

FRS Mk 1

57 navalised Harriers (Sea Harriers) for RN
New raised cockpit and Blue Fox radar
Air-to-air record of 22–0 in Falklands conflict in 1982
FF: 20 Sep 78
GW: 26,200lb
Engine: Pegasus 11 Mk 104 of 21,500lb thrust

FRS Mk 2

1988: MoD to convert all FRS Mk 1s to FRS Mk 2 standard
16 new a/c ordered
Same as FRS Mk 1 except:
– Wing extended 16in and BVR Blue Vixen radar added
– Engine: Pegasus 11 Mk 106 of 21,500lb thrust

AV-8C

47 AV-8As that underwent Mid-Life Improvement, inc.:
– SLEP increased airframe life from 3,000 to 4,000hr
– CILOP added: LIDs, OBOGS, RWR, chaff/flare dispensers
Engine: Pegasus 11 F402-RR-402 of 21,500lb thrust

TAC(A)/ FAC(A)

Possible USMC desig-nation: OAV-8B
TAV-8B with all avionics and weapon capabilities of the AV-8B Night Attack, plus ability to command and coordinate other combat aircraft
Engine: Pegasus 11-61 F402-RR-408 of 23,800lb thrust

T Mk 10

12 Harrier II trainers for the RAF
Same as TAV-8B except:
– Avionics of GR Mk 7
– FLIR, ARBS, digital moving map, 8 underwing pylons
– Engine: Pegasus 11-21 Mk 105 of 21,750lb thrust

EAV-8B

Spanish Navy desig-nation: VA.2 Matador II
12 Harrier IIs built for the Spanish Navy
Same as AV-8B except:
– Engine: Pegasus 11-21 Mk 152-42 of 21,450lb thrust

TAV-8B

24 trainer version of AV-8B ordered for USMC
Only 2 wing pylons, no attack avionics, larger vertical tail
FF: 21 Oct 86
GW: 31,000lb
Engine: Curr. 1–15: Pegasus 11-21 F402-RR-406A of 21,450lb thrust; curr. 16–24: Pegasus 11-61 F402-RR-408 of 23,800lb thrust

AV-8B Night Attack

66 Night Attack version of AV-8B for USMC
FSD: Curr. 87 (FF 27 Jun 87)
Production: Curr. 167 (FF 8 Jul 89)
Same as AV-8B except:
– FLIR, major cock-pit upgrades, NVG-compatible lighting
– Engine: Pegasus 11-61 F402-RR-408 of 23,800lb thrust

Harrier II Plus

Weather penetration day or night multi-role Harrier II
Same as AV-8B Night Attack except:
– ARBS removed and replaced by APG-65 multi-mode radar
– Associated system upgrades
Engine: Pegasus 11-61 F402-RR-408 of 23,800lb thrust

YAV-8B

2 AV-8As modified to test AV-8B improve-ments, inc.:
– Larger composite wing, LIDs and elliptical inlet design
FF: 11 Sep 78
Engine: Pegasus 11 F402-RR-404 of 21,700lb thrust

AV-8B

USMC Harriers IIs with twice the range-payload of Harrier Is
New larger compo-site wing and forward fuselage
Elevated cockpit with bubble canopy, LIDs and ARBS
FF: 5 Nov 81
GW: 31,000lb
Engine: Pegasus 11-21 F402-RR-406A of 21,500lb thrust

T Mk 4N

3 RN aircraft used for land-based training
1 a/c destroyed in 1985
Engine: Pegasus 11 Mk 103 of 21,500lb thrust

T Mk 8N

Trainer for RN FRS Mk 2
Same as T Mk 4A except:
– FRS Mk 2 cockpit without radar
– Engine: Pegasus 11 Mk 106 of 21,500lb thrust

GR Mk 5

41 Harrier IIs ordered for the RAF
Same as AV-8B except:
– Increased bird-strike resistance, outrigger pylons, Zeus ECM
– FF: 30 Apr 85
– GW: 31,000lb
– Engine: Pegasus 11-21 Mk 105 of 21,750lb thrust

GR Mk 5A

Interim specification of RAF a/c
Curr. 42–60
Same as GR Mk 5 except:
– Minor changes to simplify future conversion to GR Mk 7

GR Mk 7 Nightbird

34 new build, plus MoD will convert all 60 GR Mk 5/5A to GR Mk 7 standard during the 1990s
Same as AV-8B Night Attack except:
– Increased bird-strike resistance, Zeus ECM
– Engine: Pegasus 11-21 Mk 105 of 21,750lb thrust

TAV-8A

UK export desig-nation: Mk 54
8 trainers for USMC
Same as T Mk 4A except:
– Equipped to US specification
– FF: 16 Jul 75
– Engine: Pegasus 11 F402-RR-402 of 21,500lb thrust

T Mk 60

4 trainers for Indian Navy
Same as T Mk 4A except:
– Complete FRS Mk 1 (Mk 51) avionics except radar
– Engine: Pegasus 11 Mk 151 of 21,500lb thrust

TAV-8S

Spanish Navy desig-nation: VA.1 Matador
UK export desig-nation: Mk 58
2 ordered through US Govt for Spain
Same as TAV-8A except:
– Engine: Pegasus 11 Mk 150 of 21,500lb thrust

Abbreviations

ARBS	angle rate bombing system
BVR	beyond visual range
CILOP	Conversion in Lieu of Procurement
ECM	electronic countermeasures
FF	first flight
FRS	Fighter/Reconnaissance/Strike
GR	Close Support/Reconnaissance
GW	gross weight
LID	lift improvement device
LRMTS	Laser Ranger and Marked-Target Seeker
NVG	night vision goggles
OBOGS	on-board oxygen generating system
RWR	radar warning receiver
SLEP	Service Life Extension Program
V/STOL	vertical/short take-off and landing

APPENDIX C: PRODUCTION

P.1127 Prototypes *Built by HSA 1958–60*
XP831   First hover 21/10/60; to RAF Museum, Hendon, 1973.
XP836   First flight (ff) 07/07/61; w/o Yeovilton 14/12/61 when cold nozzle detached in flight.

P.1127 Development Batch *To HMG contract*
XP972   ff 05/04/62; crash-landed Tangmere.
XP976   ff 12/07/62; trials of inflatable intake lips and radio; shell used at Royal Tournament and Edinburgh Tattoo 1968; to 71 MU for spares, fuselage to Wittering.
XP980   ff 05/63; fitted with anhedral tail, new wingtips; overturned and damaged at A&AEE and cannibalized; used, with Harrier wing, by Tarrant-Rushton for radio-controlled barrier trials; to FAA Museum, Yeovilton, 09/03/89.
XP984   ff 10/63; revised, swept wing (Harrier type). Used for HMS *Bulwark* trials 06/66 and RAE/A&AEE trials of HUD, 'nozzle inching' and yaw autostabilization; crash-landed RAE Bedford 31/10/75; n use at RN engineering, Manadon 1993; offered at auction, Sothebys, 1994.

Kestrel FGA Mk 1
XS688   ff 07/03/64; flew at SBAC, 1964; No 8 in Tripartite Evaluation Sqn (TES); became XV-6A BuNo 64-18262; fitted with larger tailplane; displayed at USAF Museum, Wright-Patterson AFB, Ohio.
XS689   ff 28/05/64; No 9 in TES; became BuNo 64-18263, then NASA 512 for VIFF trials.
XS690   ff 05/08/64; No 10 in TES; became BuNo 64-18264, flew USS *Guam* trials; scrapped 1968.
XS691   ff 05/09/64; No 1 in TES; became BuNo 64-18265; USAF trials at Edwards AFFTC; scrapped 1968.
XS692   ff 07/11/64; No 2 in TES; became BuNo 64-18266; Tri-Service Trials; used for spares.
XS693   ff 15/11/64; No 3 in TES; did first VTO at night (01/02/65); allocated BuNo 18267 serial but kept in UK and used at CFE; did Pegasus 6 trials at Filton; crash-landed Filton 21/09/67.
XS694   ff 10/12/64; No 4 in TES; became BuNo 18268; Tri-Service Trials, seriously damaged; scrapped.
XS695   ff 17/02/65; No 5 in TES; at 1966 Hanover Air Show; crash-landed at Boscombe Down; used at RNAS Culdrose 'dummy deck' handling school; moved to Air Engineering School, HMS *Daedalus*, after nosewheel collapse; used to restore RAF Museum P.1127.
XS696   ff 05/03/65; No 6 in TES; ground-looped on take-off at West Raynham with US Army pilot aboard and crashed 01/04/65.

Harrier GR Mk 1 Development Batch (DB)
XV276   ff 31/08/66; did initial handling trials; crashed after flame-out 10/04/73
XV277   ff 09/11/66; used by R-R/BAe Filton to test zero-scarf nozzles, Sea Harrier nose shape, stores clearance trials, RWR tail; stored Filton 1982, then to Yeovilton AMG 1989.
XV278   ff 31/12/66; trials of LRMTS nose (1972) and various stores including Paveway LGB; to Gütersloh for weapons loading trainer.
XV279   ff 04/03/67; used for engine and performance trials Dunsfold and Filton; to Wittering BDRT as 8566M.
XV280   ff 29/04/67; engine trials at Patchway, A&AEE and RAE, including PCB trials 1985; dumped at Foulness 1980, scrapped.
XV281   ff 14/07/67; used for trials at Dunsfold and Filton 1967–70; to RAE for all-weather and ski-jump trials 1977; VIFF trials Filton; sea trials HMS *Eagle*; to A&AEE 1981 and Wittering Fire Section thereafter.

Harrier GR Mk 1 Production
First Batch   XV738–762, XV776–810 (60) and XW630 (replaced XV743, crashed in HSA use with US pilot); ordered 1966; Pegasus Mk 100; 41 converted to GR.1A with Pegasus Mk 102.
Second Batch   XW916–924, XW763–770 (17); Pegasus Mk 101; 61 of above GR.1/1A converted to GR.3 (those not converted were involved in accidents before conversion, including XV739, 743, 749, 750, 777, 780, 791, 794, 796, 797, 798, 799, 802, 803, XW918, 920—total 16).

Harrier GR Mk 3 Production
First Batch   XZ128–139 (12); ordered 1974; Pegasus Mk 102, LRMTS nose, RWR.
Second Batch   XZ963–973, XZ987–999 (24); ordered 1978; Pegasus Mk 103, LRMTS, RWR.
Third Batch   ZD667–670 (4); Falklands War attrition replacements.

Total GR.1/GR.3: 118

Harrier T Mk 2 Development Batch
XW174   ff 24/04/69; used as HSA trials aircraft; crashed at Larkhill 04/06/69.
XW175   ff 14/07/69; used by HSA Dunsfold for handling and development trials, HUD development, ski-jump trials (RAE Bedford) and by Flight Systems; in use DRA Bedford 1995 as VAAC test-bed.

Harrier T Mk 2/2A/4 Production
First Batch   XW262–272 (T.2), XW925–927 (T.2A) (12 aircraft in all); ordered 1967; Pegasus Mk 101.
G-VTOL   ff 19/09/71; HSA-owned demonstration aircraft (had reserve serial ZA250).
Second Batch   XW933–934 (2); T.4; Pegasus Mk 103, LRMTS nose.
Third Batch   XZ145–147, XZ445 (4); T.4; no LRMTS; for Royal Navy.
Fourth Batch   ZB600–603 (4); T.4; Mk 103 Pegasus, LRMTS, RWR.
Fifth Batch   ZD990–993 (4); T.4; Mk 103 Pegasus, LRMTS, RWR.

Total T.2/T.2A/T.4: 28

Harrier GR Mk 5/7

Development Batch	ZD318-319 (DB1, 2). Upgraded to GR.7.
First Batch	GR.5 ZD320–330, ZD345–355, ZD375–380, ZD400–412 (Build Nos P1–41) GR.5A ZD430–438, ZD461–470 (Build Nos P42–60).
Second Batch	GR.7 ZG471–480, ZG500–512, ZG530–533, ZG856–862 (Build Nos P61–94)
Concurrent Batch	Progressive conversions of GR.5/5A to GR.7; see main text.

Total GR.5/GR.7: 96

Harrier T Mk 10

TX001/ZH653	ff 07/04/94; BAe development aircraft.
TX002/ZH654	To A&AEE.
TX003/ZH655	ff 19/08/94; to A&AEE.
TX004/ZH656	Delivered by 26/05/95
TX005/ZH657	Delivered 20/01/95.
TX006/ZH658	Delivered 02/95.
TX007/ZH659	Delivered 17/02/95.
TX008/ZH660	Delivered 06/03/95.
TX009–013/ ZH661–665	In production or under delivery.

Original T.10 batch of 14 reduced to 13 aircraft listed above.
Total T.10 so far: 13

Sea Harrier FRS Mk 1

Pre-Production Batch	XZ438–440 (3); ff 30/12/78–06/06/79
First Production Batch	XZ450–460, XZ491–500 (21); deliveries up to 22/04/82
Second Production Batch	ZA174–195 (10); delivered between 16/11/81 and 24/04/82.
Third Production Batch	ZD578–582, ZD607–615 (14); delivered between 27/03/85 and 20/06/86.
Fourth Production Batch	ZE690–698 (9); delivered between 13/11/87 and 31/09/88

Total FRS.1: 57

Harrier T Mk 4N

ZB604–606	Delivered between 21/09/83 and 05/01/84.

Total T.4N: 3

Sea Harrier FRS Mk 2 (F/A Mk 2)

New-Build Aircraft	NB01–NB013/ZH796–808 (13 to date; serials in the range ZH809–813 also have already been allocated to allow for five additional F/A.2s).

Total FRS.2 to date: 13

Development Batch and conversions	DB1/ZA195 (ff 19/09/88); DB2/ XZ439; DB2/XZ439; P1/XZ497; P2/ ZE695; P3/ZD615; P4/XZ495; P5/ ZE582; P6/ZA176; P7/ZD612; P8/ XZ455; P9/ZE696; P10/XZ457; P11/ ZE697; P12/ZE698; P13/ZD608; P14/ZD579; P15/ZD611; P16/ ZD613; P17/ZD580; P18/ZD459; P19/ZE691; P20/XZ492; P21/ ZE692; P22/ZD578; P23/ZA175; P24/ZE693; P25/ZD607; P26/ ZD614; P27/ZD610; P28/ZE694; P29/ZD698; P30/XZ499; P31/ XZ494; P32/ZD581

Total FRS.2 conversions: 32

Sea Harrier T Mk 8 (conversions)

No1/ZB605	ff 27/07/94; delivered to OEU 10/94, delivered to Yeovilton 03/05/95.
No2/ZD992	

Total T.8 conversions: 2

INDIAN NAVY

Sea Harrier FRS Mk 51

INS serial	B' class /military serial allocation pre-delivery	Delivery date	Fate
IN 601	G-9-478	05/10/84	w/o 5/88
IN 602	G-9-479	12/07/84	
IN 603	G-9-480	13/12/83	
IN 604	G-9-481	13/12/83	
IN 605	G-9-482	13/12/83	
IN 606	G-9-483	12/06/84	
IN 607	ZG941	24/06/90	
IN 608	ZG942	14/12/89	
IN 609	ZG943	10/04/90	
IN 610	ZG944	14/12/89	
IN 611	ZG945	14/12/89	
IN 612	ZH230	10/04/90	w/o 09/12/94
IN 613	ZH231	24/06/90	
IN 614	ZH232	24/06/90	
IN 615	ZH233	23/04/91	
IN 616	ZH234	17/09/91	
IN 617	ZH235	17/09/91	
IN 618	ZH236	23/04/91	
IN 619	ZH237	23/04/91	w/o
IN 620	ZH238	17/09/91	
IN 621	ZH239	17/09/91	
IN 622	ZH240	?	
IN 623	ZH241	07/03/92	

Total FRS Mk 51: 23

Sea Harrier T Mk 60

IN 651	G-9-484	15/03/84	
IN652	G-9-485	18/04/??	w/o 02/08/94
IN 653	ZG984	10/04/90	
IN654	?	?	

Total T Mk 60: 4

AV-8/TAV-8A

First Batch of 12 AV-8A (Mk 50), FY 1971; Pegasus Mk 102, later Mk 103 in ten retrofits

BuNo	Orig. desig.	First flight	Delivery to USMC	Conv. to C?	Known units	Fate
158384	A	20/11/70	19/01/71	Yes	VMA-513, NATC	w/o 05/09/80
158385	A	24/12/70	05/02/71		VMA-513, -231	NASA N716NA
158386	A	03/02/71	15/03/71		VMA-513	w/o 18/06/71
158387	A	16/02/71	12/03/71	Yes	VMA-513, TPS	
158388	A	16/04/71	11/05/71		VMA-513	w/o 27/03/73
158389	A	07/04/71	30/04/71		VMA-513	w/o 07/03/80
158390	A	20/05/71	10/07/71	Yes	VMA-513, -231, -542	w/o 09/12/83
158391	A	07/05/71	28/05/71	Yes	VMA-513, -231, -513	AMARC 7A-034 02/87
158392	A	19/06/71	13/07/71	Yes	VMA-513, -231, -513	AMARC 7A-035 02/87
158393	A	28/10/71	29/11/71	Yes	VMA-513, -231	AMARC 7A-026 10/86
158394	A	23/12/71	31/01/72		YAV-8B 1974	YAV-8B No 1; NASA N704NA
158395	A	18/03/72	21/03/72		YAV-8B 1975	YAV-8B No 2; w/o 15/11/79

Second Batch of 18 AV-8A (Mk 50), FY 1972; Pegasus Mk 103, Ferranti 541 INAS

BuNo	Orig. desig.	First flight	Delivery to USMC	Conv. to C?	Known units	Fate
158694	A	12/04/72	04/05/72		VMA-513	
158695	A	11/05/72	31/05/72		VMA-513, -542	Display Quantico
158696	A	06/06/72	13/07/72	Yes	VMA-513, -231	w/o 28/06/83
158697	A	23/06/72	10/07/72	Yes	VMA-513	AMARC 7A-025 10/86
158698	A	18/07/72	19/09/72	Yes	VMA-513, -231, -513	AMARC 7A-036 02/87; El Centro NAF
158699	A	22/08/72	22/09/72	Yes	VMA-513, -231	w/o 22/09/83
158700	A	08/08/72	06/09/72	Yes	VMA-513, -542, -513	AMARC 7A-027 10/86
158701	A	30/08/72	07/09/72	Yes	VMA-513, -542	AMARC 7A-010 05/86
158702	A	18/09/72	11/10/72		VMA-513, -231, -542	AMARC 7A-014 05/86
158703	A	21/09/72	06/10/72		NATC trials	w/o 26/06/81
158704	A	20/10/72	11/12/72		VMA-542	w/o 03/12/81
158705	A	06/10/72	26/10/72	Yes	VMA-542, -513	AMARC 7A-028 10/88
158706	A	16/10/72	07/12/72	Yes	VMA-513, -542	w/o 28/02/85
158707	A	27/10/72	29/11/72		VMA-542	
158708	A	17/11/72	28/12/72		VMA-542, -231	w/o 29/11/77
158709	A	18/11/72	29/12/72		VMA-542, -513	w/o 10/01/76
158710	A	22/11/72	02/01/73		VMA-513, -231	
158711	A	27/11/72	19/12/72		VMA-542, -231	

Third Batch of 30 AV-8A (Mk 50), FY 1973; Ferranti 541 INAS (except for BuNo 158977)

BuNo	Orig. desig.	First flight	Delivery to USMC	Conv. to C?	Known units	Fate
158948	A	29/12/72	02/02/73		VMA-542	w/o 05/06/74
158949	A	28/12/72	22/01/72	Yes	VMA-542, -513	AMARC 7A-003 10/88
158950	A	17/01/73	20/02/73		VMA-542, -231	w/o 26/06/84
158951	A	13/02/73	13/03/73	Yes	VMA-542, -513	AMARC 7A-029 10/86
158952	A	06/02/73	0 8/03/73		VMA-542	w/o 03/02/78

158953	A	06/03/73	27/03/73		VMA-542	w/o 27/07/77
158954	A	13/03/73	06/04/73	Yes	VMA-542	w/o 03/04/85
158955	A	28/03/73	17/04/73		VMA-542, -513	w/o 01/12/82
158956	A	18/04/73	18/04/73	Yes	VMA-542	w/o 04/03/82
158957	A	18/05/73	09/07/73		VMA-542	w/o 27/08/76
158958	A	11/05/73	28/06/73		VMA-542, -513	w/o 25/01/81
158959	A	25/05/73	05/07/73	Yes	VMA-542, -513	AMARC 7A-002 10/85
158960	A	13/06/73	17/07/73		VMA-542	
158961	A	02/07/73	27/07/73		VMA-542, -513	w/o 06/10/78
158962	A	03/07/73	31/07/73	Yes	VMA-542, -231	w/o 24/09/82
158963	A	24/07/73	30/08/73		VMA-542, -513	
158964	A	27/07/73	07/09/73	Yes	VMA-542	AMARC 7A-005 11/85
158965	A	07/08/73	30/08/73		VMA-513	
158966	A	23/08/73	21/09/73		VMA-513, -231	AMARC 7A-001 10/85
158967	A	18/09/73	04/10/73		VMA-542	w/o 11/02/77
158968	A	21/09/73	02/11/73		VMA-513	w/o 26/01/82
158969	A	26/09/73	26/10/73	Yes	VMA-513, -231, -513	AMARC 7A-030 10/86
158970	A	01/11/73	30/11/73		VMA-513	w/o 06/09/77
158971	A	22/10/73	09/11/73		VMA-513	AMARC 7A-008 10/88
158972	A	07/11/73	28/11/73	Yes	VMA-513, -542	AMARC 7A-011 05/86
158973	A	16/11/73	07/12/73	Yes	VMA-513, -542	AMARC 7A-012 05/86
158974	A	21/11/73	20/12/73		VMA-513	w/o 30/08/76
158975	A	11/12/73	22/01/74	Yes	VMA-513, -231, -513	AMARC 7A-038 02/87 Pima Air Museum
158976	A	07/12/73	04/01/74		VMA-513	Display Cherry Point
158977	A	07/12/73	07/02/74	Yes	Baseline trial NATC, VMA-542	AMARC 7A-013 05/86

Fourth Batch of 30 AV-8A (Mk 50), FY 1974; Pegasus Mk 103; all Baseline systems equipped

159230	A	02/01/74	25/01/74		VMA-513	w/o 06/12/76
159231	A	19/12/73	25/01/74	Yes	VMA-513, -231	w/o 25/04/85
159232	A	11/01/74	13/02/74	Yes	VMA-513, -542	AMARC 7A-006 03/86; USS *Intrepid* museum
159233	A	20/03/74	05/04/74		VMA-231	FAA Museum, Yeovilton
159234	A	20/03/74	05/06/74			w/o 20/04/81
159235	A	21/03/74	21/06/74		VMA-231	w/o 13/12/75
159236	A	22/03/74	19/06/74		VMA-231	w/o 04/07/75
159237	A	03/04/74	10/07/74		VMA-231 w	w/o 16/06/76
159238	A	03/04/74	26/06/74	Yes	VMA-231, -513	AMARC 7A-024 10/86
159239	A	11/04/74	30/07/74		VMA-231, -542	AMARC 7A-016 05/86
159240	A	26/04/74	23/07/74	Yes	VMA-231, -513	AMARC 7A-033 02/87
159241	A	03/05/74	29/08/74	Yes	VMA-231, -513	AMARC 7A-009 03/86; Pima Air Museum
159242	A	24/05/74	15/08/74		VMA-231	w/o 01/05/80
159243	A	19/06/74	13/09/74	Yes	VMA-231, -542, -513	AMARC 7A-031 10/86
159244	A	26/06/74	20/09/74		VMA-231	w/o 04/07/75
159245	A	16/07/74	07/08/74		VMA-231, -542	w/o 09/10/74
159246	A				VMA-231	w/o 18/03/81
159247	A	25/07/74	05/09/74		VMA-231	
159248	A	21/08/74	27/09/74		VMA-231	
159249	A	10/09/74	04/10/74		VMA-231	
159250	A	23/09/74	22/10/74		VMA-231	w/o 12/07/77
159251	A	08/10/74	06/11/74		VMA-231, -513	w/o 13/08/80
159252	A	25/10/74	18/11/74		VMA-231, VMAT-203, VMA-542	AMARC 7A-022 05/86
159253	A	08/11/74	18/12/74	Yes	VMA-513, -231	w/o 02/02/83
159254	A	27/11/74	23/12/74	Yes	VMA-542	
159255	A	13/12/74	13/01/75		VMA-231, NATC, VMA-542	AMARC 7A-023 05/86
159256	A	04/02/74	06/01/75		VMAT-203	w/o 13/03/80
159257	A	19/12/74	20/01/75	Yes	VMAT-203, VMA-542, -513	AMARC 7A-032 10/86
159258	A	07/01/75	30/06/76	Yes	VMA-542	AMARC 7A-004 11/85
159259	A	24/01/75	03/03/75			w/o 27/11/77

Fifth Batch of 12 AV-8A (Mk 50), FY 1975; Pegasus Mk 103; Baseline systems equipped

159366 VMA-542	A	25/03/75	20/06/75		VMAT-203,	AMARC 7A-018 05/86
159367	A	24/05/75	27/06/75		VMAT-203, VMA-542	AMARC 7A-019 05/86
159368	A	13/05/75	30/06/75		VMAT-203	w/o 19/01/81
159369	A	24/06/75	25/07/75			w/o 11/11/79
159370	A	05/08/75	11/09/75	Yes	VMAT-203, VMA-542, -513	AMARC 7A-037 02/87
159371	A	20/08/75	17/10/75		VMAT-203, VMA-542	AMARC 7A-008 03/86
159372	A	12/09/75	28/10/75		VMAT-203	w/o 06/04/77
159373	A	02/07/76	04/08/76		VMAT-203, VMA-542	AMARC 7A-015 05/86
159374	A	24/08/76	08/10/76		VMAT-203, VMA-542	AMARC 7A-020 05/86
159375	A	06/11/75	05/01/76		VMAT-203, VMA-542	AMARC 7A-017 05/86
159376	A	11/75	01/76		VMAT-203, VMA-542	AMARC 7A-021 05/86
159377	A	12/12/75	29/01/76		VMAT-203	w/o 19/03/77

8 TAV-8A (Mk 54)

159378	TA	16/07/75	01/10/75	VMAT-203	AMARC 7A-043 11/87
159379	TA	17/10/75	16/01/76	VMAT-203	AMARC 7A-042 11/87
159380	TA	12/12/75	06/02/76	VMAT-203	w/o 12/08/87
159381	TA	19/01/76	12/04/76	VMAT-203	w/o 27/04/83
159382	TA	10/08/76	16/09/76	VMAT-203	AMARC 7A-040 11/87
159383	TA	04/06/76	28/06/76	VMAT-203	AMARC 7A-039 11/87
159384	TA	1976	1976	VMAT-203	w/o 01/08/80
159385	TA	07/10/76		VMAT-203	AMARC 7A-041 11/87

6 AV-8S Matador (Harrier Mk 55) on USN contract, ordered 1973

BuNo	Orig. desig.	First flight	Delivery to USMC	Units	Code	Fate
159557	S	18/09/75	07/11/75	Esc 008	008-1	w/o 28/05/80
159558	S	14/04/76	10/05/76	Esc 008	008-2	w/o 11/06/76
159559	S	11/06/76	07/07/76	Esc 008	008-3	
159560	S	18/09/75	07/11/75	Esc 008	008-4	
159561	S	24/10/75	12/12/75	Esc 008	008-5	w/o 11/06/76
159562	S	03/12/75	22/01/76	Esc 008	008-6	

5 AV-8S Matador (Harrier Mk 55) ordered via USN in 1977

161174	S			Esc 008	008-9	
161175	S			Esc 008	01-810	w/o 13/05/94
161176	S			Esc 008	008-11	
161177	S			Esc 008	008-12	
161178	S			Esc 008	008-13	

2 TAV-8S 2 (Mk 58) ordered via USN 1973

159563	TA-S	21/01/76	25/02/76	Esc 008	008-7
159564	TA-S	28/05/76	05/07/76	Esc 008	008-8

AV-8B Block Numbers

Block	AV-8A BuNos	TAV-8B BuNos	EAV-8S BuNos
1	161396–161573		
2	161574–161579		
3	161580–161584		
4	162068–162076		
5	162077–162088		
6	162721–162734		
7	162735–162746	162747	
8	162942–162964		
9	162965–162973	162963, 162971	163010–163021
10	163176–163195	163180, 163186, 163191	
11	163197–163519	163196, 163202, 163207	
12	163659–163673	163856–163857	
13	163674–163855	163858–163861	
14	163862–163872		
15	163873–164116		
16	164117–164122	164113–164113, 164122	
17	164123–164135	164138	
18	164139–164547	164540–164542	
19	164548–164571		
21	165001–165006		

USMC Procurement

FY	1985 Plan	1986 Plan	1989 Plan	Actual
1979	4 FSD a/c			
1982	12 Pilot production a/c			
1983	21			21
1984	27			27
1985	32			32
1986	40	46		32
1987	47	42		14
1988	48	42		32
1989	60	42	24	32
1990		42	24	42
1991		42	24	32
1992			32	6

Actual total: 286 excluding remanufactured AV-8B+

Serial allocations

USMC

FY	Total	AV-8B BuNos	TAV-8B BuNos
1979	4	161396–161399	
1982	12	161573–161584	
1983	21	162068–162088	
1984	27	162721–162746 (26)	162747 (1)

1985	32	162942–162962 (21)	162963 (1)
		162964–162970 (7)	162971 (1)
		162972–162973 (2)	
1986	32	163176–163179 (4)	163180 (1)
		163181–163185 (5)	163186 (1)
		163187–163190 (4)	163191 (1)
		163192–163195 (4)	163196 (1)
		163197–163201 (5)	163202 (1)
		163203–163206 (4)	163207 (1)
1987	14	163419–163426 (8)	
		163514–163519 (6)	
1988	32	163659–163690 (32)	
1989	32*	163852–163855 (4)	163856–163861 (6)
		163862–163883 (22)	
1990	42	164113–164119 (7)	164120–164122 (3)
		164123–164154 (32)	
1991	32	164540–164571 (32)	164563–5 to Italian order
1992	6	165001–165006 (6)	

USMC total = 286 TA/AV-8B
*163853 and up = AV-8B (NA)

Cancelled USMC batches

1983	3	162089–162091
1984	5	162748–162752
1987	47	163348–163394

Remanufactured AV-8B+

165305–165312 (8)*

*Includes 165305 (ex 162728), 165306 (ex161581) and 165307 (ex 161583)

Spanish *Arma Aérea de la Armada*

Code	EAV–8B BuNos	
01-901	163010	w/o 18/12/89
01-902	163011	
01-903	163012	
01-904	163013	
01-905	163014	
01-906	163015	
01-907	163016	
01-908	163017	w/o 26/11/93
01-909	163018	

01-910   163019
01-911   163020
01-912   163021

EAV–8B+ BuNos
165028–165035 (8)

TAV-8B BuNo
165036 (1)

Spanish total : 21 TA/EAV-8B

Italian *Aviazione per la Marina*

AV-8B+ BuNos   *TAV-8B BuNos*
164563–164565 (3)   164136–164137 (2)
165007–165028 (22)

Italian total: 27 TA/AV-8B+

An AV-8S of Spain's *Esc 008* formates with an 899 NAS Sea Harrier FRS.1 over the coast of southern England. (BAe)

APPENDIX D: ATTRITION

Date	Type	Serial	Unit	Circumstances
P.1127 and RAF Harrier				
14/12/61	P.1127	XP836	2nd p'type	Cold nozzle detached on approach to Yeovilton; Bill Bedford ejected.
01/04/65	Kestrel	XS696	TES	Crashed at West Raynham when US Army pilot with 10hr on jets forgot to remove parking brake; ground-looped on take-off and caught fire, pilot unhurt; aircraft scrapped.
	Kestrel	XS694	USA	As BuNo 64-18268/NASA 520, ground-looped, damaged and scrapped in USA (was designated XV-6A and assigned to Tri-Service Test organisation).
21/09/67	Kestrel	XS693	HSA	Crashed *en route* Filton to Boscombe Down with engine locked in surge; Sqn Ldr Hugh Rigg escaped unhurt.
27/01/69	GR.1	XV743	HSA	Crashed at Cranleigh, nr Dunsfold; USMC pilot Maj. Charles Rosberg lost control in transition while taking off into sun, probably lost sight of yaw vane, entered intake stall and uncontrollable roll; first fatality in programme.
04/06/69	T.2	XW174	HSA	Crashed nr Larkhill, Wilts., during delivery flight to A&AEE after fuel system fault; test pilot Duncan Simpson ejected and injured.
11/07/70	T.2	XW264	HSA	Forced landing using RAT at Boscombe Down after engine failure following fuel system fault; test pilot Barry Tonkinson unhurt but aircraft burnt out.
06/10/70	GR.1	XV796	No 1 Sqn	Flamed out after fuel pump failed; Neil Wharton ejected; crashed nr Ouston, Co Durham, on finals; first RAF loss.
23/04/71	GR.1	XV798	No 20 Sqn	Loss of control on approach to vertical landing nr Wildenrath and sideslip leading to roll and crash; pilot ejected through trees; fuselage rebuilt for R-R PCB trials in 'flying' rig at Shoeburyness, then to R-R Heritage Trust.
03/08/71	GR.1	XV803	No 1 Sqn	Crashed following nozzle control failure on take-off; USAF pilot Capt. Louis Distelzweig killed attempting landing (failed to eject, possibly because seat safety pins still in place).
12/01/72	GR.1	XW918	No 3 Sqn	Hit farm building at Tuschenbroich, nr Wildenrath, when pilot failed to recover from dive during demonstration; pilot killed.
21/03/72	GR.1	XV802	No 20 Sqn	Flew into trees nr Stadtoldendorf, Hanover; pilot killed.
26/04/72	GR.1	XV749	No 1 Sqn	Pilot ejected after birdstrike nr Theddlethorpe, the Wash.
01/05/72	GR.1	XV777	No 1 Sqn	Pilot ejected after loss of control during decelerating transition to vertical landing at Wittering.
04/05/72	GR.1	XV794	No IV Sqn	Pilot ejected after birdstrike; aircraft flew on for 40min before running out of fuel and crashing nr Hutten, W. Germany.
20/06/72	GR.1A	XW920	No 3 Sqn	Pilot ejected after low-pressure governor shaft in engine failed; wreck dumped at Decimomannu.
27/06/72	GR.1A	XV780	No IV Sqn	Pilot ejected after birdstrike nr Wesel, Germany.
12/09/72	GR.1	XV799	No 233 OCU	Flew into the ground nr Kyle of Lochalsh; pilot Gp Capt. Jeremy Hall killed.
10/04/73	GR.1	XV276	HSA	Flamed out and crashed on farm at Cranleigh nr Dunsfold; Swiss pilot closed HP cock instead of moving nozzle lever, cutting off fuel to engine, ejected; first pre-production GR.1.
09/07/73	GR.3	XV791	No 20 Sqn	Multiple birdstrikes on take-off at Wildenrath; pilot ejected; aircraft burnt out.
30/07/73	GR.1A	XV805	No 20 Sqn	Birdstrike over Coesfeld, W. Germany, caused engine to explode; pilot, Maj. Gibson USMC, ejected at 500ft.
06/09/73	GR.3	XV750	No 20 Sqn	Crashed at Roermond, Netherlands, after engine failure; pilot ejected with minor injuries.
24/09/73	GR.1A	XV739	No 1 Sqn	While rehearsing at air show at Episkopi aircraft went out of control due to excessive pitch-down in a vertical climb; pilot ejected but sustained broken leg.
24/01/74	GR.3	XV797	No IV Sqn	During ACM over Vreedepeel, Netherlands, fuel pump failed and also flap drive mechanism; pilot ejected in steep dive but killed due to parachute harness failure.
26/03/74	GR.3	XV785	No IV Sqn	Pilot lost control during landing at Wildenrath.
16/05/74	GR.3	XV800	No IV Sqn	Flamed-out after birdstrike at 50ft on take-off at Wildenrath; pilot ejected; aircraft beyond repair.
09/04/75	GR.3	XV776	No 1 Sqn	Main engine bearing failure at 33,000ft caused flame-out; pilot ejected, aircraft crashed at Church Stretton.
31/10/75	P.1127	XP984	RAE	Badly damaged in crash at Bedford and SOC; offered for sale at Sothebys late 1994 but withdrawn.
01/12/75	GR.3	XV788	No 1 Sqn	Struck eagle while on detachment to Belize; engine surged and flamed-out at 450kt and 1,000ft; Flt Lt Scott ejected.
19/01/76	GR.3	XV745	No 233 OCU	Crashed nr Nantwich, Chesire, after mid-air collision with XV754; pilot killed.

19/01/76	GR.3	XV754	No 1 Sqn	Crashed after mid-air collision with XV745; pilot killed.
12/03/76	GR.3	XV746	No 233 OCU	Hit mountain 125 miles from Tromsø, Norway, during NATO exercise 'Atlas Express'; No 1 Sqn pilot killed.
06/07/76	GR.3	XW770	No 3 Sqn	Engine flamed-out at 600 ft nr Borken, W. Germany; pilot ejected.
15/12/78	GR.3	XV801	No 3 Sqn	Pilot ejected after losing control at Ennigerloh, nr Gütersloh, but killed.
12/06/79	GR.3	XV781	No 3 Sqn	Pilot ejected after engine fire on approach to short landing at Gütersloh.
18/07/79	GR.3	XZ137	No IV Sqn	Struck houses nr Wissimar, W. Germany; US exchange pilot killed.
21/09/79	GR.3	XV757	No 1 Sqn	Crashed on to houses at Ramnoth Rd, Wisbech, Cambs., killing three, injuring seven and demolishing three houses; touched wingtips with XZ128 during close formation; pilot Wg Cdr R. Duckett (ex *Red Arrows*) ejected.
21/09/79	GR.3	XZ128	No 1 Sqn	Flt Lt C. Gowers ejected after mid-air contact with XV757 and consequent loss of control.
04/10/79	GR.3	XW766	No 3 Sqn	Lost engine power and crashed into wood nr Ravensburg, W. Germany; pilot ejected.
08/11/79	GR.3	XV756	No 1 Sqn	Hit by ricochet from own rocket while performing attack on Holbeach range, Lincs.; pilot ejected, aircraft crashed on beach.
12/03/80	GR.3	XW765	No 3 Sqn	Pilot ejected after birdstrike nr Lampeter, Dyfed, during low-level training to prepare for 'Maple Flag' visit.
14/10/80	GR.3	XV792	No 3 Sqn	Gütersloh-based aircraft on approach, during transition; pilot lost control, aircraft entered uncontrollable roll and he ejected outside the seat's effective envelope and was killed (aircraft probably experienced intake stall).
28/10/80	GR.3	XV761	No IV Sqn	On DACT with 601 TCW OV-10A nr Bitburg, suffered loss of power after unidentified piece of metal passed through HP compressor, shearing a blade; pilot ejected at 300ft after two re-light attempts; aircraft crashed in wood.
26/05/81	GR.3	XW923	No 1417 Flt	Pilot lost control during STO, Belize Airport, and ejected; forward fuselage rebuilt as 8724M for RAF recruitment.
14/07/81	GR.3	XV807	No 1417 Flt	Crashed in Cayo area of Belize after tailplane link disconnected; pilot killed.
25/08/81	GR.3	XZ139	No 3 Sqn	Pilot ejected 24 miles west of Alhorn, W. Germany, after tailplane link failure.
12/02/82	GR.3	XZ973	No 233 OCU	Hit ground in Berwyn Hills, N. Wales, during low-level navigation exercise in low cloud; USAF exchange pilot killed.
21/05/82	GR.3	XZ972	No 1 Sqn	Hit by Argentine guns nr Port Howard, Falkland Islands, during solo armed recce; Flt Lt Glover ejected.
27/05/82	GR.3	XZ988	No 1 Sqn	Hit by Argentine guns while attacking Goose Green airfield, Falkland Islands; Sqn Ldr R. D. Iveson ejected.
30/05/82	GR.3	XZ963	No 1 Sqn	Damaged by Argentine small-arms fire nr Stanley Airport and ran out of fuel on return to HMS *Hermes* due to fuel leaks; Sqn Ldr J. J. Pook ejected 30 miles from *Hermes*.
08/06/82	GR.3	XZ989	No 1 Sqn	Made heavy landing on Port San Carlos FOB ('Sid's Strip') after loss of power during vertical landing; pilot Wg Cdr P. Squire uninjured; Aircraft used for spares, then moved to Gütersloh rescue section as 8849M.
29/06/82	T.4	XW272	No IV Sqn	On take-off from FOB on Bergen Hohne range, W. Germany, pilot distracted by taxying on boggy ground and forgot to extend flaps; aircraft failed to gain height and flew into trees (grass debris on take-off prevented onlookers from seeing flaps); pilot, CO of No IV Sqn, killed in crash; aircraft became 8783M.
06/11/82	GR.3	XW767	No 1453 Flt	Sqn Ldr P. Squire ejected off Cape Pembroke, Falkland Islands, after engine failure.
23/02/83	GR.3	XV795	No 3 Sqn	Flt Lt D. Oakley ejected nr village of Eye nr Peterborough after mid-air collision with XW926 in formation during ACM.
23/02/83	T.4	XW926	No 233 OCU	Crashed nr Peterborough after mid-air collision with XV795; Flt Lt John Leeming (ex 800 NAS during Operation 'Corporate') and Fg Off. D Haigh killed.
22/03/83	GR.3	XV787	No 1453 Flt	Engine failure caused by detached rivet entering engine and damaging three HP blades; crashed into Port William Sound, Falkland Islands, on approach to Stanley; pilot ejected but sustained major spinal injury.
03/05/83	GR.3	XZ134	No 3 Sqn	Engine failure after weld failure in outer casing of combustion chamber, blowing off upper engine bay doors, during formation attack sortie from FOB while aircraft in transition to hover; pilot ejected but injured.
28/10/83	GR.3	XV742	No 233 OCU	Pilot probably incapacitated by ricochet from 30mm cannon shell while strafing Holbeach range; aircraft crashed in salt marshes before ejection cycle completed.
19/11/83	GR.3	XV762	No 1453 Flt	Hit high ground at Lafonia, nr Goose Green, Falkland Islands, during ACT; pilot killed.

03/06/84	GR.3	XZ135	No IV Sqn	Water pump failed, severing fuel and hydraulic lines while aircraft displaying at Aschaffenburg, W. Germany; fire broke out nr main undercarriage; pilot landed aircraft and ejected but seat killed spectator in crowd; cockpit section became 8848M at RAF Abingdon.
29/11/84	GR.3	XZ992	No 1453 Flt	Hit southern giant petrel during simulated attack on Stanley airfield at 180kt and 200ft; canopy 'obscured by red matter'; pilot ejected but hit water before chute fully deployed, rescued by Gemini dinghy but almost drowned. (Auto-inflation of safety equipment introduced.)
12/02/85	T.4	XW933	No 3 Sqn	Mid-air collision over Bad Rothenfelde, W. Germany, with MFG-2 F-104G whose pilot was map-reading and did not see Harrier against dark background; rear-seater in T.4 killed, front-seater injured, F-104 pilot ejected.
20/11/85	GR.3	XW922	No 233 OCU	Rolled over on landing at Wittering and seriously damaged; became 8885M at MoD/ROF Enfield.
02/04/86	GR.3	XV784	No 233 OCU	Badly damaged (Cat-5) at Wittering; became 8909M for BDR, then moved to Abingdon and Boscombe Down.
17/06/86	GR.3	XW916	No IV Sqn	Pilot ejected after major electrical failure on short finals to Yeovilton; aircraft crashed just short of runway; wreckage removed by road 22/06/86.
28/06/86	GR.3	XW769	No IV Sqn	Pilot lost control at end of flying display at Chèvres, Belgium, at low level and ejected but was killed.
22/10/87	GR.5	ZD325	BAe	Crashed into sea 250nm SW of Ireland after inadvertent bale-out of pilot, Taylor Scott, when parachute rocket ejected pilot through canopy without seat and killed him. (See text.)
02/11/87	GR.3	XV790	No 3 Sqn	Flt Lt David Sunderland killed after mid-air collision with XZ136 due to lack of deconfliction over Otterburn during Exercise 'Mallet Blow 87/3' at low level.
02/11/87	GR.3	XZ136	No 3 Sqn	USMC exchange pilot (Number Two in the Flight) killed in mid-air with XV790.
11/11/87	GR.3	XV747	No 233 OCU	Crashed through perimeter fence on landing at Wittering, ending up in lane near Easton Lodge Farm; pilot ejected; aircraft to Coltishall BDRF.
20/05/88	GR.3	XV809	No 3 Sqn	Flt Lt Paul Adams killed when aircraft hit house on take-off from Gütersloh in low cloud/poor visibility.
18/08/88	GR.3	XW921	No 3 Sqn	Pilot ejected after loss of power on approach to Gütersloh.
20/06/89	T.4A	XW925	No IV Sqn	On delivery to Gütersloh from St Athan, suffered loss of thrust on approach due to empty water tank and pitched nose-down in hover; Army officer in rear seat ejected, RAF pilot ejected but hit ground in seat and was killed; aircraft somersaulted into Ems Canal.
17/10/90	GR.5	ZD355	No 1 Sqn	Blade failure in 2nd stage LP compressor caused engine flame-out; pilot attempted four re-lights before ejection shortly after take-off from Aalberg, Denmark; aircraft crashed near Karup.
29/05/91	GR.7	ZG743	No IV Sqn	Crashed six miles from Gütersloh after fire in main wiring loom and generator failure; pilot ejected. (See text.)
15/09/91	T.4A	XZ147	No 233 OCU	Crashed near Driffield after gull hit canopy, incapacitating pilot who ejected at 125ft; female Cambridge UAS back-seater ejected at 90ft, landed in burning wreck but rescued by pilot (first woman to eject from RAF aircraft).
30/09/91	GR.5	ZD412	No 3 Sqn	Left runway during landing at Gütersloh; penetrated barrier and perimeter fence, went into Ems Canal; pilot ejected.
14/05/92	GR.3	XZ990	No 233 OCU	Engine fire on approach due to FOD-damaged compressor blade being ingested by engine; pilot made heavy landing and fire spread; pilot rescued unconscious from cockpit with broken legs.
07/08/92	GR.5	ZD350	No 1 Sqn	Stator vane failed due to metal fatigue and passed through engine, causing surge when aircraft was at 50ft AGL on take-off; pilot ejected at 25ft and received cuts and bruises. (Second stage stators subsequently reinforced.)
28/06/93	GR.7	ZD430	No 3 Sqn	Pilot ejected after birdstrike on right wing caused fuel leak and fire; aircraft crashed nr Heckington, Lincs., *en route* from Leeming to Laarbruch.
23/11/93	GR.7	ZD432	No IV Sqn	Engine surged while pilot refuelling from VC-10 during Operation 'Warden', 80 miles S of Iraq–Turkish border; pilot immediately shut off HP fuel cock, causing engine to shut down. ejected at 1,500ft nr Dahuk.
14/01/94	GR.7	ZD349	No 20(R)	USMC pilot failed to hear low-altitude warning signal during low-level four-ship ACM sortie, flew too low as he approached another Harrier for simulated AIM-9 launch and hit ground nr Aston Somerville, Worcs., in 3-degree dive; pilot killed.
01/06/95	GR.7	ZG475	SAOEU	Wg Cdr Nicholas Slater killed while on equipment evaluation trial from Boscombe Down over Wigtown Bay; flew into sea. ('Slats' Slater was CO of SAOEU.)

19/02/96	GR.7	ZG476	No 1 Sqn	Crashed at Wansford, nr Wittering, on return from Cyprus; pilot ejected.

Sea Harrier

01/12/80	FRS.1	XZ454	800 NAS	Pilot (Lt-Cdr Mike Blissett) performing slow pass for BBC TV crew when port outrigger hit ski-jump on HMS *Invincible* and pilot lost control and ejected; wreck used by RN divers off Lizard for practice.
04/05/82	FRS.1	XZ450	800 NAS	Shot down by Argentine guns while attacking Goose Green airfield, Falkland Islands; Lt Nick Taylor killed. (Aircraft was 'on loan' from MoD PE.)
06/05/82	FRS.1	XZ452	801 NAS	Lost in mid-air collision with XZ453, 53°S 57°W in fog during sea-search off Falklands; Lt-Cdr Eyton-Jones killed.
06/05/82	FRS.1	XZ453	801 NAS	Lost in mid-air collision with XZ452; Lt Alan Curtis killed.
17/05/82	FRS.1	XZ438	809 NAS	Failed to become airborne from ski-jump at RNAS Yeovilton while testing 330gal ferry tank fit; Lt-Cdr R Poole ejected; aircraft SOC 12/04/83 (was under MoD PE jurisdiction at the time).
23/05/82	FRS.1	ZA192	800 NAS	Hit sea and exploded shortly after take-off from HMS *Hermes* for attack on Stanley Airport; Lt-Cdr Gordon Batt killed.
29/05/82	FRS.1	ZA174	801 NAS	Slid off HMS *Invincible* while taxying due to rough sea, wind and ship turning sharply; Lt-Cdr Mike Broadwater ejected.
01/06/82	FRS.1	XZ456	801 NAS	Hit by Argentine Roland missile while on armed recce off Port Stanley; Flt Lt Ian Mortimer ejected.
21/01/83	FRS.1	ZA177	899 NAS	Crashed nr Cattistock, Dorset, after failing to recover from inverted spin; Lt Fox ejected with spinal injury.
15/06/83	FRS.1	XZ500	801 NAS	Aircraft entered uncontrollable spin over Bay of Biscay during test flight from HMS *Illustrious*; pilot (Lt Hargreaves) ejected at 9,000ft and was picked up by 820 NAS Sea King after 26min in sea.
20/10/83	FRS.1	ZA194	899 NAS	USMC exchange pilot (Maj. O'Hara) ejected nr Dorchester after aircraft exhibited control restriction; aircraft crashed at West Knighton.
16/03/84	FRS.1	XZ496	800 NAS	Engine fire on approach to HMS *Illustrious* off Norway caused loss of power; pilot ejected, aircraft sank in 6,000ft of water.
01/12/84	FRS.1	XZ458	800 NAS	Birdstrike by seagull at low level during Exercise 'High Tide' with Dutch Marines in Loch Linnhe; pilot (Lt Collier) ejected; aircraft crashed on Kilmonivaig Farm, Gairlochy, and was later dumped at Lee-on-Solent.
07/02/85	T.4N	ZB606	899 NAS	Crashed on A37 road at Sticklebridge Farm, Charlton Adam, Somerset, after loss of control; both crew killed.
16/04/86	FRS.1	XZ491	801 NAS	Pilot (Lt-Cdr Sinclair) ejected after aircraft ran out of fuel during sortie from HMS *Ark Royal*; crashed near Benbecula; pilot rescued by helicopter.
15/10/87	FRS.1	ZA190	801 NAS	Birdstrike caused engine fire during sortie from HMS *Ark Royal* in Irish Sea; pilot ejected, picked up 13min later.
04/10/89	FRS.1	ZA191	801 NAS	Hit mast of HMS *Ark Royal* during low-level exercise over Lyme Bay; Lt Paul Simmonds attempted to return to Yeovilton but damage to wing meant aircraft had to be dived into Lyme Bay and he ejected; wreck recovered by HMS *Cattistock* and HMS *Challenger*.
30/11/89	FRS.1	XZ451	801 NAS	Forward RCS vale seal failed due to fatigue, detached and jammed controls during ACT off Sardinia; pilot elected not to land, attempted to free control restriction but all controls jammed and aircraft entered 10-degree dive at 400kt; Lt Michael Auckland ejected and was injured.
28/02/90	FRS.1	XZ495	899 NAS	Undershot on landing at Yeovilton.
08/05/90	FRS.1	XZ460	800 NAS	Crashed into sea during Exercise 'Dragon Hammer' off Sardinia; Lt Steve Holmes killed. ('Missing man' formation flown over HMS *Invincible* by F-14 Tomcats from USS *Eisenhower*.)
09/05/90	T.4A	XZ445	899 NAS	During night-flying exercise, main undercarriage failed to extend and aircraft settled on nose gear only, suffering major damage; used for spares but later rebuilt and returned to 899 NAS.
10/05/91	FRS.1	ZD609	801 NAS	Aircraft was on three-ship recce sortie near Chepstow when pilot felt control restriction at 300ft due to FOD in control system; pilot ejected at 100ft, breaking ankles in airstream. (RN flying boots redesigned.)
28/05/92	FRS.1	ZA193	800 NAS	Control malfunction while aircraft was hovering beside HMS *Invincible* off Cyprus caused nose to pitch down; pilot (Lt Wilson) ejected.
05/01/94	FRS.2	XZ495	SHOEU	FOD damage to compressor blades caused engine failure while aircraft was doing weapons trials on Lundy range; pilot ejected and picked up by Wessex XR518 after 7min in sea.

16/04/94	FRS.1	XZ498	801 NAS	Shot down by Bosnian Serb SA-7 missile W of Gorazde during air strike in support of UNPROFOR; pilot ejected, rescued by SAS and French Puma helicopter.
15/12/94	FRS.1	XZ493	800 NAS	Suffered loss of power on return to HMS *Invincible*; pilot ejected over Adriatic, rescued by helicopter from *Príncipe de Asturias*; wreck returned to accident investigation unit at Yeovilton May 1995.
20/10/95	F/A.2	XZ457	899 NAS	Aircraft positioned for take-off on Runway 22, Yeovilton, at 1845 when several internal explosions occurred as throttle was advanced; Lt-Cdr Bayliss (senior pilot of 899NAS) ejected; aircraft taken to AIU Hangar for inspection (thought to be Cat-5).
14/02/96	F/A.2	XZ455	801 NAS	Crashed into Adriatic on approach to HMS *Illustrious* after mission over Bosnia.
23/02/96	T.4	XZ445	899 NAS	Hit Blackdown Hills nr Church Stanton at flat angle; both crew members killed.

USMC Harrier

18/06/71	AV-8A	158386	VMA-513	Failed to recover from dive over Chesapeake Bay; pilot Mike Ripley killed.
27/03/73	AV-8A	158388	VMA-51	Birdstrike, crashed at NAS Beaufort; pilot ejected.
05/06/74	AV-8A	158948	VMA-542	Crashed on landing; pilot ejected but killed.
09/10/74	AV08A	159245	VMA-231	Crashed and burned out at Cherry Point.
13/02/75	AV-8A	159235	VMA-231	Crashed during vertical landing at Cherry Point; pilot killed.
04/07/75	AV-8A	159236	VMA-231	Hit ground near NAS Beaufort; pilot killed.
04/07/75	AV-8A	159244	VMA-231	Engine failed at low-level; pilot ejected.
10/01/76	AV-8A	158709	VMA-542	Crashed on landing at Jacksonville; pilot ejected.
16/06/76	AV-8A	159237	VMA-231	Engine failed at 600ft; aircraft rashed in sea near Mayport, Virginia; pilot ejected.
27/08/76	AV-8A	158957	VMA-542	Crashed at Cherry Point after engine failure; pilot ejected.
30/08/76	AV-8A	158974	VMA-513	Ran out of fuel, crashed in sea near Iwakuni; pilot ejected.
06/12/76	AV-8A	159230	VMA-513	Crashed in sea near Iwakuni; pilot killed.
11/02/77	AV-8A	158967	VMA-542	Engine failed at high altitude and would not re-light; pilot ejected.
19/03/77	AV-8A	159377	VMAT-203	Crashed during transition to VTO; pilot ejected.
06/04/77	AV-8A	159372	VMAT-203	Crashed during transition to landing; pilot killed.
12/07/77	AV-8A	159250	VMA-231	Crashed off Cape Hatteras during range ops from USS *Saratoga*; pilot killed.
27/07/77	AV-8A	158953	VMA-542	Crashed at Cherry Point; pilot killed.
06/09/77	AV-8A	158970	VMA-513	Hit mountain near Yuma during dive on range; pilot killed.
27/11/77	AV-8A	159259	VMA-231	Crashed at Kadena, Okinawa.
29/11/77	AV-8A	158708	VMA-231	Crashed after engine failure at night off Kadena, Okinawa.
03/02/78	AV-8A	158952	VMA-542	Crashed after engne failure; pilot ejected but injured.
06/10/78	AV-8A	158961	VMA-513	Crashed nr Yuma, Arizona.
11/11/79	AV-8A	159369	VMA-513	Crashed on landing.
15/11/79	YAV-8B	158395	NATC	YAV-8B No 2; crashed near Lake of Ozarks after engine problems; pilot ejected.
07/03/80	AV-8A	158389	VMA-513	Crashed during sortie from Cherry Point.
13/03/80	AV-8A	159256	VMA-513	Crashed during ACT sortie from Yuma.
01/05/80	AV-8A	159242	VMA-513	Crashed during transition from VTO.
01/08/80	TAV-8A	159384	VMAT-203	Crashed near Cherry Point following engine failure; two ejected.
13/08/80	AV-8A	159251	VMA-231	Crashed.
05/09/80	YAV-8C	158384	NATC	Crashed off USS *Tarawa* near San Diego; pilot ejected.
19/01/81	AV-8A	159368	VMAT-203	Crashed at Cherry Point.
25/01/81	AV-8A	158958	VMA-513	Crashed on approach after engine failure.
18/03/81	AV-8A	159246	VMA-513	Loss of control during landing.
20/04/81	AV-8A	159234	VMA-513	Crashed on take-off from USS *Nassau*.
26/06/81	AV-8A	158703	NATC	Crashed.
03/12/81	AV-8A	158704	VMA-513	Crashed on range sortie.
26/01/82	AV-8A	158968	VMA-513	Lost control during landing at NAS Yuma, Arizona.
04/03/82	AV-8A	158956	VMA-54	Lost control on wave-off from Bogue Field, North Carolina.
24/09/82	AV-8A	158962	VMA-231	Crashed into Baltic from USS *Nassau*.
01/12/82	AV-8A	158955	VMA-513	Failed to recover from bomb run at Yuma.
02/02/83	AV-8A	159253	VMA-513	Engine failure on approach to Twenty-Nine Palms; pilot injured; wreck stored at Cherry Point 1995.
27/04/83	TAV-8A	159381	VMAT-203	Crashed at Cherry Point during transition; one crewman killed.
28/06/83	AV-8C	158696	VMA-513	Lost power on approach; pilot ejected.
22/09/83	AV-8C	158699	VMA-513	Departed runway on take-off at Yuma and crashed; pilot ejected.
09/12/83	AV-8C	158390		Lost control Oregon inlet, North Carolina; pilot ejected.
28/02/85	AV-8C	158706	VMA-542	Crashed after engine fire on take-off.

03/04/85	AV-8C	158954	VMA-542	Crashed on take-off from LPH *Guadacanal* nr Cherry Point; RAF exchange pilot ejected.
24/04/85	AV-8C	159231	VMA-231	Lost control during ACT nr NAS Fallon, Nevada; pilot killed.
31/05/85	AV-8B	161578	VMAT-203	In-flight fire; crashed in sea nr Long Island, New York; pilot ejected.
17/01/86	AV-8B	162724	VMA-231	Birdstrike nr Yuma, Arizona; pilot ejected.
27/02/86	AV-8B	162079	VMA-331	Pilot lost control nr Cherry Point and ejected.
04/11/86	AV-8B	162745	VMA-542	Mid-air collision with VMFA-122 F/A-18A; pilot ejected.
12/01/87	AV-8B	162746	VMAT-203	Crashed on take-off at Cherry Point; pilot ejected.
05/06/87	AV-8B	162073	VMA-331	Crashed in Barnegat Bay, New Jersey, after flame-out; pilot ejected.
24/07/87	AV-8B	162075	VMA-331	Departed runway on landing; pilot ejected.
10/09/87	AV-8B	162961	VMA-542	Crashed on approach to Twenty-Nine Palms; pilot ejected (for second time in six months!)
11/02/88	AV-8B	162071	VMA-331	Engine flamed out while on attack sortie; pilot ejected.
01/03/68	AV-8B	163182	VMA-542	Crashed in sea 15 miles off Cherry Point; pilot killed.
13/07/88	AV-8B	161582	VMAT-203	Crashed on take-off; pilot killed.
08/10/88	AV-8B	162952	VMA-331	Crashed in sea off Turkey with engine fire; RAF exchange pilot ejected.
05/11/88	AV-8B	163184	VMA-542	Departed runway at Maxwell AFB, Alabama, on landing; pilot ejected.
03/05/89	AV-8B	163185	VMA-542	Crashed on take-off Parris Island, South Carolina, during Exercise 'Solid Shield 89'; pilot killed.
28/08/89	TAV-8B	163202	VMAT-203	Crashed on finals to Cherry Point; two ejected.
31/10/89	AV-8B	163666	VMA-311	Crashed at Twenty-Nine Palms with engine fire; pilot ejected.
06/12/89	AV-8B	163667	VMA-311	Inverted on landing.
26/01/90	AV-8B	162942	VMA-542	Ditched 25 miles NE of Thejima Island, Japan; pilot killed.
02/02/90	AV-8B	163671	VMA-311	Crashed on Chocolate Mountain range, El Centro, California; pilot ejected.
12/02/90	AV-8B	163187	VMA-223	Crashed north of Twenty-Nine Palms range, Mojave desert; pilot killed.
21/02/90	AV-8B	163685	VMA-311	Loss of power on take-off from carrier, crashed nr San Diego; pilot ejected.
21/04/90	TAV-8B	163856	VMAT-203	Crashed after low-level flight (suffered birdstrike); two ejected.
04/05/90	AV-8B	162078	VMAT-203	Engine fire on finals to Cherry Point; pilot ejected.
08/08/90	AV-8B	162970	VMA-513	Engine failure nr Yuma; pilot ejected.
02/10/90	AV-8B	162734	VMAT-203	Crashed during low-level training flight; pilot ejected but was killed.
06/11/90	AV-8B	163878	VMA-211	Engine flame-out nr Yuma; pilot lost control and ejected.
22/01/91	AV-8B	162954	VMA-331	Crashed during night approach to USS *Nassau*.
28/01/91	AV-8B	163518	VMA-311	Combat loss; Capt. M C Berryman ejected and made POW. (See text.)
04/02/91	AV-8B	163873	VMA-314	Crashed on Twenty-Nine Palms range, Mojave Desert.
09/02/91	AV-8B	162081	VMA-231	Combat loss; Capt. R. A. C. Sanborn ejected and made POW. (See text.)
23/02/91	AV-8B	161573	VMA-542	Combat loss; Capt. J N Wilbourne KIA. (See text.)
25/02/91	AV-8B	163190	VMA-542	Combat loss; Capt. S. Walsh ejected and was recovered. (See text.)
27/02/91	AV-8B	162740	VMA-331	Combat loss; Capt. R. C. Underwood KIA. (See text.)
19/03/91	AV-8B	162743	VMA-331	Crashed in sea off USS *Nassau* during night launch; pilot ejected.
15/05/91	AV-8B	163420	VMA-513	Slipped off deck of USS *Tarawa* in Bay of Bengal and not recovered.
11/11/91	AV-8B	162727	VMA-223	Crashed on sortie from Rota while on Det from USS *Wasp*; pilot ejected but was killed.
06/03/92	AV-8B	163882	VMA-214	Crashed into Palm Plantation, Jahore, Malaysia; pilot ejected.
12/04/92	AV-8B	164120	VMA-211	Mid-air crash with 164133 on Barry Goldwater range; aircraft destroyed.
12/04/92	AV-8B	164133	VMA-211	Mid-air crash with 164120 on Barry Goldwater range; aircraft destroyed.
29/06/92	AV-8B	163875	VMA-214	Crashed on take-off from Davenport, Iowa, after air show; pilot ejected but was killed.
13/07/92	AV-8B	163684	VMA-311	Crashed on landing at Yuma and inverted; pilot slightly injured.
17/08/92	AV-8B	164118	VMA-211	Crashed in Kuwaiti desert at night from USS *Tarawa*; pilot killed.
19/08/92	AV-8B	163514	VMA-231	Hit sea on low-level tactical sortie nr Cherry Point; pilot killed.
09/12/92	AV-8B	163181	VMA-214	Engine flamed-out and would not re-light; pilot ejected nr Yuma.
12/05/93	AV-8B	164125	VMA-211	Engine failure on low-level sortie nr Yuma; pilot ejected.
10/08/93	AV-8B	162955	VMA-231	Crashed on airfield at Cherry Point during circuit practice.
22/09/93	AV-8B	163425	VMA-231	Hit trees on landing at Camp Lejeune, North Carolina; pilot ejected and injured.
15/10/93	AV-8B	163421	VMA-231	Birdstrike at low-level nr Raleigh, North Carolina; pilot ejected.
25/05/94	AV-8B	163679	VMA-542	Crashed in Pimlico Sound, North Carolina, after engine surge; pilot ejected.
21/06/94	AV-8B	163177	VMA-231	Crashed on landing at Cherry Point after engine failure; pilot ejected.
17/08/94	AV-8B	163681	VMA-311	Crashed.
27/09/94	AV-8B	162966	NAWC	Crashed nr China Lake NAWC, California; pilot ejected.
00/10/94	AV-8B			Crashed off coast of Somalia while operating from USS *Essex*.
14/01/95	AV-8B	164541	VMAT-203	Crashed *en route* to Seymour-Johnson AFB, North Carolina.

| 30/01/95 | AV-8B | 164547 | VMA-214 | Crashed in Red Sea off USS *Essex* with 13th MEU; pilot killed. |

Other Harrier losses

11/06/76	AV8A(S)	159561	*Esc 008*	Spanish Navy. Pitched up during STO at Whiteman AFB, Missouri, during initial training of AV-8A crew; pilot ejected.
28/05/80	AV8A(S)	159557	*Esc 008*	Spanish Navy. Crashed into sea off Majorca.
05/12/89	EAV-8B	163010	*Esc 009*	Spanish Navy. Crashed 4 miles from Rota on GCA approach; pilot killed (bad weather on approach).
13/05/94	AV8A(S)	161175	*Esc 008*	Spanish Navy. Lost at sea S of Balearic Islands during Exercise 'Dynamic Impact'; pilot Lt Frederico Garcia ejected and was rescued.
02/08/94	T.60		300 Sqn	Indian Navy. Sea Harrier two-seater crashed at Goa-Dabolim on training flight; both crew killed.

APPENDIX E: HARRIER STORES

The original Harrier I was equipped with five pylon hardpoints, including outboard (O/B) and inboard (I/B) wing stations and a centreline (C/L) fuselage station. Stores attached to all five pylons could be jettisoned in flight. In addition, the aircraft was equipped to carry two underfuselage Aden 30mm gun pods. Stores loading had to be symmetrical for take-off, but the aircraft could carry mixed loads of up to 5,500lb (2,500kg approx) at combat load factors of 7g at what Hawker Siddeley described as 'over target weights' (i.e. after a quantity of fuel had been consumed, *en route* to the target).

The five weapons pylons each had the No 119 Ejector Release Unit (ERU) fitted. The pylons, supplied by ML Aviation in the UK and McDonnell-Douglas in the USA, were single-store capable, but with the later addition of the ML Aviation Twin Store Light Weight Carrier, two stores of up to 1,000lb (450kg) could be carried on the same pylon. American aircraft used the Douglas TER (Triple Ejector Rack). The various stores configurations available to RAF Harrier Is is shown below.

In RAF use, the operational weapon load would typically comprise the Hunting Engineering BL.755 cluster bomb or the Royal Ordnance Mk 10, 13, 18 or 20 1,000lb (450kg) HE bomb fitted with a Portsmouth Aviation No 114 low drag ballistic tail unit or the Hunting Engineering No 117 high-drag retarded tail unit. From 1982 onwards the 1,000lb warheads could also be adapted with Portsmouth Aviation Paveway II CPU-123/B laser-guided 'smart' bomb 'kits'. The nitrogen gas-cooled AIM-9G Sidewinder was used originally, this being superseded by the all-aspect, argon gas-cooled AIM-9L following Phase VI modifications later in the RAF GR.3's career.

The RAF GR.1/3 and T.2/4 aircraft also carried French SNEB 68mm unguided air-to-ground rockets in launchers fitted to the underwing pylons. Two types of rocket were carried: a high-xplosive shaped charge warhead model for operational use, capable of penetrating armoured vehicles and giving off a secondary fragmentation effect, or an inert-filled warhead model for target practice purposes. The HE rockets were fired from the expendable Matra Type 116 19-tube launcher and the rockets and launcher were supplied as a ready-to-load unit. The practice rockets were carried in the reusable Matra Type 155 18-tube launcher.

For practice bombing sorties, RAF Harriers were fitted with an M L Aviation Carrier Bomb Light Stores (CBLS) No 100 bomb carrier. This was fitted with four No 122 ERUs for the carriage and release of 4lb or 18lb practice bombs. These bombs, which possessed the same ballistic qualities as the BL.755 CBU and 1,000lb HE bombs, were filled with a pyrotechnic compound which gave off a flash and a small cloud of smoke on impact, to mark the accuracy of the delivery. The Harrier II GR.5/7 and T.10 aircraft use the newer 3kg or 14kg practice bombs to the same effect.

The daylight reconnaissance pod fitted to the C/L pylon was originally configured with four F95 Mk 7 cameras (supplementing the nose-mounted port oblique F95 fitted to all Harrier Is and Sea Harriers) and a single F135 camera, collectively providing stereoscopic horizon-to-horizon optical coverage on conventional film taken at heights of between 200ft and 2,000ft (60–600m) AGL at speeds of up to Mach 0.85. Cameras comprised three arrays—port, starboard or vertical—any or all of which could also be selected individually in the cockpit, while a signal data converter in the pod annotated the borders of the exposed

Stores configurations available to the Harrier GR.1.

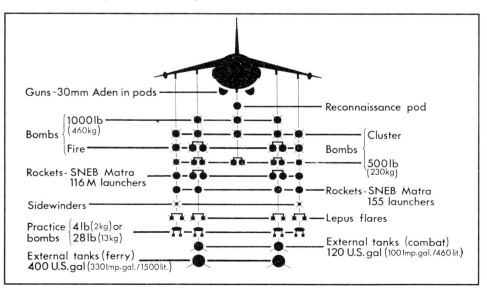

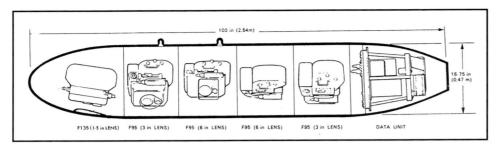

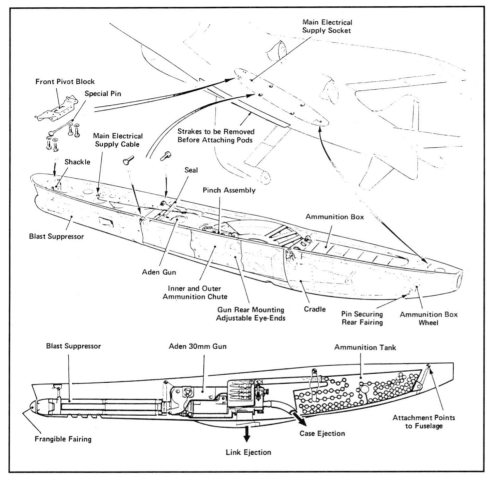

F135 (1·5 in LENS)   F95 (3 in LENS)   F95 (6 in LENS)   F95 (6 in LENS)   F95 (3 in LENS)   DATA UNIT

100 in (2.54m)

16·75 in (0.47 m)

Left, upper: Equipment arrangement in the reconnaissance pod.

Left, lower: 30mm Aden gun pod arrangement.

Right: SNEB rockets ripple from a No 1 Squadron GR.7 over the Pembrey Range off the Welsh coast. (BAe)

Front Pivot Block
Special Pin
Main Electrical Supply Socket
Main Electrical Supply Cable
Strakes to be Removed Before Attaching Pods
Shackle
Seal
Pinch Assembly
Ammunition Box
Blast Suppressor
Aden Gun
Inner and Outer Ammunition Chute
Gun Rear Mounting Adjustable Eye-Ends
Cradle
Pin Securing Rear Fairing
Ammunition Box Wheel

Blast Suppressor
Aden 30mm Gun
Ammunition Tank
Attachment Points to Fuselage
Frangible Fairing
Link Ejection
Case Ejection

film using coordinates furnished by the aircraft's INAS, to ease subsequent photo-interpretation.

Recce pods remain in service today for use by RAF GR.7s, including several specially reconfigured by Vinten: the Vicon 18-603 GP pod which contains a 91cm LOROP (long-range oblique photography) camera, the Vicon 18-403 with IR linescan and a panoramic camera, and the Vicon 57 multi-sensor/LOROP pod.

Each of the Aden 30mm cannon pods were pre-aligned and harmonised in the Armoury workshop, so that spares could be pre-loaded and taken out to dispersed sites and then fitted straight on to the Harrier's (factory jig-aligned) attachment points. This

enabled a crew of three to attached them in under 25min with no further alignment checks. Ammunition comprised up to 130 rounds of armour-piercing (AP), high explosive (HE) or training/target practice (TP) rounds, sufficient for about 6½sec of firing time based on 1,200rds/min and offering a muzzle velocity of 2,500fs (800m/sec). Either port or starboard or both guns could be selected. Frangible plastic caps protected the gun muzzles *en route* to the target and were blown off the front of the pods with the first burst of fire.

American AV-8A Harrier Is employed a different array of 'iron', cluster and fire bombs or rockets, as noted below for the Harrier II.

The American AV-8B Harrier II employed seven stations including C/L, port and starboard wing O/B and I/B, and an extra Intermediate (INT) station in between, each incorporating McDonnell-Douglas BRU-36/A (Bomb Release Units). Multiple stores carriage was available by means of the BRU-42 ITER (Improved Triple Ejection Rack) for carriage of 2–3 smaller-category weapons per station, such as the Mk 81 or Mk 82 'iron' bombs. TAV-8Bs have only two underwing stores pylons.

In RAF use, all Harrier II aircraft (including T.10 OCU trainers) are fitted with eight underwing and one C/L pylon hardpoints (wing stations comprising port and starboard O/B, INT, Outrigger and I/B), all but the Outrigger pylons being fitted with the ML Aviation No 126 ERU, capable of carrying stores up to 1,000lb (450kg) in weight. Outrigger pylons are conformal with the outrigger wheel fairings, incorporating Frazer-Nash common launch rails, and are used exclusively for Sidewinder missiles. Although USMC aircraft have long been equipped to use Outrigger pylons (known to the USMC as stations 1A and 7A), they were not certified for use until the advent of the AV-8B+. Previously, AV-8Bs employed Sidewinder LAU-7 rails on alternative BRRUs (Bomb Rack Replacement Units) on the O/B pylons instead, and also optionally on the INT pylons when fitted with ADU-299 adaptors. Both services now utilise the all-aspect AIM-9L/M gas-cooled models of Sidewinder, with the RAF destined to switch to the off-boresight-capable BAe/Hughes AIM-132 ASRAAM (Advanced Short-Range Air-to-Air Missile) during 1998 and the USMC to the AIM-9X at the turn of the century. USMC AV-8B+ Harriers may employ the Hughes AIM-120 AMRAAM on the dual-use LAU-7 pylons, for a theoretical maximum of six missiles. At the time of writing the St Louis Phantom Works is evaluating wingtip extensions and rails for AIM-9M/X carriage.

New 25mm Aden (Royal Ordnance, Nottingham) gun packs designed for the GR.5 were designed to be capable of using up to 100 rounds each comprising AP, HE,

AP Discarding Sabot (APDS) and APHE incendiary rounds, plus TPs and MPs (Multi-Purpose types). Muzzle velocity was increased to 3,450fs (1,050m/sec), with a combined rate of fire of 1,650–1,850rds/min. These are of the disintegrating link variety, fed through a revolver and percussion-fired in the cannon. However, they were never cleared for use on the RAF GR.5 and in the follow-on GR.7 the starboard pod has been replaced by an outwardly similar one containing the GEC-Marconi Zeus radio-frequency spectrum electronic countermeasures (RF ECM) system. USMC Harrier IIs feature the A/A49E-10 gun pod package, the port housing the GAU-12/A 25mm Equalizer in a GAK-14 'gun pak' and the starboard its ammunition in a GFK-11 'ammo pak', both fitted with ventral strakes. If the pods are not installed, giant strake-like LIDs (lift improvement devices) are fitted to help harness the thrust.

RAF Harrier II stores station/weight configurations, usually comprising symmetrical loads of the items listed under the original Harrier variants (except where noted subsequently) are shown below. Canadian CRV-7 70mm rockets in 19-shot pods have superseded the Matra 155 system. It is also intended to fit the SR(A).1236 Advanced Anti-Armour Weapons and the SR(A).1238 Conventionally Armed Stand-Off Missile (CASOM) when they are introduced into service in the late 1990s.

USMC Harriers employ a wider array of air-to-surface ordnance, including the Mk 81 250lb, Mk 82 500lb or Mk 83 1,000lb bomb, fitted with LDGP (low-drag general-purpose) fins; in addition, the smaller Mk 81/82 bombs may be fitted with Mk 14/15 Snakeye (respectively) or BSU-86 (Mk 82) high-drag retard fins, and the Mk 83 with a BSU-85 AIR (Air Inflatable Retarder) tail unit. These bombs may be attached to ITERs, the only loading restriction being that the station adjacent to the fuselage or a fuel tank must be left empty.

Other ordnance includes the Mk 20 Rockeye II cluster bomb, CBU-72 FAE (fuel–air explosive) cluster bomb, Mk 77 Mods 4/5 fire bombs (napalm)a and GBU-12 (Mk 82-adapted) and -16 (Mk 83-adapted) Texas Instruments Paveway II laser-guided bombs. Rockets embrace the the LAU-10 (containing four 5in Zunis), LAU-61 (19 x 2.75in rockets) and LAU-68 (7 x 2.75in rockets). The primary anti-tank/bunker missile is the Hughes AGM-65E laser-homing Maverick, fitted to single LAU-117 rails carried on the I/B or INT pylons. SUU-25F flare dispensers and the MXU-648 baggage pod may also be carried. Practice ordnance includes full-sized inert examples of the Mk 80-series (such as the BDU-45 Mk 82 equivalent) as well as Mk 76 'blue bombs' (low-drag ballistics) and Mk 106/BDU-48 'beer can' (high-drag).

The Harrier II+ is also configured for the McDonnell Douglas AGM-84 Harpoon anti-ship missile. Other stores include the Sanders AN/ALQ-126C podded RF ECM or replacement Lockheed-Martin (Sanders) AN/ALQ-164, usually carried on the otherwise seldom-used AV-8B/B+ C/L pylon. Chaff/flare/decoy fits are internal, based on the Tracor AN/ALE-39 'round hole' dispensing system.

Sea Harriers employ substantially the same freefall ordnance as the RAF Harrier I, except that the I/B pylons were fixed in place to incorporate the intricate fuse option wiring for the carriage of nuclear weapons (WE.177 or American Mk/B-57 depth charge), these beefed-up stations also being able to take a pair of Martel anti-radar or Sea Eagle anti-ship missiles. The nuclear anti-submarine capability was deleted in 1991, and WE.177 at around the same time. The F/A.2 may be fitted with two dedicated ventral fuselage LAU-106 AIM-120 AMRAAM missile launch rails in lieu of the Aden gun pods or LIDs. All four wing pylons are similarly configured either for fuel tanks, bombs/rockets or additional common launch rails for Sidewinder and AMRAAM.

APPENDIX F: HARRIER DISPLAY

John Farley joined the RAF in 1955, flew Hunters and then became a flying instructor at RAF Cranwell before joining the Empire Test Pilots' School, Farnborough, in 1963. His acquaintance with the Harrier began in 1964 when he became RAE Project Pilot on the prototype P.1127 at RAE Bedford. He completed nineteen years of Harrier programme test flying, becoming Chief Harrier Test Pilot in 1978. He flew all versions of the Harrier family from 1963 to 1984, converting the USMC evaluation pilots, assisting subsequent USMC service units and flying Harriers from eleven different types of ship. He flew the initial Sea Harrier and ski-jump trials and took part in YAV-8B and AV-8B trials in the United States (including two hours' gliding in the AV-8B!). In 1983 he became Manager of BAe's Dunsfold facility and he has been a freelance test pilot and aeronautical engineer since 1990. In a flying career encompassing more than 80 aircraft types, he was also (in 1990) the first Western test pilot to fly the MiG-29 fighter.

It is appropriate here to end this book with a first-hand account from a Harrier test pilot whose enthusiasm and skill with the aircraft has done so much to promote it over the years. John F. Farley describes his display routine:

'People sometimes ask whether the aim of my Harrier displays was airshow spectacle or technical message. In fact I always tried to provide both. The case for spectacle is obvious, but technical points can need explanation. It may seem surprising today, but there were periods back in the early 1970s when rumours got around that the Harrier was difficult to control in the VSTOL regime. Some suggested that if you let only a little sideslip develop (by not keeping the nose exactly into wind during VSTOL manoeuvres) you would quickly roll inverted out of control. Others worried about (or bad-mouthed) angle of attack limits necessary to avoid a stall of the wing at times when the aircraft was being kept up by a combination of engine thrust and wing lift.

'As a manufacturer's test pilot, I was keen to do what I could to bolster the confidence of those service pilots who had done all their conversions on single-seaters. (The USMC took delivery of 94 Harriers before taking any two-seaters!) I tried to do this by showing in public displays that there was a very large envelope inside which the aircraft was easy to control and safe to fly. Indeed, with the

Hawker two-seater G-VTOL it was possible actually to show various interested parties how easy the whole thing really was.

'Two manoeuvres are perhaps worth a mention in this context: a pedal turn with forward speed and a steep climb from VTO. To show sideslip of 90 degrees was quite safe at 50kt. I used to accelerate from the hover to this speed, then reselect the nozzle lever back to the hover position (to prevent the speed increasing further) and immediately do a 360 degree pedal turn. After 90 degrees of this turn, the aircraft was doing some 50kt sideways at 90 degrees of sideslip. This showed the safety margin that surrounded the service recommendation of "minimizing sideslip above 30kt". What made this manoeuvre totally safe was the fact that the wings were kept level and the nose flat throughout. For Harrier drivers the message was simple: "Please understand it is a *combination* of sideslip, speed, angle of attack and bank angle that leads to trouble; keep any one of the critical elements zero and the product of the combination becomes zero, leaving the pilot in control."

'With the steep climb from a VTO the aim was to demonstrate precise control of attitude close to the ground and to show the importance of a Harrier pilot understanding the difference between angle of attack and attitude. It also showed that higher thrust was available if the intakes were protected from re-circulation of hot exhaust gases by pointing the nozzles away from them as soon as possible after lift-off. To the casual spectator it also looked eye-catching.

'The manoeuvre was very easy to perform, again providing you understood the rules. Rule one was to keep the thrust pointing straight down towards the ground (how else would it hold you up?), and rule two was to raise the nose so that the aircraft pointed in the direction it was moving (that way the angle of attack was kept very low, eliminating any chance of stall effects).

'This was much easier to do than write about. Following a flat lift off at full throttle, the left hand leaves the throttle to select the wheels up and then goes on to the nozzle lever. Now the right hand pulls back on the stick to raise the nose and at the same time the left hand pushes the nozzle lever forward to rotate the nozzles in the fuselage (towards the tail), so keeping the thrust pointing straight down. Success depends on coordinating the back stick with the forward nozzle. How is this coordination judged? Just by the seat of the pants: you needed to *feel* as if *nothing* was happening. (If you overdo the back stick the aircraft can be felt rushing off backwards, while if you overdo the nozzles it darts forwards.)

'So much for the basics, but there are other points to this manoeuvre. At an air show it looks best if the aircraft climbs away with its top surface pointing towards the crowd. This is also safer, because if the engine should fail the aircraft is already moving away from the people. So, depending on the wind direction, you may need to put in a flat turn after lift-off to get on the correct climb heading before you pull the nose up. Finally, and very importantly, the Harrier's reaction controls, which are needed throughout the climb, are automatically turned *off* as the nozzles move through their last 20 degrees of travel. Forget this and you will be left with the nose dropping uncontrollably, unless you move the lever back slightly to turn them on again. Indeed this did happen to one early RAF pilot, who then chose to eject as he had not realised why the nose had dropped. This unhappily led to the manoeuvre being banned by the RAF. However, the Royal Navy have always included the climb in their Sea Harrier displays.'

Left: GR.7 ZD408/WK, with Sidewinders and camera pod, on patrol over northern Iraq. (BAe)

Below: A Wittering pilot displays the current Harrier Force garb. (MoD)

Glossary

AAA	anti-aircraft artillery	DB	Development Batch
A&AEE	Aeroplane & Armament Experimental Establishment	DCM	dissimilar air combat manoeuvring
		DDI	detail display indicator
AC	army cooperation	DECS	Digital Engine Control System
ACM	air combat manoeuvring	DRA	Defence Research Agency
ACMI	ACM instrumented (range)	DSARC	Defense Systems Acquisition Review Council
ADV	Air Defence Variant	DSL	depressed sight-line
AED	Air Engineering Department	ECM	electronic countermeasures
AEW	airborne early warning	EFA	European Fighter Aircraft (Eurofighter 2000)
AFB	Air Force Base	FAA	*Fuerza Aérea Argentina*; Fleet Air Arm
AGL	above ground level	FAC	forward air control
AMG	Aircraft Maintenance Group	FADEC	Full Authority Digital Engine Control
AMRAAM	Advanced Medium-Range Air-to-Air Missile (AIM-120)	FEBA	forward edge of battle area
		FFAR	folding-fin aerial rocket
AOA	angle of attack	FIDAE	Ferie Internacional del Aire y del Espacio (Chilean International Air & Space Fair)
APC	Armament Practice Camp		
APU	auxiliary power unit	FIN	Ferranti Interial Navigation (set)
ARBS	angle-rate bombing system	FLIR	forward-looking infra-red
ASRAAM	Advanced Short-Range Air-to-Air Missile (AIM-132)	FOB	forward operating base
		FOD	foreign object damage
ASTOVL	Advanced Short Take-Off and Vertical Landing	FONAC	Flag Officer Naval Air Command
		FSD	Full-Scale Development
ASR	Air Staff Requirement	FWOC	Forward Wing Operations Centre
ASW	anti-submarine warfare	GLO	ground liaison officer
ATAF	Allied Tactical Air Force	GOR	General Operational Requirement
AWI	Air Weapons Instructor	G-VTOL	Civil registration of HSA Harrier two-seat demonstrator
BAe	British Aerospace		
BAI	battle area interdiction	HarDet	Harrier Detachment
BDA	bomb damage assessment	HARM	High-Speed Anti-Radiation (radar) Missile
BE	Bristol Engines	HCT	Harrier Conversion Team
BIT	built-in test	HERO	hazards of electromagnetic interference to ordnance
BuNo	Bureau of Aeronautics Number		
BVR	beyond visual range	HMG	Her Majesty's Government
CADs	cushion air devices	HMS	Her Majesty's Ship
CANA	*Comando Aviacion Naval Argentina*	HOTAS	hands-on-throttle-and-stick
CAP	combat air patrol	HP	high pressure
CAS	close air support	HS	Hawker Siddeley
CASA	Construcciones Aeronauticas SA	HSA	Hawker Siddeley Aircraft
CBU	cluster bomb units	HSF	Harrier Servicing Flight
CCA	carrier-controlled approach	HUD	head-up display
CCIP	continuously computed impact point	HUD/WAC	HUD weapons aiming computer
CFE	Central Fighter Establishment	IDF/AF	Israeli Defence Force/Air Force (*Heyl Ha'Avir*)
CG	centre of gravity		
CILOP	Conversion In Lieu of Procurement	IFTU	Intensive Flight Trials Unit
CNI	Communications, Navigation, Interrogation	INAS	inertial navigation and attack set
		IP	initial point
CNO	Chief of Naval Operations	IR	infra-red
CO	Commanding Officer	I/WAC	interface/weapons aiming computer
CTP	Chief Test Pilot	JAST	Joint-Service Advanced Strike Technology
CWP	central warning panel	JSF	Joint Strike Fighter
DASC	Direct Air Support Centre	JTIDS	Joint Tactical Information Distribution System

KES	Kestrel Evaluation Squadron	QFI	Qualified Flight Instructor
Kb	kilobyte	RAE	Royal Aircraft Establishment
kVA	kilovolts alternating current	RAF	Royal Air Force
LDGP	low-drag general-purpose	RAFG	Royal Air Force Germany
LERX	leading-edge wing root extension(s)	RAT	ram-air turbine
LIDs	lift improvement devices	RCS	reaction control system
LOX	liquid oxygen	RCV	reaction control vent
LP	low pressure	RN	Royal Navy
LPRF	low PRF	RNAS	Royal Naval Air Station
LRMTS	Laser Rangefinder and Marked Target Seeker	RNAY	Royal Naval Air Yard
McAir	McDonnell Aircraft; McDonnell-Douglas Aerospace	RNR	Royal Navy Reserve
MADGE	Microwave Aircraft Digital Guidance Equipment	RWR	radar warning receiver
MAG	Marine Air Group	SAM	surface-to-air missile
MAWS	missile approach warning system	SAS	Special Air Service
MCAS	Marine Corps Air Station	SATS	short airfield tactical support
MDC	mild detonating cord	SAP	simulated attack profile
MIRLS	miniature infra-red linescanner	SBAC	Society of British Aerospace Companies
MLU	Mid-Life Update	SCADS	Shipborne Containerized Air Defence System
mmh/fh	maintenance man-hours per flight hour	SCS	sea control ship
MoD(PE)	Ministry of Defence (Procurement Executive)	SHOEU	Sea Harrier Operational Evaluation Unit
MPD	multi-purpose display	SHSU	Sea Harrier Support Unit
MPRF	medium PRF	SOR	Specific Operating Requirement
MTBF	mean time between failures	STO	short take-off
MU	Maintenance Unit	STOL	short take-off and landing
MWDP	Mutual Weapons Development Programme	STOVL	short take-off and vertical landing
MWDT	Mutual Weapons Development Team	SUM	scheduled unit maintenance
NA	Night Attack	TDC	target designator control
NAS	Naval Air Squadron	TES	Tripartite Evaluation Squadron
NASA	National Aeronautics and Space Administration	TET	turbine entry temperature
NASU	Naval Air Support Unit	TIALD	Thermal Imaging & Laser Designator
NATC	Naval Air Test Center	TIC	troops in contact
NATO	North Atlantic Treaty Organisation	TMR	thrust measuring rig
NAVHARS	navigation, heading and attitude reference system	TRNS	terrain-referenced navigation system
NAWC	Naval Air Weapons Center	TWU	Tactical Weapons Unit
NBMR	NATO Basic Military Requirement	USAF	United States Air Force
NDC	navigation display computer	USMC	United States Marine Corps
NPE	Navy Preliminary Evaluation	USN	United States Navy
NVG	night vision goggles	USS	United States Ship
OBOGS	on-board oxygen generating system	VAAC	Vectored-thrust Advanced Aircraft Control
OCU	Operational Conversion Unit	VIFF	(thrust) vectoring in forward flight
OEU	Operational Evaluation Unit	VMA	Fighter, Marine Attack (Squadron)
PCB	plenum chamber burning	VMAT	Fighter, Marine Attack, Training (Squadron)
PIA	pilot-interpreted approach	V/STOL	vertical/short take-off and landing
PPC	present position computer	VTO	vertical take-off
PPI	plan position indicator	VTOL	vertical take-off and landing
prf	pulse repetition frequency	WAC	weapons aiming computer
PSP	pierced steel planking	WGAF	West German Air Force (*Luftwaffe*)

Index

Page references in *italic* type refer to illustrations